A DICTIONARY OF BOOK HISTORY

A Dictionary of
BOOK
HISTORY

JOHN FEATHER

New York
OXFORD UNIVERSITY PRESS
1986

© John Feather 1986
Oxford University Press
200 Madison Avenue
New York, N.Y. 10016

Library of Congress Cataloging-in-Publication Data

A Dictionary of book history.

    1. Bibliography — Dictionaries. 2. Books — History —
Dictionaries. I. Feather, John.
Z1006.D52   1986   002'.0321   86-12860
ISBN 0-19-520520-0

CONTENTS

ACKNOWLEDGEMENTS

I am grateful to Alice D. Schreyer for her valuable comments on many entries, and particularly for a number of useful suggestions on the American dimension of this book. I, of course, remain responsible for the selection, and for any errors which remain.

Jonathan Price of Croom Helm Ltd has been a model Editor, displaying the patience and understanding which authors always seek but rarely find.

INTRODUCTION

'Bibliolexicography' is a word which is not defined in this book; indeed it is unknown to the *Oxford English Dictionary* and should perhaps remains so. The concept, however, is better than the term. Bibliography has, like all subjects, developed its own technical vocabulary which is as indispensable to the expert as it is baffling to the tyro. One of the purposes of this *Dictionary* is to explain that vocabulary by offering not only simple definitions but also reasoned explanations. The technical language of bibiliography is derived largely from that of the book trade, and especially of printing. Indeed, twentieth-century bibliographers have consciously adopted that vocabulary in their concern to root the study of books firmly in the soil of the printing house where books are produced. On the other hand, there have been subtle adaptations of the meanings of many of the borrowed terms. When a bibliographer writes of an 'edition' he means something specific and unambiguous; the term comes from the book trade but the trade uses it more loosely. Similarly, to a bibliographer a 'forme' is not only what it is to a printer, but also has a derived meaning which is more commonly intended. This vocabulary is defined here from the point of view of the bibliographer, while never ignoring its origins in the trade.

The *Dictionary* is not, however, confined to the technical vocabulary of bibliography. The study of books is far more wide-ranging than that, and extends into many cognate fields. First among these is the history of the book trade itself, so that many entries here are for trade practices, aspects of trade history, trade organisations and the printers, publishers and booksellers themselves. Secondly, within the history of the trade there is the more specialised subject of the history of book production: the technologies of graphic and textual reproduction, printing, papermaking and bookbinding. These too have their place here. Thirdly, the books which we study are those which have been preserved by collectors and libraries, so that they are here as well.

At this point, the user should be warned of what he will not find. First, it has, of course, been necessary to be selective, especially in dealing with persons and libraries. In general, the selection is based on an assessment of the importance of the subject, and on the likelihood of its being found in the literature. Such an assessment, while it cannot avoid a degree of subjectivity, was essential if the whole *Dictionary* were not to become merely a list of publishers, book collectors and libraries. In general, the need for selectivity has also compelled a certain concentration on British and American topics, although other parts of the world are not entirely neglected. Secondly, this is not a lexicon of the technical vocabulary of contemporary printing, and even less an instruction manual in its techniques. The *Dictionary* is for the historian of the book, and its approach is historical. Technical explanations are offered when they are necessary, but while the user who wishes to know the history and basic principles of offset lithography should be satisfied, he will not learn how to adjust the blanket cylinder on such a press to obtain the best impression. Nor is this a dictionary of the history of libraries or librarianship. The libraries listed here gain their place from their importance as repositories of the sort of books in which book historians are generally interested. Similarly, the librarians are here for their importance in the history of bibliography, so that many who have made equal or greater contributions to their profession are omitted.

For ease of use, the *Dictionary* is arranged in conventional alphabetical order, but its structure is more complex than that might imply. Certain topics which are central to the subject have been treated at considerable length; these include 'bibliography' itself, 'bookbinding', 'collation', 'illustrated books' and 'papermaking', among others. These essays are intended to provide both an introduction and an overview. The user is therefore often referred to them from shorter entries for those topics for which they provide the broader context. On the other hand, the longer essays have not been over-burdened with detail, so that the user who finds an unexplained term should go to the list of cross-references at the end of the entry and thence to the entry for the relevant topic. The cross-references are indeed the key to the proper use of the *Dictionary*. Although repetition between entries cannot be wholly eliminated, it has been avoided as far as possible. Thus, for example, there is an entry for 'Gothic type' to which the user is referred whenever the term is used in the *Dictionary*; in this way, the entries are not filled with detail which is not immediately relevant to the topic.

The entries for persons also require some explanation. Those selected fall into six broad categories: members of the book trade, illustrators, bookbinders, inventors or developers of techniques or equipment, book collectors and bibliographers. In most cases, the entry takes the form of a brief biography together with a more detailed explanation of the person's significance to the historian of the book. In other cases, however, the personal entry leads only to a reference to an entry on a topic. This has been done where the person's importance for the present purpose relates entirely to one matter and is better explained in context. It should not be taken to imply that William Morris is less important in the history of printing than Charles Ackers. It should also be added that, with two inescapable exceptions, all the persons listed are dead; this implies no disrespect to the living but rather reflects the difficulty of assessing the achievements of men and women who are still active in their various fields. The same principle has generally been applied to private presses, since, as with living scholars, it is difficult to assess the full extent of their achievement and importance while they are still active.

No reference work of this kind can be comprehensive even on the topics which are selected for inclusion. In recognition of this, every entry, with a few minor exceptions, concludes with at least one reference to a source to which the user can go for further information. In selecting the references, the principal consideration has been to direct the user to the most comprehensive and reliable work whenever such a work exists. Additionally, an attempt has been made to select references which themselves have adequate bibliographies to permit yet further investigation.

Finally, on a more personal note, I have to conclude by saying that no compiler of a reference book has ever let his work go forth without some trepidation. Somewhere in this book is my humble equivalent of Dr Johnson's 'pastern'. I can only ask for tolerance in the belief that this book will help the beginner and the more advanced student alike in a subject which is becoming more fascinating as it becomes more complex.

John Feather
Loughborough University

LIST OF ABBREVIATIONS

ABMR	*Antiquarian Book Monthly Review*
AGB	*Archiv für Geschichte des Büchwesens*
ALJ	*Art Libraries Journal*
BC	*The Book Collector*
Bibl.	*The Biblotheck*
Bibliog.	*Bibliographica*
BIHR	*Bulletin of the Institute of Historical Research*
BJECS	*British Journal of Eighteenth-Century Studies*
BJRL	*Bulletin of the John Rylands Library*
BLJ	*British Library Journal*
BLR	*Bodleian Library Record*
BNYPL	*Bulletin of the New York Public Library*
Bowers	Fredson T. Bowers, *Principles of Bibliographical Description* (1949)
BQR	*Bodleian Quarterly Record*
CBS	Cambridge Bibliographical Society
DNB	*Dictionary of National Biography*
ed.	edited
edn	edition
ELIS	*Encyclopaedia of Library and Information Science*
Gaskell	Philip Gaskell, *A New Introduction to Bibliography* (1972)
HLB	*Harvard Library Bulletin*
HMC	Historical Manuscripts Commission
JPHS	*Journal of the Printing Historical Society*
Libr.	*The Library*
monogr.	monograph
Moxon	Joseph Moxon, *Mechanick Exercises on the Whole Art of Printing (1683–4)*, ed. Herbert Davis and Harry Carter (2nd edn, 1962)
NQ	*Notes and Queries*
OBS	Oxford Bibliographical Society
OBSP	*Oxford Bibliographical Society Papers*
occ. pub.	occasional publications
OHS	Oxford Historical Society
PBA	*Proceedings of the British Academy*
PBSA	*Papers of the Bibliographical Society of America*
PCQ	*Print Collectors' Quarterly*
PH	*Publishing History*
RBGN	*Library Association Rare Books Group Newsletter*
rev.	revised
SB	*Studies in Bibliography*
SEC	*Studies in Eighteenth-Century Culture*
ser.	series
TBS	*Transactions of the Bibliographical Society*
TCBS	*Transactions of the Cambridge Bibliographical Society*
TLS	*Times Literary Supplement*
ULR	*University of Leeds Review*

A DICTIONARY OF BOOK HISTORY

In Memory of
John Jolliffe
Friend and Colleague

Abbey, John Roland (1896–1969)

Book collector and patron of bookbinders. Abbey assembled a superb collection of illuminated manuscripts, illustrated books and bookbindings. The illustrated books, described in a four-volume catalogue (1952–57), were sold to Paul Mellon, and donated by him to the Yale Center for British Art where, substantially augmented, they form the core of the rare books collection. The modern British bookbindings were bequeathed to the British Museum (British Library); the remainder of the bookbinding collection was sold at auction (Sothebys, London) in 1964, and the books are now scattered in collections and libraries throughout the world. The basis of the manuscript collection was the purchase *en bloc* of the manuscripts of C.H. St John Hornby, founder of the Ashendene Press, in 1946. Abbey's books were always superb *objets d'art*, for in his fields he was perhaps the outstanding collector of his generation.

A description of the collections, by A.R.A. Hobson and A.N.L. Munby, is in *BC* (1961), p. 40. In addition to Abbey's own catalogues, the English bindings were catalogued by G.D. Hobson (1940), the modern English and French bindings by the Arts Council (1949), and the Italian manuscripts by J.J.G. Alexander and A.C. de la Mare (1969). The Sothebys sale catalogues are important documents of reference for the Abbey bindings.

See also **Ashendene Press**

Ackermann, Rudolph (1764–1834)

Artist and publisher. A German, Ackermann came to London in 1795, and set up as a printseller. He gained a reputation as an aquatint engraver, but is chiefly associated with the introduction of lithography into England. Having experimented with coloured lithographs as early as 1808, in 1817 he established the first proper lithographic press in England. One of his earliest books was the first English version of Senefelder's *Complete Course* (1819). His reputation, however, rests on his topographical prints, notably of the universities of Oxford (1814) and Cambridge (1815), and on a series of books on Europe and South America in the 1820s and his *Repository of Arts*, a highly successful part book which he started in 1809. He was also responsible for *Forget-me-not* (1825), the first of the gift book annuals.

There is an account of him in *DNB*; and in Michael Twyman, *Lithography* (1970).

See also **Aquatint**; **Gift books**; **Lithography**; **Senefelder, Alois** (1771–1834)

Ackers, Charles (1702/3–1759)

Printer in London. Ackers was not particularly distinguished, although he was printer (and part-owner) of the *The London Magazine*. He has, however, achieved an important place in book-trade history through the fortuitous survival of a financial ledger from the period 1732–48. Detailed records of this sort are rare from the eighteenth century or earlier, and, to date, the Ackers ledger is the only such document to have been published in full. It was edited by D.F. McKenzie and J.C. Ross (OBS, new series, 15. 1968).

See also **Bowyer, William** (1663–1737) **and Bowyer, William** (1699–1777); **Strahan, William** (1715–1785)

Adams, Herbert Mayour (d. 1985)

Librarian of Trinity College, Cambridge, from 1924 to 1958. In 1967 Cambridge University Press published his *Catalogue of Books Printed on the Continent of Europe 1501–1600 in Cambridge Libraries*, now a standard work of reference. It has some faults and inconsistencies, chiefly derived from the divergent cataloguing practices of the college libraries, but is invaluable as by far the largest list (*c.* 30,000 entries) of continental European books of the sixteenth century. It is cited in the form **Adams A1**.

Advertisements

Advertising has been important to the book trade from the beginning of printing, since the printed book is, *ipso facto*, a mass-produced article which has to be marketed widely if it is to be commercially successful. Advertisements from the fifteenth century are naturally rare, but there is a famous example printed by Caxton in 1477, of which two copies are extant (one in the Bodleian Library, Oxford; the other in the John Rylands University Library of Manchester). This advertisement was posted on the door of the shop and elsewhere, and no doubt other such documents existed. At a slightly later date, as the London trade began to concentrate in St Paul's Churchyard, it became the common practice to post the title-pages of new books in this way, a custom which has sometimes been taken to be the origin of the very full imprints which are a feature of English books from the middle of the sixteenth century until the second half of the eighteenth. It was one of the apprentice's duties to change the posted title-pages each Saturday evening, and in the eighteenth century parcels of them were sent to the provincial booksellers for the same purpose. The use of title-pages as advertisements continued until at least the middle of the eighteenth century, and possibly longer in the provinces. In the nineteenth century, posters were sometimes printed to advertise individual titles, a practice particularly associated with W.H. Smith's railway bookstalls. Such posters are still issued for a few titles, although usually for display in bookshops rather than on expensive public sites.

Separate advertisements have, however, long since been displaced as the principal advertising medium for books. The printers', booksellers' and publishers' catalogues, which originated in the sixteenth century, and were later supplemented by trade catalogues and bibliographies, and newspaper advertisements, which share the mid-seventeenth century origin of the newspaper itself, are of far greater importance. Indeed, from the middle of the eighteenth century onwards, the newspaper advertisement has been by far the most important means of advertising new books. The catalogue survived most conspicuously in two forms: as a complete list of a publishers' available output; and printed on the final leaves at the end of a book. The latter fall into two categories. Some were printed with a particular edition, on a final page (or pages) which would otherwise have been blank. Others were on a separate sheet, folded to the same format as the book, and inserted in it. The latter may, of course, be found in copies of many different books of the same size, especially in the mid-nineteenth century when this practice was at its height. Another feature of many nineteenth-century books, especially those in series, was the use of the endpapers for advertising purposes. The derivatives of these practices include the list of an author's previous works opposite the title-page, or elsewhere in the prelims, and the use of part (usually the back) of the book jacket for advertising other books by the same author or publisher.

There has also, however, been a distinct shift in the audience which book advertisements were intended to reach. As the trade became more complex in the seventeenth century, and especially after the rapid development of the provincial trade in the period 1700–50, it came to be aimed primarily at booksellers who were (and are) the publishers' immediate customers, rather than the general public. By the middle of the twentieth century, public advertising, especially in the newspapers, was widely regarded in the trade as little more than a sop to the author's vanity, although some publishers, notably Victor Gollancz, did consider it important in establishing a firm's public image. Today, the public advertising of books may occasionally be spectacular, with media hyping of a few carefully selected titles, and even television advertisements for books (or more often series) with a sufficiently large potential market, but it is atypical. The great bulk of modern publishers' promotional budget is devoted to persuading the booksellers to take copies for stock.

A history of book advertising is a great desideratum, for none exists. The best substitute, which deals with a broader range of topics than its title suggests (up to the year 1800) is Graham Pollard and Albert Ehrman, *The Distribution of Books by Catalogue* (1965).

See also **Catalogues**; **Caxton, William** (1422?–1491); **Endpapers**; **Imprint**; **Newspapers**; **Prelims**; **Prospectus**; **St Paul's Churchyard**; **Smith, William Henry** (1792–1865) **and Smith, William Henry** (1825–1891); **Subscription**; **Title page**; **Trade bibliography**

Agenda format

Bibliographical format. The phrase is used by bibliographers for a book which is printed in any format, but with the lines printed at a right-angle to the usual direction. Thus in octavo, which is the most common agenda format, the lines are parallel to the longer rather than to the shorter sides. Agenda formats were used for printed forms, and sometimes for accountancy tables and similar works.

See William Savage, *A Dictionary of the Art of Printing* (1841, repr. 1968), who illustrates what he calls 'broad' formats.

See also **Format**; **Octavo**

Aitken, William Maxwell, 1st Baron Beaverbrook (1879–1964)

See **Newspapers**

Albion press

An iron hand-press, possibly invented by G.W. Cope in 1820, but never patented. No doubt because of that, it was made by almost all pressmakers from about 1830, the latest example dating from 1940. The Albion was highly regarded by printers in its hey-day, and in England was the standard book press until the mechanised presses displaced it in the 1850s. For long afterwards, and indeed until the 1960s in a few cases, Albions were used for jobbing work. The Albion was 'revived' by Morris at Kelmscott, and consequently acquired something of a mystique among private printers.

Its real value lay in its simplicity, for, except in an early version which was soon abandoned, the Albion uses a screw rather than a counterweight mechanism to raise and lower the platen. With a screw press it is easier to achieve acceptable results with comparatively little skill or preparation. Many Albions still exist, and many are indeed in use in schools and colleges, and among amateur printers.

A well-illustrated article on the Albion, by the distinguished engraver Reynolds Stone, appeared in *JPHS* (1966), p. 58.

See also **Columbian press**; **Common press**; **Kelmscott Press**; **Stanhope press**

Aldus Manutius (*c.* 1450–1515)

Printer and publisher. Aldus established a business in Venice in about 1490, and produced his first book in 1495. Thereafter, he was a prolific publisher, especially of classical texts. In particular, his series of low-priced octavo editions of Greek and Roman authors were of great importance. They were edited by leading scholars of the day, and established new standards of both textual accuracy and typographical excellence. Indeed, in the early sixteenth century, Aldus was presiding over something not unlike an academy of classical scholarship. Technically, Aldus made a major innovation, for the first italic fount was cut for him, reflecting his dislike of the often clumsy and illegible Gothic types then in common use. The Aldine Greek of 1501 is still regarded as one of the best ever cut.

There is a substantial literature on Aldus: Martin Lowry, *The World of Aldus Manutius* (1979) is a wide-ranging study, which can be supplemented with Curt F. Buhler, 'Aldus Manutius: the first five hundred years', *PBSA* (1950), p. 205; and Edward Robertson, 'Aldus Manutius, the scholar–printer, 1450–1515', *BJRL* (1950), p. 57.

See also **Gothic type**; **Italic**

Allen Press

Private press. The Allen Press is one of the many private presses which have been established in California in recent years. It was founded in 1939 by Lewis and Dorothy Allen, with the intention of producing books which were distinguished not only for their typography but also for their illustration, design and binding. The Allens have never hesitated to experiment, and if all these experiments have not been successful they have certainly stimulated an interest in their work. Like a number of modern American presses, the Allen Press can be criticised for its elevation of form above content, but in its field the Press is one of the best of its kind.

The Allens have written their own assessment of their work in *The Allen Press Bibliography MCMLXXXI*, which the Press published in 1981.

See also **Private press movement**

Almanacs

An almanac is a table of astronomical events and associated astrological predictions for the coming year. Almanacs were issued from the earliest days of printing, including one which may be by Gutenberg himself; they rapidly became very popular and were consequently printed in large numbers. Few survive, however, for they are by their nature ephemeral documents. Until the early seventeenth century, almanacs were almost invariably printed in a broadside format, but from that time they began to be issued as small books usually in duodecimo or octavo format. The contents of the almanac also underwent some change, although the basic pattern of astronomical and astrological predictions was constant. The latter, however, was often exploited for political purposes, containing implicit comment which would have been unacceptable in any other context. This technique was used in England in the seventeenth century, and revived in America in the late colonial period, notably by Franklin in his *Poor Richard's Almanack* (1733–66). Almanacs were also increasingly filled with non-political information on history, literature, popular medicine, and the like. Moreover, the almanac began to take on the characteristics of a modern appointments diary, with blank spaces left against each day for notes by the owner.

Because almanacs were so popular, they were very valuable commercial properties. In the late seventeenth century, a single title in England was printed in annual editions of 25,000–30,000; and in the late 1680s it was estimated that some 350,000 almanacs were printed each year. English almanac printing was a jealously guarded monopoly of the Stationers' Company as part of its English Stock. Despite growing protests, and some piracy, the almanac monopoly remained substantially intact until it was challenged at law by Thomas Carnan in 1775, and the courts found in his favour.

Bibliographically, almanacs are a complicated subject, not least because so few survive of the millions which were printed. The standard work on early English almanacs is E.F. Bosanquet, *English Printed Almanacks and Prognostications. A Bibliography to the Year 1600* (1917), updated in *Libr.* (1937–38), p. 195. The list is brought down to 1700 by Bernard Capp in his *Astrology and the Popular Press* (1979), an excellent study of English almanacs from the sixteenth to the eighteenth centuries, which largely displaces Bosanquet's article in *Libr.* (1929–30), p. 361. For the trade history of almanacs, see two articles by Cyprian Blagden: 'The distribution of almanacks in the second half of the seventeenth century', *SB* (1958), p. 107; and 'Thomas Carnan and the almanack monopoly', *SB* (1961), p. 23. On the American tradition, see Marion Barber Stowell, *Early American Almanacs* (1977).

See also **Broadside**; **Duodecimo**; **Ephemera**; **English Stock**; **Franklin, Benjamin** (1706–1790); **Gutenburg, Johann** (1394/99–1468); **Octavo**; **Piracy**; **Stationers' Company**

American Antiquarian Society

See **North American Imprints Program**; **Thomas, Isaiah** (1749–1831)

American Book Collector, The

Bibliophilic periodical. It began publication in 1932, but ceased in 1935. The title was revived in 1950, but it again ceased publication. The present periodical began in 1976, when it was called first *The Bibliognost* and then *Book Collectors' Market*. A new series, under the title *American Book Collector*, started in 1980. It is now published monthly by the Moretus Press, New York City. Its contents, by their concern with modern first editions and private press books, reflect the preoccupations of contemporary American collectors. The new series has included a number of valuable author checklists, including John Updike, John Fowles and Saul Bellow. The editor is Bernard McTigue.

American Book Prices Current

Annual listing of auction prices. *ABPC* began publication in 1895, and is now the most important general source of auction prices, widely used in the trade, and by collectors and librarians, for establishing the monetary value of collectable books. *ABPC* is published annually, but it is held in a data-base which is available on-line through the BOOKLINE network. This is described by Daniel J. Leab in *ABMR* (1980), p. 528.

See also **Auction sales**; **BAMBAM**; *Book Auction Records*

American Printing History Association

Learned society. Founded in 1974, APHA is concerned with all aspects of the history of printing in the United States and throughout the world. It holds an annual conference which has become a major event on the American book scene, and also has regional chapters which meet regularly. It publishes *Printing History*.

The Society's address is P.O. Box 4922, Grand Central Station, New York, NY 10163.

See also **Printing History**

Americana

Books about the Americas. This generic term is used by the trade and collectors for all books relating to the Americas, an important field of collecting especially in the USA. Not all Americana are published in the Americas; indeed the earliest material (e.g. the *Columbus Letter*) is necessarily of European origin.

See also **Evans, Charles** (1850–1935); **North American Imprints Program**; **Sabin, Joseph** (1821–1881)

Ames, Joseph (1689–1759)

Bibliographer. Ames, son of a naval captain and himself a ship's chandler, was largely self-taught under the guidance of the Rev. John Lewis, a clergyman in Wapping where Ames lived. Lewis had been making collections for a history of printing which he handed over to Ames. In 1739–40, Ames compiled and printed a preliminary list of English printers up to 1700, which, in a greatly expanded form, grew into his *magnum opus, Typographical Antiquities* (1749). Ames had studied many thousands of early English books, and *Typographical Antiquities* represents the first stage of the cataloguing of them which was to culminate with the publication of *STC* in 1926. A revised version was published by William Herbert (1785), and further revision was issued by Dibdin (1810). Ames was a remarkable pioneer of bibliographical studies in England, and deserves a fuller life than that in *DNB*, at present the only published account of him.

He was also a substantial collector; the bulk of his library was sold by auction in 1760 (Langford, London), but important manuscript collections are in the British Library, along with the collection of early title pages which he assembled and used for *Typographical Antiquities*.

See also **Dibdin**, **Thomas Frognall** (1776–1847); *STC*

Analytical bibliography

The study of the printing of a book, based on the evidence afforded by the book itself. A bibliographical analysis is concerned primarily with the physical history of a book. The process normally begins with an analysis of format, and the writing of a collational formula. Thence it proceeds to an analysis of the printing itself, using, for example, the evidence of skeletons to establish the order of formes to the press, and the collating of multiple copies to identify press variants and possible proof-reading procedures. In fact, almost any feature of a book may yield some evidence, although it may be ambiguous, as when, for example, press figures are studied. In its minutest form, as practised, for example, by Hinman, it may even be concerned with individual pieces of type. It is argued that such a study, using what Bowers calls 'mechanical' evidence, provides an objective approach which will produce results with a high degree of certainty.

A less certain analytical procedure, which has been very prominent in the bibliographical scholarship of the last 30 years, is the attempt to analyse the typesetting of a book and to identify individual compositors. In English books of the sixteenth and early seventeenth centuries, this is done by identifying the spelling preferences of the compositors in certain phonemes where the flexible orthography of the period permitted variation, such as -y/-ie terminations. Sometimes, however, the samples are too small to yield statistically valid results, and in any case, in practice, there are many technical restraints on the compositor, such as the length of the line, which also have to be considered, and which have too often been ignored. A more fruitful line of inquiry, which has been followed with some eighteenth-century books, may be to study the purely technical habits of compositors, such as spacing in the direction line.

Analysis is a necessary preliminary stage of bibliographical description, since it is only by the analysis of multiple copies that the description of an 'ideal' copy can be evolved. Analytical bibliography in its present form was developed by Greg, but it has subsequently been greatly elaborated by Bowers, Hinman and Tanselle.

The procedures are best studied in Fredson Bowers, *Bibliography and Textual Criticism* (1964); and in the introductory section of Charlton Hinman's *The Printing and Proof-reading of the First Folio of Shakespeare* (2 vols, 1963).

See also **Bibliography**; **Bowers, Fredson Thayer** (1905-   ); **Compositor**; **Descriptive bibliography**; **Direction line**; **Format**; **Greg, Sir Walter Wilson** (1875-1959); **Hinman, Charlton Joseph Kadio** (1911-?); **Ideal copy**; **Press figures**; **Press variants**; **Proofs**; **Skeleton forme**; **Textual criticism**; **Typesetting**

Annual Bibliography of the History of the Printed Book and Libraries

Current bibliography of publications on library and book history. *ABHB* is published for the Rare and Precious Books Committee of the International Federation of Library Associations by Nijhoff, The Hague, under the editorship of H.D.L. Vervleit. Volume 1 covers publications of the year 1970, and subsequent volumes have been published annually, usually somewhat in arrears. It is compiled by editors in individual countries, and both the comprehensiveness and quality of the entries varies significantly from one to another. Nevertheless, *ABHB* is an invaluable tool, used by all serious scholars of the book, for it indexes the bulk of the periodical literature, and (most valuably) reviews of relevant books. New users should, however, read the Introduction to vol. 1, and the critique by B.J. McMullin in *SB* (1980), p. 1.

Antiquarian Book Monthly Review

Bibliophilic periodical. *ABMR* first appeared in February 1974 and has succesfully established itself as a magazine for collectors and the trade. Each issue contains two or three articles, usually well illustrated, on subjects of bibliophilic interest which, while they neither aspire to nor attain the highest standards of scholarship, are informative and often well written. About half of each issue is devoted to notes on the trade, recent sales, and general news about bibliophilic matters. This section frequently contains information not readily available elsewhere, and includes an invaluable listing of newly-issued antiquarian booksellers' catalogues.

Antiquarian Booksellers Association

Trade association of the antiquarian book trade in the UK. ABA was founded in 1906 to act as a forum for the antiquarian trade. Members are elected only after at least five years' experience in the trade, and on the strong recommendation of other members. The ABA expects a high standard of business ethics among its members, who include almost all of the leading firms. One of its most important activities, and certainly its most conspicuous, is to organise the Antiquarian Book Fair which has been held in London each summer since 1958. Its full title is Antiquarian Booksellers Association (International), and there are members in some dozen overseas countries. ABA is affiliated to the

International League of Antiquarian Booksellers. A list of members can be obtained from ABA, 154 Buckingham Palace Road, London SW1W 9TZ.

See also **International League of Antiquarian Booksellers**

Antiquarian Booksellers Association of America

Trade association of the antiquarian book trade in the USA. ABAA was founded in 1949 to encourage interest in rare books and manuscripts, and to maintain a high ethical standard in the trade. There are upwards of 400 members, including almost all of the leading firms. It is affiliated to the International League of Antiquarian Booksellers. ABAA is organised in regional 'chapters' (e.g. New England, Midwest, Southern California), which organise events, publish directories, etc. ABAA itself organises two major book fairs each year, one in New York City (since 1960), and one which alternates between San Francisco and Los Angeles (since 1967). A list of members can be obtained from ABAA, 50 Rockerfeller Plaza, New York, NY 10020.

See also **International League of Antiquarian Booksellers**

Antwerp Bible

See **Bibles**

Aquatint

An intaglio process of graphic printing, invented by J.B. le Prince, but named, and first described, by Paul Sandby in 1775. The essence of the process is that the plate is etched through an even film of resin dust, later replaced by a ground of liquid resin and alcohol. A variation is to use sugar as the basis of the ground. In either case, the resultant plate will print with continuous tones; with a sugar ground, the blacks and whites are reversed to give the effect of a negative.

Its tonal qualities made aquatint exceptionally popular, and it was the dominant process from *c.* 1790 to *c.* 1830. It was used especially for reproductions of oil paintings, and for topographical works, but it is also associated with the cartoons of Rowlandson and others. Rudolph Ackermann and John Boydell were among the leading publishers of books with aquatint illustrations. They are often found as separate prints from broken copies, and are sometimes hand coloured.

A description and history of the process was published by Michael Shane, in *ABMR* (1978), p. 500, and (1979), p. 2.

See also **Ackermann, Rudolph** (1764–1834); **Boydell, John** (1719–1804); **Intaglio**

Arber, Edward (1836–1912)

Scholar. Arber started his career as a civil servant, but his interest in literature led to a lectureship at Kings College, London, and, in 1881, to his appointment as Professor of English at Mason's College, Birmingham (now Birmingham University). Arber was a prolific editor of early printed literature, especially in its more obscure manifestations, but he also made one monumental contribution to book history. This was his *Transcript of the Registers of the Company of Stationers of London 1554–1640* (5 vols, 1875–94), the first full and accurate publication of this key document. Apart from the Register itself, Arber included scores of other documents from the Company's archives, although there were a few which he was not allowed to print, and a few which he missed. Many of these were subsequently edited by Sir Walter Greg in *A Companion to Arber* (1967). Arber's *Transcript* (as it is usually called) belongs to that select company of works of scholarship which, despite being a pioneering effort, is so good as to preclude the need to repeat the exercise. Of only slightly less importance is his transcript of the *Term Catalogues* (3 vols, 1903–6), although the standard of the work is not so high. Arber was a pioneer even in the manner of his death, for he was an early victim of a motor-car accident.

There is an account of him in *DNB*.

See also **Stationers' Company**; **Stationers' Register**; **Term catalogues**

Archiv für Geschichte des Büchwesens

Bibliographical periodical. *AGB* published by the Historischen Kommission des Borsenvereins des Deutschen Büchhandels, vol. 1 appearing in 1958. It is an important journal of German and international book history. An index to vols 1-20 is in vol. 20 (1979).

Arrighi, Ludovico degli (d. *c.* 1527)

Writing master and calligrapher. Little is known of his life, but Arrighi's *Imparare di scrivere littera cancellaresca* (1522) is a key document in the history of handwriting. It is an account of the hand developed in the Papal Chancery in the early fifteenth century, which was the basis of the italic type of the early Italian printers. Arrighi himself was briefly a printer (1524–27) using types designed by himself based on this hand.

There is an elaborate facsimile of his writing books, entitled *The Calligraphic Models of Ludovico Arrighi*, by Stanley Morison and Beatrice Warde (1926); and a general study by James Wardrop in *Signature* (1939), p. 26.

See also **Italic**

Ars moriendi

An early fifteenth-century popular religious text, much printed in the fifteenth and sixteenth centuries. In its original form it was entitled *Tractatus artis bene moriendi*, but it achieved real fame in the abbreviated version known as the *Ars moriendi*. In this form, it provided the text for some of the earliest block books, and is associated with a famous series of woodcuts. The first block book edition may have appeared before 1450, and others followed. From the mid-1470s onwards many editions were printed typographically, in Latin, German, French, Italian, Spanish, English (by Caxton (1490) and others), Swedish and Polish. The *Ars moriendi* spawned a whole tradition of devotional literature on death, of which the most famous English example is Jeremy Taylor's *Rule and Exercises of Holy Dying* (1651).

See Mary C. O'Connor, *The Art of Dying Well* (1942), which includes a very full study of the manuscripts and early printed versions; and for the English tradition Nancy L. Beatty, *The Craft of Dying* (1970).

See also **Block books**

Ashbee, Charles Robert (1863–1942)

See **Essex House Press**

Ashburnham, Bertram, 4th Earl of (1797–1878)

Collector of manuscripts. In 1881, the Historical Manuscripts Commission admirably understated the achievement of Ashburnham, by assessing his library as being of 'remarkable interest'. In fact, there were four libraries in one. The first was the Libri manuscripts, bought from the Count Libri, an Italian who had stolen them from various French libraries and archives, although Ashburnham could not have known that at the time; these were chiefly historical documents. Secondly, there were the Stowe manuscripts, bought from the 2nd Duke of Buckingham in 1848, a remarkable collection of English documents dating back to Anglo-Saxon times. Thirdly, Ashburnham owned the Barrois manuscripts, bought from J.B.J. Barrois in 1849; these were mainly French, and especially strong in medieval poetry and romance. Like many of Libri's books, some of Barrois's more properly belonged to the government of France. Finally, there were Ashburnham's individual purchases, always known as the 'Ashburnham Appendix'. The Appendix contained some of the grandest of all his books, including a ninth-century Gospel Book and a fifteenth-century manuscript of the York Miracle Plays. The whole library was one of the best ever assembled in England. After the Earl's death, the Stowe MSS. were sold to the British Museum, some of the Libri and Barrois MSS. returned to the Bibliothèque Nationale, Paris, and other libraries and archives in France, and the rest of the collection was dispersed. Some of the finest manuscripts are now in the Pierpont Morgan Library, New York.

There are accounts of Ashburnham by A.N.L. Munby in *HLB* (1969), pp. 5, 279; and in *Connoisseurs and Medieval Miniatures* (1972). The MSS. were listed in HMC, 8th Report, App. 3 (1881).

Ashendene Press

Private press. Established by C.H. St John Hornby in 1894, under the influence of Morris, first at Ashendene House, Hertfordshire, and then (1899) at Shelley House, Chelsea. From 1896, Hornby used Fell types from Oxford, but in 1902 had his own type cut. This was called Subiaco, and was based on the face used by Sweynheym and Pannartz at their press in 1465. It was a modified Gothic, as was a later type, the Ptolemy, based on a German design of the 1480s. Hornby regarded the Press as his chief concern, although he was also a distinguished collector, especially of medieval manuscripts. In all, over 40 books and a number of ephemeral items were issued, of which the best examples are editions of Dante (3 vols, 1902–5) and of *Don Quixote* (2 vols, 1927–28).

The Press ceased to operate in 1935. The founder's son sold the archives and other remains to Southern Methodist University, Texas, in the mid-1970s. Hornby's Albion, which was included in this sale, had for many years previously been on loan to the Bodleian Library, Oxford, where it was used for teaching and demonstration purposes.

A bibliography of Ashendene books, by Hornby and Arundel Esdaile, was published in 1935.

See also **Albion press**; **Fell, John** (1625–1686); **Gothic type**; **Private press movement**

Atlases

An atlas is a volume containing maps of a uniform size, intended to be comprehensive of the area which it covers, whether this is the whole world or a part of it. The first true atlas was Abraham Ortelius's *Theatrum orbis terrarum* (1570), followed by Gerard de Jode's *Speculum orbis terrarum* (1578). Gerard Mercator's *Atlas sive cosmographicae meditationes de fabrica mundi et fabricati figura* was published in three parts between 1585 and 1595. This not only gave its name to the genre, but also introduced Mercator's Projection, still used for the great majority of world maps. It was reprinted many times, and is the true ancestor of the modern atlas. Its first and greatest rival was Joan Blaeu's *Atlas maior* (1635, and many later editions) which was the standard atlas of eighteenth-century Europe.

See Leo Bagrow, *History of Cartography*, ed. R.A. Skelton (1964); and C. Koeman, *Blaeu and his Grand Atlas* (1970).

See also **Map printing**

Auction sales

The essential feature of an auction is that there is competitive bidding, and the bidder who offers the highest price is the buyer of the item. Books have been sold by auction since the late sixteenth century, and arguably for much longer. The auction appears to be Arabic in origin, and to have reached Europe through Moslem Spain, where sales are recorded as early as the eleventh century. Although it has been argued that these were not true auctions (lacking, for example, catalogues), the element of competition was certainly present. By the fourteenth century, sales 'by candle' were common in Spain, and by the mid-sixteenth century were also to be found in Northern Italy. The practice was for a candle to be lit, and the last bid before it went out was successful. In the 1590s, Dutch booksellers adapted this method by cataloguing the items to be sold, numbering the lots, and substituting the hammer for the candle. From this there evolved the modern practice of indicating the end of the bidding by the banging of a gavel, although in book auction houses today the gavel is a residual stump, and 'banging' is too violent a verb to convey the nature of the auctioneer's action.

It is traditionally asserted that the first book auction in the modern style was held at Elzevier's house in Leiden in 1604, but it is clear that sales had been held in the Netherlands for some time before that date. The first English book auction was held by William Cooper at Lazarus Seaman's house in London on 31 October 1676, when Seaman's books were sold. Over the next few years both Cooper and Edward Millington held a number of auctions in London, Oxford and Cambridge. By the middle of the eighteenth century the auction had become, as it remains, the principal means of selling large libraries. The first specialist auctioneers were the Sothebys whose firm still exist.

For the early history of the auction, see Anthony Hobson, 'A sale by candle in 1608', *Libr.* (1971), p. 215; and Albert Ehrman and Graham Pollard, *The Distribution of Books by Catalogue* (1965). John Lawler's *Book Auctions in England in the Seventeenth Century* (1891) is still of some value. For lists of British sales, see *List of Catalogues of English Book Sales now in the British Museum* (1915), superseded for the seventeenth and eighteenth centuries by A.N.L. Munby and Lenore Coral, *British Book Sale Catalogues 1676–1800* (1977).

See also **Elzevier**; **Sothebys**

Audubon, John James (1785–1851)

Ornithologist and book illustrator. The illegitimate son of a French seafarer and a serving girl, Audubon was born in Santo Domingo (Haiti), but in 1789 was taken first to the USA and then to France by his father. In 1802–3 he studied drawing under David in Paris, but returned to America in 1803, and there began his life-long studies of birds as well as becoming involved in various business ventures. He spent a brief period in the French navy, but finally settled in the USA, in 1806. He now began to make a series of drawings of American birds, and by the early 1820s was looking for patrons to enable him to publish them. He failed in the US, but took his drawings to England and exhibited them there. As a result he acquired a considerable reputation as an artist, and in 1827 was able to issue a prospectus for *Birds of America.* Publication began in the same year and was completed in 1838.

Birds of America is perhaps the most spectacular book ever printed. It is a massive elephant folio, the drawings are superb, and the quality of the engraving equal to them. In many copies they have been hand coloured. Copies can be seen on exhibition in many research libraries in the USA; needless to say, the book is now very rare and phenomenally expensive. Audubon published other books, but he never again reached these standards. He died, alone and insane, in 1851.

See Francis Hobart Herrick, *Audubon the Naturalist* (2 vols, 1938), which includes a competent bibliography. Alton Lindsey, *The Bicentennial of John Audubon* (1985) is a useful recent work.

See also **Prospectus**

Authorised Version

See **Bibles**

Bagford, John (1650–1716)

Book collector and destroyer of books. A shoemaker by trade, Bagford began to collect books and to deal in them. His finest collection was of single-sheet ballads, of which he collected hundreds, many of them unique. After his death they were bought by Harley, and they went to the British Museum (British Library) with his manuscript collections where they are now bound in three volumes (C.40. m.9.-11.). A selection was edited for the Ballad Society by J.W. Ebsworth (1878). Less creditably, Bagford dismembered thousands of books, and pasted their title pages and other fragments into guard books, now also in the British Library. His intention, never fulfilled, was to write a history of printing. There is a 'rough list' of the contents of the Bagford collection in *TBS* (1902–4), p.23, and a catalogue of the title-pages by Melvin H. Wolf (1974).

A life of Bagford will be found in *DNB*; and his own account of his collecting activities was printed by Robert Steele in *Libr.* (1907), p.223.
See also **Ballads**; **Harley, Robert, 1st Earl of Oxford** (1661–1724) **and Harley, Edward, 2nd Earl of Oxford** (1689–1741)

Bale, John (1495–1563)

Bibliographer. Bale was an early convert to Protestantism, who rose high in the Church under Edward VI, was exiled under Mary I, and returned to

England in 1558. He was a virulent and controversial theologian, and a mediocre dramatist whose plays are of some historical interest. He compiled the first list of British books and authors, published as *Illustrium maioris Britanniae scriptorum summarium* (1548). This work, in its second, enlarged edition (1557, 1559), remained a standard work of reference for some two centuries, and is still of some value for medieval books.

There is a life of Bale in *DNB*; and a bibliography of his writings by W.T. Davies, *OBSP* (1940), p. 201, and J.G. McManaway, *OBSP* (1949), p. 44.

Ballads

Songs written for public performance, usually in the street or in taverns, and often sung to traditional tunes. Ballad singers existed for centuries before the invention of printing, but almost all medieval ballads, whose transmission was largely oral, have been lost. A few were, however, written down, and survive. The earliest surviving printed ballads date from the early sixteenth century, but earlier examples may have been lost. Indeed, most of the extant printed ballads are unique, and it is known that many thousands of copies of each were normally printed, suggesting that whole editions have vanished without trace. Ballads were usually printed as broadsides, although in the eighteenth century half sheets and quarter sheets (known as 'slip-songs') were used.

Some ballads were on traditional folk subjects such as Robin Hood, but others were on contemporary political or religious themes, and used for propaganda purposes, especially among the illiterate and the poor. The political purpose came to predominate, especially after the middle of the seventeenth century. The printed ballad declined in popularity in the second half of the eighteenth century. For political purposes it was displaced by the newspaper, and the traditional popular literature, whether prose or verse, was more usually printed in chapbook format. In the early nineteenth century, however, the ballad was revived in print by two publishers, James Catnach (1792-1841), and John Pitts (1765-1844). It finally expired in the later nineteenth century, displaced by the new popular songs of the music hall. The 'ballad' of contemporary popular music is usually a sentimental story, quite unlike its robust, earthy predecessors.

The trade in printed ballads was highly lucrative, and during the seventeenth century became the jealously guarded monopoly of a small group of London booksellers, known as the 'Ballad Partners'. This arrangement residually survived the Copyright Act 1710, but finally came to an end in 1732 when the pre-1710 copyrights expired, although by that time the ballad was already in decline. It was, however, to some extent taken up by the provincial printers, some of whom printed large numbers for local and regional sale. The surviving ballad trade in London was largely in the hands of William and Cluer Dicey, who were also dominant in the closely related chapbook trade. Although the ballads were sold in bookshops, they were also, and probably more commonly, sold in the streets. Indeed, because of the political content of so many ballads, legislation in the seventeenth century attempted to regulate street sales of ballad sheets. In practice, however, control proved difficult if not impossible to enforce, and the ballad became an important medium for the expression of political dissent until its eclipse in the 1740s. In the last 20 or so years of its active existence, it was particularly associated with the Jacobite cause.

Ballad sheets were collected as early as the seventeenth century by such collectors as Anthony Wood, whose collection is now in the Bodleian Library, Oxford, and, somewhat later, by John Bagford. The scholarly study and reprinting of ballads, as examples of folk poetry, began in the late eighteenth century; the pioneers were Thomas Percy and Joseph Ritson. They had many successors, and during the nineteenth century many collections of ballads were published, and the interest in them, especially as documents of the social history of a class whose history is rarely recorded elsewhere, has, if anything, increased in the last 30 years.

The literature of balladry is vast. Victor E. Neuburg, *Popular Literature* (1977) is a useful general introduction, and has an annotated bibliography. More specific, and more scholarly, are Willa Muir, *Living with Ballads* (1965); and M.J.C. Hodgart, *The Ballads* (1950). Among the major volumes of reprints, most with introductory matter, are those of Percy (ed. H.B. Wheatley, 1886); Ritson (3rd edn, by W.C. Hazlitt, 1877); Robert Bell (1857); and Hyder E. Rollins (*The Pack of Autolycus* (1927)). On the ballad trade, the classic paper is by Cyprian Blagden, *SB* (1954), p.161, supplemented on the Diceys by Neuburg, *Libr.* (1969), p.219, and on Pitts by Leslie Shepard, *John Pitts* (1969). Earlier works still of some value are those by Charles Hindley, *The Life and Times of James Catnach* (1878); and *The History of the Catnach Press* (1887).

See also **Bagford, John** (1650–1716); **Censorship**; **Chapbooks**; **Copyright**; **Half sheet**; **Quarter sheet**; **Slip songs**

BAMBAM

Acronym of Bookline Alert — Missing Books And Manuscripts. It is an on-line system whose data-base contains details of stolen and missing rare books and manuscripts, and is used increasingly by libraries and the trade in the USA to combat this problem. Subscribers can input details of missing items, or check items which are offered to them. The system is linked to BOOK-LINE, and run from the same office. It is part of an elaborate security network evolved by librarians and booksellers in the USA, described in John H. Jenkins, *Rare Books and Manuscript Thefts* (1982). UK libraries and dealers can use BAMBAM, but there is also a separate, less elaborate and non-computerised British system, described in *RBGN* (September 1979), p.18.

See also **American Book Prices Current**

Bar

See **Common press**

Bartlett, Roger (c. 1639–1712)

Bookbinder. Bartlett began his career in London, but moved to Oxford in 1666, having lost his shop in the Great Fire. He had some initial difficulties with the University authorities, but he established his business successfully, and was responsible for a number of fine gold-tooled bindings. These included the University's official gifts to Cosimo d'Medici (1674).

The broad outlines of Bartlett's career were established by I.G. Philip, 'Roger Bartlett, bookbinder', *Libr.* (1956), p. 233; and supplemented by H.M. Nixon, 'Roger Bartlett's bookbindings,' *Libr.* (1962), p. 56. Philip's paper has illustrations of the Medici bindings, and other examples of Bartlett's work can be found in Howard M. Nixon, *Five Centuries of English Bookbinding* (1978); and the Bodleian Library exhibition catalogue entitled *Fine Bindings, 1500–1700, from Oxford Libraries* (1968).

See also **Bookbinding**

Bartolozzi, Francesco (1727–1815)

See **Stipple engraving**

Baskerville, John (1706–1775)

Printer and type designer. Baskerville trained as a carver of letters in stone (for monuments), and subsequently made a fortune in the japanning trade in Birmingham. In the mid-1750s, already a wealthy man, he began to interest himself in printing, and designed and cut his first punches, of which a specimen was issued in 1754. His first book was an edition of Virgil (1757), an astonishing production often regarded as his masterpiece. There followed editions of Milton (1758, 1759, 1760), Congreve (1761), Addison (1761), and a number of classical authors including Horace (1762), Lucretius (1772), Terence (1772) and Sallust and Florus (1773). In 1758, Baskerville became Printer to the University at Cambridge, and in that capacity produced four editions of the *Book of Common Prayer* (1760, 1761, 1762), and the great folio Bible of 1762. Although Baskerville did undertake work for commercial publishers, he was always more concerned with quality than with profit. He experimented not only with new type designs, but also with laid paper, and with various modifications to the common press itself. His perfectionism, and the fact that he was wealthy enough to indulge it, made him perhaps the finest printer in English history. His type designs are still in use, and are indeed highly regarded for their elegance and legibility. His punches survive, having been bought by Caron de Beaumarchais for his type foundry in 1779; after almost 200 years in France, they returned to England in 1953, and are now, appropriately, at Cambridge University Press.

The standard work on Baskerville is still that by Ralph Straus and Robert K. Dent, *John Baskerville* (1907), but F.E. Pardoe's *John Baskerville* (1975) is also useful. There is a bibliography by Philip Gaskell (rev. edn, 1973), and a history of the punches by John Dreyfus in *Libr.* (1950–51), p. 26.

See also **Cambridge University Press**; **Common press**; **Papermaking**; **Typecasting**; **Whatman, James** (1702-1759) **and Whatman, James** (1741-1798)

Bastarda

Type design. One of the four basic groups of Gothic type. It is a rounded letterform, based on the cursive hand used for vernacular documents in Germany in the fifteenth century. The first use of it was by Gutenberg in his 1454 and 1455 indulgences, and it won widespread favour in both Germany and France in the fifteenth and sixteenth centuries. Caxton's first type was a Bastarda, and his example was imitated by other English printers to *c.* 1540. Its longest survival was as Fraktur, which remained the normal book face in Germany until the end of World War II. Granjon's design called 'La Bâtarde' (1567) is more properly a Civilité than a Bastarda, although the two are related.

See also **Caxton William** (1422?-1491); **Civilité**; **Gothic type**; **Gutenberg, Johann** (1394/99-1468)

Baxter, George (1804-1867)

Colour printer. Baxter trained as a wood-engraver, and learned the new art of lithography, before he began to experiment with colour printing. His process, which he patented in 1835, combined his two skills. He made a lithographic drawing or engraved a copper plate, including tiny marks to indicate the boundaries between colours. Impressions were then taken on wood, one for each colour, and the blocks were engraved. Each was then printed in turn, in its own colour, with the marks ensuring correct register. Baxter also developed improved oil-based inks, which gave an excellent impression. The process was first used in Robert Mudie's *Feathered Tribes of the British Islands* (1834), and in 1835-37 a number of other books were published with Baxter prints. After that year, he concentrated on separate prints, the two most famous being of Queen Victoria's coronation, and her arrival to open her first Parliament (both published in 1841). Baxter's process, despite the patent, was used by others, and indeed it has been claimed that he had no right to patent it, since a similar process had been in intermittent use since the middle of the sixteenth century. Baxter, however, was a perfectionist, and the results far outshone those of his distant predecessors. In 1849, Baxter renewed his patent, but thereafter granted licences to other printers to use the process. Some of the licensees modified the process, but none achieved results as good as Baxter's own. By that time, however, the Baxter process was being displaced by chromolithography.

21

He died an undischarged bankrupt.

There are accounts of Baxter in Joan M. Freidman, *Color Printing in England 1486–1870* (1978); Martin Hardie, *English Coloured Books* (1906); and Ruari McLean, *Victorian Book Design and Colour Printing* (1972).

See also **Chromolithography**; **Colour printing**; **Impression**

Bay Psalm Book

The first extant book printed in North America. The printer was Stephen Daye of Cambridge, Massachusetts, who issued the book in 1640. In itself, it is unremarkable, containing a metrical translation of the Psalms by a number of colonial ministers, including Richard Mather and John Cotton. Its primacy, however, has made it one of the great books of the world, and it commands astronomical prices on the rare occasions when a copy appears in the market. At present, 11 copies are known, all but one of them (in the Bodleian Library, Oxford) in the USA.

The best recent account of the book is by Zoltan Haraszti, *The Enigma of the Bay Psalm Book* (1956), which includes a facsimile of the 1640 edition.

Beatty, Sir Alfred Chester (1875–1968)

Book collector. Chester Beatty made his fortune as a mining engineer in Africa in the early years of the twentieth century. He began collecting as a young man, but his real interest in manuscripts was aroused during a visit to Egypt in 1913. Thereafter he assembled a large and superb collection, especially notable for its oriental manuscripts. These included 70 Armenian manuscripts (the largest private collection in Europe), over 100 Turkish manuscripts and many separate miniatures, and some 3500 Arabic manuscripts, including some especially notable Qurans. The crown of the collection, however, was the group of Biblical papyri, dating from the second to the fourth centuries, which are of the utmost importance in the history of the Greek text of the Bible, especially of the Pauline Epistles. He owned a series of papyri of Coptic texts, notably of the 'lost' books of the Manichees, and other items varying from cuneiform tablets to excellent medieval western manuscripts.

Chester Beatty was born an American, but became a British subject in 1933. In 1950 he moved to Dublin, believing Britain to be in the irreversible grip of socialism which he hated. He became an Irish citizen, and bequeathed his library to the Republic of Ireland. It is housed in the building he constructed for it in a suburb of Dublin.

There is an account of the collection by R.J. Hayes in *BC* (1958), p. 253, and of Chester Beatty himself in his obituary in *The Times* (22 January 1968). The Arabic manuscripts have been catalogued by A.J. Arberry (1955-66), and the Biblical papyri edited by Sir Fredric Kenyon (1934-41).

Bentley, Richard (1794–1871)

Publisher. Bentley was born into the trade, being the nephew of John Nichols, and the son of the proprietor of the *General Evening Post.* He was trained by Nichols, and in 1819 joined his brother's printing firm. In 1829 he went into partnership with Henry Colburn (d. 1855), a formerly successful publisher of popular novels whose business had been badly damaged in the financial crisis of 1825–26. Bentley gradually put the firm back on its feet, but the partners disagreed violently, and in 1832 Bentley bought out Colburn's share. Bentley now entered his most successful period. His series of *Standard Novels* reprinted older fiction, such as Jane Austen, while his new titles included works by Bulwer-Lytton, Harrison Ainsworth and Maria Edgeworth, all immensely popular with contemporary readers. In 1842, however, he found himself in financial difficulties, and the firm never really recovered, although it survived in a poor state until 1898 when it was bought by Macmillan.

Bentley's archives survive, although they are divided between the British Library and the University of Illinois at Urbana, Ill., USA, and a few lesser repositories. This archive formed the basis of Royal A. Gettman, *A Victorian Publisher* (1960), a valuable study of many aspects of nineteenth-century publishing. See also Michael Sadleir, *Bentley's Standard Novel Series. Its history and achievements* (1932). For the early years, see John Sutherland, 'Henry Colburn, publisher', *PH* (1986), p. 59.

See also **Nichols, John** (1745–1826)

Berne Convention

International copyright agreement. The Berne Convention was the first systematic attempt to make a general international agreement on copyright. The Convention was evolved at a conference of the major European countries held at Berne, Switzerland, in 1885, and came into force in 1887, with the UK as one of the signatories. The USA, however, was not a signatory, and because of the peculiarities of American copyright law she has never signed. This remained a fundamental gap in international copyright protection until the Universal Copyright Convention was produced by Unesco in 1957. The basic principle of the Berne Convention is that all works published in any of the signatory countries are protected under the law of all signatory countries as if they had first been published there. The Convention has been revised several times (1896, 1908, 1928, 1948, 1967, 1971); together with the Universal Copyright Convention it is the foundation of international copyright law.

See R.F. Whale and Jeremy J. Phillips, *Whale on Copyright* (3rd edn, 1983).

See also **Copyright**; **Universal Copyright Convention**

Bewick, Thomas (1753–1828)

Wood engraver. Bewick was born at Ovingham, Northumberland, and in 1767 was apprenticed to Ralph Beilby, an engraver in Newcastle upon Tyne. Beilby was primarily a metal engraver, but Bewick became attracted to the declining art of wood engraving. In 1777, three years after the end of his apprenticeship, he joined Beilby as a partner, and began his wood engraving on a commerical basis. He was responsible for two crucial technical innovations: he engraved the end of the plank rather than along the line of the grain; and used an elaborate 'white-line' cross-hatching technique to achieve fine detail. The result of these techniques, together with his skill as an artist, allowed Bewick to achieve perhaps the best results of any wood engraver. He was by instinct a countryman, and his most famous works are a by-product of his interest in natural history: *A History of Quadrupeds* (1790), and *A History of British Birds* (2 vols, 1797, 1804). The latter is widely regarded as his masterpiece, and was often reprinted in the nineteenth century. The text for both books was written by Beilby, although heavily revised by Bewick himself. The books, however, represent only a small part of Bewick's total output, for he was always a commercial engraver, and produced book illustrations through the whole spectrum from luxury editions to chapbooks, as well as such work as letterheads, banknotes, and the like.

Large numbers of Bewick's blocks survive, but they are widely scattered in collections throughout the world. The best collection in public hands is probably the Pease Collection in Newcastle Central Library. In recent years, there has been a revival of interest in Bewick, but the best published collection of prints from his blocks probably remains that by Julia Boyd, *Bewick Gleanings* (1886). Bewick's autobiography (ed. Iain Bain, 1975) is the best account of his life and work. There is a bibliography by Sydney Roscoe (1973).

See also **Wood engraving**

Bibles

The Bible is the sacred book of Christians, consisting of the Old and New Testaments. The books which now form the Old Testament were brought together in their present form and order by Jewish scholars in *c.* 100 AD, but some 200–300 years earlier large parts of this had been translated from Hebrew into Greek. The New Testament was written in Greek by various writers during the first century AD. In the Middle Ages, the Bible was used in Western Europe in the Latin translation of St Jerome (made 382–404), known as the Vulgate, and it was this version which was first printed by Gutenberg in 1450–55. Bibles were among the most common products of medieval scriptoria, and those intended for use in church were among the largest and most splendid of medieval books. As well as complete Bibles, the New Testament was often written separately, as were the four Gospels. Early printers were equally prolific in Bible production, but the first century of printing also coincided with a more critical approach to the accuracy of the text itself, and a revival of interest in, and knowledge of, both Greek and Hebrew. The beginning of this process is associated with the Dutch scholar, Desiderius Erasmus (*c.* 1466–1536) who in 1516 published a newly-edited Greek New Testament which revolutionised Biblical studies. At the same time, the Complutensian Polyglot (Alcala, 1522) made available early texts in other ancient Christian languages such as Coptic and Syriac. The Greek text was finally established in Estienne's edition of 1550.

The translation of the Bible into European vernaculars was largely a consequence of the Reformation in the mid-sixteenth century, although there had been earlier attempts. The most notable was the English Bible of John Wycliffe, written in 1382–88, which was banned and burned by the Church. The Protestant churches, however, encouraged Bible reading, and translation was consequently one of their major activities. The first English version of the sixteenth century was that by William Tyndale (Cologne, 1526), which was revised by Miles Coverdale in 1535. This was the first English Bible published officially in England; in a revised form, known as the Great Bible (1539), it was ordered to be used in churches, and remained standard until it was displaced by a new official translation (the Authorised Version, or King James's Bible) in 1611. This was used in the Church of England (and by many dissenting churches) until the middle of the twentieth century, although the Revised Version (NT, 1881; OT, 1885), which 'updated' it, was sometimes preferred. It has now been replaced by a scholarly, but ill-written, translation into 'modern' English, the New English Bible (NT, 1961; OT, 1970). There are, of course, many other English translations, both old and new.

The history of Biblical translation into other languages is equally complex, and in some cases further complicated by the Roman Catholic Church's long-standing objections to vernacular versions. The first vernacular Bible was Mentelin's German version (Strassburg, 1466), although it was ultimately replaced by Luther's classic translation (Wittenberg, 1534). Next came a Dutch version (Delft, 1477), followed by Czech (Prague, 1488), and Jacques le Fèvre's French translation (Antwerp, 1530), known as the Antwerp Bible. The establishment of the Protestant churches of Northern Europe led to the making of official translations like those published in England. Among these are Christian III's Bible in Danish (Copenhagen, 1550), which was in fact translated from Luther's German and was replaced in 1559 by Frederick II's Bible, and, in Sweden, Gustavus Vasa's Bible (Uppsåla, 1541), revised in 1618.

The history of the Bible is a vast subject; the non-specialist however, is well served by the *The Cambridge History of the Bible* (3 vols, 1963–70), which includes good bibliographies. For the bibliographical history of the English Bible, see T.H. Darlow and H.F. Moule, *Historical Catalogue of Printed Editions of the English Bible, 1525–1961*, revised by A.S. Herbert (1968); vol. 2 of the original edition (1911) lists foreign language editions then in the Library of the British and Foreign Bible Society.

See also **Estienne, Robert** (1498/99–1559); **Gutenberg, Johann** (1394/99–1468); **Textual criticism**

Biblia Pauperum

See **Block books**

Bibliographica

Bibliographical and bibliophilic periodical. It was published in three volumes. (1895–97) under the editorship of A.W. Pollard. In fact, *Bibliographica* was not so much a conventional periodical as a collection of lengthy essays published serially, for it was never intended to go beyond three volumes. The format is a generous quarto and it was lavishly printed. There are articles on a wide range of topics, although book illustration is predominant. There is an index to the whole series in vol. 3 (1897).

See also **Pollard, Alfred William** (1859–1944)

Bibliographical Society

Founded 1892. The moving spirits behind the foundation of the Bibliographical Society were Copinger and J.Y.W. (later Sir James) MacAlister, the Secretary of the Library Association. Their hope was that the Society could specialise in those bibliographical matters which were, inevitably, only a part of the LA's concerns. In practice, this soon came to mean an almost total concentration on historical bibliography in all its aspects. The pattern of the Society's activities has not changed substantially since 1892; it holds monthly meetings in London during the winter, and publishes a periodical and various series of monographs. From its inception, the Society has spread its wings widely, and has always included not only scholars and librarians but also the amateurs of the book world who have so enriched and enlivened bibliographical studies. Inevitably, the Society was closely associated with the British Museum, and for many years (1893–1924) Pollard was either Secretary or Joint Secretary. Together with Greg and McKerrow, of whom the latter was Secretary or Joint Secretary from 1912 to 1940, Pollard was the major influence on the development of the Society during its formative years.

The first volume of the *Transactions* was published in 1893; in 1920 the Society took over the name and goodwill of the *The Library*. The first monograph was published in 1894, and there has also been a series of monographic supplements to the *Transactions*, the first in 1891. A new series of occasional monographic publications began publication in 1985. The Society's most important publication is *STC* (1926), and it has also been responsible for planning and organising the revised edition.

There is a history of the Society by F.C. (later Sir Frank) Francis in *The Bibliographical Society 1892–1942. Studies in Retrospect* (1945). The same volume includes lists of office-holders and publications, and a series of essays by Greg and others on the Society's role in the development of bibliography during the period.

The address of the Society is British Library Reference Division, Great Russell Street, London WC1E 3DG.

See also **Bibliography**; **Copinger, Walter Arthur** (1847–1910); **Greg, Sir Walter Wilson** (1875–1959); **Historical bibliography**; *Library, The*; **McKerrow, Ronald Brunlees** (1872–1940); **Pollard, Alfred William** (1859–1944); *STC*

Bibliographical Society of America

Founded 1904 by Aksel G.S. Josephson and other members of the Bibliographical Society of Chicago. It exists to promote the study of bibliography, but the sheer size of the USA inevitably means that this is done almost entirely through publications, although in recent years it has also promoted fellowships for bibliographical studies. An annual meeting is held in New York City, and occasional meetings elsewhere. The first volume of its *Papers* was published in 1904, and many monographs have also been issued. Among the most important is the *Census* of incunabula in the USA (1919, 1940, 1964), most recently revised by Goff. BSA is also the sponsor of Blanck's *Bibliography of American Literature*.

An account of the Society by J.M. Edelstein was in *PBSA* (1979), p. 389, and to commemorate its 75th anniversary the Society published *The Bibliographical Society of America 1904–79. A Retrospective Collection* (1980).

The Society's address is P.O. Box 397, Grand Central Station, New York, NY 10017.

See also **Blanck, Jacob** (1906–1974); **Goff, Frederick Richmond** (1900–1982); *Papers of the Bibliographical Society of America*

Bibliographical Society of Australia and New Zealand

Founded 1970. It publishes a quarterly *Bulletin* (1970–   ), which is not entirely confined to matters of Australasian interest.

Bibliographical Society of Canada

Founded 1962. The Society exists to promote bibliographical study in and of Canada. It publishes (in French and English) *Papers* (1962–   ). There are index to vols 1-5 (vol. 6, p. 3), 5-10 (vol. 11, p. 3), and 11-15 (1982).

Bibliography

A much-abused word. Strictly, 'bibliography' is 'the writing of books', but it has come to mean 'writing about books', and by extension 'the compiling of lists of books' and 'lists of books' themselves. In common usage it is the latter meaning which is most familiar, but in the twentieth century bibliography has been an academic growth area, and its practitioners have added a whole range of other meanings. The modern convention is to consider bibliography to have several branches, including enumerative, descriptive, analytical, historical and textual (or critical). Only the first two of these are primarily concerned with lists of books. To compound the confusion, we must also distinguish between bibliography and *a* bibliography. The latter is a list of books which attempts to be comprehensive within its chosen field; the former is the method used in compiling such a list. For centuries, the two were substantially identical, but in the last 100 years they have become increasingly distinct.

The earliest book lists were probably inventories of libraries, although bibliographies were compiled in antiquity and in the Middle Ages. It was, however, the invention of printing, and the consequent increase both in the number of titles and in the number of copies of each title, which made bibliography a necessity for scholars and the book trade alike. Gessner, 'the father of bibliography', published the first edition of his *Bibliotheca universalis* in 1545; it was the first attempt at a universal bibliography. Gessner had followers and imitators, including Bale in England. The early bibliographers were practising what is now called enumerative bibliography.

By the early eighteenth century, the invention of printing and incunabula were themselves beginning to be of interest as historical phenomena, and the history of bibliography from that time until the late nineteenth century is indissolubly linked with that of incunable studies. The pioneer was Maittaire whose *Annales typographici* was published in five volumes between 1719 and 1741. It was the first attempt to list the books of the fifteenth century. Succeeding generations of incunabulists continued to work along the same lines; Panzer, Hain, Copinger and Reichling all attempted to complete the published record of incunabula, an effort which reached its climax in the establishment of the Kommission für Gesamtkatalog der Weigendrücke in 1908.

Meanwhile, however, other approaches were being evolved. In France, the confiscation of libraries during the Revolution led to a higher standard of cataloguing of sixteenth- and seventeenth-century books, as the public custodians of these libraries tried to make inventories of the nation's newly-acquired property. In England, nearly a century later, a small group of incunabulists introduced revolutionary new techniques into the study of books. The pioneer, and the founding father of modern bibliography, was Bradshaw. Although his published output was comparatively slight, he was immensely influential through his personal contacts and his wide correspondence. He turned his attention to type and what he called 'type families'; by identifying the type used by a particular printer, he was able to trace that printer's work in books without an imprint, of which there was a great number in the fifteenth century. His example was followed by Proctor, whose

Index to the Early Printed Books in the British Museum (1898) was the first-fruit
of what Bradshaw himself called 'scientific' bibliography, and others the
'natural history' method, both designations reflecting the fashionable
Darwinism of late nineteenth-century Cambridge.

The influence of the late nineteenth-century incunabulists was reflected in
two ways outside their own specialist field. First, in general terms, they had
shown that a rigorous and logical methodology could yield fruitful results.
Secondly, and more specifically, they had directed the attention of bibliographers away from the title-page and into the body of the book itself. The
great triumvirate of modern bibliography, Greg, Pollard and McKerrow, took
up the implicit challenge of scientific bibliography. From the 1890s until, in
Greg's case, the 1950s, they developed a new bibliographical methodology,
rationale and terminology, which they applied chiefly to English books of the
sixteenth and seventeenth centuries. Although both Greg and Pollard were
primarily interested in the textual applications of bibliographical study, their
work laid the foundations of our understanding of early printed books. All
three men insisted on the crucial importance of understanding how books
were made, and from their knowledge of printing-house procedures they were
able to detect in the printed book itself the clues to its own history and
manufacture. Thus they evolved what is now called analytical bibliography, a
term probably coined by Greg, who also used these techniques as the basis of
a more detailed and informative descriptive procedure.

They were all active in the promotion of bibliography. Although none was
ever a teacher, all of them did a good deal of lecturing, and both Greg and
Pollard were prolific writers. McKerrow was perhaps less of a public figure,
but as the first editor of *The Review of English Studies* he helped to set new
standards of scholarship in the rapidly developing field of English literature.
The early history of the Bibliographical Society is largely the story of these
three, and Pollard was, for many years, editor of *The Library*.

To some extent the initiative in bibliography passed to the United States
after World War II. Fredson Bowers' *Principles of Bibliographical Description*
(1949) is the bible of its subject; in it, Bowers systematised and elaborated
(some might say over-elaborated) the work of the previous half-century. It
remains the most enduring monument of early twentieth-century bibliography, embodying the belief that a book properly studied will yield all the
information necessary for that study.

Bibliography has not, however, stood still. Over the last 20 years, doubts
have been expressed about the validity of some of the work of the first half of
the twentieth century, although those doubts have concerned its procedural
applications of inferential logic rather than its basic principles. The doubts
turn on essentially two points: first, whether some of the minuter procedures
of analytical bibliography produce worthwhile or even, in some cases, accurate,
results, and secondly, whether it is indeed the case that a book can (or should)
be studied in isolation. The first point could be seen as a challenge to the
central doctrine of the bibliographical creed, for it has been shown from
external documentary evidence that inferences from observed features of
books are not always an accurate guide to, for example, typesetting and
printing procedures. This line of argument is particularly associated with the

work of D.F. McKenzie on the early archives of Cambridge University Press, published as *The Cambridge University Press 1696–1712* (2 vols, 1966). The second objection, that books cannot be studied in isolation, is related to a broader development in modern historiography which argues that the past can only be understood as a whole; this is thought particularly pertinent to the history of the book, for the book is a societal object and must therefore be understood in a societal context. The concept of total history is French in origin, and its application to book history is associated with the name of Henri-Jean Martin, who, in 1958, completed and published *L'apparition du livre* (translated into English as *The Coming of the Book* (1976)), planned by his late teacher, Lucien Febvre, himself a pioneer of *histoire totale*. It is an approach increasingly favoured by younger scholars in both Britain and the United States.

Arguments about the meaning of the word 'bibliography' can be somewhat sterile, for what is important is the study of the subject itself. If a definition must be offered, perhaps it had better be that bibliography is what bibliographers do. What do bibliographers do? They study books. And that is what bibliography is: the study of books.

There is a large theoretical literature of bibliography. For the history of the subject, see Rudolph Blum, *Bibliographia — eine Wort-und Begriffsgeschichte Untersuchung* (1969) (translated into English as *Bibliographia. An inquiry into its definition and designation* (1980)); and Theodore Besterman, *The Beginnings of Systematic Bibliography* (1935). A useful recent work is Bernard H. Breslauer and Roland Folter, *Bibliography: its history and development* (1984). Greg's evolving position will be found in two papers: 'What is bibliography?', *TBS* (1914), p. 39; and 'Bibliography — an apologia', *Libr.* (1932–33), p. 113, both reprinted in his *Collected Papers* (1966). A useful introduction to bibliographical practice is Roy Stokes' *Function of Bibliography* (2nd edn, 1982), but for a complete survey of the field Philip Gaskell's *New Introduction to Bibliography* (1972) is indispensable. For the more recent trends in book history, see G. Thomas Tanselle, *The History of Books as a Field of Study* (1981).

See also **Analytical bibliography**; **Bale, John** (1495–1563); **Bibliographical Society**; **Bradshaw, Henry** (1831–1886); **Catalogues**; **Copinger, Walter Arthur** (1847–1910); **Descriptive bibliography**; **Enumerative bibliography**; *Gesamtkatalog der Weigendrücke*; **Gessner, Conrad** (1516–1566); **Greg, Sir Walter Wilson** (1875–1959); **Historical bibliography**; **Incunabula**; *Library, The*; **McKerrow, Ronald Brunlees** (1872–1940); **Maittaire, Michael** (1668–1747); **Panzer, Georg Wolfgang Franz von** (1729–1805); **Pollard, Alfred William** (1859–1944); **Proctor, Robert George Collie** (1868–1903); **Textual criticism**

Bibliography Newsletter

Bibliographical periodical. *BiN* first appeared in January 1973 as a monthly publication; it has been somewhat irregular from time to time, but has now settled into a quarterly pattern. In its early years it carried short notes on bibliography and book-trade history, but recently has become what its name implies, a news service of matters relating to bibliography and rare book librarianship. As such it is unique and invaluable. It also carries lists of new books in the field, and sometimes trenchant reviews of them. The publisher is Terry Belanger of Columbia University, New York City, and the editors are Belanger and Daniel Traister.

Bibliography of American Literature

See **Blanck, Jacob** (1906–1974)

Bibliomania

Literally 'madness caused by books'. In fact, the term is applied to a remarkable period in the history of English book collecting in the first two decades of the nineteenth century, and was coined for the purpose by Dibdin. It began when books from France flooded onto the English market in the late 1790s, and was spearheaded by two remarkable collectors, Earl Spencer and the Duke of Roxburghe. Its climax was the sale of the latter's library in 1812, at which prices were paid which, in some cases, were not to be equalled until the twentieth century. The bibliomaniacs were collectors of incunabula, fine bindings and fine printing of all periods, and by their interest in these fields changed the whole direction of English bibliophily.

There is an account of the period in Seymour de Ricci, *English Collectors of Books and Manuscripts (1530-1930)* (1930), but its flavour is best tasted in the works of Dibdin himself.

See also **Book collecting**; **Dibdin, Thomas Frognall** (1776–1847); **Roxburghe Club**; **Spencer, John Charles, 2nd Earl Spencer** (1782–1845)

Bibliotheca Lindesiana

The library of Alexander, 25th Earl of Crawford (1812–80), his son, Ludovic (1847–1913), and his daughter Jane (1862–1948). Crawford began collecting as a schoolboy, and then as a young man decided to form a collection which would relate to the very distinguished history of the Lindsay family. He broadened this into a library of all aspects of literature and history to be kept at the family home at Haigh Hall in Lancashire. He bought heavily at the Heber sales (1834), and thereafter was one of the mainstays of the London antiquarian book trade. His association with Quaritch was long and fruitful, and he also did a great deal of buying during trips to the Continent. The library came to be one of the greatest collections ever formed; it was particularly strong in ballads, Bibles and liturgies, Royal Proclamations and other single-sheet materials, early printing, materials relating to the French Revolution and Napoleon, and oriental and medieval manuscripts. Various catalogues were published, most notably that of the printed books (1910–13). There were some sales after the 25th Earl's death, including the oriental manuscripts which were bought by Mrs Rylands for her new library in Manchester. Ludovic, however, shared his father's interests and maintained the library substantially intact, whilst also arranging for it to be professionally catalogued. The bulk of the library remained at Haigh until it had to be sold to pay death duties in 1947–48 (Sotheby, London).

There is a history of the library by N.J. Barker, *Bibliotheca Lindesiana* (1977).

See also **Heber, Richard** (1774–1833); **John Rylands University Library of Manchester**; **Quaritch, Bernard** (1819–1899)

Bibliotheck, The

Bibliographical periodical. *The Bibliotheck* has been published since 1956 by the Scottish Group of the University, College and Research Section of the Library Association. It is almost entirely devoted to bibliographical articles and reviews of Scottish interest or with Scottish connections. Since 1969, an *Annual Bibliography of Scottish Literature* has been published as a supplement. An *Index* to vols 1-10 was published in 1985. The present editor is G.D. Hargreaves.

Birmingham Bibliographical Society

Founded 1973. In addition to holding meetings for members, the Society is compiling and publishing a series of *Working Papers for an Historical Directory of the West Midlands Book Trade to 1850*. Five parts, covering the period to 1819, have so far been published. This is a useful work, which has been used as a model for similar projects elsewhere in the UK.

The Society's address is Main Library, University of Birmingham, Birmingham B15 2TT.

See also **Liverpool Bibliographical Society**

Black letter

Type design. It is the generic name for the common form of Gothic type used in England from the sixteenth century onwards, ultimately derived from Caxton's Texturas.

See also **Caxton, William** (1422?–1491); **Gothic type**; **Textura**

Blades, William (1824–1890)

Bibliographer. A printer by trade, Blades took an intense interest in the history of his craft, and especially in Caxton. He made many important archival discoveries about Caxton, and was the first systematic student of his types. In this he was greatly influenced and helped by Bradshaw. His researches were published as *The Life and Typography of William Caxton* (2 vols, 1861, 1863) which was the foundation of all subsequent Caxton studies, and is still an important work. He was also the leading light in planning the Caxton quartercentenary celebrations, and largely responsible for the catalogue of the associated exhibition at the Victoria and Albert Museum (1877). He was a prolific writer on bibliographical matters; his most enduring work, apart from *William Caxton*, was *The Enemies of Books* (1881). After his death, his very considerable library was sold to the newly-established St Bride Foundation, and is now in the St Bride Printing Library.

There is an account of Blades in *DNB (Supplement)*; and an excellent article on him by James Moran in *Libr.* (1961), p. 251. His connection with Bradshaw was discussed by Robin Myers in *Libr.* (1978), p. 265.

See also **Bradshaw, Henry** (1831–1886); **Caxton, William** (1422?–1491)

Blake, William (1757–1827)

Artist, poet, engraver and printer. The son of a London hosier, Blake showed an interest in art at an early age, and was apprenticed to the engraver, James Basire (1730–1802). His first major task was to draw and engrave the illustrations for Richard Gough's *Sepulchral Monuments* (1776); the plates are now in the Bodleian Library, Oxford. He studied briefly at the Royal Academy schools, but in 1778 he became a trade engraver and by 1784 had his own print shop. He also began to write poetry, and in 1789 published his *Songs of Innocence*, a remarkable production which he printed himself. He used a process which he called 'illuminated printing', which is in fact a process of relief etching. The result is strikingly beautiful, with an engraved text surrounded by Blake's own illustrations printed in full colour. Many of his subsequent books were printed in the same way, although he also continued to make conventional engravings for the booksellers.

There is a huge literature on Blake, who is one of the major figures in the history of English art and a significant poet. For the bibliographer and book historian, however, the starting-point is Geoffrey Keynes, *A Bibliography of William Blake* (1921), flawed as it is. From Keynes, one turns to the less humane but more scholarly work, G.E. Bentley Jr, *Blake's Books* (1977). Keynes' *Blake Studies* (1949) deals with various aspects of his work.

See also **Colour printing**; **Etching**; **Illustrated books**; **Relief printing**

Blanck, Jacob (1906–1974)

Bibliographer. Blanck, a librarian at Harvard University, was the instigator of the *Bibliography of American Literature* which is often referred to by his name. *BAL* lists first and other significant editions of the works of American authors of literary importance down to 1930. The entries are detailed and informative, and are in alphabetical order. Volume 1 was published in 1955, and Blanck lived to see the publication of vol. 6 (1973). Volume 7 was edited by Virginia L. Sturgen and Michael Winship, who will continue the work to its completion. *BAL* is sponsored by the Bibliographical Society of America and has attracted substantial support from foundations.

See also **Bibliographical Society of America**

Blanket

See **Common press**

Blind tooling

See **Bookbinding**

Block books

The name given to a group of fifteenth-century books printed entirely from woodcut blocks rather than type. They are sometimes called *xylographica*. The origin of the block book is a matter of some controversy. In particular, it is still unclear whether some may have been produced before the invention of typographic printing by Gutenberg in the mid-1450s. The extant examples, which are rare, are generally dated no earlier than the 1460s, but dating is difficult,and these examples may in any case have had predecessors which do not survive. The block books usually consist of whole-page illustrations, sometimes with a very short text as a caption. Among the most typical are the *Ars moriendi* and the so-called *Biblia pauperum*. The latter is a set of illustrations of key episodes in the Bible designed to instruct the illiterate.

See Heinrich T. Munger, 'Xylographic Books', in H.D.L. Vervleit (ed.), *The Book through Five Thousand Years* (1972).

See also ***Ars moriendi***; **Gutenberg, Johann** (1394/99–1468); **Woodcut**

Blurb

Book trade term. The blurb is the description of the book printed on the dust jacket as a promotional aid. This is often written by the author himself, although sometimes modified by the publisher. The other form of blurb consists of extracts from reviews printed on the jacket of a second or subsequent printing. Blurbs were first used at about the turn of the nineteenth and twentieth centuries.

See G. Thomas Tanselle, 'Book jackets, blurbs, and bibliographers', *Libr.* (1971), p. 91.

See also **Dust jacket**

Boards

See **Bookbinding**

Bodleian Library

The library of Oxford University. The medieval library was despoiled in 1542, and refounded by Sir Thomas Bodley, a failed diplomat, in 1598. It opened in 1602. At present it is housed in nine buildings on five sites; its combination of buildings, ranging in date from 1470 to 1970, and its vast collections, make it unique among the world's great libraries. Although it is strong in all fields, it is particularly notable in English literature, history and topography. It has been a legal deposit library since 1662, and had limited deposit arrangements in 1610–*c.* 1640.

For the history of the library, see Ian G. Philip, *The Bodleian Library in the Seventeenth and Eighteenth Centuries* (1983), which does not entirely replace W.D. Macray, *Annals of the Bodleian Library* (1890); for the later period see Sir Edmund Craster, *A History of the Bodleian Library 1845–1945* (1952). The library's early accounts have been edited by Gwen Hampshire (OBS, new ser. 17, 1982).

See also **Broxbourne Library**; **Daniel Press**; **Douce, Francis** (1757–1854); **Johnson, John de Monins** (1882–1956); **Legal deposit**; **Malone, Edmond** (1741–1812)

Bodoni, Giambattista (1740–1813)

Printer. Born in Piedmont, Bodoni learned to print at the Papal press in Rome, where he developed an interest in type design and punchcutting. At this time, he was influenced by the work of Baskerville. In 1768, he was invited to establish an official press for the Duke of Parma and he remained there for the rest of his life. He became the leading type designer of his generation, and one of the best printers in history. From 1790, he also had a press of his own in Parma, on which he printed books for publishers from all over western Europe. In the twentieth century, Giovanni Mardersteig revived his name when he established the Officina Bodoni, and the Bodoni type faces are still in use.

An account of Bodoni in English is a desideratum; the standard work is R. Bertieri, *L'arte di Giambattista Bodoni* (1913).

See also **Baskerville, John** (1706–1775);**Officina Bodoni**; **Typecasting**

Book Auction Records

Quarterly (formerly annual) listing of auction prices. *BAR* began publication in 1903. Although it is largely confined to British sales, it does give a wide coverage, including many provincial sales not listed in *American Book Prices Current.*

See also **American Book Prices Current**; **Auction sales**

Book Club of California

Founded 1912. The Club is based in San Francisco, Ca., and is the premier bibliophilic society of the western United States. It holds regular meetings for papers and discussion, and, since 1933, has published a *Quarterly News-Letter*, which carries articles of both Californian and general interest in the field. Occasional monographs are also published. In recent years a Los Angeles chapter has been formed, which also meets from time to time.

In 1965 the Club published *Second Reading*, a selection of articles from its *News-Letter.*

Book collecting

Books have always attracted collectors as well as readers, and the collector who never reads his books has been a figure of fun since classical times. It is, however, a more worthwhile occupation than is often supposed, and most of the world's great institutional libraries have benefited from the energy and generosity of private collectors. At its best, book collecting is a scholarly pursuit with a role to play in the preservation of man's cultural heritage.

The love of books is almost as old as books themselves, although for centuries collections had an essentially practical purpose. Throughout the Middle Ages the greatest collections were those of the monasteries, cathedrals and other collegiate bodies, and it was from this tradition that there appeared the earliest work on book collecting, Richard de Bury's *Philobiblon* written in the early fourteenth century. De Bury was Bishop of Durham, and is said to have owned more books than all the other bishops in England between them. He was, however, a rare, although not unique, example of a medieval bibliophile, and the real history of book collecting begins in Renaissance Italy.

The patrons of the humanists, especially in Florence, Venice and Rome, encouraged the arts of the book, and both the development of new scripts and the earliest fine bindings were a consequence of this interest. With the invention of printing in the mid-fifteenth century, book-ownership became more widespread, although still limited, and gradually large private collections began to be formed. By the mid-sixteenth century a distinct bibliophilic tradition had developed, most notably in the circle around the French collector, Jean Grolier. Indeed, France became, and to some extent has remained, the home of the fine book, or *Livre d'art*. In Northern Europe, it was the Reformation which provided the great impetus. Although much was destroyed when the monasteries and other ecclesiastical institutions were closed, much was also saved, with the result that in both England and Germany a large percentage of the surviving medieval manuscripts first entered secular collections in the middle decades of the sixteenth century.

The break-up of the monastic and collegiate libraries laid the foundations of the English, as opposed to the French, tradition of collecting. This was essentially scholarly and pragmatic, for most of the great English collectors of the seventeenth and eighteenth centuries were men who assembled their libraries for specific scholarly purposes. At first, most were historians and antiquaries; among this group were Matthew Parker (1504–1575), Archbishop of Canterbury, whose collection is now at Corpus Christi College, Cambridge, to which he bequeathed it, and Sir Robert Cotton (1571–1631), whose books and manuscripts were later to form one of the foundation collections of the British Museum. By the eighteenth century, the antiquaries had been joined by literary collectors, of whom perhaps the most notable was Edmond Malone, whose collection of sixteenth- and seventeenth-century English literature is now one of the glories of the Bodleian.

Bibliophilic collecting in the French manner had a brief florescence in England in the early eighteenth century, most notably in the Harley and Sunderland collections; the latter was the basis of the great Spencer library at Althorp which was later to have a decisive influence in the history of English bibliophily. Both Harley and Sunderland, and some less important contemporaries, collected incunabula, fine bindings, and examples of fine printing as well as contemporary books and archival manuscripts. Despite their example, however, book collecting did not become an aristocratic tradition in eighteenth-century England as it was in France, until after the great French libraries were dispersed in the 1790s.

The period of the French Revolution and the wars which followed is as important in the history of book collecting as is the Reformation, and for a similar reason: historic collections were dispersed and huge quantities of rare and unusual books suddenly came onto the market, having lain untouched for centuries on library shelves. In England this was the period of the 'bibliomania' when a group of wealthy men suddenly discovered a passion for book collecting and, largely under the influence of Dibdin, began to collect a different kind of book from most of their English predecessors. Dibdin set a fashion for 'black-letter' books of the fifteenth and sixteenth centuries, fine bindings and fine printing, and the same group patronised the early private presses, such as those of Brydges and Johnes. These same men, led by the 2nd Earl Spencer, formed the Roxburghe Club in 1812, and their example, embodied in the writings of Dibdin, was followed by almost every major English collector of the nineteenth century. The tradition was firmly established, and book collecting largely became a matter of collecting 'great books', especially if they were old and well-bound. There were of course exceptions; the novelist William Beckford (1759–1844) formed a great collection which was largely of interest for bibliographical peculiarities and provenances, while the megalomania of Sir Thomas Phillipps defies any classification.

By the second half of the nineteenth century, the initiative was beginning to cross the Atlantic. The long line of American collectors began with J.P. Morgan, and later collectors such as Folger and Huntington followed his example in establishing research libraries in which their collections could be preserved in perpetuity. By now, book collecting was a hobby only open to the very rich, and, by way of reaction to this, the 1920s and 1930s saw the beginning of a more broad-minded approach to 'collectable' books. Victorian popular novels, detective stories, children's books and printed ephemera were a few of the categories of material in which some younger collectors began to interest themselves. Book collecting now embraces every kind of manuscript and printed book, and has become something of an industry throughout the western world.

Much of the vast literature of book collecting consists of price guides, lists of 'good' books, and collectors' self-adulatory accounts of their collections. Seymour de Ricci's *English Collectors of Books and Manuscripts (1530–1930)* (1930) is a comprehensive but dryly factual history. A more lively account, by a man who was himself both bookseller and book collector, is in John Carter's *Taste and Technique in Book Collecting* (1949). Carter had previously edited *New Paths in Book Collecting* (1934), a seminal work in the history of twentieth-century bibliophily which opened whole new fields of interest. An attempted successor, *Collectable Books. Some new paths,* ed. Jean Peters (1979) may or may not have the same influence. On the academic implications of bibliophily, see the lectures by Louis B. Wright and Gordon N. Ray, published as *The Private Collector and the Support of Scholarship* (1969).

See also **Bibliomania**; **Black letter**; **Bodleian Library**; **Bookbinding**; **British Museum**; **Brydges, Sir Samuel Egerton** (1762–1837); **Dibdin, Thomas Frognall** (1776–1847); **Folger Shakespeare Library**; **Grolier, Jean** (1479?–1565); **Harley, Robert, 1st Earl of Oxford** (1661–1724) and **Harley, Edward, 2nd Earl of Oxford** (1689–1741); **Hafod Press**; **Huntington Library and Art Gallery**; **Incunabula**; **Malone, Edmond** (1741–1812); **Phillipps, Sir Thomas** (1792–1872); **Provenance**; **Roxburghe Club**; **Spencer, George John, 2nd Earl Spencer** (1758–1834)

Book Collector, The

Bibliographical and bibliophilic periodical. The first volume under the present title was published in 1952, but it was the successor of *The Book Handbook* (1947–51). Since its inception *BC* has maintained an exceptionally high standard of both writing and illustration. As its name suggests, its primary concern is with bibliophily, and regular features have included accounts of collectors, collections, collectable books of many kinds, and a very important series of articles on bookbindings, as well as articles on many other topics. It is published quarterly by The Collector Ltd. The present editor is N.J. Barker.

An index to vols 1-10 (1952–61) was published in 1965.

Book Collectors' Quarterly, The

Bibliophilic periodical. The title was first used for a journal of which only six parts, forming one volume, appeared in 1924–26. The name was revived in 1931 for the journal issued for members of the Limited Editions Club. It was edited by A.J.A. Symons and Desmond Flower. Despite its avowedly 'popular' approach, some useful articles appeared before it closed with no. 17 (1935).

See also **Limited Editions Club**

Book fairs

Annual fairs were one of the principal market mechanisms of late medieval Europe, especially for international trade. They were usually established or protected by rulers, and merchants were given special privileges for travel to and from fairs, as well as exemption from taxation and other legal requirements for business conducted there. By the early fifteenth century, manuscripts were being sold at fairs in Western Europe, and for the early printers they were an ideal means of distribution. Much early printing was in Latin, and therefore commanded an international audience. Moreover, given the limited size of the book market, many publications were economically viable only if they could be sold internationally.

The first great book fair was at Lyons, which straddles the vital trade route between France and Italy. It was well established before the end of the fifteenth century as a twice-yearly event, and became the principal entrepôt for the exchange of books between Southern and Northern Europe. The Lyons fair continued to be important throughout the sixteenth century, when it was gradually overtaken by that at Frankfurt.

The Frankfurt Fair had its origins in the 1490s, but its great period began when Germany became the centre of interest throughout Europe during the Reformation. Frankfurt then took the lead amongst the book fairs, and also became a market-place for type, printing equipment, and indeed everything and everyone involved in the book trade. It held this position until the middle of the seventeenth century, when the combined effects of the Thirty Years War and the persecution of the Protestant booksellers reduced its importance. From 1564 onwards catalogues were printed of books available at the Fair — until 1592 by the private enterprise of Georg Willer, and after 1598 by the Town Council of Frankfurt itself. The Frankfurt Fair catalogues are of the utmost importance as historical documents.

The third great book fair was at Leipzig. This originated in the sixteenth century, and took Frankfurt's place as the leading fair in the 1640s, partly because there was religious toleration for the booksellers there. Catalogues were published from 1600 onwards.

The book fairs continued throughout the eighteenth century, but they became gradually less important after 1700. This can be principally attributed to the decline of Latin as the international language of scholarship, for the fairs had always been concerned primarily with Latin books whose market was across the whole of Europe. The Frankfurt Fair, however, still survives, and is now the chief market-place for publishers to sell copyrights, translation rights, and the like to overseas buyers.

The literature of the book fairs is large, but much of it somewhat old-fashioned. Among the most important works are Henri Estienne, *The Frankfurt Book Fair*, trans J.W. Thompson (1911); A. Dietz, *Zur Geschichte der Frankfurter Buchermesse* (1921); H. Bresard, *Les Foires de Lyon au XI et XVI siècles* (1914); and F. Hermann Meyer, 'Die Leipziger Buchermesse von 1780–1837', *AGB* (1891), p. 288. The early Frankfurt catalogues are being edited by Bernhard Fabian (1972–   ).

See also **Frankfurt Fair**

Book Handbook, The

See **Book Collector, The**

Book jacket

See **Dust jacket**

Book label

A mark of ownership on a book. It is a label printed with the owner's name, inserted in his books. Some labels also have either dates or the location of the library, or both, and later examples usually have a decorative border. Book labels were common in England in the seventeenth century, but the earliest dated example is from 1480. They continued to be used until the late eighteenth century, but by that time most collectors used book-plates.

See Brian North Lee, *Early Printed Book Labels* (1976).

See also **Book plate**

Book plate

A mark of ownership in a book. Strictly, a book plate is printed in intaglio from an engraved plate. Book plates were indeed printed from woodcuts in the fifteenth century, but it was with the development of the copperplate in the sixteenth century that they became common. They were used by most serious collectors in the eighteenth and nineteenth centuries, and are still in use today. Many carry the arms of their owner as the principal decoration. Some are also dated or have the location of the library.

Many libraries have collections of book plates; the most notable is that of Sir Augustus Franks in the Department of Prints and Drawings at the British Museum, of which there is a published catalogue (3 vols, 1903–4). There are a number of books on book plates, of which the most comprehensive is that by W.J. Hardy, *Book plates* (1893). See also Walter Hamilton, *Dated Book Plates* (1895). There is a history by G.H. Viner in *Libr.* (1945–46), p. 39; and the Victoria and Albert Museum, London, which has a large collection, has published *A Brief History of Book Plates in Britain* (1979).

See also **Book label**; **Intaglio**

Book reviews

Critical accounts of books published in newspapers and magazines. Descriptive accounts of new books, often including extracts, appeared in *The Gentleman's Magazine* from its beginning in 1732, and were imitated in other magazines. The true history of reviewing, however, begins with *The Monthly Review* founded by Ralph Griffiths (1720–1803) in 1749, and *The Critical Review* (1756) edited by Tobias Smollett. Almost accidentally, Griffiths established a new tradition of reviewing by encouraging his contributors to offer comment as well as description. One of these contributors was Smollett who carried on the tradition when he founded a rival magazine. Both the *Monthly* and the *Critical* were highly successful and survived into the nineteenth century. From the early years of that century, however, they were gradually displaced by quarterlies, most notably *The Edinburgh Review* founded by the publisher Archibald Constable in 1802, and *The Quarterly Review* founded by John Murray in 1809. Both carried long review articles from very distinguished contributors: Macaulay, a regular reviewer for the *Edinburgh* in the 1820s, is only one of several writers who established their own reputations in this way. Both periodicals survived into the twentieth century, but were effectively killed by World War I; the *Quarterly* closed in 1922, and the *Edinburgh* in the following year.

By that time, the newspaper had become the principal medium for reviews of general books, often carrying many lengthy reviews on pages wholly devoted to literature. The *Times Literary Supplement*, founded in 1902, was an outgrowth of newspaper reviewing, and is one of the few reviewing periodicals to survive. Another development of the nineteenth century was the reviewing of academic books in learned journals, an activity which has proliferated with the journals themselves.

A general history of reviewing is a major desideratum. For the eighteenth century, see Derek Roper, *Reviewing before the 'Edinburgh' 1788–1802* (1978). There is rather more on the nineteenth century: books include John O. Haydon, *The Romantic Reviewers, 1802–1824* (1969); John Clive, *Scotch*

Reviewers: *'The Edinburgh Review'*, *1802–1815* (1957); Walter Graham, *English Literary Periodicals* (1930); and H. and H.C. Shine, *The 'Quarterly Review' under Gifford* (1949).

See also **Gentleman's Magazine, The**; **Murray, John** (1778–1843)

Book Subscription Lists Project

See **Project for Historical Biobibliography**

Bookbinding

Protective cover of a book and the process of making it. Reduced to its essentials, a bookbinding is the outer covering of a book, attached to the book itself by adhesive or stitching. In its traditional form (now usually called *hardback*) there are two sheets of stiff card (the *boards*) cut to size for the front and back of the book; these are known as the *upper* and *lower* boards respectively. They are covered with a piece of vellum, leather, cloth or artificial fabric which links them to each other around the back (or *spine*) of the book. The sheets of the book itself are sewn into quires before the boards are attached.

In traditional western bookbinding, as it evolved in the early Middle Ages and is still practised by a few binders, the stitching of the quires is done with a single piece of cotton or linen thread. This is intertwined with several larger and stronger pieces of thread (called *thongs*) which are at right-angles to the stitching and are themselves threaded through and attached to the boards. The covering material is then glued to the whole structure when the sewing is complete. This produces an immensely strong book, but it is a skilled hand-work process, which has inevitably been mechanised for reasons of economy. Such bindings are still made, but only in small quantities for very expensive books or to repair older books; the process is now called *craft binding*.

The usual modern technique is called *case binding*. In this process, the quires are stitched to each other on a sewing-machine, and the boards and covers (the *case*) are made as a single unit on a case-making machine. The two parts are then brought together in a casing-in machine, where they are joined by adhesives under heavy pressure. In fact, case bindings are surprisingly strong, provided that good adhesives and other materials are used. Mass-market paperbacks, however, are usually *perfect bound*; in this ironically named technique the sheets are guillotined at the fold and are then held, usually rather temporarily, to each other and to the outer cover by glue.

The basic structure of the craft-bound codex has not changed for centuries; materials and decoration have, however, undergone great transformations, and while the latter is the particular concern of most bookbinding historians, the former is not without interest. Since the sixteenth century, the boards have normally been stiff card or strawboard, but until that time very large books were often bound in heavy wooden boards, usually of oak. The earliest covering material was vellum, but leathers of various kinds began to be used at an early date. The most common were calfskin, sheepskin and, to a much lesser extent, goatskin; other skins were used only very occasionally. Calf, the cheapest and most popular material, was normally of a darkish brown colour, but since the late sixteenth century various tanning processes have been developed to produce leathers of different qualities and colours. Deep reds and blues, and to some extent greens, have always found favour with book-binders. Cloth was first used in the 1770s for school books and chapbooks, but was introduced into the general trade only in 1830s by Leighton, after which it rapidly displaced animal skins. In recent years artificial fabrics have gradually replaced the traditional linen cloth.

The decoration of the vellum or leather for aesthetic effect is probably Arabic in origin, although it was used to a limited extent both in Byzantium and in the West in the Middle Ages. The modern European tradition of decorative binding (usually called *fine binding*) originates in Italy in the late fifteenth century, probably under Byzantine influence through Venice. The binders in North Italy began to use sheets of gold leaf, impressed into the covers under heat and pressure by patterned tools, to produce artistic designs on the binding. Various tools are used for this purposes. The largest is the *panel stamp*, often almost the size of the board itself, engraved in relief with an elaborate pattern, typically but by no means invariably an heraldic device or the owner's name motto. These are known as *panel-stamp bindings.*

By the mid-sixteenth century, they had been displaced by the typical European fine binding in which the pattern is made up by the use of smaller tools in combination. The most important of these are the *stamp* and the *fillet* (or *roll*). A stamp is a small metal head with a wooden handle, engraved or die-cast with a distinctive pattern of lines, often symmetrical, which can be used to build up a design either by repeated use or in combination with other stamps. A fillet is a small metal wheel attached to a wooden handle which is rolled along the covering material to produce lines; these will be decorated if the wheel has a serrated edge. All tools can be applied directly to the covering material (*blind tooling*) or through gold leaf to produce a gilt pattern (*gold tooling*). Designs also sometimes incorporate pieces of leather of a different colour which are either attached to the surface (*onlay*) or inserted into a prepared recess (*inlay*).

Fashions in design have, inevitably, undergone great changes in the last 500 years, although the basic pattern of the fine binding until the twentieth century has always been dictated by the rectangular shape of the board itself. A typical design is an outer box made with fillets, which contains a symmetrical design made up of stamps, sometimes with a central lozenge or ellipse for a panel stamp.

Most bindings are, of course, far less elaborate than fine bindings; ordinary (or *trade*) bindings were usually wholly undecorated or very simply blind-tooled with fillets. The traditional trade practice was for books to be sold in unbound sheets by the publisher, and then bound for the bookseller, usually in a simple trade binding, although the customer could, of course, commission a fine binding if he wished. Publishers' binding (more properly called *edition bindings*) were first used in the mid-eighteenth century, and became normal within less than 100 years. The process of case binding was evolved from the 1820s onwards, but was not fully mechanised until the first decade of the twentieth century.

The publishers' binding is of concern to the bibliographer as well as to the binding historian, since it is a part of the book as issued, and must therefore be described as part of the ideal copy. This description normally takes the form of a statement of the colour and decoration of the cloth. If more than one binding is used on an edition, each binding creates an issue.

There is a huge literature on bookbinding, but no good general history. Perhaps the best starting point is Edith Deihl, *Bookbinding: its background and technique* (2 vols, 1946); although it is now out-of-date in some respects it does at least give an overview of binding styles, and the second volume consists of an excellent account of the binding processes. Most of the literature is inevitably concerned with fine bindings; perhaps the best general work, which describes 100 bindings, is Howard M. Nixon, *Five Centuries of English Bookbinding* (1978). A Bodleian exhibition catalogue, *Fine Bindings, 1500–1700, from Oxford Libraries* (1968), is not confined to English bindings. Another exhibition catalogue, from the Baltimore Museum of Art, entitled *The History of Bookbinding 525–1950* (1957), is even more comprehensive. All of these have excellent bibliographical references, which, for earlier work, can be supplemented from A.R.A. Hobson, *The Literature of Bookbinding* (1954).

There is little on trade bindings, but on edition bindings, Michael Sadleir, *The Evolution of Publishers' Binding Styles, 1770–1900* (1930) is rightly regarded as a classic work; and Graham Pollard's 'Changes in the style of bookbinding, 1530–1830', *Libr.* (1956), p.71, is a brilliant but all too short survey by the one man who could have written the general history which is so desperately needed. The problems of the bibliographical description of bindings are explored, more generally than the title might suggest, by G. Thomas Tanselle in 'The bibliographical description of patterns', *SB* (1970), p.71.

On bookbinders, there are three useful works in English by Charles Ramsden: *French Bookbinders, 1789–1849* (1950); *Bookbinders of the United Kingdom (outside London) 1780–1840* (1954); and *London Bookbinders, 1780–1840* (1956). See also Ellic Howe, *A List of London Bookbinders, 1648–1815* (1950).

See also **Codex**; **Descriptive bibliography**; **Edition**; **Edition binding**; **Ideal copy**; **Issue**; **Leighton, Archibald** (1784–1841); **Panel stamp**; **Paperbacks**; **Quire**; **Vellum**

Bookseller

A trader who specialises in the retail sale of books. Until the late eighteenth century, however, the word was used to mean both retailer and publisher, and the two functions were indeed combined, in so far as 'publishers' were also retailers of their own products. To compound the confusion, the plural was also used in England in the eighteenth century as a generic term for the whole book trade.

See also **Publisher**

Booksellers' Association

Trade association of booksellers in Britain and Ireland. It was founded in 1895 as the Association of Booksellers of Great Britain and Ireland. It was intended to act as a focus for the trade generally, but more specifically to negotiate with the publishers on the issue of book prices and the Net Book Agreement (NBA). It still performs this function, and in the matter of the NBA, is to some extent a regulatory body for the trade. Entry to the BA is carefully controlled in an attempt to maintain high standards in the trade. It also runs various ancillary operations such as the Book Marketing Council, and Book Tokens Ltd.

The address of the Association is 154 Buckingham Palace Road, London SW1W 9TZ.

For its early history, see James J. Barnes, *Free Trade in Books* (1964). Its present activities are listed in the *Trade Reference Book* (4th edn, 1979).

See also **Net Book Agreement**; **Publishers' Association**

Bowers, Fredson Thayer (1905–)

Bibliographer. Like many post-war bibliographers, Bowers approached the subject by the way of English literature, and has spent most of his career as a Professor of English at the University of Virginia. The outstanding bibliographer of his generation, he can be seen as Greg's successor, for he developed Greg's work in analytical, descriptive and textual bibliography. He introduced a new thoroughness and rigour into bibliographical studies, which, although it has sometimes been criticised as verging on the pedantic, has been a major beneficial influence in the subject. Moreover, unlike many bibliographers, he has put his editorial theories into practice, especially in his work on nineteenth- and twentieth-century American authors, and in editing the works of Marlowe and Dekker. His major theoretical works are *Principles of Bibliographical Description* (1949), which is little less than the Bible of its subject; *Textual and Literary Criticism* (1959), an almost polemical attack against the careless use of shoddy texts by literary critics; *Bibliography and Textual Criticism* (1964), a major study of the relationship between bibliographical and textual phenomena; and *On Editing Shakespeare* (1966). He has also contributed prolifically to periodicals, not least to *Studies in Bibliography* which he has edited since its inception. The Summer 1985 issue of *PBSA* was a *festschrift* for Bowers.

See also **Analytical bibliography**; **Bibliography**; **Descriptive bibliography**; **Greg, Sir Walter Wilson** (1875–1959); *Studies in Bibliography*; **Textual criticism**

Bowyer, William (1663–1737) and Bowyer, William (1699–1777)

Printers. The elder Bowyer set up in business in 1699, and rapidly won a reputation as an excellent printer. He was responsible for many of the best books of his time, and his status in the trade is attested by the subscription of over £2500 which was raised for him when his printing house was destroyed by fire in 1712. He sent his son to Cambridge, but he went down without a degree, and joined the firm in 1722. The younger Bowyer carried on the tradition of the firm, and gained for himself a deserved reputation as a man of considerable learning. In 1729, he became Printer to the House of Commons, and in 1736 Printer to the Society of Antiquaries. He was himself elected FSA in 1737. In the same year he was involved in the foundation of the Society for the Encouragement of Learning, which was, in effect, a publishing society for learned works which could find no commercial publisher. In 1761 he also became Printer to the Royal Society. He himself wrote a number of important antiquarian works. His successor in the business was John Nichols, whose *Biographical and Literary Anecdotes of W. Bowyer* (1782), later expanded as *Literary Anecdotes of the Eighteenth Century* (1812), is the major source for his life.

In view of the importance of the Bowyers it is particularly fortunate that their business records are among the few which survive from the eighteenth-century English book trade. There are four major documents: account books for the years 1710–36, and 1738–*c.*65, a volume of miscellaneous financial documents from the period 1737–77 (all described by J.D. Fleeman in *TLS*, 12 December 1963, p.1056), and a ledger of paper stock (described by Herbert Davis in *Libr.*, 1951, p.73). The first three are in the library of the Grolier Club, New York City, and the latter in the Bodleian Library, Oxford. The documents are being edited by K.I.D. Maslen for publication by the Bibliographical Society and the Bibliographical Society of America; he has already published *The Bowyer Ornament Stock* (OBS, occ. pub., 8, 1973), and an important article in *Libr.* (1975), p.81 based on his work. There are lives of both Bowyers in *DNB*, but Nichols remains the most important account of them.

See also **Nichols, John** (1745–1826)

Boydell, John (1719–1804)

Engraver and printseller. Boydell came from a Shropshire family, but went to London to study art and to learn the trade of engraver. He set up his own business and was modestly successful in publishing landscape prints. He really made his fortune, however, in the 1790s with a series of prints of Oxford, Cambridge and elsewhere, and at the same time began to see himself as a patron of artists. As early as the mid-1780s, he was interested in establishing a school of British historical art, and in 1786 he decided to commission drawings of characters and scenes from Shakespeare's plays as the first part of this enterprise. In 1789 he opened his Shakespeare Gallery where these pictures, whose artists included Reynolds, Romney and West, were exhibited. Between 1791 and 1805 they were published as prints to illustrate a folio edition of Shakespeare which Boydell sponsored, and in 1805 they were also published separately. By this time, however, Boydell was dead, and in the last years of his life the cost of the Shakespeare enterprise, despite its *succès d'estime*, had brought him close to bankruptcy.

Boydell, was also a politician; he was an Alderman of the City of London from 1782, and Lord Mayor in 1790–91.

See the entry in *DNB*; and, for the Shakespeare Gallery, W. Moelwyn Merchant, *Shakespeare and the Artist* (1959).

See also **Aquatint**

Bradshaw, Henry (1831–1886)

Librarian and bibliographer. The son of a banker, Bradshaw was educated at Cambridge, and joined the staff of the University Library in 1856. He became Librarian in 1867 and in that post, which he held for the rest of his life, he was responsible for the modernisation of the Library's administration and became an influential figure in British librarianship. He was also a very considerable scholar, with interests as diverse as heraldry and Celtic antiquities. It was, however, as a bibliographer that he made his mark, and it is reasonable to regard him as the founding father of modern bibliography. His special interest was in incunabula, and he was the first to study fifteenth-century type in detail. From these studies, he evolved what he called 'scientific' or 'natural history' bibliography, tracing the evolution of 'families' of type. He worked on the assumption — which would not now be entirely accepted by many scholars — that when a particular type can be identified with a particular printer, then all other books in the same type can be ascribed to the same press. This revolutionary methodology laid the foundations for twentieth-century incunable studies, for it was the Bradshaw method which Robert Proctor used in the 1890s to produce the first systematic chronological listing of fifteenth-century printed books. Bradshaw himself published no full-scale work on a bibliographical subject, but he was the author of many very important articles.

Bradshaw was of Irish descent, and his important collection of Irish books and pamphlets is now in Cambridge University Library.

See his own *Collected Papers* (1889), published posthumously, which brings together his best work in several fields; and G.W. Prothero, *A Memoir of Henry Bradshaw* (1888).

Brevier

See also **Bibliography**; **Incunabula**; **Proctor, Robert George Collie** (1868–1903)

Brevier

See **Type size**

British Bibliographer, The

Bibliographical periodical. The first periodical in the English language devoted to bibliography. It ran from 1810 to 1814, and was published in parts which make up a total of four volumes. Its founder was Sir Samuel Egerton Brydges, and its editor was J.H. Haslewood, a prolific antiquary of the period. It was important as a channel of communication during the height of the 'bibliomania'.

See also **Bibliomania**; **Brydges, Sir Samuel Egerton** (1762–1837)

British Library

See **British Museum**

British Museum

Founded 1754. The British Museum was founded as both a museum and a library, a dual function which it retained until 1973. The basis of the library, the so-called foundation collections, was in four parts: the manuscripts of the Elizabethan antiquary, Sir Thomas Cotton (1571–1631), which had been confiscated by Charles I in 1624, and restored to Cotton's grandson who gave them to the nation in 1700, since when they had been shamefully neglected; the library and other collections of Sir Hans Sloane, the virtual founder of the Museum itself; the 'Old' Royal Library, assembled by successive monarchs since 1471, presented by George III in 1756; and the manuscripts from the Harleian Library, bought for the nation in 1753. With the Old Royal Library came the right of legal deposit, although this was only fitfully enforced before the middle of the nineteenth century. Other benefactions followed, most notably that of the library of George III (the 'King's Library'), presented by George IV in 1823. By the early nineteenth century, the Museum was the subject of much criticism for the inadequacy of its services, facilities and collections. In the Library departments, the reform of the Museum was largely the achievement of one remarkable man, Sir Anthony Panizzi (1797–1879), an exiled Italian revolutionary who had arrived in England as a penniless refugee in 1823. In 1831, he was appointed to the Department of Printed Books, of which he became Keeper in 1837. While in that office, until 1856, and for the next decade as Principal Librarian and Director, he persuaded Parliament to give the Museum a realistic annual grant, and was responsible for the building of the great Reading Room and its associated bookstacks, the enforcement of legal deposit, the beginning of the modern General Catalogue and, above all, the inauguration of the imaginative purchasing policies which were to make the British Museum the greatest library in the world, universal in scope. For the next century, the Museum tended to rest on Panizzi's laurels, but his legacy was indeed a magnificent one, for he had ensured the development and continuance of a tradition of humane scholarship which no library in the world could equal, in the context of a great research institution catering for all-comers.

In 1973, the library departments became the Reference Division of the newly-founded British Library.

For a general history, see Edward Miller, *That Noble Cabinet* (1973).

See also **Harley, Robert, 1st Earl of Oxford** (1661–1724) **and Harley, Edward, 2nd Earl of Oxford** (1689–1741); **Legal deposit**; **Sloane, Sir Hans** (1660–1753)

Broadside

Statement of bibliographical format, but also used to describe items printed in that format. A broadside is an unfolded whole sheet, normally printed on one side only. It was used for printing proclamations, ballads, and other documents intended for display or public reading. The term is, unfortunately, often used very loosely to describe all items printed on one side only; bibliographically, however, it should be used only for those printed on the whole sheet, whether on one side or both. Other unfolded items are (usually) half or quarter sheets. In *English Verse 1701–1750* (2 vols, 1975), D.F. Foxon uses the formula 1° for the broadside format, a practice which is being copied by others, and which ought to be encouraged.

See also **Ballads**; **Format**; **Half sheet**; **Quarter sheet**

Brotherton Library

The library of the University of Leeds. Edward Allen Brotherton (1856–1930), who became the 1st Baron Brotherton in 1929, was an industrialist who served as MP for Leeds (1902–10; 1918–22) and Lord Mayor of the city (1913–14). In 1917, he gave £100,000 to the University for a library building which was named after him. In 1922, he began to collect books himself, and in the next eight years assembled a remarkable collection of some 35,000 printed books and very many manuscripts, deeds and letters. His chief interest was in English literature before the mid-eighteenth century, and in this field the collection is outstanding. He bequeathed his books to the University, and they now form the Brotherton Collection within the Library. Thanks to his substantial endowment the collection is still regularly augmented in its main fields of interest. It is perhaps the best of the lesser-known and lesser-used rare book collections in a British university library.

See David I. Masson, 'The Brotherton Collection of rare books and manuscripts', *ULR* (1978), p. 135; and the article by D.I. Masson and B.S. Page in *ELIS*, vol 3 (1970).

Broxbourne Library

The name given by Albert Ehrman (1890–1969) to his collection; it derives from his home at Broxbourne, Hertfordshire. Ehrman was a wealthy diamond merchant who began to collect books in the 1920s. In course of time, he came to specialise in incunabula, bindings, type specimens and early printed catalogues and bibliographies. In all of these fields the Broxbourne Library was outstanding, despite the great rarity of the items which Ehrman was buying. His collecting was intelligent and scholarly, for he sought to illustrate the history of printing and the book trade, and the early development of trade binding. The catalogues were used by Ehrman and Graham Pollard for their *Distribution of Books by Catalogue* (Roxburghe Club, 1965), and the most interesting of the bindings were described by H.M. Nixon in *Broxbourne Library. Styles and designs of bookbindings from the twelfth to the twentieth centuries* (1956).

The library was inherited by Ehrman's son, John, who, in memory of his father, presented the type specimens to Cambridge University Library, and the remainder of the collection to the Bodleian Library, Oxford, where it had already been housed for some years.

Ehrman's own account of his collecting is in *BC* (1954), p. 190.

See also **Incunabula**

Brunet, Jacques Charles (1780–1867)

Bibliographer. The son of a Paris bookseller, Brunet went into the trade himself, but soon abandoned it in favour of his bibliographical work. In 1810, he published the first edition of his *Manuel de libraire de l'amateur*, a wide-ranging list of early printed books in French and other languages. In its final form (1842–44) it is still a useful work of reference. Brunet based his work on his own large collection, which was sold in Paris after his death.

There is little in English on Brunet, except an article in the 1911 edition of the *Encyclopaedia Britannica*. See *Nouvelle biographie générale*, vol. 7 (1855); and *Dictionnaire du biographie française*, vol. 7 (1956).

Brydges, Sir Samuel Egerton (1762–1837)

Bibliographer, printer and literary scholar. Brydges, the son of a clergyman, was educated at Cambridge, and called to the Bar in 1787. He turned immediately to literary pursuits, and in the next 12 years published two indifferent novels, and a volume of execrable poems. In the early years of the nineteenth century he found his true forte in editing the works of neglected early English authors. At a time when the Elizabethans and Jacobeans were virtually unknown, he edited works by Raleigh, Carew, Breton, Davison, and Greene, among others. These volumes, many of them type facsimiles of early editions, appealed to the followers of Dibdin with their passion for black letter. Typical of the age, Brydges also became interested in books *per se*, and in 1810 founded *The British Bibliographer*. His other bibliographical works, now only of antiquarian interest, include *Censuria literaria* (10 vols, 1805–9), and *Restituta* (4 vols, 1814–16).

In 1810 Brydges moved to Lee Priory, near Maidstone, Kent, for which town he was MP, 1812–18. In 1813, he established a press at his house, where he printed many of his own works. This early example of a private press, contemporary with that of Thomas Johnes at Hafod, produced some excellent work until it came to an end in 1822. By that time Brydges was living abroad for financial reasons, usually in Geneva where he died in 1837.

Apart from books and literature, Brydges's great passion in life was genealogy, chiefly his own. He claimed the barony of Chandos for his family, but the House of Lords rejected the claim. His ambition for a title was partly met by a Swedish knighthood, conferred in 1808, and, more substantially, by a baronetcy in 1814. In 1812 he published an excellent new edition of Collins' *Peerage*.

He wrote a somewhat diffuse autobiography, published in 1834, and there is an account of him in *DNB*. Both, however, are obsessed (as indeed was their subject) with the Chandos peerage case. There is an admirable study of him by M.K. Woodworth (1935), but a bibliography of the Lee Priory Press remains a desideratum.

See also **Bibliomania**; **Black letter**; *British Bibliographer, The*; **Dibdin, Thomas Frognall** (1776–1847); **Hafod Press**; **Private press movement**; **Type facsimile**

Bulletin du Bibliophile

Bibliographical periodical. *Bulletin du Bibliophile* is the oldest bibliographical journal still in existence. It was founded by J. Techener in 1834, was subsequently edited for many years by Georges Vicaire. Under Vicaire it became, and has remained, the leading French periodical in its field. Following the disruption of World War I, a new series was started in 1922. Indexes have been published for the years 1834–1906 (1907) and 1907–33 (1934). The present editor is François Chapon.

Caldecott, Randolph (1846–1886)

See **Evans, Edmund** (1826–1905)

Cambridge Bibliographical Society

Founded 1949. The Society was founded by a group which included Professor (later Sir) Roger Mynors, Sir Geoffrey Keynes and A.N.L. Munby to promote the study of bibliography. It holds regular meetings in Cambridge to hear papers and visit libraries, and also publishes annual *Transactions* and an occasional series of monographs.

The Society's address is Cambridge University Library, West Road, Cambridge CB3 9DR.

See also **Transactions of the Cambridge Bibliographical Society**

Cambridge University Library

The earliest certain reference to a university library in Cambridge is in 1416, but the University appears to have owned some books as early as 1355. The library grew in the fifteenth century, and, unlike the Bodleian, survived the Reformation. In the sixteenth and seventeenth centuries, however, it expanded only slowly, lacking a benefactor with the money and the desire to carry out the University's somewhat grandiose plans. The great turning-point in its history was George I's gift of the library of John Moore, Bishop of Ely, which contained some 30,000 volumes, in 1715. Since that time the Library has grown steadily, and is now probably the fourth largest in the British Isles. The Library had deposit privileges from 1662 to 1679 and from 1685 to 1694, becoming a legal deposit library under the Copyright Act 1710 and its successors. It moved in 1934 from its original site and buildings to purpose-built accommodation on a generous site which allowed for further expansion. A new wing was opened in 1972.

See J.C.T. Oates, *Cambridge University Library. An historical sketch* (1975). A full-scale history by J.C.T. Oates and D.J. McKitterick is in progress.

See also **Bodleian Library**; **Broxbourne Library**; **Keynes, Sir Geoffrey** (1887–1982); **Legal deposit**

Cambridge University Press

Printer and publisher. The first printer in Cambridge was John Siberch who was in the city from 1520 to 1523 or 1524, when he returned to his native Germany. Siberch had links with individual members of the University, but it was not until 1534 that Cambridge obtained letters patent which granted it the right to appoint its own printer. In practice, it was not until 50 years after this that this right was first exercised when Thomas Thomas was appointed as the first Printer to the University in 1584. The history of the Press is continuous from that time, although until the late seventeenth century the Printer merely exercised the University privilege on his own account; there was no concept of the University itself owning or controlling the Press.

This situation changed when Richard Bentley (1662–1742) took it upon himself to create a University Press in the modern sense. Bentley, at the time a Royal Chaplain but soon to be Master of Trinity College, wished to establish a Press from which learned works could be published. An agreement was reached in 1696, buildings and equipment were obtained, and the Press began to operate in 1698. During the next 15 years a number of important books were published, including a series of editions of classical authors, but the initial impetus was soon lost. Nevertheless, the Press was active throughout the eighteenth century, especially during the period when Baskerville was Printer. The revival and the modern history of the Press begins with the opening of its new Pitt Building in 1831. Bible production was its mainstay, but by the late 1830s the Syndics (the governing body of the Press) were beginning to publish books on their own account.

A major investigation of the Press in 1852 resulted in a series of important changes. The Syndics formed a partnership with George Seeley, a bookseller, and J.C. Clay, a printer, both in London, who were to run the Press's production and sales operations. From the 1870s onwards the Syndics began to publish academic books on a much greater scale, and also ventured into the field of textbook publishing for schools; the latter proved highly profitable. This pattern remains essentially unchanged, although the Syndics now have full control of the Press and, since 1976, it has been recognised as an educational charity.

Cambridge has made one vital contribution to the British book world in the twentieth century. In the 1920s and 1930s it was in the forefront of the movement to improve the quality of typography in commercial book production. Bruce Rogers and Stanley Morison were its typographical advisers; with the encouragement of Walter Lewis (Printer to the University, 1923–45) and his successor, Brooke Crutchley (Printer, 1945–74) the Press became one of the most distinguished of British book printing houses, and it still insists on a high standard of production as well as content for its books.

M.H. Black, the University Publisher, marked the Press's 'quarter-centenary' with the *Cambridge University Press 1584–1984* (1984), the only general history. S.C. Roberts, *The Evolution of Cambridge Publishing* (1956) is excellent on the nineteenth century. D.F. McKenzie, *The Cambridge University Press 1696–1712* (2 vols, 1966) is a masterly bibliographical study of the Bentley period.

See also **Baskerville, John** (1706–1775); **Morison, Stanley** (1889–1967); **Rogers, Bruce** (1870– 1957); **Siberch, John** (1476–1534)

Cancel

Bibliographical term. A cancel is a leaf which is removed from a sheet after printing, strictly called a *cancellandum,* or a leaf subsequently inserted to replace it, called a *cancellans.* It is probably better to use the Latin terms to avoid the ambiguity of the English, which is used indiscriminately for both. A leaf inserted where none has been removed is an *insert,* not a cancellans.

Case

Cancellantes and cancellanda are important in establishing the bibliographical status of a book. A cancellans title-leaf always establishes another issue, and internal cancellantes may do the same, provided that there had been a prior intention to issue copies with the cancellanda, and the intention changed after publication.

There is a classic study of *Cancels* by R.W. Chapman (1930).

See also **Issue**

Case

Printing house equipment. The case is a shallow, open tray (normally *c.* 2ft 6in × 1ft 6in, divided into rectangular compartments of varying size, in which the compositor keeps his type. One compartment is allocated to each sort, according to a set pattern. This pattern is called the *lay* of the case. The lay varies from country to country. These national variations are for the convenience of the compositor, since they ensure that the most common letters in a country's normal language are placed at the centre of the case. For each fount there are normally two cases, called a *pair*, upper and lower. The upper case contains the capital letters and the numerals, while the lower holds the miniscules, special sorts (e.g. *), punctuation, ligatures and spacing materials. In the English lay, lower-case 'k' was held in the upper case because of the historical accident that 'k' is not used in Latin, the language of most early printing.

Although cases were normally in pairs, and probably always so for book work, a single case was sometimes used in the nineteenth century, especially in the United States. This is known as the Californian Jobbing Case, and was divided into three equal parts, two of which contained the lower case and one the upper. Such cases were widely used by jobbing printers, who required small quantities of a wide range of founts.

For a history of the case, see Philip Gaskell, in *SB* (1969), p. 125. The usual English lay is illustrated by Moxon, p. 32.

See also **Compositor**; **Fount**; **Ligature**; **Moxon, Joseph** (1627–1691); **Sort**

Case binding

See **Bookbinding**

Caslon, William (1692–1766) and Caslon, William (1720–1778)

Typefounders. The elder Caslon was apprenticed to a loriner (maker of metal parts for the bridle and bit of a horse's harness) in London in 1706, and in 1716 established his own business as an engraver of metal. He specialised in the cutting of bookbinders' tools, a skill for which he gained a considerable reputation, and which established his first contacts with the book trade. He began to cut punches for type, a closely related skill, and in 1719 was invited by the Society for the Propagation of Christian Knowledge to cut an Arabic fount for a New Testamant which it proposed to print for its missionary activities in the Middle East. The success of this fount led to further commissions, and by the late 1720s Caslon was established as the leading punchcutter and typefounder in London. He served most of the trade, including the King's Printer, and the elder Bowyer. He designed and cut a whole series of founts in many sizes which were (and are) highly regarded for their elegance and utility. After his death, his son, William, inherited the firm; although he lacked his father's artistic skills, the younger William was a businessman of great acumen. He maintained the pre-eminence of the Caslon foundry, despite competition from punchcutters and designers of the calibre of Baskerville. He in his turn bequeathed the business jointly to his sons, William and Henry, but after Henry's death, William sold his share to his brother's widow, and established a new business of his own in Sheffield. That firm is now Stephenson, Blake Ltd, and still trades, being the direct successor of perhaps the greatest of all English typefounders.

There are lives of both Caslons in *DNB*; and an admirable book by Johnson Ball, *William Caslon 1693–1766* (1973). For Caslon's types, see James Mosley, 'A specimen of printing types by William Caslon. London 1766', *JPHS* (1981–82), p. 1.

See also **Baskerville, John** (1706–1775); **Bowyer, William** (1663–1737) and **Bowyer, William** (1699–1777); **Fount**; **Typecasting**

Cassell, John (1817–1865)

Publisher. Born in Manchester, Cassell received only a rudimentary education and was apprenticed to a carpenter. In 1833 he became a fervent supporter of the Temperance Movement, then sweeping Lancashire. His conversion is not without irony, since his father was an innkeeper. He gained a reputation as a Temperance speaker, and in 1836 went to London where he continued his work as a carpenter but increasingly devoted his time to the teetotal cause. After a period as a travelling lecturer, he established a wholesale tea and coffee business in 1843, and in 1846 began to issue, at his own expense, *The Teetotal Times*.

By 1848, Cassell was giving more time to this and other Temperance publications than to his tea and coffee business, and by about 1850 was in effect a full-time publisher. Most of his publications were cheap but improving periodicals intended to divert their working-class audience from the attractions of the public house and the gin palace. There was also, however, an undertone of Liberal, and even Radical, politics, as is suggested by the title of *The Standard of Freedom*, one of the earliest and most successful of these penny periodicals. Cassell was a strong and influential advocate of the abolition of Stamp Duty on newspapers at a time when the campaign against them was in its final stages, although he himself always stamped his own publications when they were liable for duty.

Cassell's later publications included the highly successful *Illustrated Exhibition*, a cheap part-book guide to the Great Exhibition of 1851. The early 1850s were indeed the high point of his career as a publisher. His *Illustrated Magazine of Art*, with a cover design by Cruickshank, was widely admired, and he also published a part-book edition (technically a piracy) of one of the great bestsellers of the day, *Uncle Tom's Cabin* (1852). His more overtly didactic purposes were served by *The Popular Educator*, and by his ultimately successful plan for a cheap Latin dictionary whose successor is still in print. By 1854, however, after three or four years of frenetic activity, he was in serious financial difficulties, and only just avoided formal bankruptcy. Although he re-established himself and continued to publish, he never regained his former energy or eminence, and died a broken man. His name lives on, however, although since his death no member of his family has been involved in the publishing firm which bears it. That firm still flourishes.

There is a brief account of Cassell in *DNB*, and a much longer one in *The House of Cassell 1848–1958* by Simon Nowell-Smith (1958), a rare example of a readable official history.

See also **Cruickshank, George** (1782–1878); **Part books**; **Piracy**; **Stamp Acts**

Casting-off

Printer's term. Casting-off (now usually called 'estimating') is the process of calculating the length of the printed book from the manuscript or typescript copy. The purpose is both to calculate the quantity of paper needed and to estimate the probable cost of production. With a verse text the process is comparatively simple, since the number of lines can be counted, and one consequence of this in the sixteenth and seventeenth centuries was the practice of setting by formes. When the copy had been cast-off, the inner forme of a quarto (i.e. pages 2,3,6,7,) could be set and printing could begin before the outer forme was set, or vice versa. This had the advantage of economising on the use of type and other equipment. It seems that a good number of quartos, especially of verse plays, were set in this way.

See Moxon, p.239; and William H. Bond. 'Casting-off copy by Elizabethan printers', *PSBA* (1948), p.281.

See also **Compositor**; **Forme**; **Quarto**; **Typesetting**

Catalogues

A catalogue is a systematic list of books or other items in a collection or group of collections. Librarians have made catalogues since classical times, as being the only way to record and hence to control the contents of their libraries. The essential feature of a library catalogue — the identification of each book and a record of its physical location — were well established in the Middle Ages. The medieval practice was to catalogue manuscripts by a 'second folio' reference, quoting the opening words of the second folio of the text, since it was assumed that no two scribes would have reached exactly the same point at the end of the first leaf. Modern cataloguing really begins with the development of the printed title-page in Italy in the fifteenth century, and cataloguing by title became the norm for some 200 years. By the late sixteenth century, simple classification schemes had been developed; a good early example is the first printed catalogue of the Bodleian Library, Oxford (1610), in which the books were divided, as they were on shelves, into Theology, Jurisprudence, Medicine, and Arts. By the late seventeenth century, alphabetical author catalogues were beginning to be compiled, although it was not until the nineteenth century that the rules for such compilations were systematised. The initial impetus for more systematic cataloguing came from the need to record the books confiscated by the French government after the 1789 Revolution, but the real progress was made in the English-speaking world, most notably in the rules devised for the British Museum catalogue by Sir Anthony Panizzi in the 1840s. More recently other codes have been developed, especially the *Anglo-American Cataloguing Rules* which, in its second edition (1978), is becoming an international standard, despite the fact that some of its provisions are as baffling to many librarians as they are to almost all library users.

Although libraries are the most obvious producers of catalogues they are by no means alone. Booksellers and publishers have issued catalogues since the sixteenth century, and they are essential to the efficient conduct of the book trade.

See Archer Taylor, *Book Catalogs: Their varieties and uses* (1957); Albert Ehrman and Graham Pollard, *The Distribution of Books by Catalogue* (1965); and Robert Collison, *Published Library Catalogues* (1973).

See also **Advertisements**; **Bibliography**; **Bodleian Library**; **British Museum**; **Title page**; **Trade bibliography**

Catchword

Bibliographical term. The catchword, printed at the right-hand end of the direction line, reproduces the first word of the following page. It was intended as a guide to the binder to ensure that the sheet was properly folded, and that the folded sheets were collated in the correct order. Catchwords are found in medieval manuscripts, and were imitated thence by the early printers. In Italy in the fifteenth century, where they were first used in print, catchwords are normally found only on the last leaf of the gathering, but elsewhere in Europe, except in France, they were normally printed on every page. There are, however, some national and local variations, which can assist the bibliographer in locating books whose place of origin is unknown. Catchwords were in use until the end of the eighteenth century, but thereafter their use decreased, and they had virtually vanished by *c.* 1850.

Catchwords are of interest to bibliographers because they can reveal irregularities of printing; see Bowers, p. 127. They can also help in identifying the place of printing; for this see Giles Barber, in *BC* (1960), p. 301; and R.A. Sayce, *Compositorial Practices and the Localisation of Printed Books, 1530–1800* (OBS, occ. pub. 13, 1979).

See also **Direction line**; **Gathering**

Catnach, James (1792–1841)

See **Ballads**

Cave, Edward (1691–1754)

See **Gentleman's Magazine, The**

Caxton, William (1422?–1491)

Publisher and printer. Although remembered as the first English printer, Caxton came to the book trade late in life, and was never fully integrated into it. He was probably of Kentish origin, but the first documentary record of him is when he was apprenticed to a London mercer, Robert Large, in 1438. Large was a cloth merchant, deeply and profitably involved in the trade between England and Flanders, then under the rule of the Duke of Burgundy. In 1444 Caxton was despatched to Bruges, the centre of the English cloth trade in the Burgundian dominions. There he prospered, and became the leading member of the English community, with the title of 'Governor of the English Nation'. In that capacity he began to undertake diplomatic missions at the Burgundian Court on behalf of Edward IV who had close links with Duke Philip the Good. Consequently, Caxton became a well-known figure at the Burgundian Court, which, under the patronage of the Duchess Margaret, was a flourishing artistic centre. Margaret's interests included both literature and the writing and illuminating of manuscripts. It was she who suggested that Caxton translate Le Fevre's *Receuil des histoires de Troie* into English in 1469. This marks the beginning of the trail which was to lead to the introduction of printing into England.

By 1471, Caxton was in Cologne where he learned the art of printing, although it is not clear that this was his reason for going there. His instructor was almost certainly Johannes Veldener. In 1474, he returned to Bruges with some trained journeymen, and in 1475–76 printed six books there, including his own translation of the *Recueil (Recyuell of the Histories of Troye)*. The suggestion that his interest in printing arose out of his own literary efforts is unproven but irresistible. Caxton was not, however, in the narrow technical sense a printer; indeed he probably never operated a press in his life. He may, like other wealthy men before and since, have been sufficiently interested to try his hand at the black art, but the serious work was done by paid journeymen. He was, in essence, a publisher who organised and financed the production and sale of books.

It was to develop this role that he returned to England in 1476, and established himself at Westminster. One reason for his return was his desire to print in English; his *Recuyell* was the first book to be printed in English, for the language was virtually unknown outside the British Isles, and no continental printer had any interest in printing books for the English market alone. As a result, England was the only country in Europe (other than Germany itself) in which printing was first practised by a native. The choice of Westminster is as significant as the decision to return to England. The latter reflects the low international status of the English language; the former tells us much about Caxton's hopes and intentions. There was already a flourishing trade in the production and sale of manuscripts in the City of London, where it was carefully regulated by the Stationer's Company. Caxton never joined this guild, nor, so far as is known, associated himself in any way with the existing book trade except as an employer of binders. At Westminster, however, he was close to his powerful patrons, including Edward IV himself, and also had a ready market of lawyers and clerics. His publications reflect this market, for they include not only the devotional tracts and liturgical books which were the stock-in-trade of every printer in Europe, but also a succession of translations of French romances and of editions of medieval English literature, including both Gower and Chaucer. These were for his courtly audience. Two groups of books which are absent from Caxton's list of publications are also significant; he printed no law books, for the common lawyers who needed the Year Books and the like were in the Inns, not at Westminster; and no classical texts, for England's meagre demand for those could easily be met by importing continental editions, a trade in which Caxton himself may have been involved. After Caxton's death, the business was inherited by Wynkyn de Worde, whom Caxton had brought from Bruges (and probably Cologne), and who, within ten years, had abandoned Westminster for the more commerical ethos of Fleet Street.

Caxton is, of course, a key figure in the history of the book in England, but not merely as what the Victorians loved to call its proto-typographer. His translations are important literary achievements, and, because they were printed, they exercised a crucial influence on the development of English as a literary language. His editions of medieval literature helped to transmit to the sixteenth century the achievements of an earlier age, and ensure that Chaucer, at least, remained a living part of the English literary tradition. On the other hand, Caxton, with his diplomatic background and aristocratic connections, was quite unlike his successors in the mudane world of English book production. He stands out, indeed, as a unique man in almost all of his multifaceted activities.

There is, inevitably, a huge literature on Caxton. The first serious attempt at a scholarly study was by William Blades, whose *Life and Typography of William Caxton*, in its revised edition (1877), is still of interest. Among the spate of books inspired by the quincentenary of English printing, those of George Painter (*William Caxton,* 1976) and N.F. Blake (*Caxton: England's first publisher,* 1976) are outstanding. Since Painter is a bibliographer and Blake a Professor of English Language, together they cover the technical, linguistic and literary sides of Caxton's work. In 1976, the Printing Historical Society held an international conference on Caxton, whose papers were published as *JPHS,* 11 (1976–77); they are, perhaps surprisingly, very readable, and represent the state of the art of Caxton scholarship at a time when activity in the field was, naturally enough, at its height. Perhaps the outstanding paper is that by Howard Nixon on 'Caxton and bookbinding' (p. 92). Work has not stopped since 1976, however, and it is expected that the researches of Lotte Hellinga and Paul Needham, to be published in a forthcoming volume of the British Library's catalogue of its incunabula, will significantly alter the accepted chronology of Caxton's books (most of which are undated), and that this will inevitably affect the arguments of Painter, Blake, and others.

See also **Blades, William** (1824–1890); **de Worde, Wynkyn** (*c.* 1455–1534); **Incunabula; Stationers' Company**

Censorship

The control or prevention of publication by ecclesiastical or secular authorities. Before the invention of printing censorship was barely necessary in any organised form, although the Church could and did ban certain texts. One example is Wycliffe's Bible in England in the fifteenth century. Widespread illiteracy and the comparative scarcity of books, however, made the task fairly simple for the authorities, whose problems did not begin until printing vastly increased the availability of books. The first initiatives were ecclesiastical, for the Church saw itself as the natural censor of ideas. As early as 1475, the Pope licensed the University of Cologne to act as a censor, and in the next two decades many bishops began to act as, or to appoint, censors for their own dioceses. More generally, in 1501 Pope Alexander VI established a general censorship in the German states, and in 1515 Leo X forbade all printing without prior permission.

It is doubtful how far these provisions were ever enforced. In 1517, Luther's protest against the Church marked the beginning of the Reformation, and thereafter Catholics and Protestants increasingly banned each other's propaganda while producing their own, and surreptitious printing became more common. The sheer bulk of printed matter made close control impossible and, partly to counteract this, control was increasingly handed over to the state. In France, for example, Charles IX took the book trade under royal control in 1563, replacing the earlier system of licensing by the Doctors of the Sorbonne. In England a series of executive decrees going back to the reign of Henry VIII (1509–1543) was formalised in 1563 to give the Stationers' Company general responsibility for control, under the guidance of the Archbishop of Canterbury and various state officials. In both Catholic and

Protestant countries, state and Church worked together, although in the Catholic states the institutions of censorship tended to be ecclesiastical after the Church began to issue its *Index librorum prohibitorum* (1559). In Protestant countries, the institutions were more often secular, and the established Church was treated as an arm of the state, one of whose functions was to restrict the propagation of books and ideas. In general, however, the Protestant states, once they were securely established, were distinctly more liberal than those under Catholic control.

The concept of a free press is of comparatively recent origin. In England, the lapse of the Printing Act in 1695 marked the end of pre-publication censorship, although prosecutions of authors and publishers for political reasons continued for over a century after that date on various legal pretexts. In most other European countries, formal censorship survived for much longer. In France, for example, censorship was, if anything, stricter under Napoleon (1797–1815) and the restored monarchy (1815–1848) than it had been under the *ancien régime*. Not until after 1870 was there a reasonably free press in France. In Germany and the Hapsburg Empire there were strict controls until 1918, and in both Germany (from 1933) and Austria (from 1936) the Nazis reimposed a very thorough system of press control. Indeed, modern totalitarian regimes of both the right and the left have been much more successful in controlling the press than have most of their predecessors.

Since the sixteenth century, censorship has been increasingly political, although the religious and political elements are difficult to disentangle in the earlier stages of the story. Like political censorship, moral censorship has ecclesiastical origins. Rabelais, for example, was put on the *Index* in 1564, and Aretino's *Il posturi* was banned by the Church in 1545. The definition of obscenity has always been difficult, and in both Britain and the USA much has been left to the discretion of judges and juries in the last 150 years. James Joyce's *Ulysses*, for example, was banned in the USA from 1918 to 1933, and D.H. Lawrence's *Lady Chatterley's Lover* was banned in England from 1929 to 1960; in both cases, court verdicts reversed earlier executive actions.

The literature on censorship is vast, but much of it is ideological. For a guide, see Ralph E. McCoy, *Freedom of the Press: a bibliography* (1968). Anne L. Haight and Chandler B. Grannis, *Banned Books* (4th edn, 1978) is a useful list of censored books from the ancient world to the present day. On earlier periods, see G.H. Putnam, *The Censorship of the Church of Rome* (2 vols, 1906). Among recent works relating to England, there are two which are outstanding: Fredrick S. Siebert, *Freedom of the Press in England 1476–1776* (1965); and Donald Thomas, *A Long Time Burning* (1969). On the USA, see Grant S. McClellan (ed.), *Censorship in the United States* (1967).

See also **Index librorum prohibitorum**; **Pornography**; **Printing Act 1662**; **Stationers' Company**

Chain lines

Technical term in papermaking. Chain lines are the marks made in hand-made paper by the chains of the mould, as an incidental consequence of the papermaking process. They are usually about 1 inch apart, and can be seen by holding the paper up to a reasonably strong light, or to daylight. The chain lines are always parallel to the shorter sides of the mould, and are thus of value in determining format. They are crossed at right-angles by thinner, more closely spaced, *wire lines*, similarly made by wire of the mould.

For the use of chain lines as bibliographical evidence, see A.H. Stevenson, in *Libr.* (1954), p. 181.

See also **Format; Papermaking**

Center for the Book

An organisation within the Library of Congress designed to promote the study of books and reading, and to emphasise the importance of the printed word. It was established by Congress in 1977, on the initiative of Daniel J. Boorstin, Librarian of Congress, but it is funded primarily by voluntary contributions from interested individuals and foundations. Its activities include lectures, publications, exhibitions, research projects and the organisation and sponsorship of meetings. Although the focus of much of its work is historical, it is also involved with the contemporary book scene in America, and has attracted some interest in the book trade. Its publications include lectures delivered under its auspices and guides to its exhibitions. The Center has played an important role in raising the profile of book history in the Unites States, and despite its comparatively brief history has become a major influence in its field.

The Executive Director is John Y. Cole.

See also **Library of Congress**

Chapbooks

Cheaply produced books, usually of 12 pages, and usually with a text of popular poetry or a traditional story. The word itself is the subject of some debate, but probably derives from the fact that the books were sold by chapmen, or travelling pedlars. A chapbook is probably best defined in bibliographical terms, and the word restricted to a half sheet duodecimo. Chapbooks in this strict sense are almost entirely an English phenomenon, although they were produced in North America in some quantities, and also, but to a much lesser extent, in France and Spain. In Britain, chapbooks were produced in London from the early eighteenth to the early nineteenth centuries, and in the provinces and Scotland from *c.*1720 to *c.*1840. In popular estimation they gradually displaced the sheet ballad as the preferred form of cheap literature, and many of the early chapbooks were probably editions of traditional ballad texts. Unlike the single sheet, however, the chapbook became a medium for prose texts, which included retellings of traditional folk-tales and legends; reprints, often textually modified, of old jest books and other compendia; and abbreviated versions of contemporary favourites such as *Robinson Crusoe*. The typical mid-eighteenth century chapbook was a 12-page book, with a crude woodcut illustration on its title page, and a closely printed text set in abominable type on the cheapest available paper. These apparent disadvantages were, of course, more than outweighed by the cheapness which they were intended to permit, and chapbooks achieved massive popularity and huge circulations, far in excess of any other printed matter in eighteenth-century England.

The production and distribution of chapbooks was not dissimilar from the arrangements for ballads. In the early years of the eighteenth century, the London market was dominated by Cluer Dicey, but by the 1720s there was a good deal of provincial chapbook printing. The provincial printers included William Dicey (Cluer's father) in Northampton, John White in Newcastle upon Tyne, and a mysterious Mr Bence in Wootton-under-Edge, Gloucestershire. Dicey certainly, and Bence probably, chose provincial remoteness in order to escape the possible wrath of the owners of the copyrights in the works which they pirated. White established Newcastle as a major centre of the chapbook trade, serving not only the North of England, but also much of Southern and Central Scotland; later in the century, his own successor, Thomas Saint, and other printers carried on the chapbook tradition on Tyneside. In the South of England, John Cheney of Banbury, from *c.* 1760, was an outstanding chapbook printer in the later part of the century, but most provincial printers (and many in London) produced chapbooks, for the market seemed capable of absorbing all that could be printed. Like ballads, chapbooks were sold in bookshops, but probably far more were distributed through travelling traders at markets and fairs. In the last quarter of the eighteenth century the London chapbook trade was dominated by Richard and John Marshall, whose printing house in Aldermary Church Yard was a veritable chapbook factory. In fact, it was a direct descendant of the Dicey business, which itself was a successor of the ballad partnership of the late seventeenth century. Perhaps the most remarkable testimony to this success both of the chapbook and of the Aldermary Church Yard firm is that the style and format of the chapbook were imitated by Hannah More in her attempt to make her *Cheap Repository Tracts* acceptable to a mass urban audience in the 1790s. Marshall was employed to print them, because no other printer could be found with the capacity to do so in the required quantities.

In the early nineteenth century, the popularity of the chapbook declined, partly because of the competition of the revived single-sheet ballad, and partly because the steam-powered presses began to flood the market with a much wider range of cheap books. In the North of England and in Scotland, however, they were still being printed in the early 1840s.

Among the earliest collectors of chapbooks was Francis Douce, whose books are now in the Bodleian Library, where there are also substantial numbers of chapbooks in other collections. Other major institutional collections include those of the British Library, Newcastle upon Tyne University Library (catalogue by Frances M. Thomson, 1969), Harvard University Library (catalogue, 1905), and the New York Public Library (catalogue by

Harry B. Weiss, 1936). Apart from these and other catalogues, the literature of chapbooks is sparse, which is not altogether surprising since the rarity of the books is compounded by the tendency of librarians not to catalogue them. A useful guide to the literature is Victor E. Neuburg, *Chapbooks* (2nd edn, 1972).

See also **Ballads**; **Copyright**; **Douce, Francis** (1757–1834); **Duodecimo**; **Half sheet**; **Jest books**

Chapel

Printers' cant word. The chapel is the collective noun for the journeymen in a printing house. Much learned ink has been spilled on its origins, from which one can only conclude that they are obscure. It was, however, in use in the fifteenth century. In England in the late eighteenth century it came to mean more specifically a group of men in the printing house who worked together in negotiations with the master. It is now used for a trade union branch in the printing industry, and the colourfully named 'Father of the Chapel' is neither more nor less than the shop steward.

The most sensible discussion of the origin of the term will be found in Moxon, p. 383.

Chase

Printing house equipment. A rectangular metal frame used to contain type pages on the bed of the press. The pages are imposed within the chase, and then held in position by strong pieces of wood (furniture) and wedges (quoins). Until the nineteenth century, quoins were made of wood, but metal quoins gradually replaced them. The latter were either wedges or, more often, expanding quoins opened and closed by the use of an internal screw. Chases vary in size, but the normal bookwork chase was about the same size as the bed of the common press. In the nineteenth century, chases of different sizes were more common, especially for jobbing work. Some very large chases have either central dividers running parallel to the shorter side, or two dividers crossing at right-angles in the middle of the chase. These dividers not only gave additional stability, but also assisted in the correct positioning of the type pages during imposition.

Moxon, p. 43 describes the typical chase of the hand-press period.

See also **Common press**; **Imposition**

Cheap Repository Tracts

See **Chapbooks**

Chemical wood

See **Papermaking**

Chiaroscuro

A relief process of graphic printing. Chiaroscuro is a colour printing technique using woodcut blocks. In its simpler form, developed in Germany in about 1500, two blocks were used. One was cut with the outlines of the illustration and printed in black; the other, cut less formally, was used to print the broad shapes of the coloured area, usually in a light brown or reddish ink. A more sophisticated form of the technique was invented by Ugo da Carpi (*c.* 1479–1533) in Italy in 1516; this involved the use of three or four blocks, each print using a different colour of ink. Chiaroscuro gives a very gentle colour, almost like a watercolour wash, and can be highly effective.

The art was rarely practised in the seventeenth century, but it was revived, with great effect, by Jackson in the middle of the eighteenth century.

See Joan Friedman, *Color Printing in England 1456–1870* (1978).

See also **Colour printing**; **Jackson, John Baptiste** (1701–1777?); **Relief printing**; **Woodcut**

Children's books

Literary genre. It could be argued that the earliest children's books were those intended for use as school books, but the term is usually reserved for books intended for use outside the classroom, although many of them do in fact have a didactic purpose.

In this sense, it is generally considered that the first children's book was *Orbis sensualium pictus* (1658, and many later editions) by Jan Amos Komensky (Comenius), a bishop of the Moravian Church in South Germany. It was overtly educational, but it combined text and illustrations in a way which was designed to make learning attractive as well as virtuous. Comenius had no immediate successors, but by the early eighteenth century publishers were beginning to issue books intended to amuse children. Many of these were simple versions of traditional stories or editions of nursery rhymes, often in chapbook format, and sometimes indeed aimed as much at adults as at children. The first specialist publisher of children's books was John Newbery, who began to publish stories and poems written for children in the late 1740s. This marks the real beginning of what has now become a vast industry.

By the mid-nineteenth century, children's books were a widespread phenomenon throughout Europe and North America, most notably in the work of the Grimm brothers (translated as *German Popular Stories*, 1823) and the Danish author Hans Christian Andersen (first translated as *Wonderful Stories for Children*, 1846), as well as many others who are less well remembered. The nineteenth century also saw the adaptation for children of such books as *Gulliver's Travels* and *Robinson Crusoe* as well as the writing of sophisticated stories which could be read on many levels and thus have an appeal to adults as well as children. Indeed, the dividing-line between children's and adults' books is often very narrow; *Alice in Wonderland* on one level and *Treasure Island* on another are examples of 'children's' books which are as avidly read by some adults as Dickens is by some children.

In the last 40 years the children's book industry has expanded greatly, and has been particularly notable for the high standard of production of many of its books, especially in the imaginative use of colour.

There is a vast literature on children's books. For a bibliographical approach, see F.J. Harvey Darton, *Children's Books in England* (2nd edn, 1958); and for a general history see Brian W. Alderson's translation of Bettina Hurlimann, *Three Centuries of Children's Books in Europe* (1967), first published as *Europaïsche Kinderbüche in drei Jahrhunderten* (1959).

See also **Chapbooks**; **Newbery, John** (1713–1767)

Chromolithography

Colour-printing process. Chromolithography was one of the most successful of several attempts to devise a system of colour lithography. It was invented by Godefroy Engelmann in 1836, and rapidly displaced the complicated Baxter process. The essence of chromolithography is that the artist prepares one stone for each colour to be printed; the problem is then a purely technical one of achieving correct register. This was difficult, but far from impossible, and some of the best coloured books of the mid-nineteenth century were printed by this method.

See Michael Twyman, *Lithography 1800–1850* (1970), p. 160; and Bamber Gascoigne, 'The earliest English chromolithographs'. *JPHS* (1982–83), p. 63

See also **Baxter, George** (1804–1867); **Lithography**; **Register**

Civilité

Type design. Civilité is based on the *lettre courante* used in France in the sixteenth century, known in England as the Secretary Hand. It was first cut by the French printer and typefounder Robert Granjon in 1557. Robert Granjon was a highly-skilled punchcutter whose founts were already in widespread use. Civilité has complex letterforms, including a large number of ligatures and very elaborate capitals; like all script types it suffers from the disadvantage of unfamiliarity to readers more accustomed to the divided letterforms of the roman, italic and black letter alphabets. Granjon intended the design to be used generally in bookwork, as a French vernacular design comparable to Bastarda in Germany and italic in Italy. This was never achieved, however, for Civilité was primarily used in France for copybooks to teach writing, and became associated in the public mind with children's books. It was still in use in school textbooks in France in the late nineteenth century. In the Low Countries, however, where it was introduced by Christophe Plantin in 1557–58, it was very widely used and was not wholly superseded until the eighteenth century. Civilité was occasionally used in England in the sixteenth and seventeenth centuries, but it was largely confined to writing manuals.

The authoritative account of the subject, including a list of books printed in Civilité, is Harry Carter and H.D.L. Vervleit, *Civilité Types* (OBS, new ser. 14, 1966).

See also **Bastarda**; **Black letter**; **Italic**; **Ligature**; **Plantin, Christophe** (*c.* 1520–1589); **Roman**; **Script types**; **Typecasting**

Clarendon Press

Imprint used by the Oxford University Press. It was first used (as 'E Typographeo Clarendoniano') in 1713, for a book printed at the recently completed Clarendon Building in which the Press was then housed, and is found in a number of Oxford books during the rest of the eighteenth century. It was in the nineteenth century, however, that the imprint became especially associated with the books published by the Delegates from the 'learned' press. In the early 1970s, the Clarendon Press was renamed the Academic Division, and the use of the imprint is now confined to the books published by that Division.

The subject is discussed by Peter Sutcliffe, *The Oxford University Press. An informal history* (1974).

See also **Imprint**; **Oxford University Press**

Clymer, George (1754–1834)

See **Columbian press**

Cobden-Sanderson, Thomas James (1840–1922)

See **Doves Press**

Codex

The traditional form of the western book, with folded and cut sheets sewn together in a series of gatherings, and normally enclosed by a binding to which they are attached. The codex originated in Rome in third century BC, when it consisted of writing tablets held together by thongs and was used as a cheap notebook. In this form it was a little regarded book, being used only for jottings, and was despised by serious collectors, writers and readers. By the first century BC, the tablets had been replaced by sheets of parchment (*membranae*). The scroll, however, still continued to be the normal form of book, although by the first century AD the use of codex was somewhat more widespread for cheap and portable books.

It was, however, among the early Christians that the codex first achieved popularity and acceptance. In Egypt, papyrus codices were used by the Christian communities around Alexandria; despite the unsuitable nature of the material, papyrus was only gradually replaced by parchment in Egypt. The attraction of the codex was its cheapness and portability, but it may originally have been adopted because the codex notebook was the form in which early Christian texts were written by their authors for transportation and copying. The codex came to be associated with Christianity and the scroll with pagan authors, and it thus gained in prestige as Christian influence increased. Even after the official conversion of the Roman Empire, however, the scroll was still in use, and it was not until the late fourth century that the codex finally displaced it.

In its original form, the codex consisted of single sheets of whatever material was used, but when papyrus and parchment began to replace tablets, the practice of folding the sheets and sewing through the fold was developed to give additional strength to these inherently flimsier materials. It was in this form that the codex survived the fall of the Western Empire, was used in medieval Europe, was imitated by the early printers, and survived to become the normal form of the printed book, as it seems likely to remain.

See C.H. Roberts and T.C. Skeat, *The Birth of the Codex* (1983).

See also **Gathering**; **Papyrus**; **Parchment**

Coffin

See **Common press**

Colburn, Henry (d. 1855)

See **Bentley, Richard** (1794–1871)

Cole, George Watson (1850–1939)

Bibliographer and librarian. Cole, born in Warren, Connecticut, was trained as a lawyer, but abandoned his profession for librarianship in 1885. He held a number of posts in New York, Chicago and New Jersey, before retiring to pursue his bibliographical researches. These covered a wide range of topics, but he was especially prolific in the field of early Americana. In 1915 he became librarian to Henry E. Huntington, a post which he held until 1924. He continued to work until his death, not least for the Bibliographical Society of America, of which he was President in 1919–21, and for which he produced the invaluable work for which he is now best known: *An Index to Bibliographical Papers Published by The Bibliographical Society and The Library Association, London, 1877–1932* (1933). A *List* of his own writings was published in 1936.

There is an account of him by Victor H. Paltsits, in *PBSA* (1939), p. 22.

See also **Americana**; **Bibliographical Society of America**; **Huntington Library and Art Gallery**

Collation

(1) *In bookbinding*, collation is the process of putting the quires in the correct order before sewing. This was formerly done by following the sequence of signatures, but has been mechanised since the end of the nineteenth century.

(2) *In descriptive bibliography*, a collation is a formulaic representation of the make-up of the book. For hand-printed books with signatures the collational formula, in its simplest form, is a register of signatures, followed by a superscript numeral indicating the number of leaves per gathering, thus: $A-H^8$. In this case, there are eight gatherings, signed A-H inclusive, each consisting of eight leaves. The signature alphabet, however, normally omits either I or J, either U or V, and W. Thus: $A-Z^8 = 23$ gatherings, not 26. The hyphen indicates that all intervening gatherings are identical in make-up, and that the 23-letter sequence is complete. Irregularities are indicated by successive sequences internally linked by hyphens, each sequence being followed by the superscript numeral to indicate the number of leaves per gathering. In this example: $A-B^8 \ D-Z^8$ there is no gathering C. In this example: $A-V^8 \ X^4 \ Y-Z^8$ gathering X has only four leaves.

The formula derives the letters from the printed signatures in the book. Prelims are often signed with a separate sequence, as in this example: $a-b^8 \ A-Z^8$. In some cases numerals or symbols may be used instead of letters in prelims (or even in text gatherings in some very early printed books): $1-3^8 \ A-Z^8$. Another example is $\star^{8}+^{8}) \ (^8A-Z^8$. Where, as often happens, the first gathering is unsigned, but the second gathering is signed B, it is assumed that the first gathering is A. This is expressed in the formula by italicising A (or underlining in typescript): $A-Z^8$. In this case, only *A* is unsigned; if B were also unsigned, the formula would be: $A^8 \ B-Z^8$. Where there is more than one sequence of identical signatures, a superscript numeral is used to indicate the second and subsequent sequences: $A-M^8 \ ^2A-P^8 \ ^3A-F^8$. Where there is a continuous sequence running through more than 23 gatherings, the practice was to use a second (or subsequent) alphabet in the form AA (AAA, etc.) or Aa (Aaa, etc). Whatever the form in the book, this is reduced to: $A-2N^8$. Cancels must also be indicated in the formula. A minus sign $(-)$ is used to indicate a cancellans, and a plus sign over a minus sign $(\pm)$ is used to indicate a cancellandum, with the plus sign alone $(+)$ for an insert. Thus, $B-G^8(-G1) \ H-K^8$ means that G1 has been cancelled, but there is no cancellans. In $B-G^8(\pm G1)$ $H-K^8$ there is a cancellans. Finally, $B-G^8(G1 + 1)$ $H-K^8$ indicates an additional leaf inserted after G1, although no leaf has been cancelled. If a leaf is inserted between gatherings, the Greek χ (chi) is used to indicate its position: $B-G^8$ $\chi1$ $H-K^8$. The insertion of a single leaf is the only instance in which an odd number is used in the formula, and it is placed on the line, not superscript. Where there are unsigned prelims preceding A or *A*, the Greek π (pi) is used: π^8 $A-Z^8$.

The formula is always preceded by a statement of bibliographical format, so that a full formula is thus: $8^0\pi^8$ $A-G^8(\pm G1)$ $H-Z^8$.

The collational formula is always part of a bibliographical description, and is based on the ideal copy.

(3) *In textual criticism*, the comparison of different versions of the same text, whether manuscript or printed. Textual bibliographers also collate multiple copies of the same edition of a printed text, in pursuit of press variants and 'mechanical' evidence for bibliographical analysis. For the latter purpose, Charlton Hinman developed the collating machine.

For the collational formula, see W.W. Greg, 'The formulary of collation', *Libr.* (1933–34), p.365; and Bowers, p.193. The underlying principles of textual collation are explained by Paul Maas, *Textual Criticism* (1958); W.W. Greg, *The Calculus of Variants*(1927); and Fredson Bowers, *Bibliography and Textual Criticism* (1964).

See also **Analytical bibliography**; **Bookbinding**; **Cancel**; **Descriptive bibliography**; **Format**; **Gathering**; **Hinman, Charlton Joseph Kadio (1911–?)**; **Ideal copy**; **Prelims**; **Press variant**; **Quire**; **Register**; **Signature**; **Textual criticism**

Colophon

The colophon is a statement of the names of the printer and/or publisher, and the date of completion, at the end of a book. The practice originated with the scribes of medieval manuscripts, who sometimes ended their task by writing their own names and the date on which the manuscript was finished. The practice was imitated, like other features of manuscript books, by the early printers, the first printed colophon being that of the Mainz Psalter in 1457. Thereafter, colophons are not uncommon, although, unfortunately for bibliographers, they were far from universal, and many incunabula have neither a colophon nor any other statement of their date and origin. With the development of the title-page in the late fifteenth century, the colophon was gradually displaced by the imprint, although colophons are found until the middle of the sixteenth century, and occasionally even today in private press books.

See A.W. Pollard, *An Essay on Colophons* (1905).

See also **Imprint**; **Incunabula**; **Mainz Psalter**; **Private press movement**; **Title page**

Colour printing

The first book printed using more than one colour of ink was a Psalter printed at Mainz by Fust and Schoeffer in 1457. In it, some capitals are printed in blue or red, a practice derived from the rubrication of late medieval manuscripts. This was achieved by impressing each sheet twice, once with black and once with coloured ink masking those parts of the forme not being printed in the colour then in use. This principle of double (or multiple) impressions is still the basis of all colour-printing processes, but with relief printing on the common press it is, necessarily, a time-consuming and expensive procedure. Even so, a number of printers did follow the example of Fust and Schoeffer, and books with title-pages, initials or woodcuts in red are not uncommon in the fifteenth and sixteenth centuries. This is particularly true of liturgical books, where the rubrication had the practical function of guiding the priest through the rite. An isolated English example of coloured illustration is in *The Book of St Albans* (1486) in which there are a number of two- and three-colour illustrations from woodcuts. Even on the Continent, however, such books were uncommon, and the experiment was never repeated in England.

Colour printing from type and woodcut was at best inconvenient, and at worst a costly method of achieving indifferent results. As early as 1507, the German artist, Lucas Cranach (1472–1533), was experimenting with a system of specially made relief blocks for colour printing, a process developed by the Italian, Ugo da Carpi (*c.* 1479–1533) who, in 1516, was granted a patent for what he called *chiaro oscuro or chiaroscuro*. Chiaroscuro was used for fine art prints and, intermittently, for book illustration, but it was too complicated to gain widespread acceptance, and the results in unskilled hands were far from ideal. In England, John Baptist Jackson used the chiaroscuro process at the end of the eighteenth century for prints, book illustrations and wallpaper.

Just as the chiaroscuro process involved multiple blocks, so the early intaglio processes necessitated multiple plates. The first of these to achieve any degree of commercial success was the three-colour mezzotint, developed by J.C. Leblon (1667–1741), from which excellent results could be obtained. It was still, however, far too costly for ordinary book work, and when the trade was faced with a demand for more colour printing at the beginning of the nineteenth century, it was necessary to evolve new methods. William Blake developed a system of relief etching, which he used in his *Songs of Innocence and Experience* (1794). Blake's methods were not copied, however, and are now only imperfectly understood. William Savage (1770–1843), Henry Shaw (1800–1873) and others did use relief printing from blocks for colour printing, in what was, in effect, a revival of the chiaroscuro process. It was, however, George Baxter who, by bringing together the old art of wood engraving and the new art of autographic lithography, created the first truly successful colour printing system.

The Baxter process held sway for about 10 years from 1835, when it was displaced by chromolithography, a fully lithographic method of colour printing. In the meanwhile, however, many other experiments had been conducted with colour, including those of Charles Knight, who first made coloured books accessible to a mass market. Most mid-nineteenth century colour printing, however, was either chromolithographic or from simple relief blocks. The latter was brought to its highest point of development by Edmund Evans, who from the mid-1850s was almost entirely a colour printer.

Coloured plates are not uncommon in nineteenth-century books, but all the processes involved expensive hand work in preparing blocks, plates or stones, even when steam-driven presses were used for the actual printing. As with monochromic illustration, it was not until the new art of photography could be adapted for use by printers that the inherent problems of graphic printing were solved in a way which was both aesthetically acceptable and economically viable. The basic principles of colour photography were understood by the early 1880s, and various experiments were then conducted to produce photomechanical blocks from colour-separated negatives. F.E. Ives succeeded (in 1881) in making a coloured half-tone, using a trichromatic process with blocks in red, green and blue. Trichromatic systems became standard and are still used, usually with the addition of a fourth block or plate to add black lines. By the end of the nineteenth century coloured half-tones were in regular use, and continue to be used in the few books still printed by relief methods.

In the present century, the trichromatic process has been used in both intaglio (as photogravure) and planography (as offset lithography). In the latter form it has made colour printing both easier and infinitely cheaper than ever before, and since the early 1960s coloured books, once the preserve of the wealthy, have become commonplace.

There is a large literature on colour printing, but the only attempt at a general history is Martin Hardie, *English Coloured Books* (1906), which is still useful. Joan M. Friedman, *Color Printing in England, 1476–1870* (1978) is admirable on the pre-photographic period, while Geoffrey Wakeman, *Victorian Book Illustration* (1973) deals, as its sub-title states, with 'the technical revolution' from pre-photographic to photomechanical processes. Wakeman, however, deals also with the monochromic processes, and these, inevitably and properly, play a larger part in his narrative. A.W. Pollard, *Early Illustrated Books* (2nd edn, 1917) deals comprehensively with the fifteenth and sixteenth centuries, including some comments on coloured books. The crucial technical developments of the early nineteenth century are discussed in massive detail by Elizabeth M. Harris, 'Experimental graphic processes in England 1800–1859', *JPHS* (1968), p. 33; (1969), p. 41; and (1970), p. 53.

See also **Baxter, George** (1804–1867); **Chiaroscuro**; **Chromolithography**; **Common press**; **Evans, Edmund** (1826–1905); **Forme**; **Impression**; **Intaglio**; **Jackson, John Baptist** (1701–*c*. 1777); **Knight, Charles** (1797–1873); **Mainz Psalter**; **Mezzotint**; **Offset lithography**; **Photogravure**; **Photomechanical printing**; **Relief printing**; **Rubrication**; **Woodcut**

Columbian press

Printing press. The Columbian was invented by George Clymer (1754–1834), a printer in Philadelphia who conducted a number of experiments aimed at improving the common press in the early nineteenth century. In 1812–14 he built the first of his iron presses, to a design whose distinctive feature was that the platen was operated by levers rather than by the traditional screw. Visually, its most striking feature, from which it derived its name, was the cast-iron American eagle used as a counterweight on the cross-bar at the top of the press. Clymer apparently made a few Columbians in the United States, but in 1817 he travelled to England, patented the press there, and began to manufacture them in quantity. First alone, and later in partnership with Samuel Dixon, Clymer remained as a press-maker in London until his death. Dixon continued the firm until 1851, and it existed in other hands thereafter until 1862–63. By then, Clymer's patent had long since expired, and Columbians were being made by many other firms. The Columbian achieved great popularity among printers and, like the Albion, was still being used by some jobbing printers in the 1960s.

There is a comprehensive study of the Columbian by James Moran, in *JPHS* (1969), p.1, with a short supplement in *JPHS* (1978–79), p.78; and there is a life of the inventor, *George Clymer and the Columbian Press*, by Jacob Kainen (1960).

See also **Albion press**; **Common press**; **Press**

Common press

Printing press. The common press is the name given to the wooden printing press which was in universal use from the invention of printing until the early nineteenth century. The press consisted of an assembly carrying the type and paper (the *bed*) which could be rolled (on the *coffin*) under a heavy wooden block (the *platen*) which was lowered onto it by means of a screw mechanism to make an impression. The type, made up into a forme, rested on a perfectly smoothed stone on the bed, and was held firmly in place by wooden wedges. Attached to one end of the coffin was a frame called the *tympan*, which was covered with a piece of parchment; an inner frame, also covered with parchment, could be inserted into this, and between the two sheets of parchment the tympan could be packed with waste paper, or similar material (the *blanket*), which assisted in achieving a good impression. The printing paper was placed on the tympan, and held in position by means of two pins (*points*). The tympan was attached to the coffin by hinges which allowed it to be moved through approximately 130° from the horizontal. Hinged at the other end of the tympan was a second, open, frame, called the *frisket*. Before printing began, the frisket was covered with a sheet of paper which had holes cut in it to correspond with the printing area of the forme. This protected the non-printing areas, and also helped to hold the paper in position on the frisket.

The platen was a wooden block, planed on its underside, and suspended parallel to the bed and slightly above it. The suspension was by means of heavy string or cord attached to the upper side of the platen and the outer casing (*hose*) of the screw mechanism. The screw itself was operated by means of a lever (*bar*) which, when pulled towards the operator (*pressman*), brought the platen into contact with the type on the bed beneath it. The pressman then pushed the bar away from him to raise the platen.

The whole press is a single unit, with the coffin assembly and the screw and platen assembly linked by uprights and cross-pieces, the former resting on the floor.

To take an impression, one pressman placed the paper on the tympan and lowered the frisket over it. Meanwhile, the second pressman inked the forme, and when this was completed the tympan and frisket were lowered gently onto the bed. The coffin was then rolled under the platen, the bar pulled, and the whole operation repeated in reverse until the printed sheet was removed. By this method it was possible to print 250 sheets an hour.

The common press had two great disadvantages. First, the screw mechanism was not reciprocating, so that the bar had to be pulled back into position after each pull. Secondly, and more seriously, the platen was only half the size of the bed, because of problems of balance and planing. Hence each sheet had to be impressed twice, with the coffin in different positions for each pull.

Despite this, however, the common press served printers well for some 350 years. The earliest iron presses, such as the Stanhope, the Columbian and the Albion, were all essentially the same design as the common press. Although both Stanhope and Clymer replaced the screw with levers and counter-weights, the Albion had a screw mechanism which was little more than a finely-tooled metal version of the device which had been in use since the fifteenth century. The iron presses only gradually displaced the common press, and a few were still in use at the end of the nineteenth century.

The classic description of the common press and its use is that by Joseph Moxon in his *Mechanick Exercises*, ed. Harry Carter and Herbert Davis (2nd edn, 1962). There is an exhaustive technical study of *The Common Press* by Elizabeth M. Harris and Clinton Sisson (1978), based on the example in the Smithsonian Institution, Washington DC, which is believed to have belonged to Franklin. Harris and Sisson also include working drawings for building a press. Harris elaborated on the restoration of the Smithsonian press in *JPHS* (1972), p. 42. Philip Gaskell, 'Survey of wooden presses', *JPHS* (1970), p. 1, describes (with photographs) the surviving presses. Gaskell's massively detailed study of *The Decline of the Common Press* is, unfortunately, available only as an unpublished Ph.D. thesis (Cambridge University, 1956), but that work gives unequalled authority to the relevant section of his *New Introduction to Bibliography* (1972), p. 118.

Companionship

See **Compositor**

Complutensian Polyglot

See **Bibles**

Composing stick

Printing house equipment. The stick is the wooden or metal hand-held tray in which type is assembled in hand typesetting. The left-hand end is adjustable to permit variations in the measure. The stick is normally about 8 inches long and $1\frac{1}{2}$ inches deep, so that it can hold up to six or seven lines of the 12-18 point type normally used in book work.

See James Moran, *The Composition of Reading Matter* (1965).

See also **Compositor**; **Measure**; **Point size**

Composition

See **Typesetting**

Compositor

Printing house worker. The compositor sets, or *composes*, type ready for printing. In hand-setting, as practised until the late nineteenth century, he held the stick in his left hand, and removed sorts from the case with his right, assembling the lines one by one. When the stick was full, he transferred the matter to the galley, and, when enough work was completed, assembled the pages and made up the forme. At this point, the forme was carried to the press, and became the pressman's responsibility, unless there were corrections to be made, in which case both the forme and the responsibility for it were returned to the compositor.

Hand composition is a highly-skilled task, and it formed the bulk of an apprentice's training. No doubt because of the skills required, compositors became an élite within the printing trade, able to negotiate successfully with the masters. This was originally done through the Chapel, and there emerged piece-work rates which varied somewhat from firm to firm, by which each man was paid according to the quantity of matter set and the size of type used. During the eighteenth century, however, the system of Companionships developed, whereby groups of compositors worked together under a supervisor, called a Clicker, and were paid collectively for the work done by the Companionship as a group. This system was already operating in France by the 1760s, and had been established in England before the end of the century. As early as 1785, however, the compositors were powerful enough to force the masters to accept standard rates of pay, known as the London Scale of Prices, throughout the trade, and the Chapels began to function as *de facto* trade unions.

The compositor's work remained unchanged until the typesetting machines were introduced in the nineteenth century. The earliest experiments, however, were not particularly successful, and it was not until the 1880s that practical machines were designed and installed. All of these involved the compositor working at a keyboard rather than handling type, and in modern systems he normally operates a keyboard linked to a computer.

The classic description of the hand compositor's work is by Moxon, p. 191; but see also James Moran, *The Composition of Printed Matter* (1965). For the companionship system and other matters relating to pay and conditions, see Ellic Howe, *The London Compositor...1785–1900* (1947).

See also **Case**; **Chapel**; **Composing stick**; **Forme**; **Galley**; **Sort**; **Typesetting**

Computer-assisted typesetting

See **Photosetting**

Conger

Book trade cant term, used in England from the late seventeenth to the mid-eighteenth centuries. The conger was an informal group of members of the trade who worked together for their common commercial benefit. Congers dealt with three matters — wholesaling, copyrights and printing — although the activities were not always mutually exclusive in any particular conger.

The congers evolved in 1680s as a means of protecting copyrights against piracy when the temporary lapse of the Printing Act, from 1679 to 1685, left the trade without copyright protection. The first stage of evolution was a conger in which the copyright owner produced an edition, and then sold the copies in bulk at a generous trade price to other leading members of the trade. They then sold them at a profit to the retail booksellers both in London and the country. Hence, if the title were pirated, all the members of the conger would be affected, not just the copyright owner. Since the members of the conger substantially controlled the trade's market outlets, it became almost impossible to sell a pirated edition through conventional book trade channels. From this self-protection there emerged a regular system of wholesaling along these lines, within a group of perhaps 15 or 20 leading London bookseller/publishers, and it continued to function until *c.* 1720.

It was a logical progression from the wholesaling conger to a conger which not only mounted a collective marketing operation but also collectively owned the copyright in the books being marketed, with each member owning one or more shares. Again this had its origins at the very end of the seventeenth century, but membership was more flexible than that of the wholesaling conger. Groups of booksellers worked together on a particular title, but the size and membership of the group was not invariable from title to title. On the other hand, these persons were normally drawn from an overall group of no more than about 20 leading London booksellers, and shares could only be bought or sold at trade sales to which only the established members of this inner circle were invited. The group was small enough to ensure that copyrights remained in a few hands, to their mutual profit, while being large enough to continue to act as a disincentive to piracy by closing the trade to piratical publishers. A number of copyright-owning congers developed, including the 'Castle' Conger and the 'New' Conger, both of which owned many valuable copies, and which survived for decades. The share-book system itself long outlived the congers which had created it, and did not finally vanish until the nineteenth century.

At about the same time as the share-book system was developed, another group of men came together to form the Printing Conger. As its name suggests, it printed books, but it also owned some copyrights. It flourished until 1723, but thereafter survived on reprint work, and had disappeared before 1740.

Our principal source of information about the existence and operation of the congers in their early years is from a financial notebook kept by two members of the wholesaling conger, Thomas Bennet and Henry Clements, from 1686 to 1719. This is now in the Bodleian Library, Oxford (MS. Eng. misc. d. 988), for which see *BLR* (1979), p. 131. This manuscript formed the basis of the standard work on the subject: Norma Hodgson and Cyprian Blagden, *The Notebook of Thomas Bennet and Henry Clements (1686–1719) with Some Aspects of Book Trade Practice* (OBS, new ser., 6, 1956). A contemporary view of the congers, from a bookseller who was excluded, can be found in the autobiographical *Life and Errors of John Dunton* (1705).

See also **Copyright**; **Dunton, John** (1654–1732); **Piracy**; **Printing Act 1662**; **Share books**; **Trade sales**

Constance Missal

*See **Missale speciale***

Copinger, Walter Arthur (1847–1910)

Bibliographer. A lawyer by training, Copinger was Professor of Law at Manchester University. Incunabula were among his many interests, and he established a considerable reputation as a bibliographer. With MacAlister, he was one of the founders of the Bibliographical Society, and was its first President. He published a number of books and papers on incunabula, of which the most important is his *Supplement* (1895–98) to Hain's *Repertorium*, which added some 6000 titles to the original list. Unfortunately, Copinger's accuracy is not always above reproach.

See the life of him in *DNB 1901–1911*, which was written by his friend Henry Guppy, the first Librarian of the John Rylands Library, Manchester.

See also **Bibliographical Society**; **Incunabula**

Copy

(1) *In printing.* Printer's copy is the manuscript used by the compositor as his exemplar when setting the text. Where such manuscripts survive, and they are few, they can provide valuable evidence for printing house techniques; this is especially useful to the textual critic. For general studies and discussion, see Francis R. Johnson, 'Printers' "copy books" and the black market in the Elizabethan book trade', *Libr.* (1946–47), p.97; and Frederick R. Pottle, 'Printers' copy in the eighteenth century', *PBSA* (1933), p.65.

(2) *In bibliography.* A copy is a single exemplar of an edition, impression or issue of a book.

(3) *In textual criticism.* The copy is the witness used by the editor as the basis for his own text. See W.W. Greg, 'The rationale of copy text', *SB* (1950–51). p.19; and Fredson Bowers, 'Greg's "Rationale of copy text" revisited', *SB* (1978), p.90.

(4) *In book trade history.* Copy was the word used until the middle of the eighteenth century for what is now called copyright.

See also **Compositor**; **Copyright**; **Edition**; **Impression**; **Issue**; **Textual criticism**

Copyright

The legal right to publish the text of a book. The possession and defence of the unique right to publish became a matter of importance after the invention of printing when large-scale financial investment became an essential part of the dissemination of a text. These investments were made by printers and publishers, and it was they, rather than the authors, who sought such protection. By the middle of the sixteenth century most European kings and princes granted such rights to individuals for particular titles on an *ad hoc* basis. In England, these were called privileges, and were granted by Letters Patent during and after the reign of Henry VIII (1507–1543). There, as elsewhere, however, the granting of such privileges was only one part of the larger effort to control the output of the press, an enterprise on which almost all European rulers embarked in the sixteenth century, as they began to realise the potential power of the printed word. Thus copyright and censorship are indissolubly linked for nearly two centuries. Nevertheless, whatever its intentions, the effect of the system of privileges was that a text came to be seen as a form of property which was owned by an individual.

The development of the modern concept of copyright took place in England, and was later adopted in other countries, and at each stage it is linked with the Crown's determination and ability to censor the press. The Charter granted to the Stationers' Company in 1557 required each new book (or 'copy') to be registered at Stationers' Hall, together with the licence to print it granted by the Crown through one of several agents. In practice, except for potentially controversial books, the licences were granted by the Master and Wardens of the Stationers' Company itself, which thus became the willing agency of the goverment in censoring the press. The reason for this compliance was the usefulness of the Register within the trade, where the licence came to be regarded as exclusive as well as permissive, conveying not a general right to print the copy, but vesting that right in the named individual who had registered it. This was the accepted position by 1600 at the latest, and thereafter the Stationers' Register records many transactions in which rights were transferred from one stationer to another by sale or bequest. It seems that such rights were defensible at law by the early seventeenth century.

The Stationers' control of the trade broke down in the revolutionary years 1640–42, and it was only partially reimposed after the Restoration (1660). Under the Printing Act 1662, the Company was again required to keep a Register, but the crucial difference was that the licences were now granted by the Secretary of State through a Licenser in his Office. The trade, however, continued to observe the older custom of regarding the licence as conferring unique rights, and regarded existing rights as defensible even when the Act was not in force from 1679 to 1685. In 1693, however, the Printing Act was again allowed to lapse, and the Company thereafter had the utmost difficulty in enforcing the registration of copies. So few were in fact registered that there was no real record of any rights which did exist, and they could be established and protected only by long and expensive suits in the Court of Chancery — a situation complicated by the silence of the law on the whole subject, and the consequent need to rely on the complex and unclear common law of property. The trade reacted first by developing such protective mechanisms as the congers, the trade sales and the share-book system; and secondly, by petitioning Parliament to renew the Act. In fact, their real interest was in copy protection; when it became apparent that the revival of the old Act was politically impossible, they changed their tack, and in 1710 their efforts were rewarded by the passing into law of the Copyright Act.

The principal provision of the 1710 Act still forms the basis of all copyright law, granting protection to the owner for a fixed period after which the copy goes into 'public domain' and may be printed by anyone. This was, however, a wholly new concept of property, quite unlike the traditional law of real, or tangible, property. As a consequence, two major legal problems developed out of the 1710 Act in the eighteenth century. The first was in defining the precise intention of the Act itself. In the 1730s, when the first batch of copies began to come into public domain, the trade started to argue that the Act was merely confirmatory of common law, and that in common law, copyright, like any other property, had a permanent existence. They considered the temporal limitations in the Act (14 years in the first instance, and a further 14 if the owner were still alive at the end of the 14th year) applied to the specific penalties for infringement, but not to the copyright itself. This issue was before the courts in one form or another for nearly 40 years, but in 1774 the House of Lords finally ruled that the Act overrode any common law rights, and that after 14 (or 28) years a copy was indeed in public domain.

The second problem arose indirectly out of this same controversy about 'perpetual' copyright, and concerned the fundamental nature of copyright as a property. The Act and its sponsors envisaged copyright as belonging to a bookseller, but the assignment of the status of property to copies inevitably raised the question of the part played by the author as the creator of the property in the first place. During the eighteenth century, authors began to exploit this by seeking higher payment for their manuscripts, and the view developed that as the creator of the property the author had total control over it until he sold it (if he chose to do so) to a bookseller. Indeed, as a general principle, it was clear that when the bookseller paid the author he was indeed buying something which the author already owned; all that the author owned was the copy which he had created, but what was in question was not the physical document which he handed over, but rather its contents. From this there developed the concept of *intellectual property*, which is the philosophic basis of modern copyright law. By 1800 this was accepted at least in principle, and agitation soon began for a reform of the law which would recognise more fully the rights of the author.

The remaining history of UK copyright law is of its extension to Ireland (in 1800), and of the gradual lengthening of the period for which it subsists, first to 28 years or the life of the author (1814); then to 42 years or the life of the author plus a further 7 years (1842); and finally to 50 years after the death of the author (1911). Over the years, it also came to be applied to graphic reproductions, printed music, recorded and broadcast sound, cinematographic film, broadcast television programmes and the typographical arrangement of a printed text. The law is now governed by the Copyright Act 1956, but this is unsatisfactory in many ways, and there is much pressure, both from publishers and from the producers of newer media such as videotapes and computer software, for a thoroughgoing revision.

Other countries followed the British lead only slowly in enacting copyright legislation. The United States passed its first federal Copyright Act in 1790, following the British pattern, and in 1793 the French republic did likewise, although in an attenuated form. Gradually, after 1815, most European countries followed suit, and in the nineteenth century the central issue of copyright controversy concerned international law. In 1837, a Prussian law gave protection in that country to foreign authors from the countries with which Prussia had reciprocal copyright agreements. The first such was with the United Kingdom, where an Act of 1838 made similar arrangements possible. A few other reciprocal agreements were negotiated between various European countries, but it was not until the signing of the first Berne Convention (1886) that a fully developed international system was evolved. Even then the USA was excluded, despite many attempts to reach bilateral agreement with the UK. The problem was largely (and deliberately) created by US laws of 1831, 1865 and 1870, under which there was a complicated registration procedure at the Library of Congress which made it almost impossible for British publishers to secure US copyright. The Chace Act of 1891 made the situation worse by granting copyright only to books published in the USA which had not previously been published elsewhere, although the Act did allow non-residents and non-citizens to obtain US copyright for the first time. The Chace Act made it impossible for the USA to sign the Berne Convention, for its domestic law did not permit the fully reciprocal arrangements with other countries which the Convention required. In fact, the USA did not join the international copyright system until 1956, when it signed the Universal Copyright Convention, which is less stringent in its demand for reciprocity than is the Berne Convention.

Copyright is a vast and complex subject. There is no comprehensive work on the development of the law, but among the relevant literature are: A.W. Pollard, *Shakespeare's Fight with the Pirates* (rev. edn, 1920); W.W. Greg, '*Ad imprimendum solum*', *Libr.* (1954). p. 242; C.J. Sisson, 'The laws of Elizabethan copyright: the Stationers' view', *Libr.* (1960), p. 8; N. Frederick Nash, 'English licences to print and grants of copyright in the 1640s', *Libr.* (1982), p. 174; R.C. Bald, 'Early copyright litigation and its bibliographical interest', *PBSA* (1942), p. 81; and John Feather, 'The book trade in politics: the making of the Copyright Act of 1710', *PH* (1980), p. 19. For the later eighteenth century, A.S. Collins, *Authorship in the Days of Johnson* (1927) is still useful, and is supplemented by Gwyn Walters, 'The booksellers in 1759 and 1774: the battle for literary property', *Libr.* (1974), p. 287. The international issues are dealt with by Simon Nowell-Smith, *International Copyright Law and the Publisher in the Reign of Queen Victoria* (1968); and James J. Barnes, *Authors, Publishers and Politicians. The quest for an Anglo-American copyright agreement, 1815-1854* (1974). For the present position, see R.F. Whale and Jeremy J. Philips, *Whale on Copyright* (3rd edn, 1983).

See also **Berne Convention**; **Censorship**; **Conger**; **Copy**; **Printing Act 1662**; **Share books**; **Stationers' Company**; **Stationers' Register**; **Trade sales**; **Universal Copyright Convention**

Coucher

See **Papermaking**

Countermark

See **Watermark**

Courtesy books

Literary genre. The courtesy book is a volume of advice on conduct, manners and education, which attained great popularity in the sixteenth and seventeenth centuries. Although there are classical precedents, notably Cicero, *De officiis*, the archetype of the Renaissance courtesy book was Castiglione's *Il courtegiano* (1528), translated into English by Sir Thomas Hoby as *The Boke of the Courtier* (1561). Apart from Hoby's *Castiglione*, there was a considerable native literature in English, beginning with Elyot's *Boke Named the Governour* (1531), and ending with Chesterfield's *Letters to his Son* (1774).

See John E. Mason, *Gentlefolk in the Making* (1935).

Craft binding

See **Bookbinding**

Crane, Walter (1845–1915)

See **Evans, Edmund** (1826–1905)

Critical bibliography

See **Textual criticism**

Crown

See **Sheet**

Cruickshank, George (1792–1878)

Engraver and illustrator. The son of a caricature artist, Cruickshank was apprenticed to his father, and himself became a caricaturist, a field in which he was highly successful. From the early 1820s, however, he turned to book illustration, usually in the medium of etching. He illustrated hundreds of books during the next 40 years, but is best remembered for his work with Dickens. It was his illustrations which provided the inspiration for *Sketches by Boz* (1836), and he also illustrated *Oliver Twist* (1838), as well as novels by Harrison Ainsworth and Barham's *Ingoldsby Legends* (1864).

See Michael Wynn Jones, *George Cruickshank: his life and London* (1978); and John Buchanan-Brown, *The Book Illustrations of George Cruickshank* (1980).

See also **Etching**; **Illustrated books**

Cuala Press

Private press. The Cuala Press was founded in Dublin in 1902, under the name of the Dun Emer Press, changing its title in 1908. The founders were Elizabeth Corbert Yeats and Lily Yeats, sisters of W.B. Yeats, and Evelyn Gleeson. Their principal motive was to train and employ Irish girls in useful work, and to produce worthwhile Irish books. Unusually among private press owners, the ladies regarded the content of the books as more important than their appearance, and they produced a number of significant books. These included both new works in both English and Irish, and translations of early Irish literature. The Press survived until the 1940s.

See Liam Miller, *The Dun' Emer Press, later the Cuala Press* (1973); and William Maxwell, *The Dun Emer Press and the Cuala Press* (1932).

See also **Private press movement**

Curll, Edmund (1683?–1747)

Publisher and book pirate. From an obscure background, Curll emerged in 1706 as an auctioneer and bookseller in London, and soon began to publish books. He gained a well-deserved reputation as an unscrupulous operator and pirate of other men's copies. In the later part of his career one of his less agreeable habits was the publication of private correspondence without the permission of the correspondents, although in fairness it has to be added that the legal position on the copyright in such documents was obscure. The most famous episode in which Curll was involved was the publication of Pope's *Letters* in 1735. The traditional version of this affair, which is that Pope surreptitiously encouraged Curll, is now discounted and it seems that Curll did indeed issue them without permission. The long-standing quarrel between Curll and Pope was rewarded by the latter in his epic poem, *The Dunciad.*

See Ralph Straus, *The Unspeakable Curll* (1927) which includes a bibliography of his publications; and J. McLaverty, 'The first printing and publication of Pope's letters', *Libr.* (1980), p. 264.

See also **Copyright**; **Piracy**

Da Carpi, Ugo (*c.* 1479–1533)

See **Chiaroscuro**; **Colour printing**

Daniel Press

Private press. The press was the hobby of the Rev. C.H.O. Daniel (1836–1919), Fellow and, from 1903, Provost of Worcester College, Oxford. Daniel began to play with type and presses while a small boy in his father's vicarage in Frome, Somerset, and in 1874 he moved his Albion to Oxford. He now began to take a serious interest in printing, and in 1876 he was the first person to revive the use of the Fell types from the Oxford University Press. This alone would give him an important place in the history of modern English typography, but in fact the quality of the pamphlets which he produced from his Press give him a claim to be one of the best of the private printers. For Daniel, the Press was never more than a hobby; unlike Morris and his successors he had no commercial or didactic motives. He produced a considerable quantity of books and ephemera before he abandoned the Press when he was elected Provost. The books included a number of first editions of poems by Robert Bridges. After his death, Daniel's Albion was presented to the Bodleian Library, where it remains; it is still used regularly for teaching bibliography students.

The first book printed on Daniel's Albion in the Bodleian was Falconer Madan, *The Daniel Press* (1921), which remains the standard work.

See also **Albion press**; **Fell, John** (1625–1686); **Kelmscott Press**; **Private press movement**

Dates

Dates in books, or the lack of them, can present some problems to the bibliographer. It was a common although not invariable practice of medieval scribes to give the date of completion of a manuscript in a colophon. This was imitated in some early printed books, although many incunabula are undated. The development of the title-page in the late fifteenth century, and the consequent replacement of the colophon by the imprint, caused the date to be moved to the prominent position which is still normally retains, either on the title-page itself or on its verso. The fifteenth-century printers followed the scribal practice of giving a full date (e.g. 1 January 1480), but gradually it became the custom to give the year only. By the mid-sixteenth century, most books were dated in this way, and have been so ever since.

The dates in the great majority of books present no problems, although there are examples of books with deliberately falsified dates to conceal piracy or to confuse censors. One trade practice, however, can cause some confusion, for since the sixteenth century it has been common, though not invariable, to give the following year's date for books published during the last two or three months of the year. A further confusion is introduced by the fact that until the mid-eighteenth century the legal year ran from 25 March to 24 March, and only gradually was the 1 January–31 December year generally accepted. Thus a book published in January 1710 (by the modern reckoning) might be dated 1709 (the legal year) or 1710 (anticipating the new year beginning on 25 March). The complexities of the change from the Julian to the Gregorian calendar, known respectively as Old Style (OS) and New Style (NS) does not generally affect the dating of books; this change took place at various times in different countries from the late sixteenth century onwards, the last European country to make it being Russia in 1917. A few books are dated by regnal years, revolutionary calendars, and the like.

Undated books can be dated within limits by numerous factors. In some cases there is external evidence such as copyright registration or advertisements; more often, we rely on internal features such as the text itself, the identity of the publisher, printer or author, and the typography.

A comprehensive study of dating, with lists of regnal years, etc. will be found in C.R. Cheney, *Handbook of Dates* (1961).

See also **Colophon**; **Imprint**; **Incunabula**; **Piracy**; **Title page**; **Verso**

de Worde, Wynkyn (*c.* 1455–1534)

Printer. de Worde, a native of Alsace, apparently worked with Caxton in Cologne in 1471–72, and came with him to England in 1476. In 1491, he inherited Caxton's business and equipment, and in 1494 began to print and publish on his own account. In 1500, he left Westminster and moved to Fleet Street in the City of London, close to the booksellers who were already gathering around St Paul's Cathedral. His motive was financial. de Worde did not have Caxton's privileged access to royal and noble patrons, nor, indeed, his monopoly of English printing, for several other printers were established in London by the end of the fifteenth century. He had to compete in a harsh commercial climate, and therefore moved to his market. In all, he published some 700 books in his lifetime, including, in the 1530s, some early Protestant books which brought him into conflict with the authorities. After his death the business was continued by John Byddell and James Gaver, and in various hands it continued into the second half of the sixteenth century.

The best account of de Worde is probably still that by Henry R. Plomer, in *Wynkyn de Worde and his Contemporaries* (1925), although James Moran, *Wynkyn de Worde* (1976) was able to take some account of more recent scholarship.

See also **Caxton, William** (1422–1491); **St Paul's Churchyard**

Dedication

The author's inscription of his work to an individual by means of a printed statement. The practice originated in the Middle Ages, and was an attempt by the author to find a patron who would offer him financial reward. It was carried into early printed books from the same motives, and became increasingly common in the sixteenth and seventeenth centuries. Despite the decline of literary patronage since the early eighteenth century as authors have come to receive more reasonable payments from their publishers, the dedication has survived to allow an author to show his gratitude or respect to a teacher, colleague, friend or relative.

See Franklin B. Williams. 'An index of dedications and commendatory verse', *Libr.* (1957), p. 11; and the same author's monumental *Index of Dedications and Commendatory Verses in English Books before 1641* (1962), with *Addenda* published as a Supplement to *Libr.*, vol. 30 (March 1975).

Demy

See **Sheet**

Descriptive bibliography

The technique of describing books in bibliographies. It is essential that the entries in a bibliography are consistent with each other. Even at the most simple level, therefore, a bibliographical description has to be properly defined. Hence, in a straightforward enumerative bibliography, it may be decided, for example, that all of an author's forenames will be given in full, or that only the first will be so given while the others are represented by initials only; in any case, some decision must be taken, and then be consistently applied. Such rules are normally explained in a preface (as, for example, in *STC*), or follow an international standard. In recent years, such a standard has been evolved for cataloguing purposes; this is the International Standard Book Description (ISBD), which has spawned a whole family of related standards, including the International Standard Book Description (Antiquarian) (ISBD(A)). These are in turn based on the *Anglo-American Cataloguing Rules* (2nd edn, 1978). The ISBD is used by some bibliographies, such as the *British National Bibliography*.

If the first principle of descriptive bibliography is internal consistency between entries, the second is that the description must be equally applicable to every copy of the book. With modern books this presents no problem, but with early books, with their cancels, press variants and other deliberate or accidental inconsistencies between copies, it is more problematic. What is actually described is the 'ideal copy' which may, in extreme cases, not actually correspond to any single extant copy of the book. Because of these complications, it is usual to give more elaborate descriptions of early books, following the prescriptions of Greg, Bowers and Tanselle. Such descriptions normally consist of a transcription of the complete title page (and the imprint information from any other page on which it may appear); the collational formula, and registers of pagination and signatures; a detailed list of contents; and a record of bibliographical features of the book, including, but not confined to, catchwords and press figures. The theory is that a sufficiently elaborate description will enable the user of a bibliography to identify precisely another copy of the book so described, even though the compiler had not seen that particular copy. In recent years there has been a sensible tendency to use photographic reproductions rather than transcriptions for the title page.

The *locus classicus* of modern descriptive bibliography is Bowers' *Principles of Bibliographical Description* (1949); Greg explained his practices in the Introduction to vol. 4 of his *Bibliography of the English Printed Drama to the Restoration* (1959). G. Thomas Tanselle's work has appeared in the form of journal articles, mainly in *Studies in Bibliography*, but his most important papers have been reprinted as *Selected Studies in Bibliography* (1979).

See also **Bibliography**; **Bowers, Fredson Thayer** (1905–); **Cancel**; **Catalogues**; **Catchword**; **Collation**; **Enumerative bibliography**; **Greg, Sir Walter Wilson** (1875–1959); **Ideal copy**; **Press figures**; **Press variant**; **Signature**; *STC*

Device

A decorative block, usually woodcut, used by a printer as a trademark, especially in the sixteenth and seventeenth centuries, although there are both earlier and later examples, and in the nineteenth and twentieth centuries devices have more often been used by publishers. They probably share a common origin with the trademark in the mark with which a medieval merchant identified his property for the benefit of the illiterate. Devices often incorporate the arms or initials of the printer, or a symbolic device of classical origin. To the bibliographer, their chief value is in identifying the printer of a book which does not have a full imprint or colophon. This technique was pioneered by R.B. McKerrow, whose *Printers' and Publishers' Devices in England and Scotland, 1475–1640* (1913) is still a standard work. There is no comparable collection for European countries, but a large selection is in H.W. Davies, *Devices of the Early Printers 1457–1560* (1935), which is a comprehensive history of the subject.

See also **Colophon**; **Imprint**; **Woodcut**

Dibdin, Thomas Frognall (1776–1847)

Bibliophile and bibliographer. Dibdin, the son of a naval officer, was born in India, but his family returned to England, and he was educated at Oxford. After a brief period at the Bar, he was ordained in 1805, becoming a curate in Kensington. He had published a few essays in the 1790s, but it was his first bibliographical book, *Introduction to the Knowledge of Greek and Latin Classics* (1802), which proved to be the turning-point of his life. It brought him to the attention of the 2nd Earl Spencer, who invited him to augment and to catalogue the library at Althorp. Dibdin transformed this into the finest private library in England. The catalogue, *Bibliotheca Spenceriana*, was published in 1814–15 in four handsome quarto volumes. Dibdin was now wholly committed to bibliophily, and in 1809 published his *Bibliomania*, an amusing and cynical account of the current craze for book-collecting among the wealthy English aristocracy. It was a craze which Dibdin himself did much to encourage both by example and by exhortation, and the title of his book is now used to describe that era of English bibliophilic history. As well as being a central figure in the social circles of the bibliographical world, and exercising much influence over collecting tastes, he began a new edition of Ames (1810), and published a number of other bibliographical works, including *The Bibliographical Decameron* (1817), and *The Library Companion* (1824). He was largely responsible for the foundation of the Roxburghe Club in 1812.

Dibdin was a notoriously inaccurate bibliographer, but his enthusiasm infected his contemporaries, and can still be felt in his ornate but strangely breathless prose.

The account of him in *DNB* is unsympathetic to the point of insult, but there is a good little book by E.J.O'Dwyer, *Thomas Frognall Dibdin* (1967), and *An Annotated List of the Publications of the Reverend Thomas Frognall Dibdin* by William A. Jackson (1965).

See also **Ames, Joseph** (1689–1759); **Bibliomania**; **Roxburghe Club**; **Spencer, John Charles, 2nd Earl Spencer** (1782–1845)

Dicey, William and Dicey, Cluer

Dicey William (fl. 1719–1754) and Dicey, Cluer (fl. 1719–1754)

See **Ballads**; **Chapbooks**

Dictionaries

Reference books. A dictionary is an alphabetical list of words or names, with definitions and/or translations. Traditionally, a dictionary is of a language, but dictionaries of subjects or of persons have become increasingly common in the last 100 years. The earliest dictionaries were compiled in antiquity; in the second century BC, Aristophanes of Byzantium compiled the first systematic Greek dictionary, followed in the next century by two Latin dictionaries by Verro and Verrius Flaccus. The first West European dictionary was the Irish *Auricept* in the seventh century, but the initiative passed to the Arabs from the eighth century onwards. Some encyclopaedic dictionaries were, however, compiled in the West, of which the most notable were Suidas's *Lexicon* (10th–11th centuries) and Joannes Balbus's *Catholicon* (13th century). The latter was the first dictionary to be printed, by Gutenberg's successors at Mainz in 1460.

The flow of dictionaries increased considerably after the mid-sixteenth century, as the vernacular languages of the West began to be systematically studied. The first bilingual vernacular dictionary was *Vocabolista italiano-tedesco* (Venice, 1477), but both English and French had to wait considerably longer even for monolingual dictionaries (1604 and 1606, respectively). In the mid-seventeenth century, the compilation of dictionaries became a more scholarly matter. The Académie Française, founded in 1635, had as one of its principal objectives the compilation of an authoritative French dictionary, but the Académie was, and is, prescriptive as well as descriptive in an attempt to preserve the purity of the French language. No such institution has ever existed in the English-speaking world, although Johnson's *Dictionary* (1755) immediately attained a massive authority which it did not lose until the publication of Murray's *New English Dictionary* (1888–1928), and supplements; since 1933 called the *Oxford English Dictionary*). The comparable work for American English is *Webster's*, first published in 1828, and many times revised.

Bibliographically, dictionaries are no different from other books, although early editions tend to be rare, having been worn out through overuse. For a general history, see R.L. Collison. *A History of Foreign-Language Dictionaries* (1982); for English, see De Witt T. Starnes and Gertrude E. Noyes, *The English Dictionary from Cawdrey to Johnson 1604–1755* (1946). R.C. Alston, *A Bibliography of the English Language from the Invention of Printing to the Year 1800*, vol. 5 (1966) is the best bibliography of the English dictionary.

See also **Gutenberg, Johann** (1394/94–1468); *Mainz Catholicon*

Direction line

Technical term in printing. The direction line is the last line of the page which contains only the catchword and, on certain rectos, the signature. These acted as guides to the binder to ensure that the sheets were correctly folded and collated.

See Moxon, p.237.

See also **Bookbinding**; **Catchword**; **Collation**; **Recto**; **Signature**

Direction Line, The

Bibliographical periodical. *DL* was first published in 1975, and appears at approximately six-monthly intervals. It contains short notes on matters of current interest, especially on technological developments such as collating machines and the detection of watermarks. There is also an annual review of the previous year's research in bibliography, and lists of works in progess. The editor is Warner Barnes, Department of English, University of Texas, Austin, Texas.

Distribution

Technical term in printing. When a forme has been printed it is returned to the compositor who unlocks it and returns the sorts to the case. This latter process is distribution. It was the first task learned by the apprentice, to teach him the lay of the case. In the typesetting machines developed in the nineteenth century the time-consuming process of distribution was dispensed with by melting down the metal after printing.

See Moxon, p.199.

See also **Case**; **Compositor**; **Forme**; **Sort**; **Typesetting**

Dobell, Bertram (1842–1914)

Antiquarian bookseller. Dobell had little education, but began to collect books at an early age, and in 1869 opened a newsagency in North London. By 1876 he was selling secondhand books, and in 1887 moved to Charing Cross Road, then the centre of the antiquarian book trade. He became a leading member of that trade during the next few years. His special field was English literature of the seventeenth century, to which he made a major contribution through his recovery of the poems of Traherne. He was also interested in contemporary poetry, and was both the patron and the publisher of James Thomson ('B.V.'). Dobell wrote some verse of his own which he published himself. After his death, his sons continued to trade (as P.J. and A.E. Dobell) until the 1970s. The firm's records, and other material relating to Dobell, are now in the Bodleian Library, Oxford, and could form the basis of an interesting study of the only bookseller who was a serious rival to Quaritch.

There is a life of Dobell in *DNB*.

See also **Quaritch**, **Bernard** (1819–1899)

Dodsley, Robert (1703–1764) and Dodsley, James (1725–1797)

Booksellers. The son of a Nottinghamshire schoolmaster, Dodsley apparently ran away from his apprenticeship and drifted into domestic service in London. He was footman when his first poem, *Servitude*, was published in 1729. The poetic footman became something of a celebrity in literary circles, and was taken up by Pope. Indeed, Pope was instrumental in setting Dodsley up in business as a bookseller in Pall Mall in 1735, although his motives were not entirely disinterested, since he wanted to circumvent the trade by establishing printers and booksellers who were beholden to him. Alone of those whom Pope helped in this way, Dodsley gained a reputation of his own. At first he published almost nothing but the work of Pope and his circle, and his own poems and plays; having established his reputation as a literary publisher, however, he went on to publish Johnson (he was one of the group which commissioned the *Dictionary*), Goldsmith, Collins, Gray, Young and Akenside, as well as reprinting works by Pope, Swift and other earlier writers in whose copyrights he owned shares. Dodsley also published two famous and important anthologies: *A Collection of Poems by Several Hands* (1748–58), and *A Select Collection of Old Plays* (1744). Like all publishers, he also made some mistakes; most famously, he refused to publish *Tristram Shandy* because he feared that it would not sell, although he did act as distributor when Sterne had the first two volumes printed in York. In about 1742, his younger brother, James, joined him in the business, and succeeded to it when Robert died. James maintained the Dodsley reputation, and died a wealthy man.

There are lives of both brothers in *DNB*, and a biography of Robert by Ralph Straus, *Robert Dodsley* (1910). On his literary activities, see Richard Wendorf, 'Robert Dodsley as editor'. *SB* (1978), p. 235, and the references cited there. James E. Tierney is preparing Robert's letters for publication.

Donkin, Bryan (1768–1855)

See **Fourdrinier**, **Henry** (1766–1854) **and Fourdrinier**, **Sealy** (d. 1847)

Double pica

See **Type size**

Douce, Francis (1757–1834)

Librarian, scholar and book collector. Douce, the son of a minor civil servant, was educated privately in London. He became a solicitor, but in 1807 joined the staff of the British Museum. He was Keeper of Manuscripts for a short time, but resigned in 1811 after a series of disagreements with the Trustees. Even as a boy, Douce had been an avid collector, and after 1811 he devoted himself almost entirely to this occupation, greatly assisted by a legacy which he received in 1823 from the sculptor, Joseph Nollekins. He was one of the leading collectors of a remarkable period. Like many of his contemporaries, he collected 'black letter' books of the sixteenth and seventeenth centuries, but he had a strong additional interest in popular and folk literature both of his own time and of earlier periods. He was also a student of English literature, and had an exceptional collection of sixteenth and seventeenth-century poetry and drama. Again in common with many contemporary book collectors, he also assembled prints, drawings and coins. His medieval manuscripts were outstanding; perhaps the most famous is the thirteenth-century Apocalypse which now bears his name.

The whole of these great collections, except for some personal papers and a collection of medieval ivories, was bequeathed to the Bodleian Library, Oxford. The ivories and the papers he left to the British Museum; the latter were to remain sealed until 1900, but after they had been opened they too were transferred to the Bodleian. The prints and drawings are now in the Ashmolean Museum, Oxford. A catalogue of the collections was published by the Bodleian in 1840.

Although Douce was a man of great learning, he published nothing after his *Illustrations of Shakespeare* (1807) received an unfairly critical review. His vast collectanea on a great variety of antiquarian topics comprised the bulk of the sealed papers which were left to the British Museum.

There is an account of Douce in *DNB*, but the best and by far the most readable discussion of the man and his work is in A.N.L. Munby, *Connoisseurs and Medieval Miniatures, 1750–1850* (1972). For his collections, see *BQR* (1934), p. 359; and *The Douce Legacy* (1984), a Bodleian exhibition catalogue.

See also **Bibliomania**; **Chapbooks**

Doves Press

Private press. The founder of the Doves Press, T.J. Cobden-Sanderson, (1840–1922) was a close associate and admirer of Morris and the Kelmscott Press. After attempting various careers, including the civil service and the Church, he established the Doves Bindery in 1894 inspired by the ideals of Morris and Walker. By 1898, however, he was broadening his outlook, and the production of the perfect book became something of an obsession. By 1900-1 he had designed his own type, known as the Doves type, and had established the Press in association with Emery Walker. The books he produced there were magnificent, but quite different from the Kelmscott books; the design was simple and unadorned, and the type was allowed to stand alone on the page without the ornaments and borders which might be argued to disfigure so many Kelmscott books. The Doves Bible (1903–5) is perhaps the greatest book produced by a British private press before 1914. The partnership between Walker and Cobden-Sanderson, which had never been easy, ended in 1909, although the Press continued until 1916. In that year, Cobden-Sanderson decided to abandon it, and to mark the end of this phase of his life he threw the punches and matrices of the Doves type into the Thames so that they could never be used again.

See Cobden-Sanderson's own *Catalogue Raisonné of Books Printed and Published at the Doves Press* (2nd edn, 1916); and Roderick Cave, *The Private Press* (2nd edn, 1983).

See also **Kelmscott Press**; **Private press movement**; **Walker, Sir Emery** (1851–1933)

Duff, Edward Gordon (1863–1924)

Bibliographer. Duff was educated at Cheltenham and Oxford where, even as an undergraduate, he began to compile a list of incunabula in the Bodleian. This became the basis of Proctor's Bodleian entries in his *Index*, and was the first of Duff's many contributions to incunable studies. The most important of these were *Fifteenth-century Printed Books* (1917), which is still useful, and *A Century of the English Book Trade* (1905), a directory of the trade from 1476 to 1576. He was appointed as the first librarian of the John Rylands Library, but resigned in 1899 before the building was opened. He was greatly involved with the Bibliographical Society, and was one of the founders of the Oxford Bibliographical Society. In his will, he instructed that his books should be sold, and the proceeds used to endow prizes and book funds at Oxford and Cambridge.

There is an obituary by Falconer Madan in *Libr.* (1924–25), p. 264.

See also **Bibliographical Society**; **Incunabula**; **John Rylands University Library of Manchester**; **Oxford Bibliographical Society**; **Proctor, Robert George Collie** (1868–1903)

Dun Emer Press

See **Cuala Press**

Dunton, John (1654–1732)

Bookseller. The son of a clergyman, Dunton was himself intended for the Church, but his father eventually despaired of educating his intelligent but wayward son, and he was, in 1674, apprenticed to the London bookseller,

Thomas Parkhurst. Even as an apprentice, Dunton was involved in politics as the leader of a group of Whig apprentices. When he was freed from his apprenticeship in 1681, he set up his own business. He began to publish a few books, chiefly Whig and Presbyterian in tone. After the accession of James II, his views became dangerous, and in 1685 he went to Boston, Massachusetts, where he tried but failed to establish a bookshop. He was back in London within a year, but fled to the Netherlands to avoid both political enemies and his creditors. He reopened his London shop after the Revolution of 1688, and for the next ten years was reasonably successful. It was during this time that he published his most innovative work, *The Athenian Mercury* (1691–98), the first popular general-interest magazine. This was a great success and spawned many imitators.

Dunton was, however, still as ornery as he had ever been. He railed against the trade's dominant oligarchy, which he was the first to describe as a conger, and their control over the distribution and sale of books. Eventually, he tried his fortune in Dublin, failed there also, and returned to London to make his living as a hack writer for the Whigs. He died in obscure poverty.

His autobiography, *The Life and Errors of John Dunton* (1705) is a major, if eccentric, source for the history of the trade in the late seventeenth century. See also Stephen Parks, *John Dunton and the English Book Trade* (1976), which includes a bibliography of his publications.

See also **Conger**; **Magazines**

Duodecimo

Bibliographical format. A duocedimo, written 12^0, is a sheet printed with 24 pages to fold to 12 leaves. Duodecimo, sometimes called 'twelvemo', produces a smallish and narrow book, rather tall for its width. Because it is economical of paper and machine time, it is usually associated with cheaper books. In the seventeenth and eighteenth centuries it was in widespread use, and after *c.* 1730 it was perhaps the most popular format in England. The half sheet 12^0, gathered in sixes, was also used, especially for chapbooks. Another common variation, especially on the Continent, was to impose for binding in alternating gatherings of 8 leaves and 4.

The best imposition diagrams for 12^0 are those in William Savage, *A Dictionary of the Art of Printing* (1841, repr. 1968).

See also **Chapbooks**; **Format**; **Gathering**; **Imposition**

Dust jacket

The outer wrapping around the binding of a book, issued with it by the publisher. The dust jacket originated in the early nineteenth century, and it has been suggested that its origin is associated with that of publishers' cloth bindings which date from the 1820s. The earliest known jacket is that for *The*

Keepsake 1883; the only recorded example was, unfortunately, lost in 1952. From the mid-1830s onwards, jackets were issued in both the USA and Britain, but they did not become common until the 1870s, and not until the end of the nineteenth century were they in regular use. The early dust jackets are entirely typographical. From the 1880s onwards illustrations began to appear on them, and by the mid-1890s some were quite elaborate. Also in the 1890s, publishers began to exploit the advertising potential of the jackets by printing 'blurbs' and catalogues on them. In the twentieth century, jackets have become eye-catching and often colourful packaging designed to attract the customer's eye in the bookshop.

For the early years, see G. Thomas Tanselle, 'Book jackets, blurbs, and bibliographers', *Libr.* (1971), p.91. There is a more general study by Charles Rosner, *The Growth of the Book Jacket* (1954).

See also **Blurb**; **Bookbinding**; **Edition binding**

Edinburgh Bibliographical Society

Founded 1890. The Society's founder, George P. Johnstone, wanted to promote the study of Scottish bibliography through publications, meetings and exhibitions. The Society's *Papers* were published from vol. 1 (1891) to vol. 15 (1935) with an Index in vol. 15. Renamed *Transactions*, a new series started with vol. 1 (1935–38) and continues. Both series contain many valuable articles on Scottish bibliographical matters.

Johnstone wrote a history of the Society in its *Papers* (1935), p.77.

Edition

(1) *Bibliographical term.* An edition consists of all those copies of a book printed from the same setting of type and intended for simultaneous issue by the publisher. This dual concept of the edition, in terms of both type and time, is fundamental to bibliography, and the word should only be used in this strict sense. Any textual variation creates, according to its extent and intention, a variant, an issue or a state, while reprinting from stereotype or lithographic plates or from standing type creates an impression. A new edition is created only when the type is completely reset. See Bowers, pp.37, 108.

(2) *Book trade term.* The trade uses the word more loosely than do bibliographers, especially in describing a reprint from the same type or plates.

(3) *Term in textual criticism.* When a text is prepared for publication by someone other than its author, this is described as an edition. The person preparing the edition may be a reviser, or he may be a textual critic attempting to restore a corrupt text to its original condition.

See also **Impression**; **Issue**; **Standing type**; **State**; **Stereotyping**; **Textual criticism**

Edition binding

The identical binding of a whole edition, usually by the publisher, before it is offered for sale. Edition binding originated in the mid-eighteenth century, and was probably first used by John Newbery for his children's books. It was not until the nineteenth century that it became the common practice with adult books. The substitution of cloth for leather in the 1820s, and the partial mechanisation of the binding process, provided the chief impetus behind the general adoption of the edition binding.

See Michael Sadleir, *The Evolution of Publishers' Binding Styles 1770–1900* (1930); John Carter, *Publishers' Cloth 1820–1900* (1935); and Douglas Ball, *Victorian Publishers' Bindings* (1985).

See also **Bookbinding**; **Leighton, Archibald** (1784–1841); **Newbery, John** (1713–1767)

Edwards, James (1756–1816)

Bookbinder and bookseller. Edwards was a bookseller, and the son of a bookseller, in Halifax, Yorkshire, and later in London, but his real fame is as a bookbinder. His father, William, developed a method of making vellum transparent, and preparing the surface so that it was suitable for painted decoration. James worked on such bindings in his father's shop, and patented the process in 1785. He moved to London, and in his shop in Pall Mall came to be regarded as the leading antiquarian bookseller of his generation. The family firm in Halifax, however, continued to produce the bindings, which James sold, until into the nineteenth century. The Halifax shop also specialised in landscape foreedge painting, which, like the bindings, attained great popularity with the book collectors of the day. Despite his long-standing business in London, James is always known as 'Edwards of Halifax'.

See H.M. Nixon, *Five Centuries of English Bookbinding* (1978); and T.W. Hanson, 'Edwards of Halifax: a family firm of booksellers, collectors, and bookbinders', *Papers of the Halifax Antiquarian Society* (1912), p. 141.

See also **Bookbinding**; **Foreedge painting**; **Vellum**

Ehrman, Albert (1890–1969)

See **Broxbourne Library**

Eighteenmo

Bibliographical format. An eighteenmo, written 18^0, is a sheet printed with 36 pages folded to form 18 leaves. It produces a small book with a distinctly narrow page. Although 18^0 is a technically difficult format, it achieved a certain popularity in the eighteenth century because it is very economical of paper. It was especially used in Wales and Scotland, where it was often bound in two gatherings of 9 leaves each.

Imposition diagrams can be found in William Savage, *A Dictionary of the Art of Printing* (1841, repr. 1968). See also Hector Macdonald, 'A book gathered in nines', *Bibl.* (1974), p. 76.

See also **Format**; **Gathering**; **Imposition**

Eighteenth-Century British Books

Reference book. *ECBB* is a cumulated catalogue of the eighteenth-century British books in the British Library, the Bodleian Library, Oxford, and Cambridge University Library, compiled from the catalogues of those libraries. It was compiled by F.J.G. Robinson, G. Averley, D.R. Esslemont and P.J. Wallis, and published in four volumes (1981). There is also a four-volume subject catalogue of the British library books (1979), and an index to the foreign and provincial imprints (1982). The entries are highly abbreviated, and reviewers have inevitably found some errors, but it is, nevertheless, a valuable work.

See F.J.G. Robinson, 'The Dawson author union catalogue and subject catalogue', *BJECS* (1982), p. 123.

Eighteenth-Century Short Title Catalogue

Reference work. The *ESTC* is intended, as the successor to *STC* and Wing, to record all British and English-language printing in the period 1701–1800. The editor is R.C. Alston. It evolved from a conference held at the British Library in 1976, and the British part of the project is based at and funded by the British Library. The first phase — an elaborate catalogue of the British Library's own holdings, held in machine-readable form — was completed in 1983, and is available both on microfiche and on BLAISE, the British Library's on-line information network. Enrichment of the file with the holdings of other libraries in Britain and overseas continues apace. In the USA, the North American Imprints Program is a related project for American books and libraries, while ESTC–North America (ESTC–NA) is the American part of *ESTC* itself.

Quite apart from its intrinsic importance, *ESTC* has provided a major impetus for both bibliographical scholarship and rare book librarianship throughout the English-speaking world.

See R.C. Alston and M.J. Jannetta, *Bibliography, Machine-readable Cataloguing, and the ESTC* (1978); and R.C. Alston, *The First Phase. An introduction to the catalogue of the British Library collections for ESTC* (1983).

See also **North American Imprints Program**; *STC*; **Wing**

Elzevier

Printers and publishers. The firm was founded by Louis Elzevier (1546/47–1617), a native of Louvain, who had been employed by Plantin in Antwerp, and set up business as a bookseller in Liège in 1567. In *c.*1581 he moved to Leiden, where the newly-founded and vigorous university provided an excellent base for his business. He now began to print and publish as well as to sell books, retaining his links with Plantin from whom he was able to obtain stock. In 1586 he became Beadle and *de facto* printer, of the university, and was highly regarded there for his programme of classical and theological publishing. The already prosperous firm now expanded even more rapidly. Soon after 1600, the Elzeviers, in the person of Louis's son, were established at The Hague and Utrecht as well as Leiden, and a branch in Amsterdam was started in 1638. It was the Leiden business, however, which was the centre of the whole enterprise in the early seventeenth century, and it was there that Abraham and Bonaventura Elzevier, who were in partnership from 1622 to 1652, produced the series of classical texts which made their name famous throughout Europe. These little books, well edited and elegantly printed, are still sought by collectors. The firm also published many other books, notably in oriental languages, for which they were probably better equipped than any other commercial printing house in Europe. After both brothers died in 1652, the Leiden house continued but the initiative passed to Amsterdam, where Louis and Daniel Elzevier were in charge. They published an increasing number of vernacular works, especially in French, including some important Cartesian texts, and Hobbes' *De Cive* (1647). When Daniel died in 1680, however, the Amsterdam house came to an end; although the Leiden branch continued for many years, the great days of the Elzeviers were over.

The standard history is that by Alphonse Willems, *Les Elseviers* (1880), but, on a more modest scale, David W. Davies, *The World of the Elzeviers 1580–1712* (1954) is useful.

See also **Plantin, Christophe** (*c.*1520–1589)

Emblem books

Literary genre. The emblem book takes the form of short poems or mottoes, each illustrated by a symbolic engraving or woodcut. Both poem and emblem are frequently obscure to the modern reader, although of great interest to historians of art and taste. The earliest examples date from the mid-sixteenth century in Italy and France, but the genre did not reach England until the early seventeenth century, when its chief exponent was the poet, Francis Quarles. Emblem books were a minority taste even at the height of their popularity, which had ended by 1650, and are now very rare.

See Mario Praz, *Studies in Seventeenth-century Imagery* (2nd edn, 1964), which includes a substantial bibliography of European emblem books; and J.R.B. Horden, *Francis Quarles. A bibliography* (OBS, new ser. 2, 1953).

See also **Woodcut**

Encyclopaedias

A work of reference which attempts to encompass systematically the whole of human knowledge. The first such was apparently that of the Athenian Speusippos (after 408 BC–333 BC), of which only fragments survive. The first major encyclopaedia was Pliny's *Historia naturalis* (AD 77), which had a number of ancient and medieval successors, notably the *Lexicon* of Suidas (10th–11th centuries), and the anonymous *Compendium philosophiae* (*c.*1315), the first encyclopaedia in the modern sense, in that it divides and presents knowledge in a systematic way. Encyclopaedias began to be printed in the fifteenth century, and the word itself was first used in Paul Scalich's *Encyclopaedia, seu orbis disciplinarum* (1559). From the early seventeenth century, the concept of the encyclopaedia became increasingly associated with conflicting theories of knowledge. Francis Bacon proposed what is essentially the modern methodology in his *Instauratio magna* (1620), and his ideas greatly influenced Bayle's *Dictionnaire historique* (1697) and Diderot's *Encyclopédie* (1751), which are key works in European intellectual history. The first English example of a Baconian encyclopaedia was that of Ephraim Chambers (1728), which still survives as 'Chambers'. The other great English-language encyclopaedia, the *Encyclopaedia Britannica*, began as a direct imitation of Diderot. The first edition (2 vols, 1769–72) was a great success, and the work has now reached its 15th edition (1974).

See Robert Collison, *Encyclopaedias: Their history throughout the ages.* (1964).

Endpapers

A constituent part of a bookbinding. A bifolium is inserted by the binder between each board and the sheets of the book itself; one leaf, the pastedown, is glued to the board, and the other, the free endpaper or flyleaf, is attached by a strip of glue to the first or last leaf of the book. Since the late eighteenth century, decorated or coloured paper has often been used for endpapers, and in the mid-nineteenth endpapers in edition bindings were often used for publishers' advertisements.

In earlier periods, binders often used waste paper from both manuscripts and printed books for endpapers, and the fragments thus preserved are frequently of some bibliographical interest. For this, see N.R. Ker, *Fragments of Medieval Manuscripts used as Pastedowns in Oxford Bindings* (OBS, new ser., 5, 1954).

See also **Bookbinding**; **Edition binding**

English

See **Type size**

English Catalogue of Books, The

Trade bibliography. The name was first used for a fortnightly list of newly-published books, with an annual cumulation, in 1860. This list, however, can trace its origin to the fortnightly lists in *The Publishers' Circular* (1837). A number of retrospective volumes were published to cover the period 1800–60.

The *English Catalogue* was published for over a century, but from 1950 it was largely superseded by the *British National Bibliography*, with its weekly, monthly and annual listings and increasingly elaborate subject index.

Graham Pollard, 'General lists of books published in England', *BIHR* (1935), p. 165, gives a brief history, and lists the various cumulations and series.

See also **Trade bibliography**

English Stock

A group of copyrights held by the Stationers' Company, by a grant from King James I. The Stock consisted of psalters, primers, almanacs and prognostications, all of which the Company thus had the unique right to print, and all of which were printed annually or in the case of the psalters and primers, more frequently. Shares in the Stock were held by members of the Company, their entitlement to shares varying according to their rank. There was an annual distribution of the considerable profits of the enterprise. Throughout the seventeenth century, and for much of the eighteenth, the Stock's monopolies remained intact, and infringements were vigorously pursued by the Company. The income was a valuable additional source of finance for many members of the London book trades. The Company lost its almanac monopoly after a court case in 1780, and thereafter the importance of the English Stock declined rapidly.

See Cyprian Blagden, 'The English Stock of the Stationers' Company', *Libr.* (1955), p. 163

See also **Almanacs**; **Stationers' Company**

Enschedé

Typefoundry. The firm began when Izaak Enschedé (1681–1761) established a printing business in Haarlem, in the Netherlands, in *c.* 1703. It prospered, and Izaak, with his son, Joannes (1708–80) became official printer to the City Council, and the owner of the town's only newspaper. In 1743, the Enschedés purchased the equipment of Hendrik Wetstein, a distinguished printer and typefounder in Amsterdam, and they then employed an excellent punch-cutter, J.M. Fleischman, to run this new side of the business. This also flourished, and the Enschedé types, like the house's printing, became synonymous with high artistic and technical achievement in typography. The firm has remained in the family through eight generations, and still exists.

An official history by Charles Enschedé (1855–1919) was published in 1908, and was translated into English by Harry Carter as *Typefounding in the Netherlands from the Fifteenth to the Nineteenth Century* (1978); it includes reprints of many type specimens. A briefer account is *The House of Enschedé 1703–1953* (1953), also published by the firm.

See also **Typecasting**

Enumerative bibliography

A list of works, usually of printed books. An enumerative bibliography lists all books (and/or journal articles, and/or manuscripts) within its chosen field. This may be defined by genre, authorship, publisher, time, place or any other appropriate criterion. Whatever criteria are used, however, the essential feature remains the same: comprehensiveness. Having defined his topic, the compiler assembles his list, which takes him into the province of descriptive bibliography.

See also **Bibliography**; **Descriptive bibliography**

Ephemera

A generic term used for printed matter other than books, magazines and newspapers; most ephemeral printing is in fact of advertising material. Such work has been produced by printers since the fifteenth century, but little has survived since it is, *de natura*, intended to have a short lifespan. Surviving ephemera, most of which is from the nineteenth and twentieth centuries, although there is a substantial number of earlier examples, is of great interest for the insight which it often gives into daily life.

A collection of ephemera printed before 1939, which probably contains millions of items, was made by John Johnson, and is now in the Bodleian Library, Oxford. Other, smaller collections are to be found elsewhere.

See John Lewis, *Collecting Printed Ephemera* (1976).

See also **Johnson, John de Monins** (1882–1956)

Eragny Press

Private press. The press was founded in 1894 by Lucien Pissaro (1867–1944), the artist and illustrator; in 1900 it moved from Epping to Hammersmith. The Eragny Press was closely associated with the Vale Press, and indeed the first 16 of the 32 books which Pissaro eventually produced were published by the Vale Press and printed in the Vale types. Eragny books were more eclectic in style than many private press books of the period. Although some are clearly in the Arts and Crafts tradition of Kelmscott, others are closer to the art nouveau style which characterises Vale Press books. The Press attracted a good deal of contemporary praise both in Britain and on the Continent. It came to an end in 1914.

See T. Sturge Moore, *A Brief Account of the Origin of the Eragny Press* (1903); and the bibliography in G.S. Tompkinson, *A Select Bibliography of the Principal Modern Private Presses* (1925).

See also **Kelmscott Press**; **Private press movement**; **Vale Press**

Esdaile, Arundell James Kennedy (1880–1956)

Librarian and bibliographer. Esdaile, educated at Lancing and Cambridge, spent the whole of his career on the staff of the British Museum (1903–40), although he also had wider interests in both bibliography and librarianship. He first worked on incunabula under A.W. Pollard, but in 1926 he became Secretary of the Museum, a post which he held until his retirement. He moved away from the fifteenth century, and perhaps his most enduring work is his *List of English Tales and Prose Romances before 1740* (1912). In 1919 he began to lecture at the newly-founded Library School at University College, London, and these lectures formed the basis of his *Student's Manual of Bibliography* (1931), which in its fifth revised edition (1981) is still in print, although it is now badly out-of-date in some respects. Unlike most librarians from his background, he played a full part in the affairs of his profession, and was for many years a powerful force in the Library Association, not least as the editor (1924–35) of its official journal, *The Library Association Record.* Perhaps it was because of this breadth of interest that he never entirely belonged to the magic inner circle of the inter-war bibliographical world, but the very scope of his activities was a valuable and often corrective influence on the various worlds which he spanned.

See James G. Ollé, 'Arundell Esdaile: a centenary tribute', *Journal of Librarianship* (1980), p. 217.

See also **Pollard**, **Alfred William** (1859–1944)

Essex House Press

Private press. The Essex House Press was founded by C.R. Ashbee (1868–1942), as part of the Guild of Handicrafts' programme for reviving craft work. The Guild was a product of the Arts and Crafts movement which had spawned the private press movement itself, and indeed Ashbee took over Morris's type and equipment when the Kelmscott Press came to an end. He also took over Morris's ideas, although he was perhaps less successful than Morris in translating them into an acceptable printed page. In 1907, the Press was taken over by A.K. Coomaraswamy, and it finally came to an end in 1910.

Estienne, Robert

See C.R. Ashbee, *A Bibliography of the Essex House Press* (1904); the account in Roderick Cave, *The Private Press* (2nd edn, 1983) is unsympathetic but not unfair.

See also **Kelmscott Press**; **Private press movement**

Estienne, Robert (1498/99?–1559)

Printer and publisher. Estienne's father, Henri, was printer to the University of Paris from 1504, and Robert entered the trade himself in *c.* 1524, after which he gradually took over his father's business. From the beginning, the younger Estienne was interested in scholarly publishing on the grandest scale, and he is now remembered for his great dictionaries and his editions of the Bible. The first of the dictionaries was his *Thesaurus linguae latinae* (1531) of which he was, substantially, the compiler as well as the printer and publisher; a revised and definitive edition was published in 1543. In 1538, he published the first edition (of many) of his *Dictionarium latino-gallicum.* Meanwhile, he was also working on an edition of the Vulgate, and his *Biblia* (1527–28) was duly published. His greatest achievement in this field, however, was his Greek New Testament (1546) which, while drawing on the work of earlier scholars, was long regarded as the authoritative text.

Estienne was closely associated with the scholars of the French Renaissance, and inevitably came to the attention of Francis I, their patron. He was appointed King's Printer in Hebrew and Latin (1539) and in Greek (1540); from 1539, he also undertook official printing in French. He was the custodian, and the first user, of Garamond's *Grecs du roi.*

In later life, Estienne was too closely associated with the Protestants, and had to flee from Paris to Geneva, although he was soon in trouble with the authorities there as well. He died in exile.

See Elizabeth Armstrong, *Robert Estienne. Royal Printer* (1954).

See also **Bibles**; **Dictionaries**; **Garamond, Claude** (*c.* 1480–1561)

Estimating

See **Casting-off**

Etching

An intaglio process of graphic printing. Etching was invented in Germany in the early sixteenth century where its first great practitioner was Albrecht Dürer; many other artists, including Rembrandt and Blake, have been attracted to it. An etching is made on a copper plate which has been coated with a ground of beeswax, bitumen and resin, and then smoked to cover it with a film of carbon. Into this ground the engraver draws his picture with needles of varying thickness; they travel easily over the plate and can therefore produce a fine line very freely drawn. Having been engraved, the plate is immersed in acid, a process called 'biting'; the acid eats into the lines along which the ground has been cut away, thus creating an intaglio plate which can be printed.

Etching was widely used for book illustrations, prints and caricatures from the sixteenth to the nineteenth centuries. It was introduced into England by the Bohemian engraver, Wenceslaus Hollar (1607–1677) in the late 1630s; later English practitioners included Hogarth, Stubbs, Gillray and Cruickshank, as well as Blake.

See Michael Shain, 'Etching: or, the art of graveing with aqua fortis', *ABMR* (1977), pp. 140, 192, 134, 174.

See also **Blake, William** (1757–1827); **Cruickshank, George** (1792–1878); **Illustrated books**; **Intaglio**

Evans, Charles (1850–1935)

Librarian and bibliographer. Evans was born and educated in Boston, Massachusetts, and held posts in a number of libraries on the East Coast and in the Mid-West of the USA. His great scholarly achievement was his *American Bibliography*, a chronological list of all American publications, which, by his death, he had carried down to the year 1799 (12 vols, 1903–34). A supplement by Clifford K. Shipton (1955) covers the years 1799–1800, and the authors and titles in the whole work were indexed by Roger P. Bristol (1959). A *Supplement* of addenda by Bristol was published in 1970, and an index to it in 1971. Bristol also compiled an *Index of Printers, Publishers, and Booksellers* (1961) in the original 13 volumes. Evans and Bristol are among the basic tools of American bibliography, although the whole work will, eventually, be replaced by the North American Imprints Program.

See also **Americana**; **North American Imprints Program**

Evans, Edmund (1826–1905)

Printer and wood engraver. Evans was apprenticed in 1840 to Ebenezer Landells one of the founders of *Punch* and *The Illustrated London News*, both of which were major users of wood engravings until the 1890s. He set up his own business as an engraver in 1847, and was also a printer by 1850. From 1852, he specialised in colour printing, and achieved very fine results from two- or three-block printing. He was particularly expert in producing long print runs for cheap books, especially the sometimes rather garish covers for 'railway' books, designed to catch the eye on station bookstalls. He also, however, printed many illustrations, and the artists he employed include Walter Crane (1845–1915) and Randolph Caldecott (1846–1886), two of the finest engravers of the century. Evans was indeed largely responsible for the

Exotics

introduction of multi-coloured printing into ordinary commercial book production.

His autobiography has been edited by Ruari McLean as *The Reminiscences of Edmund Evans* (1967), and this edition is the best source for his life; it includes a select list of his colour-printed books.

See also **Colour printing**; **Wood engraving**

Exotics

See **Typeface**

Explicit

Literally 'it ends' or 'here ends'. The formula was commonly used at the end of a medieval manuscript, followed by the title of the book and sometimes the name of the author or scribe. Explicits are sometimes found in early printed books, but were rapidly displaced by colophons.

See also **Colophon**

Facsimile

Technical term in printing. A facsimile is an exact reproduction of a former edition in all its visual aspects. Probably the earliest type facsimile was that of the Giunta Boccaccio of 1527, printed by Ponticello in Venice in 1729. There are a few isolated examples in the later eighteenth century, but the type facsimile did not become common until the early nineteenth century. The fashion for it which then developed was associated with the bibliomania, and particularly with Dibdin who was responsible for a number of such books. The Roxburghe Club also printed a number of type facsimiles in its early years. In the later nineteenth century, Blades and others used specially cut facsimile types to illustrate works on early printing, and the type facsimile became a useful scholarly tool for those who were unable to gain access to rare originals. At the same time, there developed within the antiquarian book trade the practice of supplying missing leaves in books with hand-drawn facsimiles, often of a sufficiently high standard to deceive the unwary.

In recent years, many facsimiles have been produced photographically using offset lithography, and type facsimiles have now all but vanished.

On the early history of the type facsimile, see N.J. Barker, *The Publications of the Roxburghe Club 1814–1962* (1964); and, more generally, Joan M. Friedman, 'Fakes, forgeries, facsimiles, and other oddities', in Jean Peters (ed.), *Book Collecting. A modern guide* (1977).

See also **Bibliomania**; **Blades, William** (1824–1890); **Dibdin, Thomas Frognall** (1776–1847); **Edition**; **Forgery**; **Giunta family**; **Offset lithography**; **Roxburghe Club**; **Type facsimile**

Factotum

A factotum is a relief block consisting of a decorated frame with a hole in the middle. A piece of type was inserted into the hole to print a decorated initial. Factota were in use from the sixteenth to the eighteenth centuries.

See Gaskell, p. 155.

See also **Relief printing**

Factotum

Bibliographical newsletter. *Factotum* is published by the *Eighteenth-century Short Title Catalogue* at six-monthly intervals. It contains progress reports on *ESTC* itself and short bibliographical papers on eighteenth-century matters. The editor is J.L. Wood.

See also ***Eighteenth-Century Short Title Catalogue***

Faithfull, Emily (1835–1895)

Printer and feminist. A clergyman's daughter, Emily Faithfull became involved in the mid-Victorian women's movement, and particularly in that part of it concerned with providing employment for women to enable them to achieve some degree of independence. In 1860, she opened the Victoria Press, which was to employ women only. The enterprise initially proved to be a considerable success and, in 1862, Faithfull was appointed 'Printer and Publisher in Ordinary' to Queen Victoria. There was, however, strong opposition from the trade unions in the printing industry, who objected to the employment of women in skilled jobs. In fact, the Typographical Association, the leading compositors' union, did not admit women until 1886, which effectively prevented their employment in the trade generally. The Victoria Press was also a publisher, and in 1861–63, when Faithfull's involvement was at its height, it published more than 50 titles on a variety of topics. She began to withdraw from the enterprise in 1867, perhaps because her reputation had been damaged by her involvement in a notorious divorce case, although she retained some connections with the Press throughout the 1870s.

See William E. Fredeman, 'Emily Faithfull and the Victoria Press: an experiment in sociological bibliography', *Libr.* (1974), p. 139; and James S. Stone, 'More light on Emily Faithfull and the Victoria Press', *Libr.* (1978), p. 63.

Fell, John (1625–1686)

Bishop of Oxford, and effective founder of Oxford University Press. Fell was the son of a Dean of Christ Church, Oxford, and himself became a Student of that house in 1638; he was expelled for his strong royalism and Anglicanism in 1647, remained in Oxford throughout the interregnum, and was rewarded in 1660 first with a canonry at Christ Church, and then with his late father's office of Dean. He was a wholehearted supporter of Charles II, and by the time he became Vice-Chancellor of Oxford (1666) he was the most powerful man in the University. Fell was determined to restore Oxford's scholarly reputation and educational standards, and one of his schemes was to revive the University Press.

In 1669, with three partners, he became in effect the lessee of the Press. He installed it in the newly-completed Sheldonian Theatre, and in 1672 the first book was published. Fell developed a programme of scholarly publishing which saw the Press well into the next century, and resulted in the compilation of some remarkable works of learning. Fell was concerned with form as well as matter. In 1670, he contacted Thomas Marshall, later Rector of Lincoln College, Oxford, in Amsterdam, and through him procured the matrices of what are now known as the 'Fell' types. In fact, they are perfectly ordinary Dutch types of the period, but far superior to anything then available in England. The Greek types, based on Garamond's *Grecs du roi*, were exceptionally good. Fell also imported a typefounder to cast from the matrices; he arrived from Holland in 1676, and was the first man ever to practise this art in Oxford. Fell's matrices are still at the Press, and the types cast from them are still used from time to time.

See Stanley Morison, *John Fell, the University Press and the 'Fell' Types* (1967).

See also **Garamond, Claude** (*c.* 1480–1561); **Matrix**; **Oxford University Press**

Fere-humanistica

Type design. Fere-humanistica is one of the four basic groups of Gothic type. The letterforms are more distinct than in the other Gothics, and indeed are sometimes almost Roman in appearance. They are broad and well-rounded, although the vertical strokes are truncated in a typical Gothic style. Fere-humanistica was evolved in Augsburg in the early 1460s, and used there and elsewhere in south Germany, Switzerland and Italy for about 25 years.

See A.F. Johnson, *Type Designs* (3rd edn, 1966).

See also **Gothic type**; **Roman**

Fifteener

See **Incunabula**

Figgins, Vincent (1766–1836)

Typefounder. Figgins was apprenticed to Joseph Jackson, who had himself learned the trade from William Caslon. In 1792, he set up his own business in London, and began to design and cut his own types. Although he initially followed the usual contemporary designs, in the first decade of the nineteenth century he became one of the pioneers of the 'New Style' of type faces. In particular, he abandoned the long 's', and many ligatures. His designs are notable for the large display types, of a rather heavy and squashed appearance, which are characteristic of much nineteenth-century poster printing, but his elegant book faces were also widely used for many years.

See James Moran, 'The type foundry of Vincent Figgins 1792–1836', in *Motif* (1958); and Berthold Wolpe, *Vincent Figgins' Type Specimens 1801 and 1815* (1967).

See also **Caslon, William** (1692–1766) **and Caslon, William** (1720–1778); **Jackson, Joseph** (1733–1792); **Ligature**; **Typecasting**

Fillet

See **Bookbinding**

Filmsetting

See **Photosetting**

Fine binding

See **Bookbinding**

Fine paper

Papermaker's term, used also by bibliographers. Fine paper was the highest quality of paper in the sixteenth, seventeenth and eighteenth centuries, which was somewhat heavier than the norm, and usually made of better materials and hence whiter. It was consequently more expensive than ordinary printing paper. In that period, it was an occasional practice to print a small proportion of an edition on fine paper, usually for the author to present to patrons, dedicatees and friends. These fine paper copies are usually somewhat larger in page size than ordinary copies, and are, therefore, sometimes (rather inaccurately) referred to as being on 'large' paper. Bibliographically, such copies are an issue of the edition of which they form a part, save in the rare cases where

the type was reimposed, and thus constitutes an impression.
    See Gaskell, p. 66.

See also **Impression**; **Issue**; **Papermaking**

Fine Print

Bibliophilic periodical. *Fine Print* describes itself as 'a review of the arts of the book'. It is chiefly concerned with contemporary American private presses. The first issue appeared in 1973.

First Folio

The common name for the first collected edition of Shakespeare's dramatic works, published in 1623. The first attempt at such a collection had been made in 1617–19, but failed for reasons of copyright. By 1620, however, these problems had been overcome, and John Heminges and Henry Condell prepared the plays for the press. There were still many delays and technical problems before the book was finally printed. The printer was Isaac Jaggard. Because of its importance in preserving the only text of nearly half of Shakespeare's work, and important texts of most of the other plays, the First Folio is one of the most famous (and expensive) books in the world. Ironically, it is not particularly rare for a book of its period. It has been intensively studied, both textually and bibliographically, for it is complicated in both respects, but it is unlikely that it has yet yielded all its secrets.
    The standard study of the First Folio, and one of the masterworks of analytical bibliography, is Charlton Hinman, *The Printing and Proof-reading of the First Folio of Shakespeare* (2 vols, 1963).

See also **Hinman, Charlton Joseph Kadio** (1911–?); **Jaggard, William** (d. 1623) **and Jaggard, Isaac** (d. 1627)

Flong

See **Stereotyping**

Folger Shakespeare Library

Research library in Washington, DC. The Library was founded by Henry Clay Folger (1857–1930), the millionaire President of Standard Oil Inc., to promote the study of Shakespeare and his contemporaries. It is administered by the Trustees of Amherst College. To establish his library, Folger assembled a large collection of early editions of Shakespeare, including scores of copies of the First Folio, as well as thousands of other English books of the sixteenth and early seventeenth centuries. Since the Library was opened in 1932, in a building opposite the Library of Congress, successive directors, especially John Q. Adams (in office 1934–46), have used the generous endowment to add greatly to its holdings. It is now one of the world's major repositories of *STC* books.

Folger's purchase of multiple copies of the First Folio was more than justified when they were used by Charlton Hinman in his pioneering study of that book, which would have been impossible anywhere else.

Catalogues of the Folger's manuscripts (3 vols, 1970) and printed books (28 vols, 1970, and supplement, 1972) have been published. See Louis B. Wright, *The Folger Library: two decades of growth* (1968).

See also **First Folio**; **Hinman, Charlton Joseph Kadio** (1911–?); **Library of Congress**; *STC*

Foliation

The continuous numbering of the leaves rather than the pages of a book. Manuscripts were almost invariably foliated, and the practice was followed by the early printers. By the end of the fifteenth century, however, pagination was rapidly replacing foliation, and had done so almost completely by *c.* 1550.

The transition from foliation to pagination is discussed by Rudolf Hirsch, *Printing, Selling and Reading, 1450–1550* (1967).

Folio

Bibliographical format. A folio, written 2^0 is a sheet printed with four pages, folded to make two leaves; the resultant page is very large. Folio gatherings are usually of more than one sheet to avoid excessive sewing in the binding. Folio was a common format in the fifteenth, sixteenth and early seventeenth centuries for books, such as works of scholarship, intended for permanent preservation, and for Bibles and other lectern books. Thereafter it became less common, although it continued to be used for such purposes; its inconvenient size was the principal cause of its loss of popularity.

Imposition diagrams can be found in William Savage, *A Dictionary of the Art of Printing* (1841, repr. 1968).

See also **Format**; **Gathering**; **Imposition**

Foolscap

See **Sheet**

Foreedge painting

A method of book decoration. The foreedge of the book (i.e. the open edges of the leaves) is fanned out and a painting executed on the fanned edges. When the book is closed this becomes invisible, or appears only as a pattern of thin lines. This art was first practised in England in the mid-seventeenth century, and its origin is sometimes associated with the name of Samuel Mearne. It reached its highest development, however, in the work of Edwards of Halifax, who specialised in this form of decoration. In the nineteenth century, it became something of a fashion among amateur artists, usually with unfortunate results.

See Carl J. Weber, *A Thousand and One Foreedge Paintings* (1949).

See also **Bookbinding**; **Edwards, James** (1758–1808); **Mearne, Samuel** (1624–1683)

Forgery

The forgery of a printed book is time-consuming and expensive, since, to be convincing, a substantial number of copies must be produced, and they must be given a convincing collective and individual history in terms of both bibliography and provenance. Moreover, compared to works of art, the commercial value of old books is slight, and forgery is, therefore, rarely worthwhile. In its strictest sense, the forgery of a whole edition is, happily, very uncommon indeed, and has been practised on a large scale only by T.J. Wise in the late nineteenth century. Rather more common is the replacement of missing leaves, either by leaves from another copy of the same edition (known as 'sophistication'), or by hand-drawn or specially printed facsimiles. The former is usually intended to deceive, and creates a bibliographically meaningless copy of the book. Generally speaking, however, sophisticated copies can be detected by careful collation, paying special attention to the chain lines in the paper, while hand-drawn facsimiles are apparent at least to the trained eye. A good type facsimile may be less easy to detect, but the study of type and/or paper should reveal it. Most type facsimiles are, of course, perfectly open and honest reproductions.

Before the invention of printing, forgery was more often of texts than of documents, usually to establish legal claims. The most notorious was that of the so-called *Donations of Constantine* on which the papacy in the Middle Ages based its claim to temporal authority.

See Joan M. Friedman, 'Fakes, forgeries, facsimiles, and other oddities', in Jean Peters (ed.), *Book Collecting. A modern guide* (1977).

See also **Chain lines**; **Collation**; **Facsimile**; **Wise, Thomas James** (1859–1937)

Format

Bibliographical term. Format is a statement of the relationship between a page and whole sheet of which it is, or was, a part. This is one of the basic concepts of analytical and descriptive bibliography, because all pages on each side of the sheet are printed simultaneously, and the sheet therefore constitutes the unit from which the book is constructed. The sheet is normally intended to be folded to form gatherings of a predetermined number of leaves; the fold is normally parallel to those sides of the sheet which are shorter at the time when the fold is made. The common formats in hand-printed books are folio (1 fold, giving 2 leaves and hence 4 pages), quarto (2 folds, 4 leaves, 8 pages), octavo (3 folds, 8 leaves, 16 pages) and duodecimo (4 folds, 12 leaves, 24 pages), although others were used. The formats with the fewest folds produce the largest pages.

It is crucial to remember that format is a statement relating to the original sheet. Hence if a sheet is printed to be cut before folding, or if printing is intended to be done on a previously cut sheet, the format is that of the whole sheet. Thus, for example, if a sheet is printed with 8 pages, but is cut to form 2 gatherings of 2 leaves each, it is a quarto (strictly, a half sheet quarto) not a folio. In practice, half and quarter sheets were normally used only in broadside formats.

The format of a book printed on hand-made paper can be detected from the direction of the chain lines, which always run parallel to the shorter edges of the unfolded sheet. A statement of format is the first part of the collational formula, using the notation 2^0 (folio), 4^0 (quarto), etc.

In books printed on machine-made paper, or in machine-printed books, format is less easy to detect, and often less meaningful, since larger sheets, or a continuous web, was used for printing, and the page/sheet relationship is therefore less intimate. In particular, modern trade usages such as 'Crown Octavo' are statements about page size rather than bibliographical format, and should be avoided for bibliographical purposes. For such books, it is better for bibliographers to describe the gathering (e.g., 'in 8s', etc.) rather than to attempt to determine format.

For the detection and description of format, see Bowers, p. 193.

See also **Analytical bibliography**; **Chain lines**; **Collation**; **Duodecimo**; **Eighteenmo**; **Half sheet**; **Imposition**; **Quarter sheet**; **Papermaking**; **Octavo**; **Quarto**; **Sheet**

Forme

Technical term in printing, used also by bibliographers. The forme consists of pages imposed in the chase ready for printing. Two formes, therefore, are required to print each sheet, and bibliographers refer to these as the 'outer' and the 'inner' forme, the outer being that which includes the first page of the gathering. By extension, bibliographers refer in the same way to the pages printed from each forme. Because all the pages of a forme are printed together, it is the basic unit of bibliographical analysis, as any hypothesis about one page must be applicable to all the pages of the forme, or at least not in conflict with any evidence to be found there.

In English printing-houses of the sixteenth and seventeenth centuries, the forme was also sometimes the unit of composition, especially in the larger formats. In quarto, for example, the pages of the outer forme (1, 4, 5, 8) were set before those of the inner (2, 3, 6, 7), and often, indeed, machined and distributed before the inner forme was set. The intention was to economise on type — always a commodity in short supply in the smaller shops — but casting-off was made complicated, and the practice often led to errors in that process.

See Moxon, p. 269; G.W. Williams, 'Setting by formes in quarto printing', *SB* (1958), p. 39; and Kenneth Povey, 'The optical identification of first formes', *SB* (1960), p. 189.

See also **Analytical bibliography**; **Casting-off**; **Chase**; **Imposition**; **Typesetting**

Forty-Two Line Bible

The name commonly given to the first printed book, also known as the 'Gutenberg Bible'. The name is derived from the fact that there are 42 printed lines on most pages. Work on this Bible probably began in *c.* 1450, and it was completed in 1455. The quality of the printing is astonishing, considering that Gutenberg had to solve all the technical problems of punch-cutting, typefounding, composition and imposition (quite apart from the printing itself) before the work could proceed. Some copies were printed on vellum, and illuminated and rubricated in the manner of contemporary manuscripts. Of the latter, there are outstanding exemplars at the Bibliothèque Mazarine, Paris; the British Library, London; the Pierpont Morgan Library, New York City; and the Harry Ransom Center, University of Texas, Austin. Although this book has attracted attention since the seventeenth century, it is only recently that it has been subjected to a full bibliographical analysis (by William B. Todd) with surprising results.

For the background, see Victor Scholderer, *Johann Gutenberg* (1963). There is a large technical literature, but the starting-point for all future studies must be William B. Todd, *The Gutenberg Bible. New evidence of the original printing* (1982). See also Paul Needham, 'The paper supply of the Gutenberg Bible', PBSA (1985), which breaks new ground.

See also **Composition**; **Gutenberg, Johann** (1394/99–1468); **Imposition**; **Mazarine Bible**; **Press**; **Typecasting**

Foulis, Robert (1707–1776) and Foulis, Andrew (1712–1775)

Printers and publishers in Glasgow, and Printers to Glasgow University. The Foulis brothers were the sons of a Glasgow maltster, and were educated by their mother. Robert was apprenticed to a barber, but his attempts to improve himself led him to abandon that trade, and to travel in England and on the Continent. While abroad, he bought many books, and when he returned to Glasgow in 1749, he set up a bookshop, specialising in classical studies. Andrew joined this business in 1742. Robert was appointed Printer to the University in 1743, and embarked on a programme of classical publishing. He used the professors of the University to ensure the correctness of his texts, and went to great pains to obtain the best paper and type. Indeed he was, technically, one of the best British printers of the eighteenth century. After Robert's death, his son, Andrew, took over the Press, and kept it going until 1806. By that time the Foulis Press had produced over 700 books, including many of great importance, especially in the field of classical scholarship. Robert Foulis was always interested in his craft, and was one of those who encouraged early experiments with stereotyping.

See Philip Gaskell, 'The work of the Foulis Press and the Wilson Foundry', *Libr.* (1952), pp. 77, 149; and the same author's *A Bibliography of the Foulis Press* (1964).

See also **Stereotyping**

Fount

Technical term in typefounding and printing. A fount (or, in earlier British and contemporary American usage, font) is a complete set of types of letters, numerals and other symbols, cut to the same design and cast to the same size. A fount consists of upper and lower case letters, small capitals, numerals and marks of punctuation. To these may be added accented letters and ligatures; the latter were numerous in the fifteenth and sixteenth centuries, but their use gradually decreased thereafter. Founts are distinguished and described by design and size, as in, for example, Baskerville Pica, where Baskerville is the designer and Pica the size. Sizes are now commonly described in points.

See Moxon, p. 19.

See also **Ligature**; **Point size**; **Type**; **Type size**

Fourdrinier, Henry (1766–1854) and Fourdrinier, Sealy (d. 1847)

Wholesale stationers in London. In 1800 the Fourdrinier brothers took over their father's stationery business after his retirement, and almost immediately began to interest themselves in the development of the papermaking machine.

Such a machine had been invented and built in Paris in 1796–99 by Nicholas-Louis Robert, but he was unable to find suffcient financial and technical support in France, and he brought his models to England. In 1801, the Fourdriniers agreed to help him, and employed Bryan Donkin (1768–1855) to develop the machine for them. In 1803 he produced a prototype, and by 1807 he had perfected what is still known as the Fourdrinier machine, and which is still in general use. Meanwhile, however, the Fourdriniers had over-committed themselves financially, and they went bankrupt in 1810, having spent some £60,000 on the development of the machine. Their financial problems were not alleviated for many years, and then only by a special grant voted by Parliament in 1839. Donkin, on the other hand, had a long and profitable career as a manufacturer of papermaking machinery, and indeed dominated this industry throughout Europe until the middle of the nineteenth century.

There is an account of Henry Fourdrinier in *DNB*; and a detailed study of *The Paper-making Machine* by R.H. Clapperton (1967).

See also **Papermaking**

Fournier, Pierre Simon (1712–1768)

See **Point size**

Foxon, David Fairweather (1923-)

Bibliographer. Educated at Oxford, Foxon joined the staff of the Department of Printed Books in the British Museum in 1950, and remained there for 15 years. After a brief spell in Canada, he became Reader in Textual Criticism at Oxford (1968–82). Foxon is one of the leading bibliographers of the post-war period, and has made many important contributions to the subject. His lectures on 'Pope and the early eighteenth-century book trade' (Lyell Lectures, Oxford, 1973), and 'The Stamp Act of 1710' (Sanders Lectures, Cambridge, 1978), both unpublished, are outstanding studies in the history of the book trade. His *magnum opus*, however, is his *English Verse 1701–1750* (1975), a monumental catalogue of separately printed English poetry of the first half of the eighteenth century. It seems unlikely in this age of computers and institutional research that such a project will ever again be successfully undertaken by one scholar. It became a standard work on the day of publication, and is cited simply as 'Foxon'.

For his career and publications see *Who's Who 1983*.

Frankfurt Fair

International book fair. Frankfurt was a major centre of international trade in the late Middle Ages, and books were sold at the fairs there before the end of the fifteenth century. From the early sixteenth century onwards these fairs were increasingly devoted to books, and became the most important entrepôt of the international book trade, attracting printers and booksellers not only from Germany but from all over Europe. The number approached 100 by the middle of the century. Catalogues of the books offered for sale were printed before 1500, although the continuous official series did not begin until 1564. The Frankfurt Fair catalogues are, thereafter, one of the most important primary sources for the history of publishing and the book trade in Europe in the sixteenth and seventeenth centuries. Frankfurt always had a truly international flavour, for although many German books were sold, its primary importance was as a market-place for Latin books with their Europe-wide audience. The Frankfurt Fair also became the major centre for dealing in printing type and equipment. In the middle of the sixteenth century, the fair developed a reputation as a centre for the sale of Protestant books, and this proved to be its downfall. The Catholic authorities began to place obstacles in the way of Protestant booksellers, and in the early seventeenth century they decamped to Leipzig, where no such problems existed. The Frankfurt Fair did, however, survive, although in a truncated form, only to regain its former eminence in the present century, for it is now an annual gathering at which publishers from all over the world display their wares and deal in rights sales.

For the history of the fair, see Henri Estienne, *The Frankfurt Book Fair* (tr. J.E. Thompson, 1911); and A. Dietz, *Geschichte der Frankfurter Büchermesse* (1921). The early catalogues are being edited by Bernhard Fabian (1972-　).

See also **Book fairs**

Franklin, Benjamin (1706–1790)

Printer and a founder father of the United States of America. Franklin, one of the most remarkable men of the eighteenth century, learned his trade in Philadelphia, and then went to London where he worked as a journeyman. His description of his experiences in his *Autobiography* is an important source of information about London printing house practices in the early decades of the eighteenth century. He returned to America in 1728, and established, with a partner, the New Printing Office in Philadelphia. He continued to print there until 1776, issuing many books, pamphlets and newspapers, including the famous *Poor Richard's Almanack* which had considerable influence in the development of American national consciousness in the years before the Revolution. After 1766, Franklin was increasingly involved in public affairs, although he never lost his interest in his trade, and even when he was a distinguished elder statesman representing the new nation at European courts, he still concerned himself with technical developments.

The New Printing House is now part of the Franklin Court Museum, where, amidst many spectacular presentations in several media, there is a common press operated by student volunteers when the museum is open to the public. A press which allegedly belonged to Franklin is in the Smithsonian

Institution in Washington, D.C., and was the basis for the work of Harris and Sisson.

His *Autobiography* has been reprinted many times, but the standard work on his trade activities is C. William Miller, *Benjamin Franklin's Philadelphia Printing* (1974).

See also **Common press**

Frederick II's Bible

See **Bibles**

Frisket

See **Common press**

Frisket bite

Technical term in printing, used also by bibliographers. If the paper covering the frisket is inaccurately cut, or moves during the print run, part of the type area may be covered, and hence not print. The printed sheet therefore has a blank area, usually at the outer edge of the type page. This is known as frisket bite.

Galley

(1) *Printing-house equipment.* The galley, until the early nineteenth century, was a wooden tray, *c.* 10×6 inches, into which the compositor transferred the lines of type from his stick to make them up into pages. In the early nineteenth century, this was replaced by a metal galley, considerably longer, in which several pages could be kept before being made up into pages for imposition. This was known as a 'slip' galley.

See Gaskell, p. 49.

(2) *A form of proof.* With the development of the slip galley, the practice evolved of taking proofs from the type in the galley. These galley proofs are typically long narrow sheets, each contain the text of about three pages. Galley proofing appears to have begun in newspaper houses in the early nineteenth century, or perhaps a little earlier, and to have been used intermittently in book work from about *c.* 1830. It was the normal practice to take galley proofs by the 1870s, but it began to die out in the 1960s for economic reasons. There is no evidence for proofing from the earlier wooden galleys.

See Geoffrey D. Hargreaves, ' "Correcting in the slip": the development of galley proofs'. *Libr.* (1971), p. 295, and 'British printers on galley proofs',

Libr. (1979), p.350; and John Bush Jones, 'British printers on galley proofs: a chronological reconsideration', *Libr.* (1976), p.105.

See also **Composing stick**; **Imposition**; **Proof**

Garamond (or Garamont), Claude (*c.* 1480–1561)

Punchcutter and typefounder. Garamond learned his trade in Paris, and was in business there throughout his active life. He produced his first identifiable type, a roman, in 1530–32, probably in collaboration with Robert Estienne, and thereafter cut many roman and italic faces. They were all reworked in *c.*1559, taking the form in which they were to be widely used throughout Europe. His most famous type, however, was his *Grec du roi*, a Greek type cut in the 1540s for the books which Estienne was printing for Francis I of France. Unlike some early punchcutters, Garamond also sold copies of his matrices, which were bought by printers in many countries. His work is of an outstanding quality, and his designs are still highly regarded by printers and typographers.

The only general study is J. Paillart, *Claude Garamont, graveur et fondeur des lettres* (1914), but this is superseded on technical matters by Beatrice Warde (writing as 'P. Beaujon'), 'The Garamond types, sixteenth- and seventeenth-century sources considered', *The Fleuron* (1924), p.131; Annie Parent and Jeanne Veyrin-Forrer, 'Claude Garamont: new documents', *Libr.* (1974), p.80; and the relevant passages in Harry Carter, *A View of Early Typography* (1969).

See also **Estienne, Henri** (1498/99–1559); **Italic**; **Punchcutting**; **Roman**; **Type**

Gathering

Technical term in bookbinding, used also by bibliographers. A gathering is formed when folded sheets are sewn through the fold ready for linking together in a book. In hand-printed books, a gathering normally consisted of a single sheet, but in some formats the sheet was divided into two gatherings (e.g. a duodecimo in 6s), and in folio several sheets were often gathered together, a practice known as 'quiring'.

See also **Bookbinding**; **Duodecimo**; **Folio**; **Format**; **Quire**

Ged, William (1690–1749)

See **Stereotyping**

Gentleman's Magazine, The

Periodical, published at monthly intervals (quarterly towards the end) from 1731 to 1922. *The Gentleman's Magazine* was founded by Edward Cave (1691–1754), a Post Office official who had connections with some provincial newspapers and recognised the need for a monthly periodical for provincial readers. He intended it to contain summaries of the month's news and notices, often including lengthy extracts, of new books. It was the first, and by far the most successful, general magazine of this kind. In the eighteenth century, it was the leading monthly periodical, whose contributors included some of the leading writers of the time, notably Samuel Johnson, who was associated with it for many years. Later in the century, its character began to change, especially by the inclusion of articles on antiquarian matters. To book historians it is of particular interest because Cave and his successors included very full and accurate lists of newly-published books. In the absence of any proper trade bibliographies, it is by far the best guide to such books for the middle years of the eighteenth century.

After Cave's death, *The Gentleman's Magazine* was taken over by his nephew, Richard Cave, and his brother-in-law, David Henry. John Nichols was editor from 1778 to 1816, and for most of that time was also the owner. It was Nichols who developed the antiquarian side of the magazine. It remained in the Nichols family until 1856, when it was bought by the Parkers of Oxford, although by that time it had long since lost its pre-eminence. Its final owners were Bradbury and Evans who bought it in 1865, and closed it in 1922.

The early book lists were reprinted by D.F. Foxon in *English Bibliographical Sources* (1964–67). More generally, see C. Lennart Carlson, *The First Magazine* (1938).

See also **English Catalogue of Books, The**; **Magazines**; **Nichols, John** (1745–1826); **Trade bibliography**

Gesamtkatalog der Weigendrüke

Reference book. *GW* (or *GKW*) is a general catalogue of fifteenth-century printed books. Volume I was published in 1908 in Leipzig, under the auspices of the specially established Kommission für Gesamtkatalog, but work progressed slowly, and only seven volumes had been published by 1939. Work was not resumed until the 1970s, when the State Library in East Berlin, which had inherited the Kommission's files, began to issue further fasicules. Although in some ways *GW* has already been overtaken by more recent scholarship, it is a key work of reference for incunabulists.

See also **Incunabula**

Gesner, Conrad (1516–1566)

Bibliographer. Gesner came from a poor background in Zürich, Switzerland, but he obtained an education, and became a naturalist. Later in life he turned to bibliography, and his *Bibliotheca universalis* (1545) was the first attempt at a universal bibliography since the invention of printing. He tried to list all books in a classified subject order, and to provide elaborate cross-referencing for ease of use. He came remarkably close to comprehensiveness, perhaps the last time that such an achievement was possible as the output of press grew year by year. Gesner also wrote a number of other bibliographical works, and is often called 'the father of bibliography'. Certainly he had a passion for systematic and all-inclusive book-lists which gives him a strong claim to that title.

See Theodore Besterman, *The Beginnings of Systematic Bibliography* (2nd edn, 1936).

See also **Bibliography**

Gibbings, Robert John (1889–1958)

See **Golden Cockerell Press**

Gift books

Literary genre. The gift book, as its name suggests, was intended to be used as a present. Its originator was Rudolph Ackermann, who published *Forget-me-not* (1822), the first of the gift books. This became an annual series, and also found a number of imitators, all aimed at the Christmas and New Year markets. The typical early nineteenth-century gift book contained an almanac, blank pages for use as a diary, short pieces by eminent writers and high-quality illustrations, often of fashions in clothing to interest the female readers for whom the books were primarily intended. The vogue for gift books came to an end in the 1840s, although a few continued to be published throughout the nineteenth century. In the early twentieth century, however, the gift book was revived, again as a trade gimmick to catch the Christmas market. The twentieth-century gift books are chiefly notable for having illustrations by such artists as Dulac and Rackham, who made use of the recently developed photomechanical techniques of colour reproduction. The bindings are also of a high standard. The gift book did not survive World War II.

See Anne Renier, *Friendship's Offering* (1964); and F.W. Faxon, *Literary Annuals and Gift Books: A Bibliography 1823–1903* (1912).

See also **Ackermann, Rudolph** (1764–1834); **Colour printing**; **Illustrated books**; **Photomechanical printing**

Gill, Eric Arthur Rowton (1882–1940)

Engraver and typographer. Gill, the son of a nonconformist minister, trained as an architect and became particularly interested in stone carving; this interest continued throughout his life, and after he became a Roman Catholic in 1913 he received many important ecclesiastical commissions. He was also an artist and illustrator. His first involvement with book production was when he and his wife settled at Ditchling, Sussex, in 1907. There he illustrated a number of books for the St Dominic's Press which was based in the village, and he also did a good deal of similar work for the Golden Cockerell Press. In the 1920s he designed two very successful typefaces, Perpetua and Sans Serif. The Gill Sans Serif is perhaps the only such design which is acceptable for book work. In 1924, Gill left Ditchling and settled at Capel-y-ffin, a remote mountain village in South Wales, where, with René Hague, he printed a number of books by hand. In 1936, they moved to High Wycombe, Bucks, and mechanised their press, although they continued to insist on a very high standard of work. The firm survived Gill's death and finally came to an end in 1956.

The entry for Gill in *DNB 1931–1940* says little about his work in the book world. For that, see James Davis, *Printed by Hague and Gill* (1982); and Evan R. Gill, *Bibliography of Eric Gill* (1953).

See also **Golden Cockerell Press**; **Sans serif**; **Typeface**

Giunta family

Printers. Filippo di Giunta (1450?–1517) is first recorded in the book trade in Florence in 1497, but he did not begin printing until 1503. Thereafter he produced a series of classical texts intended to compete with those of Aldus. He published well over 100 books, and after his death the business was taken over by his son Bernardo (d. 1550) who ran it for the rest of his life. He continued the tradition of classical, especially Greek, publishing.

See F.J. Norton, *Italian Printers 1501–1520* (CBS, monogr. 3, 1958).

See also **Aldus Manutius** (*c.* 1450–1515)

Glasgow Bibliographical Society

Founded 1912. The objective of the Society was to promote the study of Scottish bibliography, especially in relation to Glasgow and the West of Scotland. Its *Records*, 1 (1912–13) –13 (1939), contain some useful articles on these matters.

Goff, Frederick Richmond (1900–1982)

Librarian and incunabulist. Goff was formerly Chief of the Rare Books Division at the Library of Congress, and is best known as the compiler of one of the most useful works of reference on incunabula. His *Incunabula in American libraries. A third census* (1964) is an alphabetical listing of fifteenth-century printed books in libraries in the USA, with brief but usable entries and a full record of locations. The first version of the census was published in *BNYPL* in 1918 and in book form in 1919, under the editorship of John Thomson, George W. Harris and Clarence S. Kates. The work was then taken up by Margaret B. Stillwell, whose *Second Census* appeared in 1940. Goff assisted in this project and was the logical choice as compiler of the third edition. A *Supplement* to Goff, by the author, was published in 1972, and the main work was reprinted from the author's annotated copy in 1973.

See also **Incunabula**

Gold tooling

See **Bookbinding**

Golden Cockerell Press

Private press. The Press was started by H.M. Taylor at Waltham St Lawrence, Hertfordshire, in 1920 and produced a few competent books before Taylor's death in 1925. It was then taken over by the artist and illustrator, Robert Gibbings (1889–1958) who, during the next seven years, produced a series of magnificently printed and illustrated books. Gibbings used Caslon Old Face, and was influential in the general revival of the old face types after more than a century of neglect. He also made great use of wood engravings for his illustrations, and is an important figure in the modern history of that art. In 1933, Gibbings sold the Press to Christopher Sandford; for the next 30 years Sandford continued the Golden Cockerell tradition of producing important books in well-printed and well-illustrated editions. Under Sandford, however, Golden Cockerell ceased to print; it was merely a publisher, rather like Meynell's contemporary Nonesuch Press.

See Colin Franklin, *The Private Presses* (1969). The Press published three bibliographies of its own work: *Chanticleer* (1936); *Pertelote* (1943); and *Cockalorum* (1951).

See also **Illustrated books**; **Meynell, Sir Francis** (1891–1975); **Old face**; **Private press movement**; **Wood engraving**

Gothic type

Typeface. Gothic is one of the three major groups (or 'families') of typefaces used for the Latin alphabet, and was the first to be developed. In England it was often known as 'Black Letter'. The earliest Gothics were based on German hands of the mid-fifteenth century, which Gutenberg used as a model for his types. All Gothics are characterised by an attempt to imitate the calligraphic strokes of formal writing. The letterforms are rather squashed in appearance, have exaggerated serifs and often show superfluous lines in, for example, the vertical strokes of the capital letters. Gothic was the only typeface used in Northern Europe for many years, although romans began to appear in the sixteenth century and soon displaced Gothic everywhere except in Germany. There, Gothic continued to be used for many books until after World War II.

There are four basic groups of Gothics: Bastarda, Fere-humanistica, Rotunda and Textura.

See A.F. Johnson, *Type Designs* (3rd edn, 1966).

See also **Bastarda**; **Black letter**; **Fere-humanistica**; **Gutenberg, Johann** (1394/99–1468); **Letterform**; **Roman**; **Rotunda**; **Textura**; **Type**; **Typeface**

Goudy Frederic W. (1865–1947)

See **Village Press**

Grabhorn Press

Private press. Edwin and Robert Grabhorn established their press in San Francisco in 1915, an event which marked the beginning of the continuing tradition of fine printing in California. They did some work on commission for publishers, including the Book Club of California, but they also produced many fine editions on their own account. The typography and illustration of Grabhorn books was often experimental, frequently exciting and usually successful. The brothers worked together until 1965 when Robert, the survivor, took Andrew Hoyem as a partner. Hoyem continued to print after Robert Grabhorn's death in 1973.

See Elinor Raas Heller and David Magee, *Bibliography of the Grabhorn Press, 1915–1940* (1940); Dorothy and David Magee, *Bibliography of the Grabhorn Press, 1940–1956* (1957); and Robert D. Harlan (ed.), *Bibliography of the Grabhorn Press, 1957–1966 and Grabhorn–Hoyem, 1966–1973* (1977).

See also **Book Club of California**; **Private press movement**

Grangerisation

The insertion of additional illustrations into printed books by their owners, named after Robert Granger (1723–1776). Granger was a notable print collector, whose own *Biographical History of England* (1769) was heavily illustrated with engraved portraits, and started a fashion for such books. In the late eighteenth and early nineteenth centuries, some collectors began to insert into their books portraits and topographical prints, often on a monumental scale, creating sets in many more volumes than the original. This practice is known as grangerisation, or extra-illustration.

There is a life of Granger in *DNB*.

Granjon, Robert (*c.* 1513–1589)

Punchcutter and typefounder. Granjon, the son of a Paris printer and bookseller, began cutting types at an early age; an italic of his was in use in 1543. By 1545 he had his own business, and in 1549 he also began to publish books. He cut a vast number of founts, not only in roman and italic, but also in exotic scripts, such as Syriac, Armenian and Arabic. His italic is particularly highly regarded. He is also associated with Civilité type, of which he cut the first example in 1557. His business activities were widespread, and he had establishments in Lyons, Antwerp, Frankfurt and possibly Rome. As a consequence, his types were well known and in common use.

For the italic, see A.F. Johnson in *Libr.* (1941), p. 291. There is an account of him in Colin Clair, *A History of European Printing* (1976).

See also **Civilité**; **Italic**; **Roman**; **Typecasting**; **Typeface**

Great Bible

See **Bibles**

Great Primer

See **Type size**

Greg, Sir Walter Wilson (1875–1959)

Bibliographer. Greg was the son of the founder of *The Economist,* and, although he was never actively associated with it, it was from this source that he derived the income which absolved him from the necessity of seeking paid employment. At Cambridge he met his contemporary, R.B. McKerrow, and they, together with A.W. Pollard, whom Greg met when he joined the Bibliographical Society in 1898, became the creators of modern bibliography. Greg brought new standards of accuracy and thought to the subject, and throughout his life was notable for his coruscating reviews of books which did not match up to his exacting ideals. His special field was the English drama of the sixteenth and early seventeenth centuries. His *Bibliography of the English Printed Drama to the Restoration* (4 vols, 1939–59), now the standard work, introduced analytical procedures into bibliographical description, and exercised a seminal influence on a whole generation of bibliographers, most notably Fredson Bowers. Greg also, however, had a consuming interest in textual matters, and he made revolutionary contributions to the study of Shakespeare's text. The summation of a lifetime's work can be found in *The Editorial Problem in Shakespeare* (3rd edn, 1954), and *The Shakespeare First Folio* (1955). If some of his conclusions have subsequently been challenged, they can never be ignored. Although he rarely edited a text, save for the many type facsimiles which he prepared for the Malone Society, his paper on 'The rationale of copy-text' in *SB* (1950), p. 19, is the starting-point for all subsequent discussions of editorial theory.

There is a life of Greg in *DNB*, and an autobiographical fragment, *Biographical Notes 1877–1947* was privately printed in 1960. A list of his writings to 1945 is in *Libr.* (1945), p. 72, and is completed in *Libr.* (1960), p. 42. His *Collected Papers* have been edited by J.C. Maxwell (1966).

See also **Analytical bibliography**; **Bibliographical Society**; **Bibliography**; **Bowers, Fredson, Thayer** (1905–); **McKerrow, Ronald Brunless** (1872–1940); **Pollard, Alfred William** (1859–1944); **Textual criticism**

Gregynog Press

Private press. The Press was founded in 1921 at Gregynog House, Montgomeryshire; the house was owned by Gwendoline and Margaret Davies, two wealthy spinsters who were generous patrons of the arts in Wales. With the advice of various friends, notably Thomas Jones, a senior civil servant, they bought a press, employed a printer and began to produce a remarkable series of books. Their first, *The Poems of George Herbert*, was published in 1923; it established the Press's future pattern of producing fine editions of worthwhile works of literature in both English and Welsh. The Davies sisters employed a number of excellent artists and typographers at Gregynog, and by the time the Press closed in 1940, it was generally recognised as one of the best of the private presses.

Gregynog House is now used by the University of Wales for conferences and similar activities; the Press's equipment is still there, and is occasionally used.

See Dorothy A. Harrop, *A History of the Gregynog Press* (1980).

See also **Private press movement**

Grolier Club

Bibliophilic society. The Grolier Club was founded in New York City in 1884 by Robert Hoe, a book collector who came from a family of press manufacturers. The Club almost immediately established the pattern which it has retained. It acquired premises in Manhattan where a library was formed and meetings and exhibitions were held. Some of the catalogues are of great scholarly value. Membership is by election only, and is strictly controlled; the library, however, is opened to serious scholars, and contains, among other things, a very important collection of book auction and booksellers' catalogues.

See the addresses by C. Waller Barrett and Alexander Davidson Jr in *An Exhibition Celebrating the Seventy-fifth Anniversary of the Grolier club* (1959). A history of the Club will be found in *The Grolier Club 1884–1984: its library, exhibitions, & publications* (1984). The Club publishes a regular *Gazette*.

Grolier, Jean (1479?–1565)

Bibliophile and patron of bookbinders. The son of a French courtier, Grolier himself entered the royal service and spent much of his time before the late 1520s in Italy on various missions. There he established contacts with the leading humanists, and patronised many of them. He also began to collect books on a large scale. No doubt he had a genuine interest in their (usually humanistic) contents, but he was also greatly concerned with their bindings. In this respect, he established a pattern which characterised French bibliophily for centuries to come: he bought well-printed modern books and had them beautifully bound by the best workmen available. These Grolier bindings are the basis of his reputation today.

His Italian bindings follow the usual contemporary pattern, but gradually the distinctive Grolier style evolved, with gold-tooled lines to form a panel around the edge of the board and curved or flowing lines within the panel, usually with a central stamp of the author's name or the title of the book, and Grolier's own motto (GROLIERII [later IO. GROLIERII] ET AMICORUM) stamped at the foot. This style was perfected after Grolier's return to France by Claude de Picques, the Royal Bookbinder, who bound nearly all of Grolier's books after 1538. Grolier's bindings have always attracted other collectors, and examples are to be found in most of the world's major libraries.

See H.M. Nixon, 'Grolier's binders', *BC* (1960), pp. 45, 165; and the same author's anonymous British Museum exhibition catalogue *Bookbindings from the Library of Jean Grolier* (1965).

See also **Book collecting**; **Bookbinding**

Gustavus Vasa's Bible

See **Bibles**

Gutenberg Bible

See **Forty-two Line Bible**

Gutenberg Jahrbuch

Bibliographical annual. *GJ* has been published since 1926 by the Gutenberg-Gesellschaft, Mainz, although with some irregularity during and immediately after World War II. As its title suggests, *GJ* is concerned with incunabula, and it has carried many very important articles on this subject. Its principal language is German, although there are occasional articles in English and French. An index to the volumes from 1926 to 1975 was published in 1981.

See also **Incunabula**

Gutenberg, Johann (1394/99–1468)

Inventor of typographic printing. Gutenberg was born in Mainz, in the Rhine Valley, but in 1428 he left the city for political reasons and settled in Strasbourg. There he learned several crafts, including that of gem-cutting, but it seems that he also began to experiment with printing. His skills as an engraver doubtless helped him in punchcutting, the first of the skills which he had to invent and perfect. Indeed, the invention of type and the means of making it lies at the heart of Gutenberg's achievement. He had, in effect, realised that the 23 letters of the alphabet used for printing Latin, with their constant repetition in different combinations, made it possible to think in terms of identical, but reusable, type, rather than woodcut blocks. The latter were possibly already in use for printing illustrations, in the so-called 'block books'.

His experiments continued for several years, but apparently with no concrete results. He returned to Mainz, in *c.*1445, and in 1449 borrowed a large sum of money from Johann Fust to finance further work. It was this which enabled him, in 1450–55, to produce the Forty-two line Bible, the first book printed from type. To do so, he had to develop methods of typesetting, imposition and printing. Although it is the latter which has attracted attention, the pre-printing stages were in some ways more difficult, for they involved wholly new techniques and equipment. The press itself was in fact a derivative of the presses used in the Rhine Valley since Roman times for winemaking and, indeed, for bookbinding.

After finishing the Bible, Gutenberg was unable to repay Fust, and in 1456–57 he had to hand over all his equipment to him. Fust and a new partner, Peter Schoeffer, then continued to print with this for several years. Eventually, Gutenberg received some financial aid from the Archbishop of Mainz, and died in reasonable comfort, but he never again had any contact with the craft which he had invented and which was to revolutionise the world into which he had been born.

For a brief account of Gutenberg, see Victor Scholderer, *Johann Gutenberg*

(1963). The sources for his life and work are printed (in English translation) in D.C. McMurtrie, *The Gutenberg Documents* (1941). More recent work, especially on technical matters, will be found in Aloys Ruppel, *Die Technik Gutenbergs und ihre Vorstüfe* (1961), but for his Bible, see William B. Todd, *The Gutenberg Bible. New evidence of the original printing* (1982).

See also **Block Books**; **Common Press**; **Compositor**; **Forty-two Line Bible**; **Imposition**; *Mainz Catholicon*; **Mainz Psalter**; **Mazarine Bible**; **Press**; **Typecasting**

Hafod Press

Private press. Established in 1802 by Thomas Johnes (1748–1816) at his house at Hafod, Cardiganshire. Johnes was a wealthy landowner, much concerned with agricultural improvement, whose hobby was book-collecting. His interests were wide-ranging, but the immediate cause of the establishment of the Press was his desire to publish his own translation of Froissart's *Chronicle*. There was no competent printer in Wales, and Johnes disliked dealing with the distant printers of London. He first employed a man who left after six months, but his successor, James Henderson, presided over the Press throughout the rest of its life. The *Chronicle* was published in five volumes (1803–5), and was followed by a number of other books. These books were elegantly printed on good paper, and attracted considerable attention from contemporary bibliophiles. After a disastrous fire at Hafod in 1807, Johnes experienced severe financial difficulties, and the Press closed in 1810. It is difficult to assess the importance of the Hafod Press, but its products were certainly known to Dibdin and his circle, and Johnes may have inspired Sir Samuel Egerton Brydges in establishing the Lee Priory Press.

See James A. Dearden, 'Thomas Johnes and the Hafod Press, 1803–10', *BC* (1973), p. 315.

See also **Brydges, Sir Samuel Egerton** (1762–1837); **Dibdin, Thomas Frognall** (1776–1847); **Private press movement**

Half profits

A system of payment to authors, whereby the author and the publisher share equally in the profits of the book after all expenses have been met. It was widely used in the mid-nineteenth century, but was gradually displaced by the modern system of royalty payments. Although from the author's point of view half profits was a distinct advance on the older practice of outright sale of copyright, it had the disadvantage that if the book made a loss the author shared the liability equally with the publisher.

See James Hepburn, *The Author's Empty Purse* (1968).

See also **Royalty**

Half sheet

Bibliographical term. Literally, it is half of the full sheet of paper used in hand printing. Specifically, it is used for half-sheet imposition, where all the pages for the half sheet were imposed in a single forme. The sheet was then printed on both sides: in octavo, for example, it was moved through an angle of 180° after it was turned over. This process was also known as 'work and turn'.

See Moxon, p.227; W.H. Bond, 'Imposition by half-sheet', *Libr.* (1941–42), p.163; and Keith Povey, 'On the diagnosis on half-sheet imposition', *Libr.* (1956), p.268.

See also **Forme; Imposition; Octavo**

Half-title

Bibliographical term. The half-title is the leaf before the title page on whose recto is printed the title of the book, often in an abbreviated form. In the seventeenth century, it became the practice to protect the title leaf by an initial blank, and during the eighteenth century an abbreviated title began to be printed on this leaf. It is now an almost invariable feature of a book.

See Gaskell, p.52.

See also **Recto**

Half-tone

Illustration process. Half-tone is a photomechanical system, developed in the late nineteenth century, which permits the reproduction of continuous tone in monochrome, with results which resemble a monochrome photograph. The original art work is photographed through a mesh screen, and the printing plate made from the resulting negative. The screen has the effect of dividing the picture into tiny dots, which are then etched to different depths to produce the tonal variations which are required. The plate is mounted on a block to type height, and printed by a relief method. When a very fine screen is used, as is usual in book work, the dots are invisible when the plate is printed, but in newspaper work, where a wider mesh and cheaper paper are usual, the dots are often visible to the naked eye. Half-tone techniques were developed in the USA in the 1870s, and first used in England by George Meisenbach in 1882.

See Geoffrey Wakeman, *Victorian Book Illustration. The technical revolution* (1973).

See also **Etching; Illustrated books; Photomechanical printing; Relief printing; Type height**

Halkett and Laing

Reference book. *H & L* is the standard work for the identification of anonymous and pseudonymous English books. The titles of such books are listed alphabetically, with the attribution of authorship. Samuel Halkett (1814–1871) was the Librarian of the Faculty of Advocates, Edinburgh, and began this work in the 1850s. When he died, his notes were handed over to John Laing (d. 1880), Librarian of New College, Edinburgh. The first edition was prepared for the press by Laing's daughter, Catherine, and published as *A Dictionary of the Anonymous and Pseudonymous Literature of Great Britain* (4 vols, 1882–88). A much revised and enlarged version, *A Dictionary of Anonymous and Pseudonymous English Literature,* was edited by James Kennedy, W. A. Smith and A. F. Johnson (7 vols, 1926–34). To this, Dennis E. Rhodes and Anna E.C. Simoni added vol. 8, covering the period 1900–50 (1956), and a volume of *Addenda* to vols 1–7 (1962). A third, and fully revised edition, with more elaborate entries and full indices, is now in progress, under the direction of J.R.B. Horden. The first volume, *A Dictionary of Anonymous and Pseudonymous Publications in the English Language* (1980), has been published, and covers the period 1475–1640.

For the history of *H & L,* see Horden's Preface to vol. 1 of the 3rd edition. There is a life of Halkett in *DNB.*

Hansard, Thomas Curson (1776–1833)

Printer, publisher and Printer to the House of Commons. Hansard, whose father was also Printer to the House of Commons, made some important contributions to the improvement of his craft, and wrote a competent historical and technical account of it, published as *Typographia* (1825). He is, however, chiefly remembered as the publisher of the *Parliamentary Debates.* Until 1771, the House of Commons forbade the publication of its debates, but even after that no official record was made or issued. In 1803, William Cobbet began to publish his *Political Register,* which Hansard bought in 1811. He gradually eradicated the bias which had marred the *Register* under Cobbet's editorship, and in 1829 the title *Hansard's Parliamentary Debates* began to be used for this increasingly authoritative publication. Although this was still a private enterprise, the House gradually involved itself in the publication, providing facilities for the shorthand writers, and, in the case of individual members, collaborating in ensuring the accuracy of the record. By the end of the nineteenth century it was treated, *de facto,* as an official record. In 1909, the House finally took over *Hansard,* and renamed it *Official Report.* The old name continued in common usage, however, and in 1943 was formally restored as *Hansard. Official Record of Debates.* It now covers both Houses, and is referred to simply as 'Hansard'.

For the early history of reporting, see A. Aspinall, 'The reporting and publishing of the House of Commons' debates, 1771–1834', in R. Pares and A.J.P. Taylor (eds), *Essays Presented to Sir Lewis Namier* (1956). There are lives of both Hansards in *DNB*, and a history of *Hansard* by J.C. Trewin and E.M. King, *Printer to the House* (1952).

Hardback

See **Bookbinding**

Harleian bindings

Binding style. The name is given to the distinctive style used in binding many of the books and manuscripts of Edward Harley, 2nd Earl of Oxford, mainly in the 1720s and 1730s. At its most typical, it is a red morocco binding, with a gold-tooled border surrounding a central lozenge-shaped decoration. The principal binders involved were Thomas Elliott and Christopher Chapman.

See Howard Nixon, 'Harleian bindings', in R.W. Hunt, I.G. Philip and R.J. Roberts (eds),. *Studies in the Book Trade in Honour of Graham Pollard* (OBS, new ser., 18, 1975).

See also **Bookbinding**; **Harley, Robert, 1st Earl of Oxford** (1661–1724) **and Harley, Edward, 2nd Earl of Oxford** (1689–1741)

Harleian Miscellany, The

After the death of Robert Harley, 2nd Earl of Oxford, in 1742, his manuscripts were bought for the nation, but his printed books had to be sold. The purchaser was the bookseller, Thomas Osborne, who prepared a catalogue in five volumes (1743–45). The library included some 41,000 prints and pamphlets, and a selection of the latter was edited for publication by William Oldys. This selection is *The Harleian Miscellany* (8 vols, 1744–46). The prospectus and introduction were written by Samuel Johnson.

See D.J. Greene, 'Johnson and the *Harleian Miscellany*', *NQ* (1958), p. 304.

See also **Harley, Robert, 1st Earl of Oxford** (1661–1724) **and Harley, Edward, 2nd Earl of Oxford** (1689–1741)

Harley, Robert, 1st Earl of Oxford (1661–1724) and Harley, Edward, 2nd Earl of Oxford (1689–1741)

Politicians and book collectors. The elder Harley was one of the most important politicians of the early eighteenth century. He came from the landed gentry, was educated privately, called to the Bar, and elected to the House of Commons in 1690. By the beginning of Queen Anne's reign he was the leader of the Tory Party, and for long periods her Chief Minister. He was raised to the peerage in 1711, but in 1714 he was suspected of Jacobitism, and the accession of George I marked the effective end of his political career. From 1715 to 1717 he was imprisoned in the Tower, and after his release took little part in public affairs.

Harley began to collect in about 1701, concentrating chiefly on heraldic and historical manuscripts. He rapidly accumulated a large collection, including many historical documents of great importance. He had some 3000 manuscripts by the time of his death, and the 2nd Earl, whose tastes were literary rather than political, added substantially to the collection. The younger Harley, unlike his father, also collected printed books on a large scale, and was one of the first English collectors of incunabula. He was interested in bindings, and had many books specially bound for him in what came to be known as the 'Harleian' style.

By 1740, the 2nd Earl was badly in debt, and when he died in 1741 the printed books had to be sold; these included the vast collection of pamphlets which formed the basis of the *Harleian Miscellany*. In 1754, the countess sold the manuscripts to the nation, and they became one of the foundation collections of the British Museum.

The best account of the Harleys as collectors will be found in the Introduction to C. E. and Ruth C. Wright (eds), *The Diary of Humfrey Wanley 1715–1726* (2 vols, 1966). Wanley was the Harleys' librarian, and was largely responsible for assembling and cataloguing the collection.

See also **Book collecting**; **British Museum**; **Harleian bindings**; *Harleian Miscellany, The*; **Incunabula**

Harmsworth, Alfred, 1st Baron Northcliffe (1836–1922)

See **Newspapers**

Hazlitt, William Carew (1834–1913)

Bibliographer. Hazlitt, grandson of the essayist, was educated at Merchant Taylors', and tried both the Bar and the civil service before devoting himself entirely to letters. He edited a number of texts, and wrote on subjects as various as Shakespeare and numismatics. His life's work, however, was his attempt to list early English books, which began with his *Handbook to the Popular, Poetical and Dramatic Literature of Great Britain from the Invention of Printing to the Restoration* (1867). He followed this with *Bibliographical Collections and Notes* (3rd ser., 1876–89). The whole was indexed by G.J. Gray (1893), and a fourth and final series was issued in 1903. Although superseded as a standard work, Hazlitt's *Handbook* and *Collections* are still occasionally useful for his records of copies which he had seen.

There is a life of Hazlitt in *DNB*.

Head title

Bibliographical term. The head title is the heading at the beginning of the text, or of a major textual division, such as a part or chapter. Since it is often set below the normal level of the first line, it is sometimes called the drophead, or dropped head, title.

Headline

Bibliographical term. The headline is the top line of the page, usually containing the running title and page number. The running title, in particular, can provide valuable evidence to the analytical bibliographer.

See Fredson T. Bowers, 'Notes on running-titles as bibliographical evidence', *Libr.* (1938–39), p. 315.

See also **Analytical bibliography**; **Running title**

Heber, Richard (1774–1833)

Book collector. Heber was already an avid bookbuyer before he went up to Oxford in 1791; at that time his interest was chiefly in the classics. Shortly afterwards, however, he turned to the English literature of the sixteenth and seventeenth centuries, and assembled a huge library of such books. Outside this field, he was almost equally omnivorous, and it is said that at the time of his death his library totalled over 145,000 volumes, as well as a vast collection of pamphlets. Whatever the figure, it is the case that the collection filled at least eight houses in three countries. Heber was something of a recluse and spent much of his life abroad, although he was a founder member of the Roxburghe Club, a friend of Dibdin and, briefly, MP for Oxford University (1821–1826). Heber was a great accumulator of duplicate, and indeed triplicate, copies, for he said that 'No gentleman can be without three copies of a book, one for show, one for use, and one for borrowers.' Perhaps through oversight, he made no provision for his books in his will, and they were sold at a series of 16 sales in London (Sotheby; Evans; Wheatley: 1834–36), Paris (1834–35), and Ghent (1835). The catalogues, consisting of 12 parts from the London sales, 2 volumes from Paris, and 1 from Ghent, together make up the *Bibliotheca Heberiana*, the only record of what was probably the largest collection of printed books ever assembled by one man. They are now in libraries and private collections all over the world, and can be identified by Heber's book stamp, usually on the upper free endpaper.

Heber's personal papers were acquired by Sir Thomas Phillipps, and are now with the Phillipps papers in the Bodleian Library, Oxford. A study based on them would be a major contribution to the history of English bibliophily. So far, we have to be content with A.N.L. Munby's posthumously published 'Father and son: the Revd. Richard Heber's vain attempt to stem the rising tide of his son Richard's bibliomania', *Libr.* (1976), p. 181. There is a life of

Heber in *DNB*, and an account of him in Seymour de Ricci, *English Collectors of Books & Manuscripts (1530–1830)* (1930); the latter includes details of the sales.

See also **Dibdin, Thomas Frognall** (1776–1847); **Phillipps, Sir Thomas** (1792–1872); **Roxburghe Club**

Hills, Henry (d. 1689) and Hills, Henry (d. 1713)

Printers. The elder Hills fought for Parliament in the Civil War, and was Official Printer to successive governments during the Interregnum. Later, however, he changed his allegiance and in about 1670 became King's Printer. In James II's reign he became a Roman Catholic and served as Master of the Stationers' Company in 1687–88, but found it prudent to leave England after the Revolution and died in exile. His son was freed from his apprenticeship in 1679 and immediately went into business by himself. In Anne's reign he became notorious for his piracies, especially of poems and sermons. In particular, he produced a whole batch of piracies of poetry in 1709–10 when the Copyright Act was about to come into force, advertising them as the last cheap editions which would ever be available because of the effects of the new law.

The two Hills have sometimes been confused, but the confusion was resolved in Henry R. Plomer, *A Dictionary of the Printers and Booksellers...1668 to 1725* (1922). The pirated poems are listed and indexed in D.F. Foxon, *English Verse 1701–1750* (2 vols, 1975).

See also **Copyright**; **King's (or Queen's) Printer**; **Piracy**; **Stationers' Company**

Hinman, Charlton Joseph Kadio (1911–?)

Bibliographer. Hinman was educated at Cornell and Oxford, and devoted his life to the study of the text of Shakespeare. He fulfilled the dream of Henry Clay Folger by collating the more than 90 copies of the First Folio in the Folger Shakespeare Library, in pursuit of textually significant press variants. This work is described and his results analysed in *The Printing and Proofreading of the First Folio of Shakespeare* (2 vols, 1963), one of the masterworks of analytical bibliography. To facilitate his work, Hinman developed the collating machine which bears his name, and which is now in use in many research libraries. A system of mirrors and flashing lights permits the comparison of two copies of the same edition and visually reveals press variants, progressive type damage and the like.

For Hinman's career, see *Who's Who in America (1974–1975)*.

See also **Analytical bibliography**; **Bibliography**; **Collation**; **Edition**; **First Folio**; **Folger Shakespeare Library**; **Press variant**; **Textual criticism**

Historical bibliography

The generic term used for all aspects of bibliography applied to hand-printed books, including not only printing, but also publication history and the study of book-making materials such as paper and bookbindings. Its vagueness is useful in some ways, and it is, for example, often used as the title of introductory courses in bibliography. In effect, so far as those interested in early printed books are concerned, it is synonymous with 'bibliography' itself, as in the title of Philip Gaskell's *New Introduction to Bibliography* (1972).

See also **Bibliography**

Hoe press

Printing press. An early rotary press, invented by Richard Hoe in 1845–46. Hoe belonged to a family of New York pressmakers, whose firm had already made a number of advances in printing technology. In the Hoe press, the type was held on a central revolving cylinder, which could be fed from up to ten piles of paper. Each feeder could work at speeds in excess of 2000 sheets per hour, and production rates of up to 40,000 sheets per hour were claimed for the ten-feeder press. The machine was primarily designed for newspaper work. The first was installed by the Philadelphia *Public Ledger*, followed by *La Patrie* (Paris), in 1848, and *The Times* (London) in 1858. The Hoe was one of the most successful and widely used of the early rotary machines.

See James Moran, *Printing Presses* (1973); and Frank E. Comparato, ' "Old Thunderer's" American Lightning: machinework and machinations in furnishing the first Hoe rotaries to *The Times*, 1856–60', *JPHS* (1978/79), p. 27.

See also **Press**

Hogarth Press

Private press. The Hogarth Press was founded in 1917 by Leonard and Virginia Woolf, partly as a hobby and partly as therapy for Mrs Woolf. Its books reflect the interests of the Woolfs and their circle, and consequently include some important and interesting works of literature. The most notable of these is the first edition of T.S. Eliot's *Waste Land* (1923). There was also a number of books on psychology, including English translations of Freud, and works by Ernest Jones and Melanie Klein. In later years, the Press's books were so popular that the Woolfs could no longer print them by hand, although some printing continued until 1938. Since then, the Hogarth Press has been a publisher's imprint.

See Howard J. Woolner, *A Checklist of the Hogarth Press 1917–1938* (1978). This includes a history of the Press, but the best sources are Leonard

Woolf's autobiography (*Beginning Again* (1964); and *Downhill All the Way* (1967)), and the remarkable Richard Kennedy, *A Boy at the Hogarth Press* (1972).

Hollander

See **Papermaking**

Hollar, Wenceslaus (1620–1674)

See **Etching**

Hollis, Thomas (1720–1774)

Lover of liberty and patron of bookbinders. Hollis was a wealthy and somewhat eccentric man who devoted his life and fortune to libertarian causes. He had great affection for the 'republican' writers of the seventeenth century, such as Toland whose *Life of Milton* he edited (1761). He is of interest to book historians because he commissioned special bindings for books whose authors' principles agreed with his own, and presented the books to various libraries, notably those of Harvard, Berne and Zürich universities. He had special tools cut for these 'republican' bindings; the tools were various emblems of liberty, and usually form the sole decoration on otherwise plain red morocco covers. A second set of tools was engraved in 1764–67, after the first set had been destroyed by fire.

There is a life of Hollis in *DNB*, but the only full account is Francis Blackburn's *Memoirs of Thomas Hollis* (1780). For the bindings, see Howard M. Nixon, *Five Centuries of English Bookbindings* (1978); and Charles Ramsden, 'The collection of Hollis bindings at Berne', *BC* (1958), p. 165.

See also **Bookbinding**

Horn book

An early form of school book. It is not actually a book at all, but rather a single leaf printed on one side only which is pasted to a board of wood or stiff card covered with a thin layer of horn to protect it. Normally it had a handle by which it could be held when in use. The 'text' was merely the letters of the alphabet and, usually, the Lord's Prayer. Of the millions that were printed between the sixteenth and nineteenth centuries only a handful have survived the ravages of children and time.

See Andrew W. Tuer, *History of the Horn-book* (2 vols, 1896).

Hose

See **Common press**

Hot metal

The generic name for typesetting machines which use molten type metal to cast type as part of the process of typesetting.

See also **Line casting; Monotype; Typecasting; Typesetting**

Hunterian Library

A collection within the library of the University of Glasgow. The collection was formed by William Hunter (1718–1783), a distinguished medical man who collected both in his own subject and more widely. His library reached the University only in 1902, since when it has been kept separately and administered by its own Trustees. The most striking features of the collection are the incunabula, the early Italian books and, above all, the superb medieval manuscripts.

There is a catalogue of the manuscripts by John Young and P. Henderson Aitken (1908); see also *ELIS*, vol. 10 (1973).

See also **Incunabula**

Huntington Library and Art Gallery

Research library at San Marino, California, USA. The institution was founded by Henry E. Huntington (1850–1927), a businessman who made a fortune from the Southern Pacific Railroad and from urban railways in and around Los Angeles. His serious collecting began in about 1910. He bought heavily at the Hoe (1911–12) and Huth (1911–20) sales, and in 1914 purchased a large collection of plays and playbills from the library at Chatsworth House (the Kemble–Devonshire plays). In 1917, he made his most spectacular purchase, of the entire Bridgewater House library, which its owner, the Earl of Ellesmere, was forced to sell to pay estate duties. The library was formally founded in 1919, and the building completed in 1923, but the books were not finally sorted and catalogued until 1939. Huntington's intention was to provide a research library in California comparable with those of the East Coast and Europe, and in his chosen fields of English literature before 1700 and early Americana he largely succeeded. The library's treasures, which are still augmented from the endowment and other sources, include the Ellesmere Chaucer and a superb collection of early editions of Shakespeare. An art gallery is an integral part of the institution, and the buildings are set in magnificent grounds whose gardens are of exceptional botanical interest.

See James Thorpe, Robert R. Wark and Ray Allen Billington, *The Founding of the Henry E. Huntington Library and Art Gallery* (1969); and Robert O. Schad, *Henry E. Huntington: the founder and his library* (1931).

Ideal copy

Bibliographical term. Ideal copy is one of the fundamental concepts of modern descriptive bibliography. The bibliographer describes the book as it was intended to be issued by the publisher, even though there may be no extant copy which precisely conforms to this description. The theory is that any copy can be compared to the ideal copy to establish its relationship to it. The description is of the ideal copy of the issue or impression, the smallest bibliographical grouping in which the publisher's intention can be detected. Variations which are states are considered to be accidental, and are therefore deviations from the ideal copy rather than a part of it. Because the ideal copy is derived from the bibliographer's understanding of the publisher's intention, the binding is considered only if it was issued bound. If, however, there are publishers' binding variants, each variant constitutes an issue of which there is, therefore, an ideal copy.

See G. Thomas Tanselle, 'The concept of *ideal copy*', *SB* (1980), p. 18.

See also **Bibliography**; **Bookbinding**; **Descriptive bibliography**; **Edition binding**; **Impression**; **Issue**; **State**

Illuminated printing

See **Blake, William** (1757–1827)

Illustrated books

Some of the most magnificent books of the ancient world and the Middle Ages are illuminated manuscripts, and the practice of illustration was carried over into early printed books. Although the early printers tried to imitate the illustrations of their manuscript models, technical problems made this difficult. Some early books were printed to allow space for the rubrication of initials, and copies of some incunabula are found fully illuminated in the manner of contemporary manuscripts. In general, however, early illustrated books used comparatively crude woodcuts, and they were not in general very numerous. Perhaps the most famous illustrated book of the fifteenth century is the edition of Hartmann Schedel's *Liber chronicum*, printed by Anton Koberger at Nuremberg in 1493, and always known as the Nuremberg Chronicle. There are over 2000 woodcut illustrations, although in fact only about 600 blocks were made, and many were used more than once.

Illustrated books

In the sixteenth century, woodcut was gradually replaced by intaglio processes, usually simple copperplate engraving, as the principal medium of book illustration, and illustrated books became distinctly expensive because of the high cost of intaglio printing. Indeed, until the present century, illustrated books were the exception rather than the rule, and were intended for wealthy and usually bibliophilic book buyers. In general, the quality of book illustration was improved by the transition to the more subtle intaglio processes. There is a tendency, however, for the style of book illustration to be anything up to 50 years behind stylistic developments in the other visual arts, at least until the twentieth century. Even so, artistic trends are reflected in book illustration. Perspective was gradually introduced in the fifteenth and sixteenth centuries, and there are styles of illustration in the seventeenth and eighteenth centuries which correspond with such fashions as mannerism, rococo and classicism.

In the seventeenth and eighteenth centuries, illustrations were most often used to illustrate classical legends, contemporary fiction and scientific and topographical work. The latter was particularly prominent in England in the late eighteenth century, but in fact most of the best illustrated books were of continental origin. The French, Italian and Dutch printers were especially notable for the quality of their products, and indeed the illustrated book became something of a speciality of printers and publishers in France in the middle of the eighteenth century.

The great changes in the illustrated book in the nineteenth century were a consequence of the development of new processes of graphic reproduction. Lithography was the first of these, and attracted artists because it was the first process which permitted direct drawing by an artist who was not skilled in woodcutting or engraving. The artist-engraver was not unknown in earlier centuries, for both Dürer and Blake had cut their own blocks and plates, but this was unusual. Autographic lithography changed this, and became an attractive medium even to artists of the calibre of Turner. At the same time, the first practical colour processes were developed by Baxter, Evans and the chromolithographers. Again, these attracted artists, and although books illustrated in colour were expensive, the coloured book became a reasonable technical and economic proposition for the first time.

The second half of the nineteenth century saw the beginnings of the photographic revolution. The early photomechanical processes were not ideal, but they did permit exact reproduction, while the use of half-tone made accurate tonal representation possible at least in monochrome. The trichromatic process used for colour illustration today is a more recent development, and it is the development of offset lithography which has made the coloured book the familiar object which it now is.

In general, the purpose of book illustration has barely changed since the fifteenth century. It is used to elucidate points in the text which are more easily shown than described; in its simplest form this may be merely a diagram, or it may be a reproduction of a drawing, painting or photograph. It is also, of course, used as decoration, although many book illustrations fall perhaps somewhere between the two, as when there is a portrait of the subject of a biography. The illustrated book, properly so-called, is one where the illustration is integral to the book, and perhaps even its *raison d'être*. Obvious examples are Blake's illustrated books, where the poem, the illustration, and even the page layout are part of a single artistic concept. This is the illustrated book in its purest form, but it has rarely been equalled. Later examples, however, would certainly include the great bird books of the nineteenth century, such as Audubon's *Birds of America* (4 vols, 1827–38), one of the most spectacular (and certainly one of the most expensive) books ever published. In the twentieth century, many artists, including Picasso and more recently David Hockney, have worked in the field of book illustration, but in many cases their illustrated books are really collections of their own lithographic or screen prints with commentary.

In broader terms, book illustration is one of the minor arts, but it is nevertheless of considerable interest to the historian. Before the advent of the cinema, the illustrated book was the only mass medium of graphic communication, and visual images of both men and things were derived from no other source by the majority of people who never had access to the few art galleries then in existence. In the present century it has become a more consciously artistic medium, not always to its advantage.

There is a huge literature on this subject, and no first-rate history; there are, however, two reasonably adequate general accounts: David Bland, *A History of Book Illustration* (1958); and John Harthan, *The History of the Illustrated Book* (1981). For more detailed recent work, see Sandra Hindman, ed., *The Early Illustrated Book: Essay in Honor of Lessing J. Rosenwald* (1982), published by the Library of Congress to commemorate the gift of Rosenwald's major collection of illustrated books.

See also **Audubon, John James** (1785–1851); **Baxter, George** (1804–1867); **Blake, William** (1757–1827); **Chromolithography**; **Colour printing**; **Evans, Edmund** (1826–1905); **Half-tone**; **Intaglio**; **Lithography**; **Offset lithography**; **Photomechanical printing**; **Woodcut**

Imposition

A stage in the process of preparing type for printing. When type has been set and made up into pages, the pages are arranged in a relationship to each other which will ensure that they are in the correct order when the printed sheets are folded. This is the process of imposition. In hand printing, the type pages were laid by the compositor on the imposing stone, a stone with a polished plane surface, and then locked up in a chase to make a forme. It is important that the imposition should be done on a plane surface, to ensure that all the type is at exactly the same height from the bed of the press. The arrangement of pages is, of course, crucial, and varies from format to format. In quarto, for example, the four pages of the outer forme are imposed so that pages 8 and 1 lie next to each other, with page 4 head-to-head with page 1, and page 5 head-to-head with page 8.

On imposition in general, see Moxon, p. 223. Imposition diagrams for the more common formats are in Gaskell, p. 88, and a vast range of formats is illustrated in William Savage, *A Dictionary of the Art of Printing* (1841, repr. 1968).

See also **Chase**; **Compositor**; **Format**; **Forme**; **Quarto**; **Typesetting**

Impression

(1) *Technical term in printing.* When a sheet is printed, it is said that an impression has been taken.

(2) *Bibliographical term.* In strict bibliographical usage, an impression is all the copies of a book printed from the same setting of type in a continuous print run. With hand-printed books, this is normally identical with an edition or an issue, and the term is probably better avoided. The rare instances of reprinting from standing type, unaltered in any respect, do constitute an impression, but are notoriously difficult to identify from internal evidence alone. With the introduction of stereotyping in the early nineteenth century, the concept has more bibliographical meaning, since second and subsequent printings from the plates are indeed impressions. The same is true of such printings from lithographic and other photographically generated plates.

See Bowers, p. 37

See also **Edition**; **Issue**; **Offset lithography**; **Standing type**; **Stereotyping**

Imprimatur

Literally 'it may be printed', but it has come to be used to mean 'permission to print'. An imprimatur was granted by a licenser or censor, to signify approval of the text, and was often printed in the book. Indeed at various times in various countries it was a legal requirement to print it. In England, imprimaturs are found before 1640, but they are only common from 1662 to 1695, when books had to be licensed under the terms of Printing Act 1662. In those European countries which had a stricter system of control, especially the Roman Catholic countries, imprimaturs are common from the sixteenth to the early nineteenth centuries, and are still to be found in theological works by Roman Catholic priests, which have to be licensed by the appropriate bishop.

For some early English examples, see Franklin B. Williams, 'The Laudian imprimaturs', *Libr.* (1960), p. 96.

See also **Printing Act 1662**

Imprint

Book trade term, used by bibliographers. The imprint is the publisher's name, and usually his location, printed at the foot of the title page; normally, there is also a date, although the modern fashion is to print this on the verso of the title. The imprint gradually replaced the colophon as the title page was developed in the early sixteenth century; by about 1550 it was a usual feature of almost all printed books. In its simplest form it may merely give the printer's name, but from the late sixteenth to the late eighteenth centuries, imprints in all countries tended to be long and complex, giving the names and addresses of not only the printer but also all the booksellers involved in the publication, sale and distribution of the book.

In its fullest English form, the imprint typically reads: 'Printed by X for Y and sold by Z' where X is the printer, Y is the publisher and Z is the wholesaler or distributor. All of this was vital information to the trade, and can provide valuable evidence for the book trade historian. In particular, the bookseller for whom the book was printed, the functionary whom we would now call the publisher, was normally the owner of the copyright, or if the book was printed for more than one bookseller they were the joint owners. Imprints are therefore central to the study of share books and copyright ownership. The distributor, by whom the book was sold (and who was sometimes the same as the copyright owner) was even more crucial to the trade, for it was from him that the retail booksellers could obtain trade terms, and thus maximise their profits. In studying imprints it is important to realise that 'for' and 'sold by' have these precise and unambiguous meanings.

In the nineteenth century, the shortened imprints with which we are familiar today became common. This was because of two developments in the trade. First, as publishing houses became larger and more heavily capitalised, the basic economic motives for joint publication vanished, since there was less need to protect capital by spreading the risk of a particular title. Secondly, the trade's distribution mechanisms were radically changed by the building of the railways, and wholesale houses developed which dealt with the entire output of many publishers, thus eradicating the need for named distributors for each title.

Book historians should also be aware of the danger of false imprints, which exist in considerable numbers, and were usually intended either to disguise piracy or to deceive censors. Some are obvious, such as 'Utopia, 1790', but others are less so. Clever piracies used authentic imprints of the books which they were imitating, and books printed in countries in which the text was banned often had an imprint from another country. Printers were adept at making convincing imitations of imprints from elsewhere. In general, any imprint which deviates from the norm for the place and period should be treated with some suspicion and fully investigated. At various times and in various countries imprints have been made compulsory to assist in the state in controlling the output of the press. In the United Kingdom, printers (but not publishers) have been required to put their imprints on all printed matter since 1799.

See M.A. Shaaber, 'The meaning of the imprint in early printed books',

Libr. (1943–44), p. 120; and Percy Muir, 'English imprints after 1640', *Libr.* (1933–34), p. 155. Both are, however, to some extent out of date, but the work which has superseded them, chiefly by D.F. Foxon, remains as yet unpublished. For the 1799 Act, see W.B. Todd, 'London printers' imprints, 1800–1848', *Libr.* (1966), p. 46.

See also **Colophon**; **Copyright**; **Piracy**; **Share books**; **Title page**; **Wholesaling**

Incipit

Literally, 'it begins', or 'here begins'. This formula was commonly used at the beginning of a manuscript, as in, for example, 'Incipit liber Actarum Apostolorum': 'Here begins the book of the Acts of the Apostles'. It is sometimes found in early printed books, where it has been copied from the manuscript which was the source of the text.

Incunabula

Literally, 'apparatus of a cradle', but by extension 'symbol of childhood' and 'first home' or 'birthplace'. The word is used by bibliographers of books printed in the fifteenth century, a practice which can trace its origins back to a catalogue by Cornelius Beughem, *Incunabula typographiae* (1688). The word was taken up in France (usually as 'incunabule') in the eighteenth century, and made its way into England (sometimes anglicised as 'incunable') in the mid-nineteenth century, displacing the older English term 'fifteener'. It was, however, used to mean 'early printing' in general, and was still as vague as that when it was defined by the *Oxford English Dictionary*. It is now, however, always used only to mean books printed in or before the year 1500.

Incunabula began to attract attention in the mid-seventeenth century among French book collectors, and the first systematic attempt to list them was made by Michael Maittaire in the early eighteenth century. A similar effort was made, with greater success, by Panzer in 1793–97, and by Hain in 1823–28. Hain's *Repertorium bibliographicum*, with its supplements by Copinger (1895–1902) and Reichling (1905–11), remained the standard work on the subject for almost a century. The nineteenth-century revolution in incunabula studies (and indeed in bibliography in general) began with the work of Henry Bradshaw, who studied typography in great detail, and was thus, he believed, able to date and localise books without imprints. From this Robert Proctor developed a new method of listing incunabula in catalogues, in order of place and date of printing, rather than by author or title. This practice, usually called 'Proctor order', was followed by Pollard and his successors in the British Museum's catalogue of its incunabula (1908–   ), although not by the German scholars who worked on the *Gresamtkatlog der Weigendrüke* (1908–   ).

Incunabula do indeed present special problems to bibliographers, to which special methodologies must to some extent be applied, although the conventional techniques of analytical bibliography are more applicable to these books than some incunabulists seem to realise. A very high percentage have no imprint or colophon, and can therefore only be dated from the study of type, paper and other bibliographical phenomena. The difficulties are compounded by our still imperfect understanding of the circumstances of the trade by which incunabula were produced, although we do know, for example, that many printers travelled from place to place in pursuit of business. These intrinsic difficulties are, however only enhanced by the esoteric 'Proctor order' of so many catalogues, and by the descriptions of the books in those catalogues, which are often more like the description of a manuscript than the normal cataloguing and descriptive practices employed in dealing with printed books. The conventional alphabetical arrangement of *GW* and Goff is greatly to be preferred.

Incunabula are, naturally, both rare and expensive; even institutional collections tend to be small, although those of the British Library, the Bodleian Library, Oxford, and the Bibliothèque Nationale, Paris, are outstandingly good, all containing more than 10,000 examples. Print runs were very short in the fifteenth century, often less than 250, which is the root cause of the scarcity of so many fifteenth-century books. Moreover, most of the survivors are folios, rather than the smaller and more popular books which may have been produced in larger quantities than the extant examples would suggest. They have been collected since the mid-seventeenth century, although the real craze for 'fifteeners' in England did not begin until the late eighteenth century, and received its greatest impetus from Dibdin and the bibliomaniacs.

For a general survey, see Curt F. Bühler, *The Fifteenth-century Book* (1960); and Konrad Haebler, *The Study of Incunabula* (1953).

See also **Analytical bibliography**; **Bibliography**; **Bibliomania**; **Bradshaw, Henry** (1831–1886); **Colophon**; **Copinger, Walter Arthur** (1847–1910); **Dibdin, Thomas Frognall** (1776–1847); *Gesamtkatalog der Weigendrüke*; **Goff, Frederick Richmond** (1900–1982); **Imprint**; **Maittaire, Michael**(1668–1747); **Panzer, George Wolfgang Franz von** (1727–1805); **Pollard, Alfred William** (1859–1944); **Proctor, Robert George Collie** (1868–1903)

Index librorum prohibitorum

A list of works judged heretical by the Roman Catholic Church. It was first published in 1559, by the Holy Office, or Congregation of the Inquisition. Catholics were forbidden to buy, sell, print or read the books listed in it. The *Index* was regularly updated by additions and occasional deletions until it was abolished by Pope Paul VI in 1966.

See Heinrich Reusch, *Der Index der Verbotenen Bücher* (3rd edn, 1885).

See also **Censorship**

Index to Selected Bibliographical Journals 1933–1970

Reference work. The *Index*, published by The Bibliographical Society (1982), is based on a card-index created for in-house purposes at the Bodleian Library, Oxford. It is the successor to, and continuation of, G.W. Cole's *Index to Bibliographical Papers* (1933), but it is better in that it indexes 11 major bibliographical periodicals: *BC, Book Handbook, Bibl., Edinburgh Bibliographical Society Transactions, Records of the Glasgow Bibliographical Society, JPHS, Libr., OBSP, PBSA, SB* and *TCBS*. Each article is indexed by author(s) and subject(s), and the *Index* is in a single alphabetical sequence. Bibliographical literature is (ironically) only erratically indexed elsewhere, and the *Index* is thus an invaluable tool for the researcher.

See also **Cole, George Watson** (1850–1939)

Ink

Printing ink, until the late nineteenth century, was normally made of linseed oil and lampblack, which gave it a base and a colour respectively. The lampblack could be replaced with other substances to give other colours; thus, ground vermillion was used in making red ink. The quality of ink is dependent on the quality of the materials used, especially that of the oil base, and, unfortunately, these were too often less than perfect. There were specialised inkmakers, but until the mid-nineteenth century many printers made their own ink, which was indeed the source of many of the problems of quality.

See C.H. Bloy, *A History of Printing Inks, Balls and Rollers, 1440–1850* (1967).

Inlay

See **Bookbinding**

Intaglio

Printing technique primarily used for graphic processes. Intaglio is the method of printing from an engraved plate, where the areas to be printed are beneath the level of the surface of the plate. The printing process involved inking the plate, removing ink from the surface, and forcing the paper onto the plate to collect the remaining ink from the engraved lines. This was done in a rolling press, which generates the great pressure needed for intaglio printing, a feat of which the common press was incapable.

In the simplest intaglio process, called line-engraving, the engraver drew a tool called a graver (or burin) across the surface of the plate to make his lines, and then sharpened and cleaned them with tools called the scraper and the burnisher. In this manner, intaglio plates were made from the mid-fifteenth century onwards, and line-engraving never entirely lost its popularity, largely because of its simplicity and consequent cheapness. It does, however, produce a plate which cannot convey tonal gradations, and from the mid-seventeenth century onwards other intaglio techniques were developed to overcome this problem. Those which were of greatest significance were etching, mezzotint, aquatint and stipple engraving.

Intaglio processes were used primarily for graphic purposes, although most printed music was engraved after the late sixteenth century, and there are occasional examples of whole books of text printed from engraved plates. More commonly, in the seventeenth and eighteenth centuries, a book had an engraved frontispiece and title page, the latter in addition to the letterpress title page which normally followed it.

The only intaglio technique in current commerical use is photogravure, although printmakers still use the old hand-techniques.

For a general account of the various intaglio techniques, see A.M. Hind, *The Processes and Schools of Engraving* (4th edn, 1952); and, for a more detailed account, the same author's *A History of Engraving & Etching* (3rd edn, 1923).

See also **Aquatint**; **Common press**; **Etching**; **Mezzotint**; **Music printing**; **Photogravure**; **Printing**; **Rolling press**; **Stipple engraving**

International League of Antiquarian Booksellers

International organisation of the antiquarian book trade, whose members are the antiquarian book trade organisations of the cooperating countries. ILAB was founded after World War II to bring together the trade in different countries. It coordinates various matters such as ethical standards and forms of cataloguing, and also issues an occasional directory of booksellers, of which the most recent edition was that of 1977.

International Standard Book Description (ISBD)

See **Descriptive bibliography**

International Standard Book Description (Antiquarian) (ISBD(A))

See **Descriptive bibliography**

Intertype

See **Line casting**

Irish Stock

The name given to the Stationers' Company's interests in Ireland in the seventeenth century, by analogy with the much more important English Stock. In 1618, the Company was granted the rights of King's Printer in Ireland, and this was apparently divided into shares among the members. In practice the whole Irish enterprise amounted to little more than a largely unsuccessful attempt to market English books in Dublin, and it had petered out by the middle of the seventeenth century.

See Cyprian Blagden, *The Stationers' Company* (1960).

See also **English Stock; Stationers' Company**

Issue

Bibliographical term. An issue consists of all those copies of an edition which are intended to be identical and to be published simultaneously. Both halves of this deceptively simple equation are important in determining and defining the existence of an issue.

The classic example is that of a book whose title leaf is cancelled after publication, and replaced by a cancellans. Two issues are thereby created, the first with the cancellandum, the second with the cancellans. Less clear-cut cases arise where either greater or lesser alteration has taken place. If, for example, several sheets of a book are reset and printed, and then published with the remaining sheets of the previous edition, it is probably right to argue that what is thereby created is a second issue of the previous edition, provided that the publisher was consistent in mixing the sheets of the original and reset parts of the book. Only textual collation can establish the latter point, which is crucial in determining the publisher's intention. A more complex case arises when there are cancellantes of less than a whole sheet within the book, but the title leaf is uncancelled. Again the intention of the publisher is paramount. If the cancellantes merely represent a second (or subsequent) attempt to print correctly matter which was incorrect when originally printed (in the sense that it did not correctly represent the copy used for setting the type), then this would be better treated as a state, arising from the presence of what are, *de facto*, press variants. If, however, the cancellantes contain new matter which was never intended to be in the cancellanda (or, conversely, if the cancellantes deliberately omit matter which did appear in the cancellanda) then an issue has indeed been created.

If these matters are complex with hand-printed books, they become more so after the invention of stereotyping in the early nineteenth century. When a second or subsequent printing is made from the plates, an impression is created; but it might be argued that it is also an issue, since all the copies of the impression are intended for simultaneous publication. Since, however, the intention is that the impression shall be identical to the earlier impression(s), it is probably better not to regard it as an issue. The concept of issue can then be reserved for cases where the plates were altered by, for example, changing the date on the title page. Thus an edition may have two or more issues, each consisting of two or more impressions. Conversely, in the most simple case, edition, impression and issue may be identical, when a single printing is made from a single and unaltered setting of type and the sheets are intended for simultaneous publication.

In the end, the bibliographer must apply intelligence, judgement and common sense in the most marginal cases, remembering that the object of the exercise is to clarify, not to confuse.

For a wide-ranging discussion, see G. Thomas Tanselle, 'The bibliographical concepts of issue and state', *PBSA* (1975), p. 17.

See also **Cancel**; **Collation**; **Edition**; **Impression**; **Press variant**; **State**; **Stereotyping**

Italic

Letterform. Italic derives from the cursive handwriting used in the Papal Chancery in the fifteenth century, and is characterised by a noticeable inclination to the right and exaggerated serifs. The first italic was cut for Aldus in 1501, but this was lower case only; no upper case italic was cut until the mid-1520s. In the sixteenth century in France and Italy it was not unusual to set a whole book in italic, especially if the text were in verse; thereafter, however, italic came to be used, as it is today, for emphasis or quotations and citations. Because of this development, since the seventeenth century typographers have tended to cut both a roman and an italic face for each design, intending them to be used together.

See A.F. Johnson, *Type Designs* (3rd edn, 1966).

See also **Aldus Manutius** (*c.* 1450–1515); **Roman**; **Serif**; **Typeface**

Jackson, John Baptiste (1701–*c.* 1777)

Woodcut artist. Jackson's background is obscure, but by 1725 he was in Paris, where he learned the trade of woodcutting which he then practised there. In 1731 he moved to Venice, where he learned the art of chiaroscuro. He remained in Italy until 1745, and while there produced some excellent chiaroscuro work, sometimes using as many as ten blocks for each print. He was the most important artist to work with this technique in the eighteenth century. In 1745 he returned to England, and began to produce colour-printed wall-hangings which are in fact some of the earliest coloured wallpaper. His business failed however, and he died in obscurity.

See Jacob Kainen, *John Baptiste Jackson: Eighteenth-century master of the color woodcut* (1962).

See also **Chiaroscuro**; **Colour printing**; **Woodcut**

Jackson, Joseph (1733–1792)

Typefounder. Jackson was a Londoner by birth and was apprenticed to the elder Caslon in 1748; there he learned the whole trade, including the art of punchcutting which Caslon had tried to conceal from him. He left Caslon after a quarrel, served at sea for some time, and then established his own type-foundry in London in 1765. He soon came to specialise in cutting unusual faces, including Hebrew, Persian and Bengali. Perhaps his greatest achievements were the founts he cut for two of the earliest type facsimiles: the 1783 edition of the *Domesday Book* and Woide's facsimile of the *Codex Alexandrinus* (1786). Later in life he cut some excellent romans which mark an important stage in the transition from Old face to Modern face. After his death, Jackson's foundry and punches were bought by William Caslon III.

See Talbot Baines Reed, *A History of the Old English Letter Foundries* (new edn, rev. by A.F. Johnson, 1952).

See also **Caslon, William** (1692–1766) **and Caslon, William** (1720–1778); **Fount**; **Modern face**; **Old face**; **Type facsimile**; **Typecasting**

Jaggard, William (d. 1623) and Jaggard, Isaac (d. 1627)

Printers. The elder Jaggard established his own business in about 1595, and began to publish on his own account. Among his early books were a number of literary works, including *The Passionate Pilgrim* (1599). In about 1608 he became Printer to the City of London, and in that capacity undertook the City's official printing. He is, however, best remembered for his central role in the publication of the Shakespeare First Folio, for which he seems to have had overall responsibility. In fact it is his son, Isaac, whose name appears in the imprint, for before the book was published William Jaggard was blind and terminally ill.

See Charlton Hinman, *The Printing and Proof-reading of the First Folio of Shakespeare* (2 vols, 1963).

See also **First Folio**

Jenson, Nicholas (*c.*1420–1480)

Printer, publisher and typefounder. Jenson, a Frenchman, was Master of the Mint in Tours when, it is said, Charles VII sent him to Mainz in 1468 to learn the new art of printing. If this is true, his native country did not benefit, for he went on to Venice and remained there for the rest of his life. He printed and published his first book in 1470, and was soon cutting the famous series of roman types which were to make him famous throughout Europe. He was indeed largely responsible for establishing Venice as a major centre of the trade in printed books, a reputation which was confirmed by Aldus in the next generation.

See Horatio F. Brown, *The Venetian Printing Press 1469–1800* (1891).

See also **Aldus Manutius** (*c.* 1450–1515); **Roman**; **Typecasting**

Jest books

Literary genre. Jest books are collections of jokes or humorous short stories which attained great popularity in Western Europe in the sixteenth and seventeenth centuries. There are classical precedents, but the Renaissance tradition begins with Poggio Bracciolini's *Liber facetiarum*, completed in the mid-fifteenth century and first printed in 1477. There were translations and imitations in English, French and German, and a substantial vernacular jest book literature developed in all three languages. The taste for jest books lasted for rather more than a century, but after about 1650 it was displaced, at least among more sophisticated readers, by the romances which are the ancestors of the novel.

See P.M. Zall, *A Hundred Merry Tales* (1963).

Jobbing case

See **Case**

Jobbing printing

Printing trade term. 'Job work' is the name given to the printing of all material other than books, newspapers and magazines, i.e. the production of ephemera. Such work has been undertaken since the fifteenth century, but became very common from the late seventeenth century onwards. It is now the mainstay of all but a few very large printing houses, and even some of them undertake jobbing work. Its value to the printer is that jobs can be done quickly, and produce a rapid, and often substantial, income.

See also **Ephemera**

John Rylands University Library of Manchester

The library of Manchester University. The University, founded as Owens College, has had a library since 1851, and it grew rapidly in the nineteenth century largely through the generosity of successive generations of wealthy Manchester businessmen. By 1900 it was already a major research library, and was not unimportant in establishing Manchester's pre-eminence among the civic universities of the nineteenth century. The John Rylands Library was opened in 1899, having been founded by Mrs Enriqueta Augustina Rylands (d.1908) in memory of her late husband. In 1892 she had purchased the incunabula and other early printed books from the Spencer Library at Althrop, to which she added (1899) the manuscripts from the Bibliotheca Lindesiana at Haigh Hall; these two collections alone would have made the Library a major centre for the study of medieval manuscripts and early printed books, but it went from strength to strength under the guidance of its remarkable first Librarian, Henry Guppy. The University was always closely involved with the Rylands Library, and in 1972 the two libraries were amalgamated, when the Rylands Trustees found themselves facing an increasing financial burden in maintaining their inheritance. Since that time all of the University's collections of manuscripts and rare books have been moved to the Rylands building, a very important architectural monument in the heart of Manchester. The combined Library is now probably the third largest in the UK after the British Library and the Bodleian Library, Oxford.

See Henry Guppy, *John Rylands Library, Manchester: 1899–1935* (1931); and F.W. Ratcliffe, in *ELIS*, vol. 17 (1976).

See also **Bibliotheca Lindesiana**; **Spencer, George John, 2nd Earl Spencer** (1782–1845)

Johnes, Thomas (1748–1816)

See **Hafod Press**

Johnson, John de Monins (1882–1956)

Printer and collector of ephemera. Johnson was educated at Oxford, and became a papyrologist, spending some time in Egypt from 1907 to 1914. Found unfit for war service, he returned to Oxford, and took a post at the University Press; he became Printer to the University in 1925, and held that position until he retired in 1946. His work on papyri had convinced him of the importance of preserving the ephemeral documents of our own civilisation, and he began to form what he called 'a little museum of common printed things'. He collected virtually anything printed, from pamphlets to labels, and the result was an accumulation of millions of pieces of paper which form a unique record of the use of print in everyday life from the invention of printing to the beginning of World War II. He also sought to illustrate the history of printing itself, and the collection includes many crucial items on the history of type, printing machinery and the book trade. The collection was formed at the University Press, and remained there after his death; in 1968 it was transferred to the Bodleian Library, where it can now be consulted.

See John Feather, '"The sanctuary of printing": John Johnson and his collection', *ALJ* (1976), p.23.

See also **Ephemera**; **Oxford University Press**

Johnson, Joseph (1738–1809)

Bookseller and publisher. Johnson was born into a Baptist family in Liverpool, but was sent to London to be apprenticed to the bookseller, George Keith, and remained there for the rest of his life. He had his own shop by 1761, and began to publish a few books. He was soon specialising in political and religious works mainly of a radical and dissenting nature. In 1770, he moved to new premises in St Paul's Churchyard, and his shop there became famous as a meeting-place for his authors as well as being his place of business. He was liberal in politics and Unitarian in religion, opinions which are clearly reflected in many of the works which he published in the last three decades of the eighteenth century. His most important author was Joseph Priestley, but the list also included Mary Wollstonecraft, Blake, Fuseli and Cowper. Indeed, by the 1790s he was at the centre of a small circle of writers who tried to hold out against the strong tide of reaction in the aftermath of the French Revolution. Perhaps inevitably, Johnson was eventually prosecuted, successfully, for seditious libel; the book which put him in the dock was a pamphlet by Gilbert Wakefield attacking Bishop Watson of Llandaff, despised in Johnson's circle as a former radical who had 'defected' to the Tories. After spending six months in prison in 1799, Johnson resumed his business, but he was never again as significant as he had been in the previous decade.

Despite his key place in the history of English radicalism, Johnson has attracted little attention until very recently. There is now a modestly good book by Gerald P. Tyson, *Joseph Johnson: A liberal publisher* (1979); and a number of articles, including an analysis of his publications by Leslie F. Chard, 'Bookseller to publisher: Joseph Johnson and the English book trade, 1760–1810', *Libr.* (1977), pp. 138-54.

See also **Censorship**; **St Paul's Churchyard**

Journal of the Printing Historical Society

Bibliographical periodical. The first volume was published in 1965, and it has appeared annually (sometimes somewhat delayed) since then. It carries articles on the history of the techniques and equipment of printing, generally of an extremely high standard. The Editor since its inception has been James Mosley. An index to vols 1-10 (1965–74/75) was published in 1979.

Justification

Technical term in typesetting. Justification is the means by which the typeset lines are made exactly equal in length. In all relief processes this is a technical necessity, since the forme could not be properly locked up and carried if the pages were not solid rectangles of type. In setting prose by hand, the compositor varied the width of the inter-word spacing to achieve a justified line; in verse, or with short lines in prose, spacing materials are used after the last character to fill out the line. In line casting and Monotype machines, the justification is performed automatically as part of the casting process.

See Gaskell, p. 45.

See also **Compositor**; **Forme**; **Line casting**; **Monotype**; **Typesetting**

Kelmscott Press

Private press. Kelmscott was the first of the modern private presses, founded in 1891 by William Morris (1834–1896). Morris was a remarkable man in many ways; at Oxford he had been under the influence of the pre-Raphaelites and had carried this influence into his subsequent work as an architect and designer. He was also a competent poet and prose writer. In middle life he became involved in politics and by the late 1880s was, by the standards of the day, an advanced socialist. To Morris all of these activities were part of a coherent whole; he looked back to the Middle Ages as a period when free craftsmen, untrammelled by capitalism, pursued their avocations and produced objects which were both useful and aesthetically worthwhile. He became involved with the Arts and Crafts Society, which sought to promote guild socialism to revive this lost world.

The Kelmscott Press was a product of this ethos, the immediate influence being Emery Walker's famous lecture on typography to the Arts and Crafts Exhibition Society in November 1888. Morris sought to revive what he saw as the purity of the first century of printing, and to produce what he described as books which 'would have a definite claim to beauty...[and] be easy to read'. Whether he achieved either of these objectives may be a matter for debate, but there can be no doubt of the influence of the Kelmscott Press which he founded to promote them. It marked the beginning of the modern private press movement.

The first book, Morris's own *Story of the Glittering Plain*, was published in 1891. Between then and the closure of the Press in 1894, 53 books and various ephemeral items were printed. The earlier books were in the Golden Type which Morris designed for the purpose, but by late 1892 he had produced his Troy Type which thereafter was the mainstay of the Press. Both were based on fifteenth-century Gothic designs. It is generally agreed that the finest product of Kelmscott was the edition of Chaucer (1896) printed in Troy.

The literature on Kelmscott is vast. Of recent works, perhaps the most valuable is the Pierpont Morgan library exhibition catalogue entitled *William Morris and the Art of the Book* (1976), but *A Note by William Morris on His Aims in Founding the Kelmscott Press* (1898, repr. 1969) must not be ignored. All previous bibliographies are superseded by William S. Peterson, *Bibliography of the Kelmscott Press* (1984).

See also **Gothic type**; **Private press movement**; **Walker, Sir Emery** (1851–1933)

Keynes, Sir Geoffrey (1887–1982)

Surgeon, book collector and bibliographer. Keynes, brother of the economist Maynard Keynes, was educated at Rugby and Cambridge. His profession was surgery, in which he attained great eminence. In the book world, his chief importance is as a collector. He had superb collections of Donne, Evelyn, Browne and, above all, Blake, his first and greatest love. He published bibliographies of these and other authors, but these did not, unfortunately, always maintain the neccessary standards of rigour and accuracy. His characteristically trenchant defence of his bibliographical work, 'Religio bibliographici', is in *Libr.* (1953), p.63. He did, however, make important and lasting contributions to our knowledge and understanding of Blake, consummated in his *Blake Studies* (2nd edn, 1971). After his death, his books were bought by Cambridge University Library.

His *Gates of Memory* (1981) is a fascinating autobiography, and his own catalogue of his library, *Bibliotheca bibliographici* (1964), gives a vivid picture of the range and depth of his achievement as a collector. There is an obituary in *The Times* (6 July 1982), and a tribute in *TCBS* (1982), p.139. *BC* (Spring 1972) was a Festschrift for him.

King's (or Queen's) Printer

The office was created by Henry VII for William Faques in 1504, and by the middle of the sixteenth century the King's Printer had the sole privilege of printing Acts of Parliament and the Statutes. By 1603, this had been extended to include Bibles and New Testaments, the Bible patent being shared with the Universities of Oxford and Cambridge. This made the office both profitable and contentious, for, while large sums of money changed hands to secure it in the seventeenth and eighteenth centuries, other members of the trade objected to being excluded from the publication of such certain best-sellers as the Authorised Version of the Bible. In 1769, the office came into the hands of William Strahan and Charles Eyre, and has since remained in the latter's family; the firm now trades as Eyre and Spottiswoode.

There is a brief history of the office in J.A. Cochrane, *Dr Johnson's Printer. The Life of William Strahan* (1964).

See also **Strahan, William** (1715–1785)

Kirkman, Francis (1632–c.1680)

Bookseller and publisher. Kirkman, the son of a London merchant, became a bookseller in the 1650s, but it was not until after the Restoration that he made his name. From 1661, with partners, he made something of a speciality of printing pre-1640 plays, which were once again in demand after the 19-year period during which the theatres had been closed by the Puritans. Kirkman denied being a pirate, but there is little doubt that he realised that most of the plays which he printed were actually owned by other members of the trade. Kirkman was a pioneer in two other respects: he published some of the earliest prose romances, now recognised as precursors of the novel, which were popular in the 1660s and 1670s; and he owned the first commercial circulating library in the country. He was also an author, his most notable work being *The English Rogue* (4 vols, 1665–71), which he wrote with Richard Head.

See Strickland Gibson, 'A bibliography of Francis Kirkman', *OBSP* (1947), p. 47.

See also **Langbaine, Gerard** (1656–1692); **Piracy**

Knight, Charles (1791–1873)

Author and publisher. Knight was apprenticed to his father, a bookseller in Windsor whose customers included George III. He then worked on the local newspaper, began to write verse and published an edition of Tasso (1817). In the early 1820s he was associated with a number of publishing ventures in London, and moved there in 1823. He remained in London for the rest of his life. He was printer to the Society for the Diffusion of Useful Knowledge from 1828 onwards, and after various financial vagaries established a reputation as an author and publisher of cheap but 'good' popular books. He published many part books in the hope, which was realised, that comparatively poor people would buy them. The most famous of these were his *Penny Cyclopaedia* (1833–44) published in weekly parts and, later, his *Popular History of England* (8 vols, 1856–62). Knight was also a pioneer of cheap periodicals with his *Penny Magazine* (1832–45), which was filled with well-written but simple articles on a wide variety of topics. He was liberal in politics and greatly involved in the campaign against the Stamp Duties.

The main source for his life is his autobiography, *Passages of a Working Life* (3 vols, 1864–74), which is also an important general source for the book trade historian. See also A.A. Clowes, *Charles Knight: A sketch* (1892).

See also **Colour Printing**; **Newspapers**; **Part books**; **Stamp Acts**

Koenig press

Printing press. Friedrich Koenig (b. 1774) was a German printer and bookseller, who began experimenting with the application of mechanical power to printing in about 1800. Finding little support in Germany, he migrated to London in 1806, where he received financial help from Thomas Bensley and others. He had built a primitive printing machine before leaving Germany, and in 1811 constructed another, improved version in London. This attracted the attention of John Walter II, the owner of the *The Times*, who commissioned Koenig to build a press for his newspaper. This was first used to print the issue of *The Times* for 29 November 1814, a date which marks the beginning of mechanised printing in commercial use.

The principal of the press was that a steam-powered chain-belt drove two cylinders, around which the paper passed so that it was brought into contact with the forme, and lifted away from it after the impression had been made. Koenig also developed a mechanical inking system, with a new kind of roller specially designed to cope with the speed and pressure of the steam press. The original Koenig machines could print about 600 sheets an hour, but in later versions this was greatly improved. Indeed, the early steam presses were so fast that only newspaper houses needed them, and it was another 20 or 30 years before they were used for normal book work.

See James Moran, *Printing Presses* (1973).

See also **Forme; Press**

Lackington, James (1746–1815)

Bookseller and inventor of remaindering. Lackington, the son of a drunkard, was apprenticed to a shoemaker, and subsequently practised this trade in Bridgwater and Bristol. He was converted to Methodism in his teens, and became an avid reader of religious literature. In 1773, he moved to London, intending to set up a shoemaking business there, but he also began to sell Methodist books, and was soon running a successful bookshop. He broadened his scope to cover books of all kinds as he reacted against the religious fervour of his adolescence. His particular contribution was to sell books at the lowest possible prices, making his profits by selling large quantities. Others in the trade, including his first partner, disliked this method, and consequently resented the fact that he was more successful than they. In 1793, he opened his 'Temple of the Muses' in Finsbury Square, which was (as it was intended to be) the largest bookshop ever seen in England up to that time. He now began to buy in quantity from publishers, and by his dual policy of low prices and no credit sales he rapidly made a considerable fortune. In fact, he was doing what later came to be called remaindering. He took two former apprentices into partnership, and in 1798 retired from what was now Lackington, Allen and Co. In his retirement, he reverted to the Methodism of his youth, became a lay preacher, and built and endowed a chapel.

His two autobiographies, *Memoirs of the Forty-five First Years* (1791) and *The Confessions of J. Lackington* (1804) are not only primary sources for his life, but also for the trade as a whole in the late eighteenth century. There is a good modern account of his life and work by Richard G. Landon, in *SEC* (1976), p.387.

See also **Remaindering**

Laid paper

See **Papermaking**

Lair von Siegburg, Johann (1476–1554)

See **Siberch, John** (1476–1554)

Lane, Sir Allen (1902–1970)

Publisher. After an education at Bristol Grammar School, Lane went to work at The Bodley Head, which was owned by his distant cousin, John Lane. He learned his trade with Lane, and remained there for some years. In 1934, he conceived the idea of a series of paperback reprints of worthwhile books which would retail at 6d, and, despite the misgivings of his elders, the first of these were published in 1935. He chose the name Penguin Books for his series. The first titles were published jointly with The Bodley Head, but a separate company was established later in the year. From the beginning, Penguins proved to be a major commercial success, contrary to the gloomy predictions of almost everyone else in the trade. Lane's unconventional marketing, making use of chain-stores as well as bookshops, and his long print runs which gave low prices with small profits on single copies but which resulted in huge sales, were the major economic contributors to this success. The other element, however, was his accurate prediction that there was a market for good books if they were cheap enough, and Penguins became a major cultural influence, and even something of a cult, in mid-twentieth-century Britain. Lane also developed subsidiary series, such as Pelican Books (for the more serious non-fiction), Puffin Books (for children), and series like the Penguin Specials (on current affairs), the Penguin Shakespeare, and the Penguin Buildings of England. Lane had, in effect, invented the mass-market paperback, although he himself never used the true mass-marketing techniques which were to become the dominant feature of the paperback industry, especially in the USA after World War II.

Always opinionated and idiosyncratic, Lane proved somewhat inflexible later in life, and his reluctance to make commercial and policy changes led Penguin into serious financial difficulties in the 1960s. He never found a successor whom he regarded as suitable, despite several highly-publicised attempts. Shortly after his death, Penguins became part of the Longman Group, and gradually clawed its way back into profit.

See J.E. Morpurgo, *Allen Lane, King Penguin* (1979).

See also **Longman**; **Paperbacks**

Lane William (1725?–1814)

See **Minerva Press**

Langbaine, Gerard (1656–1692)

Bibliographer. The son of the Provost of The Queen's College, Oxford (also

Gerard), Langbaine was apprenticed to the London bookseller, Nevill Simons in 1672, and may also have worked for Francis Kirkman. Very shortly afterwards, however, he returned to Oxford as an undergraduate at University College, and remained there for the rest of his short life. His chief interest was in English drama, of which he formed a large collection of printed texts. In 1687, he published *Momus triumphans*, the first history of the English stage, which included a list of printed plays. A revised version of the latter, as *A New Catalogue of English Plays*, was published in 1688, and reached its final version in *An Account of the English Dramatic Poetry* (1691), which is still a useful source for theatrical and dramatic history. Laingbaine was a passably competent bibliographer, and, although his list has long since been superseded, his spadework was useful for future generations of scholars of the English drama.

There is a life of Langbaine in *DNB*.

See also **Kirkman, Francis** (1632–*c*. 1680)

Lansdowne, William Petty, 1st Marquess of (1737–1805)

Statesman and book collector. Lansdowne, better known to historians by his Irish title of Earl of Shelburne, was an important, if unpopular, figure in British politics in the second half of the eighteenth century. He was also a major benefactor of the arts, served for many years as a Trustee of the British Museum, and was an important book collector. His collection was chiefly of English political history, and as well as thousands of printed books and pamphlets he also acquired many important archives. The latter included the papers of Lord Burleigh (1520–1598), Sir Julius Caesar (1558–1636), White Kennett (1660–1728), and Peter Le Neve (1661–1729). His printed books were sold after his death, at an 11-day sale (Leigh and Sotheby, 1806), but his manuscripts were bought for the nation and are now in the British Library (MSS. Lansdowne 1.–1245.)

There is an account of him in *DNB* and *A Catalogue of the Lansdowne Manuscripts* was published in 1819.

See also **British Museum**

Lanston, Tolbert (1844–1913)

See **Monotype**

Large paper

See **Fine paper**

Latin Stock

The name given to the Stationers' Company's organisation for the import of continental books, which was instituted in 1591, with shares held by the members of the Company. Although some dividends were paid, the enterprise was wound up in 1627 probably because individual booksellers were better able to conduct this rather specialised branch of the trade.

See Cyprian Blagden, *The Stationers' Company* (1960).

See also **Stationers' Company**

Lay

See **Case**

Layman

See **Papermaking**

Leading

Technical term in printing. During the eighteenth century, and occasionally earlier, a thin strip of lead was put in the composing stick between each line of type. This was intended to give added stability, but it also had the effect of increasing the interlinear space, and hence giving a more generous and perhaps more elegant page layout. When mechanical typesetting was developed, the same visual effect was achieved by casting type on a body which was 1 point size larger than the type itself.

See Gaskell, p. 46.

See also **Composing stick; Point size; Typecasting; Typesetting**

Leaf

In bibliographical work, the terms leaf and page must always be used with literal exactness. Each leaf has two pages.

Lee Priory Press

See **Brydges, Sir Samuel Egerton** (1762–1837)

Legal deposit

The legal requirement for publishers to give one or more copies of their books to a specified repository for permanent preservation. The earliest such law was the Montpellier Ordinance issued by Francis I of France of 1537, which required printers to send a copy of each of their books to the Royal Library in Paris. This was not imitated elsewhere until the Printing Act 1662 imposed a similar requirement on English publishers. In fact, the Bodleian Library, Oxford, had had a private arrangement with the Stationers' Company since 1610, and this was incorporated into the Act; at the same time Cambridge University Library and the Royal Library also became deposit libraries. The Copyright Act 1710 repeated this provision, increasing the list of libraries to nine; in 1814 two more were added, but in 1842 the number was reduced to five: the British Museum, the Bodleian, Cambridge University Library, Trinity College, Dublin, and the Faculty of Advocates, Edinburgh. In 1911 the National Library of Wales (founded 1907) was added, and in 1912 the Advocates' privilege was transferred to the new National Library of Scotland.

In the USA deposit in the Library of Congress has been required since 1846 and, as under the 1911 Act in Britain, deposit was made a prerequisite for the protection of copyright. Other countries have followed the Anglo-American pattern.

Publishers have been known to complain about 'giving away' their books, but legal deposit is defensible on two grounds; first it creates and maintains a national printed archive which is a vital resource for research; and secondly it provides the basis on which a national bibliography can be compiled, a tool which is as valuable to the trade as it is to libraries and scholars. These arguments have not always impressed publishers, and libraries have sometimes had difficulty in enforcing their rights. In Britain, the problem was solved in the 1830s and 1840s when the British Museum ruthlessly pursued defaulting publishers.

See R.C. Barrington Partridge, *The History of the Legal Deposit of Books* (1938).

See also **Bodleian Library**; **British Museum**; **Cambridge University Library**; **Copyright**; **Library of Congress**; **Printing Act 1662**; **Stationers' Company**

Leighton, Archibald (1784–1841)

Bookbinder. Leighton was the son of a binder, also Archibald, who had migrated from Glasgow to London to establish a business in 1764. He inherited this business from his father, and became an important pioneer of new techniques and materials in bookbinding. He is believed by some to have been the first binder to use cloth instead of animal skin as a covering material, although this is uncertain. He was certainly, however, the first to use gold blocking on cloth, and to emboss cloth to simulate morocco leather. These developments all represent significant stages in the development of the edition

Leighton, J. and J.

binding. All Leighton's sons were bookbinders, John (1822–1912) becoming well known for his elaborate fine bindings in the second half of the nineteenth century, when the firm was trading as J. and J. Leighton.

See Charles Ramsden, *London Bookbinders, 1780–1840* (1956); M. Hartzog, 'Nineteenth-century cloth bindings', *PBSA* (1967), p.114; and Michael Sadleir, *The Evolution of Publishers' Binding Styles, 1770–1900* (1930).

See also **Bookbinding**; **Edition binding**

Leighton, J. and J.

See **Leighton, Archibald** (1784–1841)

Letterform

Generic name for the shape of letters, usually interpreted to mean 'the letters of the Latin alphabet'. There are, of course, many different ways in which the 26 letters can be written, not all of which have been, or indeed can be, imitated by punchcutters for use as typefaces. The upper case letterforms of roman type are essentially those used for inscriptions in the late classical period, and have undergone few modifications; the lower case forms, and Gothic and italic, are much later in origin, and have been subjected to far more alterations.

For a general history, see Stanley Morison, *Letter Forms* (1968).

See also **Gothic type**; **Italic**; **Roman**; **Typeface**

Letterpress

See **Relief printing**

Library, The

Bibliographical periodical. *The Library* was founded in 1888 by J.Y.W. (later Sir James) MacAllister, an an official journal for The Library Association. It rapidly became bibliographical in character, and in 1899 the LA replaced it with *The Library Association Record*, which was more concerned with practical matters of interest to the public librarians who constituted the great majority of the membership. MacAllister, however, kept *The Library* alive until 1919, when it was taken over by The Bibliographical Society. The Society had been publishing its own *Transactions* since 1893, but the two were now merged. There were three series of *The Library* before amalgamation (1888–99; 1900–9; 1910–19), and one of *TBS* (1893–1920). Subsequently, there have been three further series, under the title *The Library* (1921–45; 1945–78; 1978–date). As the organ of the The Bibliographical Society, edited for many years by A.W. Pollard, *The Library* became, and remains, the leading English-language bibliographical journal. It carries articles, notes and reviews on a wide range of topics, and also includes a valuable list of recent books and articles. The present editor is Mervyn Jannetta of The British Library. Both *TBS* and *The Library* were indexed by G.W. Cole in his *Index to Bibliographical Papers...1877–1932* (1933); and *The Library* is included in the *Index to Selected Bibliographical Journals 1933–1970* (1982). There is a detailed index in each annual volume.

See A.W. Pollard, '*The Library*: a history of forty volumes', *Libr.* (1932); and Shane Godbolt and W.A. Munford, *The Incomparable Mac* (1983).

See also **Bibliographical Society**; *Index to Selected Bibliographical Journals*; **Pollard, Alfred William** (1859–1944)

Library of Congress

The library of the United States Congress, in Washington, D.C., which is, *de facto* although not *de jure*, the national library of the USA. During the eighteenth century, the members of Congress were granted access to libraries in New York and Philadelphia, but when they moved to the new Federal capital in 1800, they established their own library. By 1814 this had grown to about 3000 volumes, but in that year it was destroyed when the British army burned Washington. In 1815, Congress bought some 6000 books from Thomas Jefferson, which were the foundation of the present Library, although about half of the original Jefferson collection was destroyed by fire in 1851. Meanwhile, in 1840, the Library became the official depository for US government publications, and, in 1846, the deposit library for books printed and published in the USA. In 1865, the latter provision was extended to include all printed matter. As a deposit library, its growth was very rapid, and the long-felt need for a new building was satisfied in 1897 with the opening of the present Library of Congress on Capitol Hill, close to both the Federal Capitol and the Supreme Court. During the nineteenth century the Library also acquired many important historical collections; many were of specifically American interest, but others were more broadly based and, by 1900, the Library was a major international research resource, a role in which it continues to develop. In the late 1970s, the Madison Building was opened to cope with the voracious space requirements of a library which now contains some 20 million books, and millions of maps, manuscripts, films and other materials.

Although it is not a national library, and through the Congressional Research Service continues to provide the services to Senators and Representatives for which it was originally intended, it functions as one, being responsible for the *National Union Catalog* and housing the US Copyright Office. More recently, the Center for the Book, another division of the Library, has become an important focus for the study of book history in the English-speaking world. *The Quarterly Journal of the Library of Congress* which has, unfortunately, recently ceased publication, carried many important articles based on the collections.

John Y. Cole is engaged on a history of the Library; in the meanwhile, the article by Mary C. Lethbridge and James W. McClury in *ELIS*, vol. 15 (1975), suffices as an introduction.

See also **Center for the Book**; **Legal deposit**

Licensing Act

See **Printing Act 1662**

Ligature

Technical term in typecasting. A ligature is a sort cast with two or more characters on a single body. The most common example is 'fi' where, if the two were cast separately, the kern (overhanging curved stroke at the top of the letter) of the 'f' would interfere with the dot of the 'i'. Ligatures are unnecessary in photosetting where there is no type, but are sometimes retained for aesthetic reasons.

See Gaskell, p. 33.

See also **Sort**; **Typecasting**

Limited Editions Club

Publisher. LEC was founded in New York City by George Macy, a publisher, in 1929, to publish a 'perfectly printed and beautiful book' every month. Macy's idea was to improve the standards of American book production by giving designers and printers the opportunity to produce fine books which would, he hoped, act as an inspiration to their colleagues. Although he was much influenced by Morris's idea of the 'book beautiful', Macy was interested in contemporary rather than pseudo-medieval designs. Most of the books are editions of standard literary classics. Perhaps the outstanding achievement of the Club, which still flourishes, is the edition of Shakespeare (1939–40) designed by Bruce Rogers. The Club has fulfilled Macy's intention by becoming a major influence for the good in American printing and book design.

See *Quarto-Millenary. The first 250 publications and the first 25 years 1929–1954 of the Limited Editions Club* (1959).

See also **Book Collectors' Quarterly, The**; **Kelmscott Press**; **Rogers, Bruce** (1870–1957)

Line block

See **Photomechanical printing**

Line casting

Mechanical typesetting technique. The idea of line casting was conceived by a Frenchman called Hernan in the late 1790s, but only became a practical proposition in the hands of Ottmar Mergenthaler (1854–1899). Mergenthaler produced the first working machine in 1884, in Baltimore, Maryland.

The essence of line casting is that a whole line of type is cast on a single piece of metal, known as a 'slug'. In the final version of Mergenthaler's machine, the Linotype, which set the pattern for all commercial line casters, a set of matrices is stored at the top of the machine and linked to a keyboard. When a key is depressed, the appropriate matrix descends into a tray with wedges inserted, also by a keystroke, between words. When the line is complete, the operator presses a lever which expands the wedges and so justifies the line. Molten type metal then pours into the matrices, the whole line is cast, and the slug is expelled into a galley.

Large-scale production of Linotype machines began in 1890, and they were rapidly adopted by American printers. They continued to be used in the USA for most work until relief printing was displaced by offset lithography in the 1960s. In Europe, however, line casting was used for newspaper and magazine work, but for book printing, Monotype was generally preferred.

See L.A. Legros and J.C. Grant, *Typographical Printing-surfaces* (1916).

See also **Galley**; **Justification**; **Matrix**; **Monotype**; **Offset lithography**; **Relief printing**; **Typecasting**; **Typesetting**

Line engraving

See **Intaglio**

Linotype

See **Line casting**

Literary agent

A businessman who acts as an intermediary between author and publisher, advising on manuscripts and negotiating terms. The agent's fee is normally 10 per cent of royalties, paid by the author. A.P. Watt (1834–1914), who turned from publishing to agency in the late 1870s, is normally regarded as the first true agent. Initially, publishers were suspicious of agents, but authors found their services valuable, and they are now a recognised part of the trade in both Britain and the USA. They often play an important role, especially in advising new authors about their first efforts to break into print.

See James Hepburn, *The Author's Empty Purse* (1968), which is largely a history of literary agency.

See also **Royalty**

Lithography

Printing technique. Lithography is a planographic process, i.e. the printing and non-printing areas are in the same plane of the printing surface. Whereas in relief and intaglio processes the distinction between printing and non-printing areas is physical, in lithography it is chemical, depending upon the mutual repellance of oil and water. The basic principle is a simple one: the printing area is defined by an oil-based chemical, and the whole surface is then dampened with a water-based chemical before inking, so that the ink, which is itself oil-based, will adhere only to the oily areas which have rejected the water-based damper.

Lithography was invented by Alois Senefelder in 1798, and in the technique developed by him involved drawing with a wax crayon on a slab of washed and polished limestone. The stone was then etched and wetted before ink was applied and the impression taken. In this form, known as autographic lithography, the technique spread widely but slowly in the early nineteenth century. It was more suitable for graphic than for textual matter, but as a graphic process it proved very popular with illustrators and cartographers. Its great advantage, from the points of view of both artistic expression and accuracy of line, was that it permitted the artist or cartographer to draw directly on the stone, rather than have his work interpreted by an engraver as was necessary in all the intaglio and relief processes then in use. Engelmann's invention of chromolithography in 1836, which permitted the use of a full range of colours, further increased the artistic possibilities of the technique. Even in monochrome, however, lithography soon developed to the point at which the lithographer could achieve a full tonal range from black to white. It was widely used for topographical illustration in the nineteenth century, until it was slowly displaced by the photo-mechanical processes. In cartography, its use continued into the twentieth century, as it did in music printing, another field which it came to dominate.

The great problem with lithography was its cost. Limestone, while undoubtedly the best substance for the process, was expensive, and good lithographers were themselves a scarce commodity. For these reasons, lithography was used only for expensive books, usually those in which illustration was an essential and substantial part of the work, or even its *raison d'être*. Even in such cases it was very unusual to print the text matter lithographically, and, since a separate press was needed for printing from the stone, the cost was thus further increased.

In the second half of the twentieth century, the lithographic principle has been applied to printing from photographically-generated plates, in a process called offset lithography. This is now the standard technique used for almost all printing.

See Michael Twyman, *Lithography 1800–1850* (1970) and the same author's 'Lithographic stone and the printing trade in the nineteenth century', *JPHS* (1972), p.1. The first English treatise on the subject, Henry Bankes' *Lithography; or the art of making drawings on stone*, was published in 1813, and a second, enlarged, edition in 1816. Both have been reprinted with an introduction by Michael Twyman (1976).

See also **Chromolithography**; **Illustrated books**; **Ink**; **Intaglio**; **Music printing**; **Offset lithography**; **Photomechanical printing**; **Relief printing**; **Senefelder, Alois** (1771–1834)

Little Gidding bindings

A group of bookbindings made by members of an Anglican community at Little Gidding, Huntingdonshire, in the 1630s. The community was founded by Nicholas Ferrar (1592–1637) in 1624, and although it was not monastic, Ferrar's ideas included the Benedictine concept of useful work. The daughter of a Cambridge bookbinder, probably called Katherine Moody, taught some of the ladies the craft of binding in about 1630. They produced a number of exquisitely designed if not always perfectly executed bindings in the next few years. These included a number which were gold-tooled on velvet, as well as more conventional bindings of leather and vellum.

See Howard M. Nixon, *Five Centuries of English Bookbinding* (1978); and Cyril Davenport, 'Little Gidding bindings', *Bibliog.* (1896), p.129.

Liverpool Bibliographical Society

Founded 1979. The primary aim of the Society is to compile an historical directory of the book trade in the north-west of England. The first part, covering the city of Liverpool up to 1805, was edited by M.R. Perkin (1981), and work continues on its successors. Regular meetings are held in Liverpool during the winter.

The Society's address is Sydney Jones Library, PO Box 123, Liverpool L69 3DA.

Logography

Printing process. The principle of logography is that common combinations of letters (e.g. in English, ING, ED, TION) are cast as a single type, the theory being that this saves time in composition. The inventor was Henry Johnson, who developed the system in the 1770s. It was taken up by John Walter, the founder of *The Times*, in 1783, and in the following year Walter opened the

Logographic Press, at which he printed some 140 books between 1784 and 1792. *The Times* itself (until 1788 called *The Daily Universal Register*) was also printed logographically during these years. Although ingenious, logography was a commercial failure because, despite the claims made for it, it actually increased composition time because of the great number of sorts required and the size and complexity of the case needed to accommodate them.

The logographic principle now survives only in the logotypes, or logos, which are a familiar feature of modern trade marks and advertising.

See John Feather, 'John Walter and the Logographic Press', *PH* (1977), p. 92.

See also **Case**; **Sort**; **Typecasting**; **Typesetting**; **Walter, John** (1739–1812)

London Society of Compositors

See **Typographical Association**

London Typographical Society

See **Typographical Association**

Long Primer

See **Type size**

Longman

Publishing house. The firm, one of the oldest in the world, was founded in 1724 by Thomas Longman (1699–1755), although the bookshop which he bought ('The Ship') had existed since at least 1640. In 1725, Longman was joined at The Ship by John Osborn, to whom he had been apprenticed, and whose daughter he married. This partnership and marriage gave him an advantageous start in his career, and he quickly became a leading member of the trade, not only as a bookseller, but increasingly as the owner of shares in copyrights. Typically of the period, he functioned both as bookseller and publisher, but it was publishing which came to occupy the greater part of his time. His publishing activities were largely in the lucrative field of non-fiction; one of the major (and most profitable) enterprises in which he had shares was Chambers' *Cyclopaedia* (1734). His nephew, also Thomas (1730–1797), inherited the business, and moved into the field of literary publishing, his books including *Humphry Clinker* and other novels. He also, however, followed his uncle's practices, and was, for example, a sharer in Johnson's *Dictionary* (1755).

The family tradition was continued by Thomas Norton Longman (1771–1842), who in 1794 entered into partnership with Owen Rees, a Bristol bookseller, an event which marked the beginning of a long series of complex partnerships which characterised the firm in the nineteenth century. From this time, the retail business was gradually abandoned, and the house became purely a publisher. Thomas Norton (known in the firm as Thomas III) was the publisher of Wordsworth, while his successors included Disraeli and Macaulay among their authors. By the middle of the nineteenth century, Longmans was one of the most staid and respectable of the London publishing houses, and vastly improved its economic base by entering the expanding and lucrative field of school textbooks. This was further developed after World War I, when Longmans opened branches throughout the then British Empire, and became a major force in educational publishing overseas, especially in anglophone Africa. In 1968, the last generation of publishing Longmans took their firm into the Financial and Provincial Publishing company, a large and successful newspaper group which was then renamed Pearson Longman Ltd. This is now one of the major conglomerates of British publishing, with wide newspaper interests (including *The Financial Times*), Penguin Books and Ladybird Books, as well as Longmans itself.

The archives of Longmans from the early nineteenth century onwards, with the exception of the correspondence files which were destroyed in the Blitz in 1940, are substantially intact, and are now in the library of the University of Reading. They have been published with an index, on microfilm. The existence of this massive archive and the long family tradition have made the firm exceptionally conscious of its own history. The most substantial product to date of this interest is *Essays in the History of Publishing* (1974), edited by Asa Briggs for the firm's 250th anniversary. The same anniversary saw the publication of Philip Wallis's *At the Sign of the Ship 1724–1924* (1974), a great improvement on its bicentennial predecessor, *The House of Longman 1724–1924* (1924), by Harold Cox and John E. Chandler. C. J. Longman, *The House of Longman 1724–1800* (1936) is a detailed record of the firm's publications in the eighteenth century. Wallis includes a full account of the family, and of the bewildering succession of partnerships and associated imprints. All of these will, no doubt, be superseded by the history of the firm now being written by Asa Briggs.

See also **Bookseller**; **Publisher**; **Share books**

Lower board

See **Bookbinding**

Lowndes, William Thomas (*c.* 1798–1884)

Bibliographer. The son of a bookseller, Lowndes worked in the trade himself, but devoted most of his life to his bibliographical work. In 1834, he published

The Bibliographer's Manual, a listing of over 50,000 books published in Britain up to that time. Each entry gave the author and, if possible, the printer, and the then current price. Lowndes had access to Heber's library, and hence to many thousands of rare books. He became well known in book circles in London, but he never advanced in the trade, and in the 1850s and 1860s he worked for H.G. Bohn, a publisher, who revised the *Manual* for the edition of 1857–64 in which it is now usually consulted.

See the brief notice in *DNB*; and G.W. Cole, 'Do you know your Lowndes?', *PBSA* (1939), p. 1.

See also **Heber, Richard** (1774–1833)

Luttrell, Narcissus (1657–1732)

Book collector and diarist. Luttrell came from a wealthy background and was educated at Cambridge and Gray's Inn. He never practised any profession, however, and from the mid-1670s he devoted himself almost entirely to book collecting and to recording the public events of his time. As a collector his chief interests were in poetry and politics and he bought comprehensively in both fields. He usually recorded the date of purchase underneath the imprint in a neat and distinctive hand, and, since he normally bought his books on the day they were published, Luttrell's copies are very valuable to bibliographers and book historians. The collection was broken up after his death, and his books are now to be found in many libraries and private collections. His diary, published as *A Brief Relation of State Affairs* (6 vols, 1857) from the manuscripts in All Souls' College Oxford, is a very important source for the historian of the period.

See James M. Osborn, 'Reflections on Narcissus Luttrell (1657–1732)', *BC* (1957), p. 15.

McKerrow, Ronald Brunlees (1872–1940)

Bibliographer. McKerrow was the son of an engineer, and was intended for the family business; he worked in it briefly after leaving Harrow, but then went to Cambridge where he was a contemporary of W.W. Greg. They became firm friends, and as undergraduates generated many of the ideas on bibliography and textual criticism which they were to refine during the rest of their lives. McKerrow taught in Japan after going down, but shortly after his return, he became in 1908 a director of the publishing house of Sidgwick and Jackson where he remained until his death. He had already published the first three volumes of his great edition of Nashe (1904–5), and two more were to follow (1908, 1910). This was the first major edition in which the new 'bibliographical' techniques of textual criticism were applied, and is a landmark in English studies. McKerrow was also involved, with Greg and Pollard, in the work of The Bibliographical Society, and made many important contributions to *TBS* and *The Library*, as well as compiling three substantial works for the Society: *A Dictionary of Printers and Booksellers...1557–1640* (1910); *Printers' and Publishers' Devices in England & Scotland 1485–1640* (1913); and, with F.S. Ferguson, *Title-page Borders in England and Scotland 1485–1640* (1932). All are still standard works.

McKerrow's interest in education, first aroused in Japan, was reflected in his lectures at King's College, London, which became his classic *Introduction to Bibliography* (1927), a book which remains one of the best on the subject for beginners. He also continued to edit sixteenth- and seventeenth-century texts, and in 1925 was the founding Editor of *The Review of English Studies* which, by his exacting standards, he soon made into one of the leading journals in its field. In 1929 he was invited to edit Shakespeare for the Clarendon Press, and in 1939 he published his *Prolegomena*, a classic statement of the techniques of editing texts preserved only in printed witnesses. Greg, a more adventurous spirit, found the *Prolegomena* somewhat austere and conservative in its approach, and in fact the Oxford Shakespeare never appeared as McKerrow had intended it for, although he had apparently edited some 14 plays by the time of his death, the project was abandoned in wartime, and not fully revived until the 1970s.

Greg wrote the obituary of McKerrow in *PBA* (1940). p. 488; and F.C. Francis's list of his writings is in *Libr.* (1940–41), p. 229. Both are reprinted, the latter with revisions, in John Phillip Immroth, *Ronald Brunlees McKerrow: A selection of his essays* (1974).

See also **Bibliographical Society**; **Bibliography**; **Greg, Sir Walter Wilson** (1875–1959); **Pollard, Alfred William** (1859–1944); **Textual criticism**

Magazines

Periodicals published at intervals varying from weekly to quarterly. The word means 'storehouse', and was used in the sense of 'storehouse of knowledge' in book titles in the late seventeenth and early eighteenth centuries. It was first applied to a periodical by Cave in *The Gentleman's Magazine* in 1731, and, because of the success of that journal, became the generic term.

General interest periodicals were first published in the late seventeenth century, when they were particularly associated with John Dunton. Few were long-lived, although one or two in the early eighteenth century, notably *The Tatler* (1709–11) and *The Spectator* (1711–14), are remembered for the literary eminence of their editors and contributors. The success of *The Gentleman's Magazine* set the pattern for the eighteenth century, although the many imitators of its contents, style and periodicity never matched its popularity. A new pattern was set by *The Edinburgh Review* (1802), with quarterly publication, immensely long and learned articles, and overt political commitment. The monthlies did, however, continue to flourish throughout the nineteenth century, especially the general literary magazines such as *The Cornhill Magazine* and *Blackwood's Magazine*. These literary and general interest magazines were notable for their reviews, as well as for the publication of original articles and of fiction. Their descendants are to be found in the 'little' magazines of the literary world, and in the reviewing periodicals such as *The Times Literary Supplement* and *The New York Review of Books*.

Special interest magazines, whether for particular groups (such as women) or on particular subjects (such as music), also originated in the late seventeenth century, and proliferated in the eighteenth. The great age of such magazines, however, has been since the middle of the nineteenth century, when technological advances in printing and papermaking made it possible to produce long print runs rapidly at low prices.

The learned journal can trace its origin from *The Philosophical Transactions of the Royal Society* (1665), which still continues, but its modern history begins with the professionalisation of the academic world in the last quarter of the nineteenth century. A further development of the last 100 years has been that of journals published by professional associations, trades unions, societies and other organisations for their own members.

There is no general history of magazines, but among the specialist literature there is: C. Lennart Carlson, *The First Magazine. A history of the 'Gentleman's Magazine'* (1938); A.J. Meadows, (ed.), *Development of Science Publishing in Europe* (1980); Derek Roper, *Reviewing before the Edinburgh 1788–1802* (1978); and Cynthia L. White, *Women's Magazines 1693–1968* (1970).

See also **Book reviews**; **Dunton, John** (1654–1732); **Gentleman's Magazine, The**

Mainz *Catholicon*

Printed book. The *Catholicon* is a Latin dictionary and grammar written by Joannes Balbus in the late thirteenth century. The first edition was printed at Mainz in 1460, and some scholars ascribe it to Gutenberg himself. Others, however, consider it to have been printed by Fust and Schoeffer, Gutenberg's successors, or by Heinrich Keffer, a former employee of Gutenberg.

See Aloys Ruppel, *Die Technik Gutenbergs und ihre Vorstüfe* (1961).

See also **Dictionaries**; **Gutenberg, Johann** (1394/99–1468)

Mainz Psalter

The first dated printed book completed, according to the colophon, on 14 August 1457. It was printed by Fust and Schoeffer at Mainz using the materials and equipment which they had taken over from Gutenberg. It is a magnificent book clearly intended to imitate the manuscript Psalters then in use for liturgical purposes.

See also **Colophon**; **Gutenberg, Johann** (1394/99–1468)

Maittaire, Michael (1668–1747)

Classical scholar and incunabulist. The son of a Huguenot exile, Maittaire was educated at Westminster and Oxford, and then became a schoolmaster, and later a private tutor, in London. His classical scholarship was considerable, and highly regarded in his own day, but he is remembered now for his *Annales typographici* (5 vols, 1719–41), the first systematic attempt to catalogue and describe fifteenth-century printed books. Although long since superseded, Maittaire's *Annales* marks the starting-point of incunabula studies and, as such, is an important landmark in the history of bibliography.

There is a life of Maittaire in *DNB*.

See also **Incunabula**

Malone, Edmond (1741–1812)

Book collector and scholar. The son of an Irish barrister, Malone was educated privately and at Trinity College, Dublin, and was himself called to the Irish Bar in 1767. In 1777, however, having inherited considerable wealth from his father, he moved to London, where he was already known in literary circles, to establish himself as a man of letters. He became friendly with Boswell, and assisted in the publication of the latter's *Life of Johnson* (1791). His chief interest, however, was in Shakespeare, and his painstaking research was to revolutionise Shakespearian studies. He substantially determined the chronology of the plays in his *Attempt to Ascertain the Order in which the Plays of Shakespeare were Written* (1778), and in a Supplement to Johnson's Shakespeare (1790) he wrote the first scholarly history of the English stage. His own edition of Shakespeare was first published in 1790, and showed a wholly new approach to the preparation of the text. Malone had studied both the First Folio and the quartos with great care, and was far more consistent than his predecessors in selecting the readings which he took into his own text. He continued to work on textual problems for the rest of his life, as well as the sources of Shakespeare's plots, and on Dryden and the Restoration drama.

Malone's scholarship derived from his unrivalled knowledge of contemporary sources and literature, the latter largely based on his own library. The core of it was some 800 volumes of early editions of Shakespeare and his contemporaries, including poetry and prose as well as drama, and with some very great rarities. He bequeathed his library to his nephew, Lord Sunderlin, with the wish that it should eventually go to a public collection. Sunderlin fulfilled this request in 1821, when he presented the collection to the Bodleian Library, Oxford.

For an excellent account of Malone's life and work see Samuel Schoenbaum, *Shakespeare's Lives* (1970). See also W.D. Macray, *Annals of the Bodleian Library* (2nd edn, 1890). A catalogue of his collection was published by the Bodleian in 1836.

See also **First Folio**; **Textual criticism**

Manière anglaise

See **Mezzotint**

Map printing

Maps, with their intricate and finely-drawn lines and their need for a high level of accuracy, present many problems to the printer. Map printing from type is impossible, and from the earliest days intaglio techniques have been used. The first edition of Ptolemey's *Geographia* (Bologna, 1477), the standard ancient and medieval geography book, has 26 engraved maps. Woodcuts were rarely used, even in the fifteenth century, because the necessary detail was almost impossible to obtain with the tools and techniques then available. Various intaglio processes were used until they were replaced by lithography in the nineteenth century. Today, both cartography itself and map printing have been revolutionised by computerised techniques, and maps, like all other printed matter, are usually printed by offset lithography, often in full colour.

For a general account of the subject, see Leo Bagrow, *History of Cartography*, rev. by R.A. Skelton (1964); and R.V. Tooley, *Maps and their Makers* (1949).

See also **Atlases**; **Intaglio**; **Lithography**; **Offset lithography**; **Woodcut**

Marbled paper

Decorated paper used for endpapers or wrappers. The decoration resembles the patterns to be found in marble, from which the name is derived. It is made by soaking a sheet of paper in a bath of gum, into which a dye is then poured. The sheet is lifted out with the dye and gum on the surface, and the marbler sweeps the dye back and forth with a special comb. When the paper dries, the pattern created by the comb remains. The technique was developed in the seventeenth century, probably in France, and by the beginning of the eighteenth century it was in use throughout Western Europe.

See Rosamond B. Loring, *Marbled Papers* (1933).

See also **Endpapers**

Mardersteig, Giovanni (1892–1977)

See **Officina Bodoni**

Matrix

See **Typecasting**

Mazarine Bible

The name sometimes given to the Forty-two line Bible, because the first copy to attract general scholarly attention was that in the library of Cardinal Mazarin (1601–1661). It is a particularly fine copy, printed on vellum and rubicated, and is now in the Bibliothèque Mazarine, Paris. Its historical importance is that the Mazarine copy is signed by the rubricator, Heinrich Cremer, with the date 24 August 1456, which establishes the *terminus ante quem* for the printing of the book. The significance of this fact was first recognised by François de Bure in 1760, and published by him in his *Bibliographie instructive* (1763–82).

See also **Forty-two Line Bible**

Mead, Richard (1673–1754)

Physician and book collector. Mead was the son of a nonconformist minister, and because of his religion, was educated privately and abroad, graduating MD from Padua in 1695. He returned to London and built up a large and fashionable practice, in which he was helped by treating Queen Anne during her last illness. He was a major collector of books, manuscripts and *objets d'art*, his book collecting concentrating especially in science and medicine. He had very wide-ranging interests, however, and was known and respected in literary circles in London, Oxford and Cambridge. After his death his library was sold at a sale lasting almost 30 days (1754, 1755: Baker). The books were widely scattered and are now to be found in many libraries and private collections.

There is a good life of Mead in *DNB*. See also Austin Dobson, 'The Bibliotheca Meadiana', *Bibliog.* (1895), p. 404.

Mearne, Samuel (1624–1683)

Bookbinder and bookseller. Mearne, the son of a yeoman farmer, was apprenticed to a London bookseller, and had his own business by 1653. In 1655 he went to Holland, where he may have been in contact with the exiled Charles II. In any case, at the Restoration he became Bookbinder to the King, and had a large and successful workshop until his death; his son Charles, joined him in the firm some time before 1678. He also employed journeymen, and took a number of apprentices. Some of the finest work of this shop was done for Charles II himself, including Bibles and service books for the Chapels Royal and for the Royal Family, and for St George's, Windsor and the Order of the Garter. Many of these are now in the British Library.

Mearne's characteristic style is the so-called 'cottage' binding; on a red or blue turkey cover is a painted panel with a roof-shaped head and tail, the whole cover being elaborately gilt-tooled in symmetrical patterns. There is usually a central lozenge for the cipher or arms of the owner. The influence is French, but the style is Mearne's own, resulting in what are perhaps the most beautiful, and certainly some of the most spectacular, bindings ever executed in England.

Mearne has been the subject of considerable scholarly controversy. E. Gordon Duff, *The Great Mearne Myth* (1918), argued that he was merely a businessman who never bound a book. His rehabilitation, and the careful identification of his work and that of his employees, pupils and imitators, was the life's work of Howard M. Nixon, which reached its consummation in his *English Restoration Bookbindings. Samuel Mearne and his contemporaries* (1974), a British Library exhibition catalogue.

See also **Bookbinding**

Measure

Technical term in typesetting. The measure is the length of the typeset line, determined, in hand-setting, by the length to which the compositor sets his composing stick. The measure is normally expressed in *Pica ems*, i.e. the number of square sorts of Pica size which would fill the line.

See Gaskell, p. 44.

See also **Composing stick**; **Compositor**; **Sort**; **Type size**; **Typesetting**

Mechanical wood

See **Papermaking**

Mergenthaler, Ottmar (1854–1899)

See **Line casting**; **Typesetting**;

Meynell, Sir Francis (1891–1975)

Typographer and publisher. Meynell, the son of a literary journalist, left Trinity College, Dublin, without a degree, and took a job with Burns and Oates, the Roman Catholic publishers, with whom he had family connections. He immediately began to take an interest in book design, and also met Stanley Morison, another Burns and Oates employee at that time. Their shared religion, left-wing politics and typographical interests brought them into a close and lasting friendship. In 1914–15 Meynell established a private press at which he used, for the first time, the Fell types from Oxford. In 1916, he established The Pelican Press, where, with Morison's help and advice, he produced very fine work, in which he tried to create a distinctive style quite unlike the revived Gothicism of Kelmscott and its imitators. His greatest achievement, however, was in the work of The Nonesuch Press, a publishing house which he founded in 1923. He insisted on the highest standards of design and production for Nonesuch books, for he was determined to prove that commercial books could be as beautiful as those of the private presses and yet be economically viable and more practical. In this he wholly succeeded, and his work at Nonesuch was a key factor in encouraging the greater awareness of design which characterised British printing and publishing in the middle of the twentieth century. Meynell and Morison between them were the inspiration for this immeasurable improvement.

Meynell's autobiography, *My Lives* (1971), is the best source for his life, but see also Ian Rogerson, *Sir Francis Meynell and the Nonesuch Press* (1979). The great work on Nonesuch, however, is John Dreyfus, *A History of the Nonesuch Press* (1981).

See also **Fell, John** (1625–1686); **Kelmscott Press**; **Morison, Stanley** (1889–1967); **Private press movement**

Mezzotint

An intaglio process of graphic printing, developed in Holland in the seventeenth century, and widely used in the eighteenth century especially in England; indeed it came to be known as the *manière anglaise*. It was first described by Alexander Browne in 1675. The distinctive feature of mezzotint is that it enables the engraver to achieve continuous tone and considerable subtlety of shading. This is a consequence of the preparation of the plate with a tool called a *rocker*, on whose rounded end are closely engraved parallel lines. The plate was roughened in a cross-hatched pattern using the rocker before it was engraved, and this gave a 'soft' quality to the resultant print.

Mezzotint was widely used for the reproduction of paintings in the mid-eighteenth century, as well as for topographical and other illustrations. Coloured mezzotints, made from multiple plates, were engraved in the eighteenth and early nineteenth centuries, with some success. After about 1790, however, mezzotint was gradually displaced by aquatint, although it continued in use into the 1820s.

See Michael Shane, 'Mezzotint engraving', *ABMR* (1976), pp. 124, 180.

See also **Aquatint**; **Colour printing**; **Intaglio**

Middle Hill Press

Private press. Middle Hill was the private press of Sir Thomas Phillipps, who used it for printing the catalogue of his manuscripts and various works derived from his library. The Press was established at his house at Middle Hill, Gloucestershire, in 1822 and from that time onwards Phillipps employed a succession of printers to operate it for him. The catalogue of the manuscripts, the most important work done at the Press, was begun in 1824, although some later parts were in fact printed elsewhere. The Press continued until 1871.

Like most of Phillipps' enterprises, the Press encountered innumerable problems, which are chronicled in A. N. L. Munby, *Phillipps Studies*, vols 3 (1954) and 4 (1956).

See also **Phillipps, Sir Thomas** (1792–1872)

Minerva Press

Publishing house, specialising in novels for circulating libraries. The Minerva Press was founded by William Lane (1745?–1814), who began as a bookseller in about 1770 and started to publish in 1773. By the mid-1770s he was publishing the novels which were to make his fortune. These were Gothic fantasies, a genre then at the height of its popularity. The literary value of these works, which were usually and mercifully anonymous, is minimal, but they were a major commercial success. In 1790, Lane moved to The Minerva in Leadenhall Street, London, which gave its name both to his Press and to the novels published there. The period from 1790 to 1810 marks the highpoint of The Minerva Press, for after Lane's retirement in 1813 his successors allowed the business to decline. The name itself was dropped in 1820; although the firm continued until 1859, it was by then just another publisher of bad novels and indifferent children's books, whereas it had once been the principal purveyor of one of the great fashions of English literary history.

There is an exhaustive study of *The Minerva Press 1790–1820* by Dorothy Blakey (1939).

Miniature books

Defined by collectors as books under 3 inches in height. Although of no particular bibliographical interest, miniature books are an important, if highly specialised, field of bibliophilic activity. A few were published in the fifteenth and sixteenth centuries, and by the seventeenth century they were comparatively common. They were usually devotional books or extracts from the Bible, and sometimes Prayer Books, intended to be carried in the pocket. In the eighteenth century miniature children's books were not uncommon, and it was from the eighteenth-century miniature almanac that the modern pocket diary evolved.

See Louis W. Bondy, *Miniature Books* (1981).

Missale speciale

A missal printed for the diocese of Constance, Switzerland, which has attracted much attention from bibliographers because it was believed at one time to have been printed before the Mainz Psalter or even perhaps before the Forty-Two line Bible. This has now been disproved, and the *Missale speciale* is believed to have been printed in *c.* 1473–74, probably at Basle. In itself, therefore, it has ceased to be interesting; but the work which finally disproved the legends about it is a classic of bibliographical analysis, especially in its pioneering use of the evidence afforded by the study of paper. This book is *The Problem of the Missale speciale* by Allan Stevenson (1967).

See also **Forty-two Line Bible**; **Mainz Psalter**

Modern face

Type style. Modern face is the generic name given to a style of type design evolved in the early eighteenth century which is characterised by flattened serifs, vertical shading and rather exaggerated 'modelling' of the letterforms so that, for example, the thick parts of the 'o' are diagonally rather than horizontally opposite to each other. The first type to exhibit these characteristics to some degree was cut by Jaugeon for the Imprimerie Royale, Paris, in 1692, and it was gradually taken up by others. Notable exponents included Baskerville, in England, and Fleischman in his work for the Enschedés in the Netherlands. By the late eighteenth century, it was the normal form of both roman and italic, and, despite a revival of Old face in recent years, it has continued to be so.

See A.F. Johnson, *Type Designs* (3rd edn, 1966).

See also **Baskerville, John** (1706–1775); **Enschedé**; **Italic**; **Old face**; **Roman**; **Serif**

Monotype

Typecasting and typesetting system. Monotype, invented by Tolbert Lanston (1844–1913), an American, in 1887, is a 'hot-metal' system. The operator works at a keyboard which generates a perforated paper tape, the patterns of perforation indicating specific characters. The tape is then fed through a second machine, the caster, in which compressed air is forced in a thin stream through the perforations to release a matrix of the appropriate character. Molten type metal then pours into the matrix, and a sort is cast. When a whole line has been cast, it is automatically justified by type metal which pours into the inter-word spaces. The complete line, consisting of individual sorts, is then ejected into a galley, and thus the page is gradually assembled.

Lanston finally perfected his system in 1895, and he and his backers began to market it in the USA. It was not a great success there, however, and it was the establishment of The Monotype Corporation in the UK in 1897 which marked the real beginning of its large-scale commercial exploitation. Monotype became the standard typesetting system in British book printing until it was displaced by photosetting in the 1950s and computer-assisted typesetting in the 1970s. A very high quality of product could be achieved, not least because of the work of Stanley Morison in designing a wide range of type faces specifically for the Monotype system. It became so dominant that the word was often used to mean 'letter casting machines', although it is merely a trade name.

For an extremely lucid account of the operation of the system, see Hugh Williamson, *Methods of Book Design* (3rd edn, 1983); and, for a history, Richard E. Huss, *The Development of Printers' Mechanical Typesetting Methods 1822–1925* (1973).

See also **Galley**; **Hot metal**; **Justification**; **Matrix**; **Morison, Stanley** (1889–1967); **Sort**; **Typesetting**

Mores, Edward Rowe (1730–1778)

Antiquary and historian of typefounding. Mores, the son of a clergyman, was educated at Merchant Taylors' and Oxford; being more or less of independent means, he devoted his life to scholarship, and published a number of classical and antiquarian works which commanded some respect. The beginning of what was clearly a considerable interest in printing is difficult to document, but in 1754 he was instrumental, if somewhat lethargic, in arranging for the gift of Bowyer's Anglo-Saxon types to Oxford University Press. A crucial point in the development of Mores' typographical interests, however was his purchase in 1773, of the punches and matrices of John James (d. 1772). James was the last descendant of a family and firm whose typefounding activities and equipment can be traced back to Wynkyn de Worde. Using this remarkable collection, Mores wrote his *Dissertation on English Typographical Founders and Foundries*, which was published posthumously by Nichols in 1779. It is an erratic book but it contains a wealth of information about English typefounding before it was revolutionised by Caslon in the mideighteenth century, and Mores is often the only source of our knowledge of such matters.

A Dissertation has been edited, with a valuable preface and notes, by Harry Carter and Christopher Ricks (OBS, new ser., 9, 1961).

See also **Bowyer, William** (1663–1737) **and Bowyer, William** (1699–1777); **Caslon, William** (1692–1766) **and Caslon, William** (1720–1778) **de Worde, Wynkyn** (*c.* 1455–1534); **Matrix**; **Nichols, John** (1745–1826); **Typecasting**

Morison, Stanley (1889–1967)

Typographer. Morison had a difficult childhood and only an elementary education, and on leaving school he took a minor clerical position in the City. On 10 September 1912 he happened to see the special 'Printing Number' of *The Times*, and this accident changed the course of his life. Fascinated by what he read there about printing history and technology, and the design of type, he obtained a job on *The Imprint*, and went thence to Burns and Oates, where he met Francis Meynell. After World War I, during which he had been imprisoned as a conscientious objector (having been converted to both Roman Catholicism and Marxism, beliefs which he continued to hold simultaneously) he joined Meynell at The Pelican Press.

In 1923, he was appointed Typographical Adviser to The Monotype Corporation, with which he was to be associated until the end of his life. He already had strongly held views on typography, and was now able to put them into practice from a very influential position. He modified such classic designs as Garamond and Caslon to suit the needs of machine composition, while introducing many contemporary faces into the Monotype repertory. Because Monotype so dominated the British printing industry, Morison's designs were used in almost all British book printing for nearly half a century. He was more directly involved with the revival of fine typography at Cambridge University Press, where he became a consultant in 1925, and he was instrumental in making the Press perhaps the best printing house in the world from the points of view of typography and design. A further critical appointment was in 1929 when he was asked to redesign *The Times*. Morison's new *Times*, using the Times New Roman type which he specially designed for it, first appeared on 3 October 1933.

Morison was an enthusiastic, if occasionally impressionistic, historian of both newspapers and typography. He was the anonymous author of the official *History of The Times* (5 vols, 1935–52), and also wrote a more general history of the English newspaper (1932), as well as numerous other monographs and periodical articles. His masterpiece, of whose scholarship there is no question, is *John Fell: the University Press and the 'Fell' types*; it was published by Oxford University Press in 1967, on the day after its author's death.

There is a sparkling biography of Morison by Nicholas Barker (1972), and a *Handlist* of his writings by Tony Appleton (1976). A volume of *Selected Essays*, edited by D. J. McKitterick, was published in 1981.

See also **Cambridge University Press**; **Meynell, Sir Francis** (1891–1975); **Monotype**

Morris, William (1834–1896)

See **Kelmscott Press**

Mould

See **Papermaking**

Moxon, Joseph (1627–1691)

Printer and writer on printing. Moxon was born in Wakefield, Yorkshire, but was probably brought up in Holland where his father, James, was a printer from 1637 to 1643. James Moxon was a Puritan, and involved in printing English Bibles in Holland; he returned to London after the outbreak of the Civil War, and father and son were in partnership from 1646 to 1649. The younger Moxon then abandoned printing for map- and globe-making, and established a business in this trade and in the closely associated trade of mathematical instrument-making, in 1653. This continued to be an important part of his life, although by 1655 at the latest he was, once again, a printer. He was active in the book trade not only as a printer, but also as a publisher and as a writer. In the latter capacity, he wrote on cartography, instrument-making and mathematics. In 1678, he issued the first part of his *Mechanick Exercises*, which was published in 14 parts (and was one of the first part books) before the spring of 1680.

The second volume of *Mechanick Exercises*, which was designed as a general guide to various skills and crafts, was published in 24 parts in 1683–84, and is the work for which he is now remembered. It deals with the art of printing, and is the first detailed description of all aspects of the craft. Moxon deals with the common press itself, punchcutting and typefounding, and composition and printing, describing in great detail the equipment, materials and techniques in use in the seventeenth century. It is by far the most important source for our knowledge of all of these matters, and one of the key works in printing history.

The text has been edited, with valuable annotation and commentary, by Herbert Davis and Harry Carter (2nd edn, 1962).

See also **Common press**; **Part books**; **Punch**; **Typefounding**; **Typesetting**

Munby, Alan Noel Latimer (1913–1975)

Librarian and book historian. Munby, the son of an architect, was educated at Clifton and Cambridge, and was already collecting books on a large scale as an undergraduate. After going down he worked for Quaritch, the antiquarian booksellers, but he went off to war in 1939, and on his return, he became Librarian of his old college, King's, a post which he held for the rest of life. His great interest was in the history of book collecting, and his scholarly reputation rests on his five volumes of *Phillipps Studies* (1951–60), in which he explored for the first time the vagaries and achievements of that greatest of collectors; *The Cult of the Autograph Letter in England* (1962); and *Con-*

noisseurs and Medieval Miniatures (1972), whose title conceals a masterly study of the bibliophilic aspects of the Gothic revival of the late eighteenth and early nineteenth centuries. He also wrote many periodical articles on both book collecting and the history of the antiquarian book trade.

Munby was a sociable and humane man, with a wide circle of friends. The regard in which he was held was evident after his untimely death when an appeal in his memory rapidly raised the funds to endow the annual Fellowship in Bibliography at Cambridge University Library which bears his name. The Library also bought his substantial collection of book sale catalogues and other rare and valuable materials on the history of the trade.

A selection of his *Essays and Papers* was edited posthumously by Nicholas Barker (1977); the volume includes a list of his writings. There are tributes in *TCBS*(1974), p. 203, and *BC*(1975), p. 191.

Murray, John (1778–1843)

Publisher. Murray's father, a retired army officer, bought a bookselling business in London in 1768, but was soon more involved with publishing than with bookselling. Indeed, the elder Murray's years in the trade more or less coincided with the emergence of publishing as a distinct occupation, and he was one of the first members of the trade to whom the description 'publisher' can be applied in the modern sense. He died in 1793, and the business continued in the hands of his partner until John Murray was old enough to take over in 1799. The younger Murray laid the foundations for the firm to become one of the great nineteenth-century publishing houses, both by his perceptive recruitment of authors and by his considerable skills as a businessman. The starting-point was his association with Scott's publisher, Archibald Constable, which began in 1802. In 1809, Murray established *The Quarterly Review*, which the firm published until 1922. His most famous author, however, was Byron, whose *Childe Harold* (1812) made Murray's fortune on the same day that it made Byron famous. He continued to publish Byron, although he later besmirched the connection by destroying the manuscript of Byron's memoirs because of its allegedly scandalous contents.

On a different level, the *Family Library* series (1829–34) was one of the first major series of cheap books which took advantage of the technical advances in printing in the early nineteenth century. Indeed, there was always a streak of radicalism in Murray, although he was at heart a Tory and in later life was more cautious in his selection of books for publication. He bequeathed a flourishing business to his son, and the firm is still in the hands of the Murray family.

The firm's archives are still owned by Murrays, but access is difficult. Samuel Smiles' *A Publisher and his Friends* (1891) is a minor classic of Victorian biography, but is uncompromisingly 'official' in tone. The life of Murray in *DNB* is largely based on Smiles. Scott Bennett, who was granted selective access to the archives, has written an important article on 'John Murray's Family Library and the cheapening of books in the early nineteenth century', *SB* (1976), p. 139, but it has to be assumed that a vast amount of important and still untapped material is in the archives which, if it were more generally available, would be of great importance to the historian of the book in nineteenth-century England.

See also **Publisher**

Music printing

The printing of musical notation is almost as old as the art of printing itself but, through the centuries, it has always presented special difficulties, and consequently has become a highly specialised activity. The basic technical problem is the need to superimpose the notation, bar lines etc. on the stave lines, as well as the need to differentiate visually between notes of different values both by linking them and by having an 'open' or a 'closed' note.

The earliest printed music is in fifteenth-century service books, and here various solutions were adopted. The music might be written in by hand, as in the Mainz Psalter; the stave might be printed and the notes added by hand, or the notes printed, and the staves added by hand; or two impressions could be taken, one for the notes and one for the staves. In the late fifteenth century, the first music type was cut, with sorts for each note on each line and space of the stave and all five stave lines on each sort. Although the type was difficult both to cut and to set, typographic music printing was widely practised throughout Europe in the sixteenth and seventeenth centuries.

By the middle of the sixteenth century, Italian music printers were using intaglio processes to produce music from engraved plates. This was expensive, but the results were aesthetically preferable to typographic printing, and a careful engraver could achieve a high degree of accuracy. By the eighteenth century, intaglio was the normal process for music printing.

Lithography began to be used by music printers almost as soon as it was introduced, and by the middle of the nineteenth century it had largely displaced intaglio. Its great advantage was that the lithographer could not only work directly on the stone or plate, but could also correct his mistakes more easily. In the twentieth century, various mechanical devices have been made for setting music, including a special line casting machine and, more recently, computer-assisted photosetters.

Because of its technical diffculty and the limited market, printed music has always been expensive compared to other books, and its production and sale concentrated in a few specialised firms. Consequently its study is also specialised, and the literature often requires and assumes a considerable knowledge of musicology. For the non-specialist, a useful theoretical starting-point is Donald W. Krummel, 'Musical functions and bibliographical forms', *Libr.* (1976), p. 327. For a general survey, see A. Hyatt King, *Four Hundred Years of Music Printing* (1964); and the article by H. Edmund Poole and Donald W. Krummel in Stanley Sadie (ed.), *The New Grove* (1980), vol. 15, p. 232, which includes a bibliography. On the music trade in Britain, see Donald W. Krummel, *English Music Printing 1553–1700* (1975); and Charles

Humphries and William C. Smith, *Music Publishing in the British Isles* (2nd edn, 1970).

See also **Impression**; **Intaglio**; **Line casting**; **Lithography**; **Mainz Psalter**; **Photosetting**; **Sort**

National Graphical Association

See **Typographical Association**

Net Book Agreement

A price-fixing mechanism in the British book trade. In essence, the NBA allows the publisher to fix the price at which his books must be sold at bookshops in the UK. Booksellers who sell at reduced prices will not be supplied at trade rates, by way of 'punishment'. In practice, there are exceptions for the benefit of major groups of customers: public libraries and various societies and organisations can get a 10 per cent discount on the net price, and prices are generally reduced for all customers during the annual National Book Sale. Most school books, sold in bulk to Local Education Authorities, are non-net, and the price is negotiable between supplier and customer. Net prices do not apply to export sales.

The adoption of net prices was proposed by Alexander Macmillan (1818–1896) in 1890, as a solution to the problem of 'underselling' which had bedevilled the trade throughout the nineteenth century. Larger bookshops were able to offer larger discounts, and were demanding proportionately larger discounts from publishers; the effect was to undermine the profitability both of the smaller bookshops and, ultimately, of the publishers themselves. During the 1890s, Macmillan's idea was gradually accepted by both sides of the trade, and their two representative bodies, the Publishers' Association (founded 1896) and the Associated Booksellers (founded 1895, and now the Booksellers' Association), negotiated a mutually acceptable agreement which came into force on 1 January 1900. After initial difficulties it was accepted throughout the trade.

In 1962 the legality of the NBA was challenged under the Restrictive Trade Practices Act (1956). After a lengthy hearing the court decided that the NBA was in the public interest because it ensured the continued existence of a large number of bookshops and also enabled publishers to take risks on less profitable titles, in both cases because it defended and even guaranteed profit margins. More recently, the NBA has been questioned again, on economic grounds, and it may eventually wither away. There is no doubt, however, that it has ensured the comparative well-being, and perhaps even the survival, of the trade during the last 80 years.

Similar price-fixing arrangements have also existed in France, Sweden and Australia, but all have now been abandoned. No such system is possible in the USA, because it would be illegal under the anti-trust laws.

For the historical background, see James J. Barnes, *Free Trade in Books* (1964). The events of 1956–62 are fully chronicled in R. E. Barker and G.R. Davies (eds), *Books are Different* (1966).

See also **Booksellers' Association**; **Publishers' Association**

New English Bible

See **Bibles**

Newberry Library

Research library in Chicago, Illinois, USA. The Newberry was founded in the will of Walter L. Newberry (1804–1868), a Chicago shipping and real estate magnate; but because of his widow's life interest, the bequest became effective only in 1886 when she died. The Library opened in 1892. The original concept was of a public reference library, but even before opening the purchase of some 2500 rare books, including incunabula, from Henry Probasco set the Newberry on the road to being a specialised research library in the humanities. The Library has come to specialise in Americana (including Latin America), cartography and printing history, as well as having a large reference collection in these fields, and substantial general holdings of early printed books of all kinds other than science and medicine. There is also an active programme of Fellowships and research projects. Since 1944, the Library has published the *Newberry Library Bulletin.*

There is a history of the Newberry by Lawrence W. Towner in *ELIS,* 19 (1970), p. 450, and the same author's *A Collection of Uncommon Collections: The Newberry Library* (2nd edn, 1976) is the best guide to its great riches. There are published catalogues of the William B. Greenlee collection of Latin Americana and Portuguese material (1953); the John M. Wing Foundation collection on printing history (1961); and other collections.

Newbery, John (1713–1767)

Publisher. Newbery was the son of a farmer in Waltham St Lawrence, Berkshire, and went to work with William Carnan, a bookseller and printer, in nearby Reading. In 1737 he inherited a half-share of Carnan's business. He published a few books in Reading, but in 1744 he moved to London, where he was to remain for the rest of his life. Gradually he came to specialise in children's books, publishing not only school books but also leisure reading for young children. In the latter field he was a pioneer, and has some claim to be regarded as one of the originators of the children's book. It was for his children's books that Newbery developed the idea of the edition binding, of which he is usually considered to be the inventor. Children's book publishing proved very profitable, and Newbery's commercial success was further enhanced by his purchase of a half-share in Dr James's Fever Powder, a widely used patent medicine. Newbery also published adult literature, including Johnson's *Idler* (1761), and a number of works by Goldsmith, Smart and others.

The best account of Newbery is still that by Charles Welsh, *A Bookseller of the Last Century* (1885), which includes transcripts of many important documents, some of which can no longer be traced. Welsh's list of Newbery's publications is updated, although not with untarnished accuracy, by Sydney Roscoe in his *John Newbery and his Successors* (1973).

See also **Children's books**; **Edition binding**

Newspapers

A newspaper is usually defined as a serial publication issued at regular intervals between daily and weekly, whose primary function is to carry stories about current events. Occasional publications about such events were issued as early as the beginning of the sixteenth century, but they lack the essential element of periodicity. In its true form, the newspaper is a Dutch invention; by 1619, and possibly earlier, there was a weekly paper in Amsterdam. The first English newspaper, *Courant out of Italy*, was also published at Amsterdam (1620–21) for import into England. In 1621, Thomas Archer and Nathaniel Butter began to publish the *Courante* in London, but each issue had to be passed by the censors, and in 1632 all newsbooks, as they were usually called, were banned, despite the fact that they contained only foreign news.

The revival of the newspapers, and their entry into the field of home news, was a consequence of the disputes between Charles I and Parliament. The first of these newspapers was the weekly *Heads of Severall Proceedings* (1641). Throughout the Civil War (1642–48), both sides issued weekly newspapers for propaganda purposes, and by 1650 the newly-established republican government had its official newspaper, *Mercurius Politicus*. After the Restoration, the press was strictly controlled, only two newspapers being allowed. During the 1670s, however, the controls broke down, and after the lapse of the Printing Act in 1695, there was not even a notional pre-publication censorship.

In the freer political climate which followed the Revolution of 1688, the newspapers proliferated and flourished. The first successful daily, *The Daily Courant* started in 1702, and the eighteenth-century pattern was of daily, weekly and thrice-weekly papers published in London, the latter being widely distributed throughout the country. The provincal newspapers, which began in the first years of the eighteenth century, were weekly, and did little more than reprint news from the London papers. Politicians were not entirely happy about this proliferation of newspapers, but their popularity was such that they had to learn to live with them. There were, however, government-owned newspapers, and subsidies (i.e. bribes) for editors and proprietors were common until the middle of the nineteenth century. In addition, from 1712, there was a Stamp Duty on newspapers, which had reached punitive levels by the end of the eighteenth century, and effectively restricted circulation to the comparatively wealthy.

In the nineteenth century, the newspaper industry began to undergo a series of technological revolutions in its search for greater speed and quantity in production. The first came with steam-powered presses, an era inaugurated by the use of the Koenig press at *The Times* in 1814. Thereafter, successive generations of machines facilitated high-speed printing on machine-made paper. The introduction of mechanical typesetting in the second half of the century, and especially the almost universal adoption of Linotype, completed the first revolution in newspaper technology. The final abolition of the Stamp Duty in 1856 was the economic equivalent of steam-printing. It was now possible to produce a daily paper which sold for a penny or even a halfpenny. Indeed, the late nineteenth century was in some ways the golden age of the newspaper in Britain, with the London dailies, widely distributed by rail, supplemented by daily morning and evening papers in even quite small provincial towns.

The second revolution is more recent, and not yet complete, as proprietors and trades unions continue to struggle about such issues as direct computer input by journalists into typesetters which can generate the plates for offset lithographic printing. The cost of this new technology, like much of that introduced since the middle of the nineteenth century, has made the newspaper industry an expensive one in which to operate, and the trend is increasingly towards the ownership of many titles by a few large corporations.

Over the centuries, the appearance of the newspaper has undergone a change as radical as that in its production. The early newsbooks were in a half sheet quarto format, which remained unchanged until the second half of the seventeenth century. The adoption of the half sheet folio broadside in the 1660s marked the beginning of the modern appearance of the newspaper. By the middle of the century, the size of the sheet was increasing, and as advertising came to take up more space (and became the economic mainstay of many papers) the bifolium became the usual form of the newspaper. The speed of the steam presses made larger papers possible, and by the mid-nineteenth century the multi-paged broadside newspaper of today was already familiar.

The nineteenth-century newspaper was filled with political and foreign news of great seriousness; layout was, at best, unexciting; headlines and illustrations were unknown. All this was changed by Alfred Harmsworth (1865–1922), later Lord Northcliffe, who launched *The Daily Mail* in 1896. The *Mail* was a tabloid size, had bold headlines and prominent photographs, and used a simple and direct journalistic style which was designed to appeal to the mass audience created by mass literacy. Northcliffe's greatest imitator was Max (later Lord) Beaverbrook, who bought the ailing *Daily Express* in 1913, and turned it into one of the world's most successful newspapers while also using it to further his own political career and disseminate his ideas. These innovations affected even the 'heavy' papers like *The Times*, which began to carry photographs and revise their layouts.

The history of the British press has been largely conditioned by the *de facto* freedom which it has enjoyed, to a greater or lesser extent, since the beginning of the eighteenth century. Indeed, a free press has come to be regarded as one of the distinguishing characteristics of an open society. Consequently, the history of the newspaper in other countries has been determined by their political histories. In the British colonies in North America the situation in the seventeenth and eighteenth centuries was similar to that in Britain itself. Royal control, exercised through the Governor of each colony, was strict in the mid-seventeenth century; it gradually diminished until by the mid-eighteenth century the newspapers were playing a crucial role in moving public opinion in favour of independence. After the Revolution, press freedom was guaranteed by the First Amendment to the US Constitution, and the USA has, since then, developed an aggressively independent press, less trammelled by libel laws and governmental secrecy than anywhere else in the world. In Europe developments were slower. Official newspapers existed in the seventeenth and eighteenth centuries but, in general, a free press in the Anglo-American sense was a consequence of revolutions in the nineteenth century or later. In Germany, for example, there was no press freedom until 1945, save for the brief interlude of the Weimar Republic (1918–33). In the socialist countries and in most countries of the Third World (with the notable exception of India) the press is controlled by the organs of the state or the ruling party.

There is a huge literature on newspaper history, although adequate scholarly works are rare. Anthony Smith, *The Newspaper. An international history* (1979) is a popular and competent general history; Stanley Morison, *The English Newspaper 1622–1932* (1932) remains for all its defects perhaps the best introduction to the history of the British press. On the earliest period, see Joseph Frank, *The Beginnings of the English Newspaper 1620–1660* (1961). For the eighteenth century, the best starting-point is the essay by Michael Harris, in George Boyce, James Curran and Pauline Wingate (eds), *Newspaper History* (1978). The nineteenth century has been better worked; two central studies are Joel H. Weiner, *The War of the Unstamped* (1969); and Alan J. Lee, *The Origins of the Popular Press, 1855–1914* (1976). The bibliographical history of newspapers is highly complex. For the earliest period, see Folke Dahl, *Bibliography of English Corantos and Periodical Newsbooks, 1620–1642* (1952). More generally, R.S. Crane and F.B. Kaye, *A Census of British Newspaper and Periodicals 1620–1800* (1927) is valuable, as is *The Tercentenary Handlist of English and Welsh Newspapers* (1920).

Among the general works on the American press are John Tebbel, *A Compact History of the American Newspaper* (1963); and F.L. Mott, *American Journalism: a history 1690–1960* (1969). The European press has been well served by scholars, notably in the superb *Historie générale de la presse française* (4 vols, 1969), edited by C. Bellanger and others. For Germany, see M. Lindemann, *Die Deutsche Presses bis 1815* (1969), and for Italy, V. Castronovo and N. Tranfaglia, *Storia della stampa italiana* (5 vols, 1976).

See also **Broadside**; **Folio**; **Koenig press**; **Linotype**; **Offset lithography**; **Printing Act 1662**; **Quarto**; **Stamp Acts**

Nichols, John (1745–1826)

Printer and antiquary. Nichols, the son of a banker, was apprenticed to the younger Bowyer. Impressed by his talents, Bowyer made him partner in the business in 1767, and at his death left him a substantial legacy, including the firm itself. In the following year, Nichols bought a half-share in *The Gentleman's Magazine* from the heir of Cave's nephew, and in the next few years he gradually bought up the other shares. By 1792 he was solely responsible for *The Gentleman's Magazine*, and brought it to the height of its fame and popularity. In 1808, his printing house was destroyed by fire, and he lost his stock and £10,000 above the value of the insurance. The firm was, however, re-established, and was inherited by his son, John Bowyer Nichols (1779–1863), and his grandson, John Gough Nichols (1806–1873). As J.B. Nichols and Sons it survived until 1898.

As a printer and publisher Nichols produced many important books, but he was also a major antiquary in his own right. His masterpiece is *The History and Antiquities of the Town and County of Leicester* (8 vols, 1795–1815), the grandest and one of the best of the classic county histories. His work brought him into contact with many of his fellow antiquaries, notably Richard Gough (1735–1809), the *de facto* leader of this band of amateur scholars. His other great works were *Literary Anecdotes of the Eighteenth Century* (9 vols, 1812–15), and *Illustrations of the Literary History of the Eighteenth Century* (6 vols, 1817–31; with 2 further vols by J.B. Nichols, 1848, 1858). *Literary Anecdotes* is an expansion of his *Biographical and Literary Anecdotes of William Bowyer* (1782), and is a vast storehouse of first-hand information about the personalities of the book trade itself and the literary and antiquarian worlds of the late eighteenth century.

There is a good life of Nichols in *DNB*, and an interesting paper on him by Robin Myers in Robin Myers and Michael Harris, (eds), *Development of the English Book Trade, 1700–1899* (1981). On his involvement with *The Gentleman's Magazine*, see James M. Kuist, 'The *Gentleman's Magazine* in the Folger Library: the history and significance of the Nichols family collection', *SB* (1976), p. 307. A substantial part of his post-1806 archive is in the Bodleian Library, for which see *BLR* (1978), p. 360, and the Bodleian also has Nichols' own copy of his *Literary Anecdotes* annotated for a revised edition which was never published. A good book-length study of Nichols is a major desideratum.

See also **Bowyer, William** (1663–1737) **and Bowyer, William** (1699–1777); *Gentleman's Magazine, The*

Nineteenth-Century Short Title Catalogue

Reference work. *NSTC* is a cumulation of the catalogue entries for nineteenth-century British books in the British Library, the Bodleian Library, the National Library of Scotland, Trinity College, Dublin, Cambridge University Library, and the Library of Newcastle upon Tyne University. It started in 1983, and vol. 1, covering the letters A–C for the period 1801–15, was published in 1984. Preparation of subsequent volumes continues apace under the direction of the Editor, F.J.G. Robinson. *NSTC* is a commercial publication by Avero Publications Ltd, of Newcastle upon Tyne, which also publishes an occasional *NSTC Newsletter.*

Nonesuch Press

See **Meynell, Sir Francis** (1891–1975)

Nonpareil

See **Type size**

North American Imprints Program

Bibliographical research project. NAIP is a project which is making a detailed bibliographical record of all pre-1801 North American books, following the general principles of the *Eighteenth-Century Short Title Catalogue.* Funded by the National Endowment for the Humanities and various foundations, it is based at the American Antiquarian Society, Worcester, Massachusetts. Associated with NAIP is a program of research and conferences on the history of the book in North America sponsored by the AAS. The Project Director is John B. Hench.

See *Factotum,* no. 9 (1980), pp. 2-3 and subsequent reports in almost every issue.

See also **Eighteenth-Century Short Title Catalogue**

Number books

See **Part books**

Nuremberg Chronicle

See **Illustrated books**

Octavo

Bibliographical format. An octavo, written 8°, is a sheet printed with 16 pages folded to form 8 leaves. Octavo was a very common format in the eighteenth century, when it was used for the majority of books. The page size is convenient and well-proportioned.

The best imposition diagrams for 8° are those in William Savage, *A Dictionary of the Art of Printing* (1841, repr. 1968).

See also **Format**; **Gathering**; **Imposition**

Officina Bodoni

Private press. The press was founded in 1923 by Giovanni Mardersteig (1892–1977) in the North Italian town of Montagnola. In 1927, Mardersteig moved to Verona, and the press was then named in honour of Bodoni, a native of the town. Mardersteig was in correspondence with Morison throughout the 1920s, and shared many of his ideas on typography and book design. The Officina Bodoni came to represent all that is best in twentieth-century fine printing: page layouts were generous and tasteful, illustrations were of the highest quality and the type and paper were carefully chosen for their suitability and compatibility. The Mardersteig books are highly prized by collectors for these qualities.

See Mardersteig's own history of the press translated into English by Hans Schmoller as *The Officina Bodoni. An account of the work of a hand press 1923–1977* (1980).

See also **Bodoni, Giambattista** (1740–1813); **Morison, Stanley** (1889–1967).

Offset lithography

Printing technique. The origins of offset litho (as it is usually called) can be traced back to the 1850s, when a number of experiments were carried out in making photographic images on the metal plates which had gradually displaced the stones used in the earliest forms of lithography. In 1858 a photographic facsimile of the Second Quarto of *Hamlet* was printed by this method, and was the first photolithographic book.

The second element of the process is the offset principle, by which the impression is made from the plate onto an intervening cylinder in the press, called the *blanket cylinder*, from which the image is transferred to the paper or other material to be printed. This process was developed for printing on tin in the mid-nineteenth century; the crucial breakthrough of building an offset press to print on paper was made by Ira Rubel, an American, in 1904. The combination of photographic lithography and offset printing had many advantages, especially in the potential speed of the press. It was not possible on a large scale, however, until the development of photosetting in the 1940s offered a simple method of making the plates. Gradually offset litho began to make inroads into the entrenched position of relief printing for all kinds of work, and by the late 1970s was the normal printing method in all developed countries. Compared with letterpress it is cheap, simple and clean, and can be conducted on the scale of an office as well as that of a factory.

See Eric Chambers, *Photolitho-offset* (1967).

See also **Lithography**; **Photosetting**; **Relief printing**

Old face

Type style. Old face is the generic name given to the style of roman type in general use from the early sixteenth to the mid-eighteenth centuries. The first recognisable Old face was cut for Aldus by Francesco Griffo at the very beginning of the sixteenth century. It is characterised by open letters and rather exaggerated points on the serifs. Old face was displaced by Modern face from the middle of the eighteenth century onwards, but it was revived 100 years later. In particular, the Caslon Old Face romans were popular with nineteenth-century English printers, beginning with Charles Whittingham at the Chiswick Press in the 1840s. The Old face types came to dominate book printing in Britain in the late nineteenth century, and many were subsequently recut for Monotype by Stanley Morison.

See A.F. Johnson, *Type Designs* (3rd edn, 1966).

See also **Aldus Manutius** (*c.* 1450–1515); **Modern face**; **Monotype**; **Morison, Stanley** (1889–1967); **Roman**; **Serif**

Onlay

See **Bookbinding**

Oxford Bibliographical Society

Founded 1922. The Society was founded by a group of Oxford bibliographers and librarians, most of them associated with the Bodleian. Its aim was, and is, to promote the study of bibliography in general, and the word 'Oxford' in its title is a statement of geographical location rather than range of interest. Meetings are held regularly during the winter, and the Society has two series of publications. The main series of *Proceedings and Papers* began in 1922, and was suspended at the end of vol. 5 in 1939. This series includes many important papers read to the Society. The New Series (1 (1947)– date) is its successor, but consists of monographs, bibliographies and collection of documents each filling a complete volume. The Occasional Publications (1 (1967)– date) are of works which fall in the difficult gap between the length of an article and that of a book. From 1962 to 1967 the Society published a very valuable annual series, *Bibliography in Britain,* which indexed bibliographical literature; it was, unfortunately, abandoned.

The Society's address is Bodleian Library, Oxford OX1 3BG.

See also **Bodleian Library**

Oxford University Press

Publisher and printer. The first printer in Oxford was Theodoric Rood, a German who set up a printing house in 1477 (not 1476 as was traditionally believed). Rood was licensed by the University, but only in the sense in which it had licensed booksellers and stationers for centuries, and in any case the whole enterprise was short-lived. The continuous history of the Press could be more cogently argued to begin in 1585, when Joseph Barnes was given permission to set up a press in Oxford, and to call himself Printer to the University. In practice, however, Barnes was merely an ordinary printer and bookseller, although he and his successors did inevitably publish a few scholarly works. Despite the grandiose plans of Archbishop Laud, as Chancellor of the University, in the 1630s, there was still no recognisable University Press in the modern sense.

The true history of Oxford University Press begins in 1668, when Samuel Clarke, at the initiative of John Fell, began to equip a printing house in the recently completed Sheldonian Theatre. The first books came from Fell's press in 1672, and he prepared a long-term programme of learned publishing, while equipping the Press with punches and matrixes for the exotic scripts which would be needed for work in oriental languages. Fell had considerable success with his learned publishing, although financially the Press was sustained by exercising its right to print the Bible and almanacs, and there were always difficulties in making arrangements to sell Oxford books in London and elsewhere. From this time, the Press was divided into the Bible Side and the Learned Side, a division which became physical in 1713 when it moved to the new Clarendon Building, probably the first building in England to be specially built as a printing house. In its new premises, however, the Press lost its sense of purpose, and only a trickle of books were published. The revival began when William Blackstone, the eminent lawyer, joined the Delegacy which controls the Press in 1755. He was a highly competent man of affairs, and was responsible for the reorganisation of the Press and for setting its finances on a sounder footing. A new publishing programme began, and better arrangements were made for the sale of books.

The Press gradually expanded, and in 1825–30 moved to its present premises. The Learned Press, in particular, which was now beginning to use the imprint 'Clarendon Press', flourished in the nineteenth century, as a result of the great demand for scholarly works created by educational developments in all fields of study. The Bible Side continued to make an important contribution, however, and to sustain its finances the Press also moved into the lucrative field of school and university textbooks in which it is now one of the world's major publishers. To cope with the more popular books, the London

Business emerged, which published some books and acted as the channel for Oxford books into the book trade's distribution mechanisms. Learned publishing continued in the midst of these developments, most strikingly perhaps in the *New English Dictionary*, which the Press took over from the Philological Society in 1879; now known as the *Oxford English Dictionary* it has spawned a whole family of dictionaries, and taken the name and fame of the Press round the world. The combination of learned and semi-popular publishing continues to characterise the Press, and it is now deeply involved in such diverse fields as children's books and music, as well as maintaining its commitment to the highest standards of scholarship. Unlike the university presses of America, OUP is not subsidised by the University of which it is a part, and must survive in the harsh climate of commercial publishing.

A History of the Oxford University Press was to have been the crowning achievement of the late Harry Carter, for many years the archivist of the Press. In the event, only vol. 1, covering the period to 1780, was published (1975) before Carter's death. Unfortunately, most of the specialised studies of the history of the Press fall into the same period, so that for the years after 1780 the only general source is Peter Sutcliffe, *The Oxford University Press. An informal history* (1978), which was written for the Press's self-proclaimed 'quincentary'.

See also **Clarendon Press**; **Fell, John** (1625–1686); **Matrix**; **Rood, Theodoric** (fl.1487–1480)

Page

In bibliographical usage, page and leaf must be carefully distinguished. A page is one side of a leaf, and each leaf has two pages.

Pagination

The printed numbers of the page of a book. Pagination replaced the older practice of foliation in the sixteenth century, beginning in Italy and gradually spreading throughout Europe. It had become the almost invariable practice before 1600. Page numbers were usually printed in the headline, although after the abandonment of catchwords and signatures in the nineteenth century, they were (and are) sometimes printed in the direction line.

See Rudolph Hirsch, *Printing, Selling and Reading 1450–1550* (1967).

See also **Catchword**; **Direction line**; **Foliation**; **Signature**

Pair

See **Case**

Panel stamp

Bookbinder's decorative tool. A panel stamp is a block with a design cut on it in relief, intended to cover the whole board of a book. It is impressed in a screw press rather than by hand. Panel stamps were in use in the thirteenth century, but they were confined to Cologne and the Low Countries. Only in the fifteenth century did they become more common, and they are then found in France, England and several parts of Germany. The first introduction of panel stamps into England was probably in the 1480s, and thereafter their use increased. They were at the height of their popularity in the early sixteenth century, but had fallen into disuse by about 1560.

See G.D. Hobson, *Blind-stamped Panels in the English Book Trade c. 1485–1555* (1944), which is a wide-ranging study.

See also **Bookbinding**

Panizzi, Sir Anthony (1797–1879)

See **British Museum**; **Catalogues**

Panzer, Georg Wolfgang Franz von (1729–1805)

Incunabulist. Panzer was born at Sulzbach, Germany, and educated at Altdorf University. He became a librarian, and was a pioneer student of early printed books. His *Annales typographicae ab artis inventae ad annum MDXXXVI* (11 vols, 1793–1803) was the first attempt since Maittaire to produce a comprehensive list of early printed books. Although far from complete, and superseded by the *Gesamtkatalog*, it was a remarkable work for its time, and, with the supplements of Hain and Copinger, was standard for a century.

There is a notice of Panzer in *Allgemeine Deutsches Biographie*, vol. 25 (1887), p.132.

See also **Copinger, Walter Arthur** (1847–1910); ***Gesamtkatalog des Weigendrüke***; **Maittaire, Michael** (1668–1747)

Paper

Paper is a Chinese invention, ascribed to Ts'ai Lun, a member of the Imperial Guard, in 105 AD. Some paper of the second century has indeed been found by archaeologists working in China. The use of paper and the knowledge of papermaking spread westwards along the Asian trade routes during the next 1000 years. By the mid-seventh century it was in use in Samarkand in what is now Soviet Central Asia, and it had reached Mecca in Saudi Arabia by 707, and Egypt by 800. The Arabs now spread the use of paper throughout their growing empire, its first recorded use in Europe being in Spain in 950. In the early twelfth century it was introduced into Italy and thereafter spread through Christian Europe, reaching Germany in 1282 and England in 1309. Only gradually, however, did paper displace the traditional European writing materials of parchment and vellum, for its comparative cheapness was counterbalanced by a dislike of its apparent flimsiness. Papermaking was, however, well-established in Western Europe by the time of the invention of printing in the mid-fifteenth century, and paper was the only material which could be made in suffcient quantities to satisfy the huge demands of the printers. Since the sixteenth century paper has been the only material in regular use for both writing and printing, as well as being used for packaging and other purposes.

See Dard Hunter, *Paper Making* (2nd edn, 1947).

See also **Papermaking**; **Parchment**; **Vellum**

Paper Publications Society

Publishing society. The PPS was founded in the Netherlands after World War II to issue works on the history of paper. A series of publications entitled *Monumenta Chartae Papyraceae Historiam* began in 1950. It has now reached vol. 12 (1973). The volumes are large quartos, elaborately illustrated and immensely learned, covering many aspects of papermaking, the paper trade, watermarks and other matters. The first editor was E.J. Labarre; since 1970 it has been J.S.G. Simmons.

Paperbacks

Books bound in paper, or very thin card, rather than in boards. Books had been issued in paper covers or wrappers since the sixteenth century, or even earlier, but the history of the paperback, as the term is normally understood, really begins with the foundation of Penguin Books in 1935. Allen Lane's concept of cheap books of high quality proved to be a major commercial success and soon attracted imitators for the format if not for the quality. The major developments in the paperback since 1935 have all come from the USA, the home of the mass-market paperback, which as its name suggests is printed in huge quantities and is often sold through non-bookshop outlets to maximise sales. The USA was also the source of the glossy multi-coloured decorative covers with eye-catching designs which typify the contemporary paperback.

Paperbacks have been, and remain, one of the major cultural influences of the twentieth century, for they are cheap, portable and disposable. Lane's own idealism has not been entirely lost, and thousands of worthwhile titles are widely available in paperback form for those who cannot afford the hardback. The market is, of course, dominated, and the paperback industry financed, by fast-selling popular fiction.

Hans Schmoller, a former colleague of Lane, has written an account of

Papermaking

'The paperback revolution', in Asa Briggs (ed.), *Essays in the History of Publishing* (1974). For the American scene, see Thomas L. Bonn, *Under Cover: An Illustrated History of American Mass Market Paperbacks* (1982).

See also **Lane, Sir Allen** (1902–1970); **Yellowbacks**

Papermaking

Paper is made from a pulp of fibrous vegetable substances, such as linen rags, or wood.

Traditional hand methods, in use until the early nineteenth century, involved men working in teams of three. The first step is to beat the rags into pulp; they are soaked in water and then broken down by hammers or other heavy tools. In the late seventeenth century, a machine called a *Hollander* was invented for this purpose, and was soon in general use. The liquid pulp which emerged from the Hollander was then poured into a vat. The first workman, the *vatman*, held in his hands the *mould* in which the paper was made. The mould was an open wooden rectangular frame with an internal wire mesh. The wires parallel to the shorter side of the mould were fairly thick, and about an inch apart; these are known as chains. Those parallel to the longer sides were much thinner, and much closer together; these are known as wires. It was often the practice to sew onto the chains and wires a maker's mark, usually in the middle of one half of the mould. The vatman dipped the mould into the vat, and pulled it out filled with pulp; he then shook off the loose water and surplus pulp before handing it to the second workman, the *coucher*, who turned the sheet out of the mould onto a piece of felt. Another sheet of felt was placed on top of the paper, and thus gradually a *pile* of paper and felt was created. The function of the felt was to absorb the remaining surface water. The pile was presided over by the *layman*, who was usually an apprentice. When the pile was large enough it was put into a screw press to squeeze out the water, the felt having been removed, and the paper was dried. It was then counted out into *reams*, each ream consisting of 20 quires of 24 or 25 sheets each. To maintain continuous production, moulds were used in pairs, so that the vatman was filling one while the coucher was emptying the other. Paper made by this method is called *laid paper*, and can be recognised by the chain lines and wire lines which are visible, together with watermark formed by the maker's mark, when it is held up to the light. In the late eighteenth century, James Whatman developed a mould with a much finer mesh, which dispensed with the chains. This produced *wove paper* with no chain lines.

Papermaking remained substantially unchanged until the early nineteenth century, although in the eighteenth century various chemical bleaches were introduced to improve the whiteness of the paper, and quality depended very much on the quality of the rags which were used. The great revolution came with the introduction of the Fourdrinier papermaking machines, of which the first was built by Bryan Donkin in 1807. It is still in use, although with modifications. In its modern form, since the middle of the nineteenth century, the pulp is beaten by a powered Hollander, and then flows onto a moving conveyor on which it is thinned and dried, and any necessary additives put into it, coming off the machine as a continuous roll, or *web*, of paper. This is called the 'dry end' of the machine, while the Hollander end is called the 'wet end'.

By the middle of nineteenth century the problem was not with machinery but with materials. There was an insufficient supply of linen rags for the quantity of paper needed, especially as cotton, which is unsuitable for papermaking, replaced linen as the usual cheap fabric. Various experiments were conducted with other vegetable fibres, but none was satisfactory, for the paper discoloured very quickly. In 1860–61, however, esparto grass from the eastern Mediterranean was used successfully, and became the usual papermaking fibre in Britain for some years. Meanwhile, American papermakers were experimenting with wood pulp made from the chips of untreated logs (*mechanical wood*), a process introduced into Europe in 1871. Wood treated with sulphite (*chemical wood*) proved more satisfactory; it was first used commercially in Sweden, although it was an American invention, and by the mid-1880s was in general use, as it remains to this day.

Papermaking requires large quantities of water both for the process itself and, until the late nineteenth century, to drive the machinery. Consequently paper mills are normally sited on the banks of rivers with a reliable and fast-flowing supply of pure water. The first record of a paper mill in Europe is at Fabriano in Italy in 1276, and the early European paper industry was largely Italian, although both the French and the Germans had some mills. The first mill in England was established by John Tate near Hertford in the 1490s, but it was a commercial failure and it was another 100 years before the trade began in earnest. Even then, it was not until the middle of the eighteenth century that Britain became self-sufficient in paper, having previously imported most of its paper from Holland and France. The mechanisation of papermaking transformed it into a large-scale industry and there are now few firms involved in it, but they are large, often multinational, corporations.

The technical history of the subject is comprehensively covered by Dard Hunter, *Paper Making* (2nd edn, 1947). For the trade in Britain, see D.C. Coleman, *The British Paper Industry 1495–1860* (1958); A.H. Shorter, *Papermaking in the British Isles* (1971); and A.H. Shorter, *Paper Mills and Paper Makers in England 1495–1800* (1957). For the USA, see Lyman H. Weeks, *A History of Paper Manufacturing in the United States, 1690–1916* (1916). E.J. Labarre, *A Dictionary of Paper and Papermaking Terms* (1937) is an invaluable work of reference.

See also **Chain lines**; **Fourdrinier, Henry** (1766–1854) **and Sealy** (d. 1847); **Paper**; **Watermarks**; **Whatman, James** (1702–1759) **and Whatman, James** (1741–1798)

Papers of the Bibliographical Society of America

Bibliographical periodical. *PBSA* has been published as a quarterly since 1904. It carries articles of a high scholarly standard on a wide range of bibliographical topics, with, naturally enough, some American bias. The present Editor is John Lancaster.

See also **Bibliographical Society of America**

Papyrus

Writing material used in the ancient world. Papyrus is the dried leaves of papyrus grass, a reed which grows in profusion along the banks of the River Nile. It was used from the third millenium BC until it was generally replaced by vellum and parchment between the second century BC and the third century AD, although it was still in use for Papal Bulls as late as the early eleventh century. Papyrus is brittle and does not react well to damp, but it has good survival properties in a hot, dry climate, and thousands of ancient fragments are extant. The word 'paper' is derived from 'papyrus', but papyrus is not a paper since it is made from the whole leaf, not from pulped and processed fibres.

See N. Lewis, *Papyrus in Classical Antiquity* (1974).

See also **Paper**; **Parchment**; **Vellum**

Parchment

Writing material. Parchment, like vellum, is made from animal skin, usually that of a sheep or a goat. The skin is split, scraped and dressed with pumice stone, but not tanned. Its invention is traditionally ascribed to Eumenes II, King of Pergamon (197–159 BC), but it was in fact in use in Egypt in the sixth century BC. It was, however, manufactured in quantity at Pergamon in the second century BC because the Egyptians had banned the export of papyrus, and it was at Pergamon (from which the word parchment is derived) that the ancient manufacturing processes were refined. Parchment was widely used in the ancient world and in medieval Europe. Until comparatively recently it was still in use for legal documents, and indeed is still used today for some formal purposes, although for general use it was displaced by paper before the end of the sixteenth century.

Parchment and vellum differ both in the skin used and in the method of manufacture, and the words should not be used as synonyms. It has to be admitted however, that the substances are not easy to distinguish in older books and documents, especially when badly worn.

See Ronald Reed, *The Nature and Making of Parchment* (1975).

See also **Paper**; **Papyrus**; **Vellum**

Parliamentary Papers

Documents printed officially for the two Houses of Parliament. Official printing began in the Short Parliament of 1640, when certain documents were 'ordered to be printed' by the House of Commons; the phrase is still used. In general terms, Parliamentary Papers are those documents which the House requires for the conduct of its business, such as reports, accounts, Bills and order papers. Since 1801 they have been issued in a continuous series, more recently split into several series, as Sessions (or Sessional) Papers, but before that year they were issued separately, and complete sets probably do not exist.

Bibliographically, Parliamentary Papers are extremely complex. Sheila Lambert has edited a reprint series of eighteenth-century Parliamentary Papers (145 vols, 1975) of which vols 1 and 2 consist of an admirable introduction and a list of documents from 1715 to 1800. For the nineteenth and twentieth centuries, see P.S. King and Son Ltd, *Catalogue of Parliamentary Papers 1801–1901* (1904); and the official *General Alphabetical Index ... 1852–1899* (1909); and *General index ... 1900 to 1948–49* (1960). For an excellent map to this jungle, see P. and G. Ford, *A Guide to Parliamentary Papers* (3rd edn, 1972).

Part books

Books issued serially in numbered parts, intended to form a complete work at the end of the series. In the eighteenth century, they were sometimes known as 'number books'. The crucial distinction between a part book and other serials is that the part book is finite and, indeed, the publisher normally states at the beginning of the series how many parts it is his intention to publish. The first true part book was Moxon's *Mechanick Exercises* (2 vols, in 14 + 24 pt., 1678–83), and a few others were published in the late seventeenth century. The great age of the part book, however, began in the mid-1720s and continued for some 40 years. Most of the part books of this period were intended for a popular market, and one purpose of part publication was indeed to spread the cost of the book for the benefit of the less wealthy buyer. It seems likely that they were also issued with the provincial market in mind, since they were distributed by post, and until the late 1730s bookshops were not common outside London. The fashion for the part book ended suddenly in the late eighteenth century; among the reasons for this are the proliferation of circulating libraries, where books could be obtained cheaply, and developments in the trade which made books more widely available throughout the country. Eighteenth-century part books can be recognised by the part number which normally appeared in the direction of the first page of each part.

In the nineteenth century, the part book was revived for the publication of fiction, beginning with Dickens' *Pickwick Papers* in 1836. The publishers, Chapman and Hall, were delighted by the success of this gimmick, and all of Dickens' novels and those of many other Victorian novelists were published in this way. In the late 1850s, however, the serial novel was gradually displaced, as changed production methods brought down the price of novels in book form. More recently, part books have enjoyed another revival, beginning in the 1960s with the part publication of *Knowledge,* a children's encyclopaedia.

R.M. Wiles has written a brilliant study of *Serial Publication in England before 1750* (1957), and the nineteenth-century revival is dealt with by J.A. Sutherland in *Victorian Novelists and their Publishers* (1976).

See also **Direction line**; **Moxon, Joseph** (1627–1691)

Pastedown

See **Endpapers**

Patents

Historically, a patent is a right granted by the Crown to a person or body of persons to exercise a monopoly over an invention or over the manufacture and sale of specified goods. The monopoly system was in fact a means of raising revenue for the Crown, since a fee was charged for the Letters Patent under which these rights were granted. The system was widely used from the 1560s to the 1620s; the worst abuses were eliminated by the Statute of Monopolies (1624) after many years of parliamentary agitation. In book trade history, patents are important because the various monopolies which were brought together to form the English Stock of the Stationers' Company, and the right of the King's Printer to print Bibles and Prayer books, were in fact patents, although they are more often referred to by book trade historians as 'privileges'. All the book trade patents survived the 1624 Act, and indeed various other attempts to abolish them; they were still valuable in the mid-eighteenth century.

For the general background, see *Terrell on the Law of Patents* (13th edn, 1982). For book trade matters, see Cyprian Blagden, *The Stationers' Company* (1960).

See also **English Stock**; **King's Printer**; **Stationers' Company**

Payne, Roger (1738–1799)

Bookbinder. Payne was born at Eton to a father, Thomas, who was also a bookbinder. He joined his father in the business, but in the late 1760s he moved to London where he set up on his own. He was later joined by his younger brother, also Thomas. Payne worked for the bookseller Thomas Osborne and for other members of the trade, most notably his unrelated namesake, Thomas Payne, who was the leading antiquarian bookseller of the late eighteenth century. His bibliophilic patrons included Earl Spencer, C.M. Cracherode (1730–1799) and Thomas Greville (1755–1846). Both of the latter were to be major benefactors of the British Museum, and the British

Library consequently has many fine Payne bindings.

Payne is widely regarded as the greatest of all British bookbinders. He was deeply concerned for the quality of the materials which he used, especially his leathers, and since his reputation enabled him to charge high prices he was able to use the best. A typical Payne binding is of red or blue morocco, elegantly but simply gilt-tooled, gilt-edged, and with watered silk endpapers.

The best recent account is by Mirjam Foot in *The Henry Davis Gift*, vol. 1 (1978).

See also **Bookbinding**; **Spencer**, **George John, 2nd Earl Spencer** (1782–1845)

Pearl

See **Type size**

Pendred, John (*c.* 1742–1793)

Printer. Pendred, the son of a London baker, was never more than a journeyman, but he compiled and published *The London and Country Printers', Booksellers' and Stationers' Vade Mecum* (1785), the first directory of the book trade. As such it is a crucial document, although in many respects incomplete. In particular, the provincial section is merely a selective list of the major booksellers and printers with whom the London trade might have dealings, although the selection was carefully made, and is, in itself, significant. There is also a list of newspapers, with valuable information about their distribution and advertising arrangements.

Vade Mecum was edited by Graham Pollard as *The Earliest Directory of the Book Trade* (1955), with a marvellous preface and appendix. A more complete list of the London trade at this period can be found in Ian Maxted, *The London Book Trades 1775–1800* (1977).

Penguin Books

See **Lane, Sir Allen** (1902–1970)

Penrose Annual, The

Annual survey of developments in printing technology. It began as *The Process Year Book* in 1895, and took its present title in 1898. A.W. Penrose, for whom it is named, was a pharmaceutical chemist who assisted William Gamble, who worked in the printing industry, to develop photographic chemicals suitable for use in photomechanical printing and platemaking. Gamble manufactured both chemicals and equipment, and started *The Process Year Book* as little more than a catalogue of his own products. Very quickly, however, it became an important medium for disseminating information about the rapid developments in printing which have continued throughout the twentieth century. The articles are usually fairly non-technical and lavishly illustrated explanations of these developments, often written by those who have been directly involved in them. *The Penrose Annual* itself is beautifully printed, often with inserts in different processes on different papers, to illustrate the points under discussion. It is a crucial book for the student of contemporary printing, and the earlier volumes are an important primary source for twentieth-century printing history.

James Moran has edited a selection of articles as *Printing in the 20th Century* (1974).

Pepys, Samuel (1633–1703)

Civil servant, diarist and book collector. Pepys was educated at St Paul's and Cambridge, and through the influence of his patron, Sir Edward Montagu, became a clerk in the Exchequer after the Restoration. Almost immediately, however, he secured the office of Clerk of the Acts and was, effectively, secretary of the Admiralty. He was responsible for major reforms in the Navy in the 1660s and 1670s, continuing to hold various Admiralty offices until he retired in 1690. From 1659 to 1669 he kept the secret diary for which he is now best remembered; it has recently been re-edited, with a vast panoply of scholarship, by Robert Latham and William Matthews (11 vols, 1970–83).

Pepys was a book collector throughout his life, amassing some 3000 volumes. These include some very important books and documents on naval history, unique collections of pamphlets from the Restoration and the Exclusion Crisis and a large and important collection of broadsides and chapbooks in English, French and Spanish. Pepys also had a taste for pornography; although he destroyed some of his 'little French books', others found their way into his library and have survived. He bequeathed his books to Magdalene College, Cambridge, with a life interest to his nephew and heir, John Jackson; the College received the books in 1726, and they are still housed in the cases which Pepys had made for them by carpenters at a naval dockyard in 1666, and in a building for which he helped to pay. The Pepys Library is perhaps the most remarkable surviving library from seventeenth-century England, in that it is the collection of an educated and intelligent professional man, rather a grand aristocratic collection in a country house. It has, accordingly, attracted much attention, and is, indeed, open to tourists from time to time. A complete catalogue is in progress; so far vols 1 (Printed books, ed. N.A. Smith, 1978), 2 (Modern manuscripts, ed. R.C. Latham and C. Knighton, 1981), 3, pt. 1 (Prints and drawings, 1980), and 6 (Bindings, ed. H.M. Nixon, 1984), have been published. One aspect of the library has been studied in great detail in Edward M. Wilson and Don W. Cruikshank, *Samuel Pepys's Spanish Plays* (1980).

See also **Ballads**; **Chapbooks**

Perfect binding

See **Bookbinding**

Perfecting

Technical term in printing. Perfecting, which Moxon calls *reteration,* is the name given to the process of printing the second side of a sheet when the first side has already been printed.

See Moxon, p.306.

Pharmacopoeia

A book containing standard formularies for pharmaceutical preparations. The origin of the pharmacopoeia is to be found in the ancient and medieval herbals which dealt with the medicinal properties of plants. Manuscripts of such books were often beautifully illustrated, as were their printed successors such as *The grete herball* (1526) and John Gerard's *Herbal* (1597). Pharmacopoeias are Italian in origin, one of the earliest being the *Recettario fiorentino* (Florence, 1498); their English history begins at a rather later date. In the late 1590s, the College of Physicians began to prepare a pharmacopoeia, and this was eventually published with the College's authority as *Pharmacopoeia Londinensis* (1618); it went through nine further editions, all thoroughly revised, until 1851. In 1862 it was replaced by the *British Pharmacopoeia,* which, fully revised, is still in use, and is issued by the General Medical Council under legal powers granted to them in 1862.

See Leslie G. Matthews, *History of Pharmacy in Britain* (1962).

Phillipps, Sir Thomas (1792–1872)

Book collector, although the term seems barely adequate. Phillipps, the son of a wealthy landowner, was educated at Rugby and Oxford, and was already buying large quantities of books and manuscripts as an undergraduate and running up proportionately large debts. He inherited his father's property, including the family house at Middle Hill, near Broadway in Worcestershire, in 1818, and was created a baronet for the coronation of George IV in 1821. In 1820–25 he went on a long continental tour, during which he bought thousands of manuscripts in France and the Low Countries. Many of these came from monastic libraries which had been broken up during the Napoleonic Wars, and included both historical documents and medieval manuscripts of all kinds. On his return to England, Phillipps settled at Middle Hill, and used the London bookseller, Thomas Thorpe, as his agent to buy books and manuscripts from booksellers all over Europe. His aim was to own a copy of every book ever printed (he failed, but only just) and all significant manuscripts not in public collections. Within this somewhat ambitious programme, he did have specialist interests, notably in English and Welsh history and genealogy. By 1862, the collection had filled Middle Hill, and Phillipps moved it and his family to Thirlstane House, Cheltenham, where his long-suffering wife and daughters were set to work cataloguing and transcribing as part of a domestic routine which was often, not surprisingly, interrupted by financial crises. Phillipps had established a private press at Middle Hill, at which he printed transcripts and calendars of some of his manuscripts, and most importantly, the catalogue of them, which had reached no. 23,837 by the time of his death.

Phillipps gave much thought to the ulimate disposal of his library. He was, at his best, a very difficult man, and in the course of complicated negotiations he managed to quarrel with both Sir Frederic Madden, Keeper of Manuscripts at the British Museum, and Bulkley Bandinel, Bodley's Librarian. In fairness to Phillipps, neither institution was above reproach in its dealings with him, and had either been so, it might eventually have had the whole collection. In the end, he left Thirlstane House and its contents to his third daughter, Katherine (Mrs Fenwick), partly for the pleasure of not leaving it to his eldest daughter, Henrietta, whose husband was the Shakespearean scholar, James Orchard Halliwell, whom he hated. The Fenwicks had only a life interest, and Trustees were appointed, but the Court of Chancery broke the Trust in 1885 and the series of sales began which still continues. In 1945, the residue of the collection was sold to Lionel and Philip Robinson, the antiquarian booksellers, for £100,000. This 'residue' consisted of tens of thousands of books and documents, including Phillipps' private papers, which the Robinsons ultimately gave to the Bodleian Library.

A.N.L. Munby's *Phillipps Studies* (5 vols, 1951–60) is the standard work on Phillipps, being a study of both the man and the library. Nicolas Barker, *Portrait of an Obsession* (1967) is a highly readable adaptation of Munby's work.

See also **Middle Hill Press**

Photocomposition

See **Photosetting**

Photogravure

Intaglio printing process. Photogravure is a photomechanical technique invented by Karl Klič in Vienna in 1879. A photographic image is chemically etched onto a copper cylinder through a fine mesh screen, and the cylinder is then used in a rotary press. Ink is forced into the etched lines, and cleaned from the surface of the cylinder. The result is of very high quality. Photogravure is, however, a very expensive process, and is normally used only for colour work when long print runs and high standards of reproduction are required. For colour work, three or four cylinders are made from colour-separated negatives.

See Harold Curwen, *Processes of Graphic Reproduction in Printing* (3rd edn, rev. by Charles Mayo, 1949).

See also **Colour printing**; **Etching**; **Intaglio**; **Photomechanical printing**

Photolithographic printing

See **Offset lithography**

Photomechanical printing

The general name given to the process of printing from photographically generated blocks or plates. The first true photograph, involving a negative exposed in a camera and then chemically printed onto paper, was made by W.H. Fox-Talbot (1800–1877) in 1841. It was another 20 years before photography made a real impact on book illustration, although several processes were developed during that time. The first developments were in the making of intaglio plates, although the best intaglio process, photogravure, was not invented until 1879. It was, however, the relief processes which transformed the production of illustrated books in the last two decades of the nineteenth century. The first and simplest of these was the line block, probably invented by Charles Gillot, a Frenchman, in 1872. A sheet of zinc coated with a light-sensitive chemical is exposed to a photographic negative, and the image developed. The unprinted area is then etched away chemically, while the image protects the surface beneath it. What remains is a relief plate, with the lines of the image raised above the surrounding areas. The plate is mounted on a block to type height and can then be printed.

Line blocks, however, are only suitable for line drawings, diagrams, and so on, because the process cannot reproduce tonal variations. The second of the relief processes, the half-tone, overcame precisely this problem, for it permitted continuous monochromic tones to be printed.

Both the line block and the half-tone are still in use in relief printing, although offset lithography has largely replaced them, not least because graphic matter can more easily be reproduced by a system which depends entirely upon photographically generated plates.

See Geoffrey Wakeman, *Victorian Book Illustration. The technical revolution* (1973).

See also **Half-tone**; **Illustrated books**; **Intaglio**; **Offset lithography**; **Photogravure**; **Relief printing**; **Type height**

Photosetting

Typesetting system, although in fact no type is involved; it is sometimes called

Phototypesetting

'phototypesetting', 'photocomposition' or 'filmsetting'. As early as the 1870s, experiments were conducted in the USA to make use of photography to generate text for lithographic printing. Little came of this, but the basic principle was established of a store of characters to be photographed. The problem was to build a machine which could do this in response to an operator at a keyboard. The first machine which was actually used by a commercial printer was the Uhertype, invented by Edmund Uher in Augsburg, Germany, in 1925, but it was the Linotype Fotosetter, an American machine of 1946, which really ushered in the age of photosetting. The Fotosetter had transparent characters on a disc which revolved in front of a light source as the keyboard was struck; it also had the facility of automatic justification. This system was widely used, as was the Monophoto built by Monotype, in which the Monotype matrix case was replaced by a die case containing transparent characters.

Within 20 years of its introduction photosetting underwent, and is still undergoing, a profound revolution, by the linking of photosetters to computers. In Computer-Assisted Typesetting (CAT), the keyboarder creates a file in the computer which can be processed like any other electronic file and can generate paper print-out (for proof-reading), but can also create film negatives for making plates for offset lithography. The computer is programmed to 'format' the output for printing, so that the product looks as nearly as possible like the traditional product of the typecasting machines, and in recent years typographers have begun to produce a wide range of traditional type designs suitably adapted. Developments in CAT continue apace; perhaps the most significant at present is the rapid development of interface devices which will allow disks from word processors to drive photosetters, so that the author's own input will be printed exactly as he created it.

For a general account of photosetting, see James Moran, *The Composition of Printed Matter* (1965). The first generation of CATs are discussed by Andrew Bluhm, *Photosetting* (1969), but developments are so rapid that they can only be followed in such periodicals as *Printing World* and specialised computer journals.

See also **Justification**; **Line casting**; **Lithography**; **Monotype**; **Offset lithography**; **Typesetting**

Phototypesetting

See **Photosetting**

Pica

See **Type size**

Pierpont Morgan Library

Research library in New York City. J. Pierpont Morgan (1837–1913) was a banker whose business career was fabulously successful if not always morally or even legally unblemished. He began to collect as a schoolboy, but it was not until the 1890s that he did so seriously. Over the next 40 years he and his son, J.P. Morgan (1867–1943), assembled an astonishing collection of medieval and Renaissance manuscripts, incunabula, fine bindings, musical manuscripts and Old Master drawings. In 1906, the elder Morgan built a house for himself and his collections on 36th Street, New York, and in 1924 the son handed over the house, its contents and a large endowment to a Board of Trustees. The Morgan Library is still in its original building, and makes regular purchases of books and manuscripts of the highest quality in its chosen fields. The whole collection is superb in every respect, and access is strictly limited to serious researchers.

For the collections, see Fredrick B. Adams Jr, *An Introduction to the Pierpont Morgan Library*, rev. by Charles Ryskamp (1974), and, for Morgan himself, there is a good, if not always flattering, account by Andrew Sinclair, *Corsair. The life of J. Pierpont Morgan* (1981).

Pile

See **Papermaking**

Piracy

Book trade term. Piracy is the name given to the printing and publishing of books by persons other than the copyright owner. The practice is as old as copyright itself, and official bodies within the trade have always tried to prevent and to punish it, and to press for legislation to help them. In England, the Stationers' Company policed the trade with considerable success in the sixteenth and seventeenth centuries, and additional legal redress was given to copyright owners under the Copyright Act 1710. On the other hand, the difficulties in interpreting that Act created equal difficulties in identifying piracies and prosecuting their publishers. The word must, indeed, be used with great care; some reprints are not piracies, because the law does not apply where they are printed. For example, until 1800, English books reprinted in Ireland were not piracies unless they were sold in Great Britain, because copyright protection did not extend to Ireland.

Even today, piracy is conducted on a large scale, especially in certain Far Eastern countries where British and American textbooks are reprinted in large quantities for sale to developing countries.

The whole subject is in urgent need of further historical research, for the literature on it is sparse. Most books and articles on copyright have something to say on the subject, but in general one must search for scattered references in such books as Marjorie Plant, *The English Book Trade* (3rd edn, 1974).

See also **Copyright; Stationers' Company**

Pissarro, Lucien (1863–1944)

See **Eragny Press**

Pitts, John (1765–1844)

See **Ballads**

Planography

See **Lithography**

Plantin, Christophe (*c.* 1520–1589)

Printer and publisher. Plantin was a native of Tours, France, and learned his trade with Robert Mace in Caen. After a short spell in Paris, he moved to Antwerp in 1550, where he worked as a bookbinder until he was able to establish a press in 1555. Antwerp was at the centre of the political and religious struggles in the Low Countries, and Plantin suffered greatly from this, although even after the worst episode, the 'Spanish Fury' of 1576, he did recover. After a brief exile in 1562–63, as a result of printing an heretical book, Plantin developed his business rapidly, to the extent that by 1576 he had 22 presses, at a time when four was regarded as exceptional. His prosperity was largely based on his position as *de facto* printer to Philip II of Spain, the ruler of the Netherlands for much of Plantin's time in Antwerp. For the King, Plantin printed tens of thousands of service books for the Spanish market. He was also, however, a major scholarly publisher, and many of his books became and remained standard works throughout Europe.

Plantin bequeathed his business to his son-in-law, Jan Moerentorff (Joannes Moretus) (1543–1610), and it survived in the Moretus family until 1875 when Plantin's premises at the sign of the Golden Compasses became the Plantin-Moretus Museum.

The standard work on Plantin is Léon Voet, *The Golden Compasses* (2 vols, 1968–72).

See also **Plantin—Moretus Museum**

Plantin—Moretus Museum

Museum of printing history in Antwerp, Belgium. In 1865, the business founded by Christophe Plantin was inherited by Hyacinth Moretus–Plantin who ceased to trade and, in 1876, sold the printing house and its contents to the city of Antwerp. It was opened as a museum in 1877. During the three centuries of the firm's existence almost nothing had been destroyed, and the fine Renaissance building houses the world's greatest collection of early presses, typefounding equipment, matrices, punches and composing-room equipment. All of this is still used from time to time. In addition, the Plantin-Moretus archive is virtually intact from 1555 to 1864, and there is an almost complete collection of all the books printed by the firm throughout its history.

See Léon Voet, *La musée Plantin–Moretus* (1952).

See also **Plantin, Christophe** (*c.* 1520–1589)

Platen

See **Common press**

Plomer, Henry Robert (1856–1928)

Bibliographer and antiquary. Born in Guernsey into a formerly wealthy family which had fallen on hard times, Plomer became a bank clerk in London, but left this job to set up his own business. The business failed, and he then made his living as a copyist, a now vanished occupation which involved transcribing documents on commission from scholars, at such repositories as the British Museum and the Public Record Office. Plomer, however, had antiquarian interests of his own, and these came to focus on the book trade. In the late 1890s, he began to contribute to *TBS*, and also wrote essays for Pollard's *Bibliographica*. His first substantial work was *A History of English Printing 1476–1898* (1900), but the books for which he will be remembered are the dictionaries of members of the book trade published by the Bibliographical Society. These cover the periods 1641–67 (1907), 1668–1725 (1922), and 1726–75 (1932; completed and edited by G.H. Bushnell and E.R. McC. Dix). He wrote dozens of papers for *TBS* and *The Library* in his later years, many of them based on previously unknown documents.

The Bibliographical Society had an unfortunate attitude to this distinguished contributor to its publications; copyists were not regarded as scholars (or gentlemen) and, astonishingly, Plomer was never elected to membership of the Society which he served so well. This attitude can be judged from the somewhat patronising tone of Pollard's notice of Plomer in the Introduction to the posthumously published 1726–1775 *Dictionary* (1932).

See also **Bibliographica**; **Bibliographical Society**; **Pollard, Alfred William** (1859–1944)

Points

(1) *In printing*, points are the pins used to hold the paper onto the tympan in the common press.
(2) *In typography*, points are the unit of measurement of type.
(3) *In bibliography*, points are the distinguishing characteristics which differentiate between issues or impressions of the same edition.

See also **Common press**; **Edition**; **Impression**; **Issue**; **Point size**

Point size

The unit of measurement of the body size of type. Until the early eighteenth century, type sizes were differentiated by such names as Pica or Primer, but these were necessarily imprecise and non-standard. In 1737, the French typographer, Pierre Simon Fournier (1712–1768), worked out a system of 'Corps des Caractères', or points, taking a standard unit of measurement and defining each type size in relation to that. In his system, 1 pt = 0.34875 mm. The system was revised by the Parisian typefounder, Firmin-Didot, in about 1770; he took the *pied de roi* (the French foot = 12.7897 imperial inches), and worked on the basis of 72 pt = 1 inch. This gives 1 pt = 0.376 mm, which became the standard European measurement. In practice, however, the point system, logical and simple as it is, was adopted only slowly, and many systems were developed with minute deviations from the Didot points. In 1886, when Didot had become the European standard, American typefounders agreed to adopt a measure of 1 pt = 0.351 mm. Through the influence of the American typecasting machines then being introduced, this became the standard in Britain in the 1890s, and has remained so.

See L.A. Legros and J.C. Grant, *Typographical Printing-surfaces* (1916).

See also **Type size**

Pollard, Alfred William (1859–1944)

Librarian and bibliographer. Pollard was educated at King's College School and Oxford where he was a contemporary and intimate of A.E. Housman. In 1883, he joined the staff of the British Museum, where he remained until his retirement in 1924; he became Keeper of Printed Books in 1919. During his early years at the Museum he turned himself into a bibliographer; he produced a number of bibliophilic books, conceived and edited *Bibliographica*, and reviewed for *The Library*. In 1893, he became Honorary Secretary of the newly-founded Bibliographical Society, a post which he held, either alone or with McKerrow, until 1934. His greatest achievements as a scholar were in the field of Shakespearean textual criticism, which he set on a wholly new basis, as was readily admitted by both Greg and McKerrow. From his knowledge of early printing and of the Elizabethan book trade, Pollard was able to challenge the guess-work of earlier generations with hypotheses which were developed out of provable facts. *Shakespeare Folios and Quartos* (1909) was the first major product of his work in this field; like *Shakespeare's Fight with the Pirates* (1917, rev. edn. 1920), it was a landmark in Shakespearean studies, for Pollard was able to illuminate subjects as diverse as copyright, and the 'good' and 'bad' Quartos, as well as discussing the formal transmission of texts.

In his work for the Bibliographical Society, he was largely responsible for the Society taking over the ailing *Library*, which he then edited for many years. He was also the progenitor, and with G.R. Redgrave the joint compiler, of the *Short-Title Catalogue* (1926). In his official capacity at the Museum, he took over the catalogue of incunabula after Proctor's death, and although the work did not greatly appeal to him, he had set it on a firm footing before he handed it over to others in 1913.

Pollard held two key posts, one at the British Museum and the other in the Bibliographical Society, for the greater part of his life, and is one of the central figures of modern bibliography, both as a practitioner and behind the scenes. He was a good administrator, and a great encourager of younger scholars. He was also a man of great intellect (he had taken a First in the very examination which Housman failed), and was always willing to take intellectual risks, a quality which makes his work as exciting as it is exacting.

The memoir by J. Dover Wilson in *PBA* (1945) is a vivid account, which supplements the more formal notice by Greg in *DNB*.

See also **Bibliographica**; **Bibliographical Society**; **Bibliography**; **Greg, Sir Walter Wilson** (1875–1959); **Incunabula**; *Library, The*; **McKerrow, Ronald Brunlees** (1872–1940); **Proctor, Robert George Collie** (1868–1903); *STC*

Pollard, Henry Graham (1903–1976)

Bibliographer. Pollard, the son of the historian, A.F. Pollard, was educated at Shrewsbury and Oxford. His undergraduate interests, which included good living, left-wing politics and book collecting, did not extend to the Honours School of Modern History; he was awarded a Third and refused to take his degree. In 1942, he became a partner in Birrell and Garnett, a firm of antiquarian booksellers in London, where he remained until 1938, when he became Reader in Newspaper History at London University; in 1942, he joined the Board of Trade, and worked there until his retirement in 1959.

His book collecting had begun even before Oxford, but he laid the foundations of his wide-ranging bibliographical scholarship at Birrell and Garnett. His first major work was the Birrell and Garnett catalogue of *Typefounders' Specimens* (1928), now itself a collector's piece, which virtually inaugurated the serious study of that subject. There followed papers in *The Library* on the early history of the Stationers' Company, on medieval binders and binding and on the size of the sheet, all of which broke new ground. He had a special interest in the history of the book trade, both generally and in Oxford. His

Oxford studies extended to the history of both the university and the city. His masterpiece, however, and his only full-scale publication on book trade history, is *The Distribution of Books by Catalogue* (1964), a survey, based on the Broxbourne Library, of book advertising and distribution in Europe up to the year 1800. Pollard was also, with John Carter, the author of *An Enquiry into the Nature of Certain Nineteenth-century Pamphlets* (1934), whose carefully understated title concealed the startling revelation that T.J. Wise was a forger.

A Festschrift for Pollard was published by the Oxford Bibliographical Society in 1975, under the title *Studies in the Book Trade*; it includes a list of his writings, and a memoir by John Carter.

See also **Broxbourne Library**; **Stationers' Company**; **Wise, Thomas James** (1859–1937)

Pornography

Sexually explicit literature intended to titillate and arouse the reader. The definition of pornography is notoriously difficult, because ideas of what constitutes unacceptably explicit text and pictures varies between places and periods. The book historian can merely follow the vagaries of civil and ecclesiastical authorities in their attempts to exercise moral control over the output of the press. Historically, obscene literature has been treated as a moral offence, and hence until the seventeenth century (and later in some places) was a concern of the Church rather than the state, although as in other areas of censorship the balance between Church and state varied between different countries. Some books were put on the Catholic Church's *Index* on moral grounds in the sixteenth century but they were not, on the whole, books which were intended by their authors to be pornographic. The deliberate writing of pornography did not, apparently, begin until the late sixteenth or early seventeenth centuries in Europe, a phenomenon for which Jung offered the explanation that Protestantism, by its emphasis on the individual rather than the Church, made individuals more willing to take their own moral and political decisions.

Whatever the psychological reasons may be, by the mid-seventeenth century pornography was being written and published, one of the most notorious examples being a French book called *L'école des filles* (1655); Pepys bought a copy in London in 1668. There is evidence for the publication of obscene literature in England in the second half of the seventeenth century, including a translation of *L'école des filles* as *The School of Venus* (1688). The most notorious example was Jean Barrin's *Vénus dans le cloître* (1683), translated as *Venus in the Cloister* (1683). In 1724–25, Robert Samber and Edmund Curll produced another English edition, for which they were prosecuted; this was the first successful prosecution on purely moral grounds in an English secular court.

Pornography is, inevitably, largely published *sub rosa*, and its history difficult to trace. It seems, however, that it was not uncommon in the eighteenth

212

century and by the nineteenth century it was widespread. In 1787, George III issued a Royal Proclamation condemning vice, including pornography, and The Proclamation Society was founded by William Wilberforce (1759–1833) and others to prosecute offenders. Its successor, The Society for the Suppression of Vice (founded 1801), was active in the same cause for most of the nineteenth century, when the increased output of pornography coincided with a far greater public emphasis on morality. The law, however, was obscure, and offenders could only be prosecuted in King's Bench for obscene libel, a common law offence with many loopholes. In 1857 the law was clarified in the Obscene Publications Act (known as Lord Campbell's Act), which defined obscenity in terms of its tendency to 'deprave or corrupt'. This also proved difficult to interpret, and both judges and juries tended to be swayed by the prevailing moral climate. The 1857 Act was amended by the Obscene Publications Act 1959, which retained the 1857 definition, and all its difficulties, but added the further difficulty of permitting a defence on the grounds of literary merit. The courts were now, therefore, called upon to be literary critics as well as moral censors. For all its faults, however, the 1959 Act has at least spared the world the spectacle of British courts condemning the works of Joyce, Lawrence and Zola, as they had under the 1857 Act. The 1959 Act has, however, proved powerless, as any legislation must inevitably be, to prevent the publication and sale of hard-core pornography, especially of the visual kind, and recent developments in video technology have probably made what was once a difficult task into a wholly impossible one.

Donald Thomas has written a fascinating and learned history of literary censorship in Britain, under the title *A Long Time Burning* (1969); for the early period, see David Foxon, *Libertine Literature in England 1660–1745* (1964).

See also **Censorship**; **Curll, Edmund** (1683?–1747); *Index Librorum Prohibitorum*; **Pepys, Samuel** (1633–1703)

Pot

See **Sheet**

Prayer books

A generic name for liturgical works, but normally used only to refer to the *Book of Common Prayer* of the Church of England. The evolution of the English prayer book began in the reign of Henry VIII, under the influence of Archbishop Cranmer, but the first complete English liturgy was that of 1549, known as the First Prayer Book of Edward VI. A revised version in 1552 was more Protestant in tone, and was essentially the same as that whose use was required by the Act of Uniformity 1559. The next revision was undertaken after the Restoration, and first published in 1662. The 1662 Prayer Book remained in use until very recently; a proposed revision in 1922 was rejected by Parliament, and not until 1980 did the Church of England finally produce its *Alternative Service Book* which the General Synod proceeded to impose upon generally reluctant congregations.

The printing of the *Book of Common Prayer* is a privilege reserved by patent to the King's Printer and the University Presses of Oxford and Cambridge. Hundreds of editions have been published in formats varying from large folio for the lectern to sixteenmo and even smaller for personal use. The editions are meticulously listed in F.E. Brightman, *The English Rite* (2 vols, 1915), although for the period before 1640, *STC-2* should be consulted under the heading **Liturgies – Church of England**. For a general history, see Francis Procter, *A New History of the Book of Common Prayer* (rev. edn by W.H. Frere, 1901).

See also **Cambridge University Press**; **Folio**; **Format**; **King's (or Queen's) Printer**; **Patents**; **Oxford University Press**; **Sixteenmo**; *STC*

Prelims

Book trade term. The prelims (or 'preliminaries', but only the abbreviation is ever used) are all the pages which precede the first page of the main text of a book. These include, for example, the half-title, title page, Contents, Preface, and so on. The bibliographical significance of prelims is that, except in a reprint, they are normally printed after the rest of the book, since they are usually the last part of the book to be written.

See Gaskell, p. 52

See also **Half-title**; **Title page**

Press

The machine on which an impression is made from a prepared surface onto paper or some other material, using ink. The common press, in use from the fifteenth century, was a hand-operated wooden machine, which in the early nineteenth century was gradually displaced by hand-operated iron presses such as the Stanhope, the Albion and the Columbian. At the same time, the steam-powered press was developed by Koenig, and during the nineteenth century the equipment was increasingly mechanised, leading to the high-speed rotary presses of today.

For an historical overview, see James Moran, *Printing Presses* (1973).

See also **Albion press**; **Columbian press**; **Common press**; **Impression**; **Ink**; **Koenig press**; **Stanhope press**

Press figures

The numbers which appear in the direction line of some seventeenth- to nineteenth-century English and American books. They were intended to indicate to the master printer or his foreman which press or pressman was responsible for machining the forme, a unique number being assigned to each man or machine. There is still some debate about whether it was the machine or its operator to which the press figure referred, but there is evidence to suggest that in practice the two were closely and continuously associated with each other. It seems likely, however, that it was the man rather than the machine who was intended, since the only rational explanation for the existence of press figures at all is that it enabled the master printer to calculate piece-rate wages. Because of this uncertainty about their meaning, the interpretation of press figures, *per se*, is difficult, although it is generally assumed that they do give some evidence of the number of presses or pressmen engaged on machining a particular book. As a spin-off, however, they can assist in differentiating between impressions, since the press figures had to be changed for each impression to provide an accurate record of the machining of that particular impression. Press figures were an English and American practice, and are most common, although they were never universal, in the eighteenth century. The earliest example, however, is that of a Bible printed in London in 1629.

See Philip Gaskell, 'Eighteenth-century press numbers', *Libr.* (1950–51), p. 149; G. Thomas Tanselle, 'Press figures in America: some preliminary observations', *SB* (1966), p. 123; and B.J. McMullin, 'The origins of press figures in English printing 1629–1671', *Libr.* (1979), p. 307.

See also **Direction line**; **Forme**; **Impression**; **Press**; **Pressman**

Press numbers

See **Press figures**

Press variants

Alterations to the text of a book, revealed by collation of multiple copies. Variants within an impression were usually created by corrections made during the print-run, which was interrupted while the compositor worked on the forme on the bed of the press. They are sometimes known as *stop-press corrections*. In fact, this was merely the final stage of proof correction, and consisted of a last reading of the text while the forme was being machined. It seems that such corrections were normally made without reference to the copy, and they are, therefore, of bibliographical rather than textual interest and significance. There are exceptions, however, and for that reason most editors of printed texts now collate multiple copies of their witnesses to discover the press variants, if any. Variants create a state of an impression, but the state is of the forme rather than book as a whole, since within any given copy of the book there will be a random collection of corrected and uncorrected formes.

See Gaskell, p. 215; and, for a classic investigation of a complex example, W.W. Greg, *The Variants in the First Quarto of 'King Lear'* (1940).

See also **Collection**; **Copy**; **Edition**; **Forme**; **Proofs**; **State**; **Textual criticism**

Pressman

See **Common press**

Printing

The process of reproducing textual, numerical or graphic matter by mechanical means. The fundamental principle is that an image is transferred from one surface to another when the first surface is inked and the two are then brought together under pressure. There are three basic printing techniques: relief, in which the image is raised above its surroundings; intaglio, in which the image is recessed beneath its surroundings; and planography, or lithography, in which the printing and non-printing areas are in the same plane but are distinguished chemically.

The first process to be developed was relief printing, which was in use in China in the ninth century AD. The process was independently invented in the West in the fifteenth century, and used for printing from woodcuts (the so-called 'Block books') and, after 1454, from metal type. Typographic printing, invented by Gutenberg, was the great breakthrough in the history of printing, for it created the printed book as we know it. Intaglio processes, usually used only for graphic reproduction, began to be developed in the sixteenth century and were greatly improved over the next 250 years. Lithography was a much later innovation, being invented by Senefelder in 1798.

All of these are hand processes. The mechanisation of printing began with the building of the first operational Koenig press in 1814, and in the later nineteenth century typesetting was also mechanised. The other great development of the nineteenth century was in the use of photographic techniques in the preparation of the printing surface. These photomechanical processes were first applied to graphic reproduction, but with the development of offset lithography from 1904 onwards, the photographic processes have gradually taken over from mechanical printing.

For a general history see S. H. Steinberg, *Five Hundred Years of Printing* (1960); and James Moran, *Printing Presses* (1973). Colin Clair, *A Chronology of Printing* (1969) is a useful work of reference.

See also **Block books**; **Gutenberg, Johann** (1394/99–1468); **Ink**;
Intaglio; **Koenig press**; **Lithography**; **Offset lithography**; **Photo-
mechanical printing**; **Relief printing**; **Senefelder, Alois** (1771–1834);
Type; **Typesetting**

Printing Act 1662

Legislation controlling the English book trade. The Printing Act (sometimes
known as the Licensing Act) was one of a series of measures passed in the
early 1660s designed to reinforce the Crown's control over various activities
and to replace the executive decrees which had fallen into desuetude during
the Civil War and Interregnum. The Act restored some of the pre-1640
privileges of the Stationers' Company, including restrictions on the numbers
of both Master Printers and apprentices. Printing was permitted only in
London, in Oxford and Cambridge (under the control of the universities) and
in York (under the control of the Archbishop). The great innovation of the
Act, however, was the creation of the office of Surveyor of the Press. The
Surveyor's duty was to license books before publication, under the direction
of the Secretary of State, or in the case of books on such dangerous subjects
as theology and law, in consultation with appropriate authorities, such as the
Archbishop of Canterbury or the Lord Chief Justice. The Act was substantially enforced, although some unlicensed printing took place, and some
books were licensed which were not as innocuous as they seemed. Nevertheless, during the first period when the Act was in force (1662–79) the English
press was controlled more closely than at any other time in its history. In
1685, the Act was revived but Parliament failed to renew it when it came up
for confirmation again in 1694, and from 1695 onwards the whole system of
controls vanished for ever. Although this did not create a 'free' press, it did
create the circumstances in which such a press could develop.

See Fredrick Seaton Siebert, *Freedom of the Press in England 1476–1776*
(1965); Timothy Crist, 'Goverment control of the press after the expiration of
the Printing Act in 1679', *PH* (1979), p. 49, and Raymond Astbury, 'The
renewal of the Licensing Act in 1693 and its lapse in 1695', *Libr.* (1978), p. 296.

See also **Censorship**; **Stationers' Company**

Printing Historical Society

Founded 1964. The Society exists to promote the study of printing history. It
holds regular meetings in London, and publishes *JPHS*, a *Bulletin* for its
members, and occasional monographs. A Northern Group caters for members
in the North of England and holds its own meetings. The Society's address is
St Bride Institute, Bride Lane, Fleet Street, London EC4Y 8EE.

See also ***Journal of the Printing Historical Society***

Printing History

Learned journal. *Printing History* is published by the American Printing History Association; it contains articles on the history of printing, well illustrated and with a strong American flavour. The Editor is Susan O. Thompson of Columbia University, New York.

See also **American Printing History Association**

Private Press Books

Annual listing of books printed at private presses, published by the Private Libraries Association. The first volume appeared in 1959. The coverage is world-wide, and a list of recent publications on private presses is also included. The present editor is David Chambers.

See also **Private press movement**

Private press movement

A private press can be defined in general terms as a press operated for pleasure rather than for profit, although the word 'pleasure' should not be taken too literally since many such presses have a very serious purpose. Wealthy and not so wealthy men (and a few women) have amused themselves with printing as a hobby since the sixteenth century, and have sometimes printed important books which could not find a commercial outlet. By the mid-eighteenth century, however, the development of subscription publishing had largely overcome the problem of financing scholarly works, and the private press became, in the words of its most recent historian, 'an aristocratic plaything'. In England, the most notable of these aristocrats was Horace Walpole, whose Strawberry Hill Press was at work from 1757 to 1789. It was not, however, until the first decade of the nineteenth century that we find a few examples of private presses in the style which was later to become familiar. The most important of these were the Hafod Press of Thomas Johnes and the Lee Priory Press owned by Brydges. Throughout the middle decades of the nineteenth century there were a few presses which followed this pattern, among them Phillipps' press at Middle Hill and the Daniel Press in Oxford.

In the late nineteenth century, the private press became a more widespread and more self-conscious phenomenon. The 'movement' began in 1888 when Emery Walker delivered a lecture condemning (not unfairly) contemporary standards of commercial book production. This lecture was Morris's inspiration for the establishment of the Kelmscott Press in 1891, the first of the modern private presses. Kelmscott set the fashion followed by most private presses before 1939. The first and greatest concern was for the physical quality of the product in terms of paper, ink, type, design and binding.

Morris, reacting against the aesthetics of a mechanised society, reverted to traditional methods of book production and reached far into history for the models for his types and page layouts. On the other hand, Morris was also an evangelist and could only achieve this objective by disseminating his books as widely as possible. Here too he established a pattern. Although edition sizes were small, Kelmscott books were commercially available.

The Kelmscott achievement is unique; Morris had disciples and successors but no real imitators. The first follower of the Kelmscott tradition was the Essex House Press (1898), but perhaps more important was the Vale Press, less directly indebted to Morris but certainly benefiting from the cultural climate which he was instrumental in creating. Associated with Vale was the Eragny Press; both were close in spirit to Art Nouveau. After World War I, the tradition was inherited by the Ashendene Press, whose founder was directly influenced by Walker as well as being an admirer of Morris. Morris's influence also crossed the Atlantic, and was indirectly very important to Bruce Rogers.

Ashendene was the last of the heirs of Kelmscott, but the tradition of fine printing by small presses continues. In the 1920s and 1930s the Golden Cockerell Press and the Gregynog Press in Britain and the Grabhorn Press in the USA continued to maintain the highest standards, while since World War II small presses have proliferated throughout the developed world.

Private presses and their books command an almost fanatical admiration from some bibliophiles, although their wilder extremes are not perhaps to everyone's taste. The historical importance of the private press movement is not so much in what the presses produced but rather in their less tangible achievements. For all their vagaries and eccentricities the private press owners cared about books, book production and book design. Modern typography, encapsulated in the work of Meynell, Morison and Rogers, is in many ways remote from Morris, but it was Morris and his associates and successors who had first criticised nineteenth-century printing and had tried to do something about it. Their pseudo-medievalism may not have been the right solution to the problem, but at least it drew attention to the fact that a problem did exist.

There is a vast literature on private presses. For a sympathetic, comprehensive and scholarly account, see Roderick Cave, *The Private Press* (2nd edn, 1983), which includes an excellent bibliography. For the books themselves, see G.S. Tompkinson, *A Select Bibliography of the Principal Modern Private Presses* (1928); Will Ransom, *Private Presses and Their Books* (1929); William Ridler, *British Modern Press Books* (new edn, 1975); and *Modern British and American Private Presses. Holdings of the British Library* (1976).

See also **Ashendene Press**; **Allen Press**; **Brydges, Sir Samuel Egerton** (1762–1837); **Daniel Press**; **Eragny Press**; **Essex House Press**; **Golden Cockerell Press**; **Grabhorn Press**; **Gregynog Press**; **Hafod Press**; **Kelmscott Press**; **Meynell, Sir Francis** (1891–1975); **Middle Hill Press**; **Morison, Stanley** (1889–1976); **Rogers, Bruce** (1870–1957); **Strawberry Hill Press**; **Vale Press**; **Village Press**; **Walker, Sir Emery** (1851–1933)

Proctor, Robert George Collie (1868–1903)

Librarian and incunabulist. Proctor was educated at Marlborough, Bath College and Oxford, where as an undergraduate at Corpus Christi College he made a list of incunabula in the College library. This brought him into contact with Duff, who helped him with his first publication, and recommended him to Bodley's Librarian to compile a list of the Bodleian's incunabula. In 1893 he took a post at the British Museum and was encouraged to work on incunabula. His chief concern was to list the Museum's holdings, an activity which bore its first fruits in his *Index to the Early Printed Books in the British Museum: From the invention of printing to the year MD* (1898). The *Index* also includes Bodleian holdings, based on Proctor's earlier work in Oxford. Proctor applied Bradshaw's 'natural history' principles of typographical analysis to his work, and listed the books in an order of his own devising, now known as 'Proctor order'. Countries are listed in the order in which printing began there; thus Germany comes first, followed by Italy, and so on. Within each country, the towns are arranged in a similar order, as are printers within each town. Although Proctor order presents difficulties to the non-specialist, and no modern catalogue of incunabula should use it, it did have the advantage of making clear the distinction between the work of Proctor and that of all his predecessors except Bradshaw, and of clarifying what he had achieved. That achievement was, in fact, quite astonishing, for to establish his order Proctor had to be familiar with every type fount used in the fifteenth century. It was a monumental task, and although he inevitably and forgivably made a few mistakes, the *Index* built much of the edifice of twentieth-century incunable studies. The British Museum's great *Catalogue of Books Printed in the XVth Century*, which was intended to be the full-dress version of the *Index*, began publication only after Proctor's death, under the guidance of his colleague, A.W. Pollard. Proctor himself had intended to take the *Index* down to 1520, and was hard at work on this when he was killed, in somewhat mysterious circumstances, during a walking tour in the Tyrol.

In Proctor's memory, Pollard edited *Bibliographical Essays* (1906), to which he prefixed a memoir. See also Barry C. Johnson, *Lost in the Alps. A Portrait of Robert Proctor* (1985).

See also **Bibliography**; **Bradshaw, Henry** (1831–1886); **Duff, Edward Gordon** (1863–1924); **Incunabula**; **Pollard, Alfred William** (1859–1944)

Project for Historical Bio-Bibliography

Research project. PHIBB, under the direction of P.J. Wallis of the University of Newcastle upon Tyne, began in 1972 as the Book Subscription Lists Project (BSLP), whose objective was to catalogue all British books with lists of subscribers, and to analyse the lists themselves using advanced automated techniques for data-processing. This phase reached its climax with the publication of *Book Subscription Lists. A revised guide* (1975) by Wallis and F.J.G.

Robinson. After 1975, BSLP was transformed into PHIBB which worked to a much wider brief. The concept itself was a bold and good one; the names in the subscription lists were to be compared with *DNB* and other biographical sources in an attempt to analyse the social, economic and cultural composition of the reading public, especially in the eighteenth century. While this ambitious objective was never entirely achieved, many of PHIBB's publications broke new ground in social history, and the whole project has made scholars more aware of the need for such analyses, and indeed of the value of subscription lists as historical source material.

PHIBB has published hundreds of reports and papers as well as the very substantial *Eighteenth-century British Books*.

See also **Eighteenth-century British Books**; **Subscription**

Proof

A proof is an impression taken for the purpose of being read to check its accuracy, with a view to correcting the type before machining begins. There are normally three stages of proof. The first proof, which since the late nineteenth century has been made from the type in galley, is necessarily the least accurate, and is read with great care both by the author himself and within the printing house. The Corrector of the Press was a familiar figure before the end of the fifteenth century, and by the seventeenth century Moxon prescribed for him a complex and important role. When the type had been corrected, and made up into pages if this had not aleady been done, a second proof, called a *revise*, was taken. When this had been read and corrected, it was normal, although not invariable, to take a *second revise* and to make final corrections from that. It was this third and final stage which produced the press variants revealed by collation in some English books of the sixteenth and seventeenth centuries.

These practices have developed slowly over the centuries, and have been followed unevenly, but proof sheets do survive from the early sixteenth century, and proofing of some sort must always have been a feature of the printing process. Revises were common by the mid-eighteenth century at the latest, and it seems from Moxon that they were in use 100 years earlier. By the late nineteenth century, cheap printing and low labour costs made many stages of proof an economic possibility, and authors developed the habit, which would be more than a little alarming to a modern publisher, of leaving their last stage of revision until they received the galleys.

Percy Simpson's *Proof-reading in the Sixteenth, Seventeenth and Eighteenth Centuries* (1935) is a classic, although it needs major revision. For a briefer, but more up-to-date account, see Gaskell, p. 110.

See also **Galley**; **Impression**; **Moxon, Joseph** (1627–1691); **Press variants**

Prospectus

Book trade term. A prospectus is a pre-publication advertisement for a book which, in its classic form, is soliciting subscriptions to finance publication. The first true prospectus was that issued in London by John Minsheu in 1610 for his *Glosson Etymologikon*, and thereafter he was imitated by a growing number of authors and booksellers. By the middle of the eighteenth century, the practice of issuing a prospectus was comparatively common both in England and in Continental Europe, especially for scholarly works which commanded a small audience and were unattractive to commercial publishers. The situation changed in the nineteenth century, as printing became cheaper and learned societies began to take over much academic publishing, but the private presses revived the use of the prospectus in the 1890s, and it is their successors who are its principal users today.

See John Feather, *English Book Prospectuses. An illustrated history* (1984).

See also **Private press movement; Subscription**

Provenance

The history of the ownership of a book or manuscript. The evidence normally takes the form of a book plate, book label or inscription of some kind. The latter may be a signature, or perhaps a note of presentation by the author or some other donor. In rarer cases, there may be a binding associated with a particular collector or library, or an identifiable shelf-mark. Provenance is highly prized by book collectors, especially when it establishes a link with, for example, a famous collector or the author of the work. It is also, however, of some scholarly importance, in permitting the reconstruction of a collection, or an analysis of a person's book reading and bookbuying habits.

There are essays on the scholarly dimension of provenance by Robert Nikirk and Salvatore J. Iacone, in H. George Fletcher (ed.), *A Miscellany for Book Collectors* (1979).

See also **Book collecting; Book label; Book plate**

Provincial printing

Printing in England outside London. In fact, London has always been the only real centre of the English book trade, and most provincial printers have been concerned with the production of non-book materials (so-called 'ephemera'). The first press outside London was that of Theodoric Rood at Oxford in 1478/79, followed by others at various towns including St Albans (1479/80), York (1509) and Tavistock (1525). All of these were associated with some local institution, such as a university, school or monastery, and all were short-lived, for the English market for books was still small at the beginning of the sixteenth century and could easily be satisfied by the London printers and with books imported from the Continent. After 1557 provincial presses were discouraged; from 1586 to 1695, with a short gap during the Civil War, they were illegal. When the lapse of the Printing Act in 1694 allowed presses to be established outside London, Oxford, Cambridge and York, reprinting began in some of the major provincial towns, beginning with Bristol. By about 1730 most of the towns had a printer, and by the end of the eighteenth century there were few towns of any size which did not have at least one. Those who were successful, however, were the printers who built their businesses on the printing and publication of local newspapers, and they became the keystones of the whole system for the distribution of London books in the provinces. Most printers confined themselves to producing catalogues, handbills, advertisements, and the like for local tradesmen; although a few provincial books were printed, most were of purely local interest.

A good deal of work has been done on the history of the provincial press; it is listed in John Feather, *The English Provincial Book Trade before 1850. A checklist of secondary sources* (OBS, occ. pub. 16, 1981). The same author's *The Provincial Book Trade in Eighteenth-century England* (1985) is a study of the crucial period in the growth of the trade.

See also **Ephemera**; **Printing Act 1662**; **Rood, Theodoric** (fl. 1478–1486)

Publisher

A specialist within the book trade. By derivation, the word means 'to make public'. In the book trade, the term began to be used in the late seventeenth century, when it was applied to booksellers who specialised in the wholesaling of pamphlets and newspapers. It is important to realise that these early publishers did not own copyrights; if their names appear in imprints they do so to conceal the name of the copy owner rather than to reveal it. By the late eighteenth century, however, the word was beginning to take on its modern meaning of the copyright owner who financed and organised the publication of a book or newspaper. It was fully established in this sense by about 1820, displacing the word 'Bookseller' which had formerly had this meaning. The change in meaning corresponded with the separation of the two roles of publisher and retail bookseller.

See Michael Treadwell, 'London trade publishers, 1675–1750', *Libr.* (1982), pp. 99–134; and Terry Belanger, 'From bookseller to publisher: changes in the London book trade, 1750–1850', in Richard G. Landon (ed.), *Book Selling and Book Buying* (1978).

See also **Bookseller**; **Copyright**

Publishers' Association

The trade association of the British publishing industry. The PA was founded in 1896 on the initiative of C.J. Longman, John Murray and Frederick Macmillan. Its original purpose was to provide a common front for the publishers in the negotiations with the booksellers which culminated in the signing of the Net Book Agreement in 1899. From the beginning, however, the PA has been concerned with wider issues which affect the trade, especially the law of copyright. In recent years, the PA has collaborated with the Booksellers' Association not only in defending the sacred writ of the Net Book Agreement but also in various promotional schemes both in Britain and abroad.

There is an admirable history of the PA by R.J.L. Kingsford, a former President, under the title *The Publishers' Association 1896–1946* (1970).

See also **Booksellers' Association; Net Book Agreement**

Publishing History

Learned journal. The first issue of *PH* appeared in 1977, and it is now published twice yearly. It gives scope for articles which are longer than those which are usually to be found in such journals, thus enabling its contributors to present their evidence as well as their conclusions at some length. Perhaps because of this generosity of space it has rapidly established itself as the leading journal in the field, with articles of an almost uniformly high standard. The editor is Michael L. Turner.

Punch

See **Typecasting**

Pynson, Richard (*c.* 1435–1530)

Printer. Pynson was a Frenchman, who may have been in London as early as 1482. By the late 1480s he apparently had the Law Patent, although he also had a flourishing printing business in other fields. His non-legal work included an edition of Chaucer (1491). Pynson was indeed one of the most prolific and successful of the early English printers. In 1508 he became King's Printer, and when he died he left a considerable amount of property.

See E.G. Duff, *A Century of the English Book Trade* (1905); and H.R. Plomer, 'Richard Pynson, glover and printer', *Libr.* (1922/23), pp. 49-52.

See also **King's (or Queen's) Printer; Patents**

Quads

Composing-room equipment. Quads are pieces of type-metal cast to large sizes to fill out the space at the beginning and end of indented and short lines.
See Moxon, *Mechanick Exercises*, p. 217.

Quaerendo

Bibliographical journal. *Quaerendo* was first published in 1971, and appears at quarterly intervals. It is published in Amsterdam and is chiefly concerned with topics relating to the history of books and the book trade in the Low Countries. Its principal language is English, although there are some articles in Dutch and French.

Quaritch, Bernard (1819–1899)

Antiquarian bookseller, Born in Germany, Quaritch arrived in London in 1842 after serving his apprenticeship with a bookseller in Nordhausen. He worked for H.G. Bohn, another German immigrant, who was an antiquarian bookseller, remainder dealer and publisher. In 1848, Quaritch established his own business, and within ten years was already one of the most highly regarded antiquarian booksellers in London. By the mid-1870s he was unquestionably the leading man in the trade. He bought heavily at all the major sales in the last quarter of the nineteenth century, and consequently his customers included all the important collectors of the period, including the Americans who were beginning to have a great influence on the market for early books. His magnificent catalogues of his huge stock became standard works of reference, although they reflected the qualities of his staff rather than those of Quaritch himself, for he was always a businessman before he was a bookman. His last great catalogue, entitled *General Catalogue of Old Books and Manuscripts* (12 vols, 1887–97), is still of some value as a source of bibliophilic information. Quaritch also published some books, chiefly on behalf of learned societies, although his early ventures into publishing included the first edition of Fitzgerald's translation of the *Rubaiyat* of Omar Khayaam.

His son succeeded to the business after his death, and the firm still trades as Bernard Quaritch, although there is no longer a family connection.

There is a life of Quaritch in *DNB (Supplement)* but a history of the firm is a desideratum, and would be a major contribution to the history both of the trade and of book collecting.

Quarter sheet

Bibliographical format. It is, as the name suggests, an item printed on one-fourth of the full sheet of paper. Sometimes such items were printed in pairs by half sheet imposition. Quarter sheets were rarely used, and the few recorded examples are at least semi-clandestine, mainly Jacobite.

Several items are listed by D.F. Foxon, *English Verse 1701–1750* (2 vols, 1975).

See also **Format**; **Half sheet**; **Sheet**

Quarto

Bibliographical format. A quarto, written 4°, is a sheet printed with 8 pages to fold to 4 leaves. It was a common format in the sixteenth and seventeenth centuries, when it was used for pamphlets, plays (including the first editions of many of Shakespeare's plays) and newsbooks. As the standard size of the sheet increased, however, quartos became inconveniently large for normal purposes, and by the middle of the eighteenth century the use of the format was generally confined to books such as topographical works or poems where some typographical display or illustration was desired.

The best imposition diagrams for quarto are those in William Savage, *A Dictionary of the Art of Printing* (1841, repr. 1968).

See also **Format**; **Imposition**

Queen's Printer

See **King's Printer**

Quire

(1) *Papermaker's term.* A quire consisted of 24 (or sometimes 25) sheets; 20 quires = 1 ream.

(2) *Bookbinder's term.* In the fifteenth, sixteenth and early seventeenth centuries, books were sometimes printed so that a single gathering consisted of more than one sheet. The sheets were bound so that each, when folded, was inserted into the centre fold of the other. This is called quiring, and the gatherings are called quires. The practice was perhaps most common with folios, where, for example, three sheets might be quired in this way. Thus in the outermost sheet are pages 1, 2, 11 and 12; the second sheet has pages 3, 4, 9 and 10; and the inner sheet pages 5, 6, 7 and 8. Quiring was also used in quarto and octavo.

See Edith Diehl, *Bookbinding* (2 vols, 1946).

See also **Folio**; **Gathering**; **Octavo**; **Papermaking**; **Quarto**

Quoin

See **Chase**

Radcliffe, John (1652/53–1714)

Physician and book collector. The son of an attorney in Wakefield, Radcliffe graduated from Oxford in 1669, was briefly a Fellow of Lincoln College, took his MD in 1682, and in 1684 established a medical practice in London. He was highly successful in his profession, becoming one of the physicians to Queen Anne. He wrote little or nothing, but formed a large collection of medical and scientific books and manuscripts. He bequeathed this collection, and a large sum of money, to Oxford University, and his Trustees built a library to house them. This building, the Radcliffe Camera, was built (1737–49) adjacent to the Bodleian Library but not as a part of it. The Radcliffe Library continued to develop as Oxford's scientific library, and with the growing importance of science in the nineteenth century it became necessary to rationalise the arrangements between the Radcliffe and the Bodleian. In 1861, the Radcliffe collection was transferred to the new University Museum, the core of what is now the 'Science Area' of the University, and the Camera itself was made available to the Bodleian as its first undergraduate reading room. Not until 1927, however, did the Camera legally become part of the Bodleian. Radcliffe's own collection is now housed in the Radcliffe Science Library, built in 1902 and extended in 1934 and 1976.

See Sir Edmund Craster, *History of the Bodleian Library 1845–1945* (1952); and *Bibliotheca Radcliviana 1749–1949* (1949).

See also **Bodleian Library**

Rare Books and Manuscripts Section

A section of the Association of College and Research Libraries, which is itself a division of the American Library Association, the professional association of librarians in the United States. RBMS holds a well-supported annual conference, sometimes with speakers and participants from outside the USA, and acts as a forum for rare book librarians. It publishes *Rare Book and Manuscript Librarianship*, a recently-founded journal, which fills an important gap in the literature of both librarianship and bibliography.

RBMS's address is A.L.A., 50 East Huron Street, Chicago, Ill. 60611.

Rare Books Group

A group of the Library Association, the professional association of librarians in the United Kingdom. The group brings together British librarians concerned with rare books by holding regular meetings and by publishing a

Newsletter. The *Newsletter* contains papers read to the Group, and notes and news on matters of rare book interest. The Group also sponsored *A Directory of Rare Book and Special Collections in the United Kingdom* (1985), edited by Moelwyn Williams, a unique and invaluable guide to rare book resources.

Reader

(1) *In printing,* the reader is the proof-reader who reads the first and subsequent proofs against copy. Since the mid-nineteenth century this has been a preliminary to sending a set of proofs, marked up by the reader, to the publisher. Before then, however, it was frequently the only proofing that was done.

See Percy Simpson, *Proof-reading in the Sixteenth, Seventeenth and Eighteenth Centuries* (1935).

(2) *In publishing,* the reader is the person who reads an author's manuscript on behalf of the publisher to assess its suitability for publication. Until the early nineteenth century, this person was usually the publisher himself, and indeed in smaller houses this practice still continues. By the 1830s, however, it appears that publishers employed readers, usually on the basis of a fee paid for each manuscript read. The late nineteenth century was the great age of the publisher's reader, especially in fiction publishing. Some of them, notably Sir Arthur Quiller-Couch (1863–1944) and, above all, John Morley (1851–1923) exercised immense influence. Morley was a reader for Macmillan from the 1860s until World War I; his discoveries included Hardy and Kipling. In recent years, the reader has been somewhat superseded by the in-house editor, although academic books are usually assessed by a scholar who is paid a fee for his trouble.

See Linda Marie Fritschner, 'Publishers' readers, publishers, and their authors', *PH* (1980), pp. 45-100.

See also **Editor**; **Proof**

Ream

See **Papermaking**

Recto

The right-hand page of an open book; the left-hand page is called the verso.

See also **Page**

Register

Printing term.
(1) *In hand-printing*, when the sheet is returned to the press for perfecting, it has to be placed so that the second side correctly backs up the first side. Correct back-up is called *register*. See Gaskell, p. 131.
(2) *In colour printing*, register is the correct superimposition of colour-separated blocks. See Gaskell, p. 261.
(3) *In early printed books*, the printer sometimes printed a list of the signatures in the correct order as a guide to the binder. This was especially the case when the signatures were symbols rather than letters or numbers. This list is called a *register*. By extension, bibliographers use the term for a formulaic list of the signatures in a book when only a single copy has been examined so that the description is of that copy rather than the ideal copy. See Bowers, p. 201; and Gaskell, p. 52.

See also **Collation**; **Colour printing**; **Ideal copy**; **Perfecting**; **Printing**; **Signature**

Relief printing

Printing process. Until the last 20 years, relief (or letterpress) was the normal technique for almost all printing. The basic principle is a very simple one: the area to be printed is raised above its surroundings so that, when the forme is inked, the ink will adhere only to the printing area. The ink is then transferred to the paper under pressure on a printing press.

The fundamental principle pre-dates Gutenberg's invention of typographic printing in the mid-1450s, having been used in China, Korea and elsewhere in the East for centuries; it may also have been used in Western Europe for printing from woodcut blocks. All typographic printing, whether set and printed by hand or by machine, has worked on exactly the same principle ever since. The chief technical diffculties of relief printing arise from the need to ensure that the entire printing surface is in exactly the same plane; on the common press, with its wooden bed, this was difficult to achieve and uneven impressions are often to be found in books printed on such presses. With the invention of the iron press in the early nineteenth century, this problem was eased since the use of more sophisticated machine tools and the greater stability of iron ensured that the Stanhope and its successors had more perfectly planed beds. The invention of stereotyping, and the later development of steam-driven and rotary presses, raised relief printing to a high standard of technical perfection in the later part of the nineteenth century.

A related problem was that of illustration, for the blocks had to be at type height. For centuries, this was possible only by using woodcut and wood-engraved blocks. In the second half of the nineteenth century, however, photomechanical processes were developed, of which the most important were the line block and the half-tone.

In recent years, the development of offset lithography has almost entirely displaced relief as a commercial process. Although the quality of the product is not as high, offset lithography has two great advantages: it permits a more flexible combination of text and graphics, and plates are a great deal easier to handle and to store than are formes of type or stereotype plates.

The classic description of relief printing by hand is that in Moxon, p. 252; for modern processes, see Hugh Williamson, *Methods of Book Design* (3rd edn, 1983).

See also **Block books**; **Common press**; **Forme**; **Gutenberg, Johann** (1394/99–1468); **Half-tone**; **Impression**; **Offset lithography**; **Photo-mechanical printing**; **Printing**; **Stanhope press**; **Stereotyping**; **Type height**; **Wood-engraving**; **Woodcut**

Remaindering

Bookselling term. Books are remaindered when the publisher judges that there is no further market for the title at its full published price. He then sells the remaining copies to wholesalers or booksellers for retailing at a much lower price. This clears his warehouse space, and also generates some income. The inventor of the practice was James Lackington at the end of the eighteenth century, and it has subsequently become common (some would say too common) in the trade throughout the world. In Britain, remaindering is regulated under the Net Book Agreement.

For Lackington, see Richard G. Landon, in *SEC* (1976), p. 387. Some very early examples are noted by Kenneth Muir, 'Elizabethan remainders', *Libr.* (1958), p. 56.

See also **Lackington, James** (1746–1815); **Net Book Agreement**

Revise

See **Proofs**

Revised Version

See **Bible**

Revue française d'histoire du livre

Learned journal. The new series of *RFHL*, which began in 1971 under the joint auspices of the Société des bibliophiles de Guyenne and the Société française d'histoire du livre, has been a major influence in the development of the history of the book as an academic discipline. The first article in vol. 1 was entitled 'Le livre, ce ferment', and surveyed the evolution and present state of historical studies of the book as a social and cultural phenomenon. This established the tone and direction of the journal's editorial policy, and in subsequent issues there have been many very important articles, chiefly by younger French scholars, which book historians ignore at their peril. *RFHL* is published quarterly.

Richardson, Samuel (1689–1761)

Novelist and printer. Descended from an old Kentish family which had gone into trade, Richardson was apprenticed to John Wilde, a London printer, in 1706. He was freed in 1715, and set up his own business in 1719. He was highly successful as a printer, and became a leading figure in the trade. In 1754 he was Master of the Stationers' Company, and in 1760 became a partner in the Law Patent which added yet further to his prosperity. He is, of course, best remembered as one of the earliest and one of the greatest of English novelists, especially for his *Pamela* (1741) and *Clarissa* (1748).

Richardson has attracted much attention from literary scholars; for a full-scale biography, see T.C. Duncan Eades and Ben D. Kimpel, *Samuel Richardson* (1971). His career in the trade, however, is best studied in William M. Sale, *Samuel Richardson: Master Printer* (1950) which includes a detailed bibliography of his output.

See also **Patents**; **Stationers' Company**

Robert, Nicholas-Louis (1761–1828)

See **Fourdrinier, Henry** (1766–1834) **and Fourdrinier, Sealy** (d. 1847)

Rogers, Bruce (1870–1957)

Book designer and typographer. Rogers, born in Lafayette, Indiana, graduated from Purdue University in 1892 and began to work for the *Indianapolis News*. By 1894 he was already working as a freelance book designer, and from 1895 to 1912 he worked for the Riverside Press in Cambridge, Massachusetts, which, under his influence, became one of the best book-printing houses in the world. It was during this time that he designed his most famous type, Centaur, which was widely used in the mid-twentieth century. In 1917, he visited England for the first time, met Emery Walker, and became, briefly, typographic adviser to Cambridge University Press. At Cambridge he did little work, but his devastating report on the Press's typographic standards paved the way for the appointment of Morison a few years later. In 1920, he returned to the USA as adviser to Harvard University Press where his work was comparable with that of Morison at Cambridge.

For the context of his American work, see James M. Wells, 'Book typography in the United States of America', in Kenneth Day (ed.), *Book Typography 1815–1965* (1965).

See also **Cambridge University Press**; **Morison, Stanley** (1889–1967); **Walker, Sir Emery** (1851–1933)

Roll

See **Bookbinding**

Rolling press

Printing equipment. The rolling press was used for hand-printing from intaglio plates and was designed to apply the extremely heavy pressure required in such work. The earliest rolling presses were made of wood. A bed was held between two posts, or cheeks, and heavy rollers fixed between them above and beneath the bed. An X-shaped handle was attached to the outer side of one cheek and to the bed. The plate was placed face upwards on the bed and after it had been inked the paper laid on it. The handle was then turned so that the bed passed between the rollers and the paper was pressed down into the inked plate thus making the impression.

The wooden rolling press is apparently a Dutch invention of the late sixteenth century; it came into use throughout Europe during the next 50 years. Various improvements were attempted, but there were no major changes until the first iron rolling presses were built in the 1830s. They were of essentially the same design, although the machinery of the rollers and the screw mechanism of the handle were more precise in operation. Some nineteenth-century rolling presses are still in use.

See H. Meier, 'The origins of the printing and roller press', *PCQ* (1941), p. 173; and Anthony Dyson, 'The rolling press: some aspects of its development from the seventeeth century to the nineteenth century', *JPHS* (1981/2), p. 1.

See also **Impression**; **Intaglio**

Roman

Letterform. Roman, which is now the standard typeface for the Latin alphabet throughout the world, is derived from a style of handwriting evolved by the Italian humanists in the fifteenth century. This was itself based on the Carolingian Miniscule of the ninth century. When Sweynheym and Pannartz set up the first printing press in Italy at Subiaco, near Rome, in 1464/65, they cut a type based on the humanist hand; this was the first roman. Roman soon became popular throughout Italy, especially for setting Latin texts, and the first of the great romans was cut by Jenson as early as 1470. At about the same time, roman began to be used in France, and it gradually displaced Gothic type throughout Europe except in Germany. Gothics had all but vanished in Italy by the end of the fifteenth century, although in France, the Netherlands and England they survived rather longer.

There are two basic groups of romans: Old face, which derives from the design cut by Griffo for Aldus, and Modern face, which began to evolve in the late seventeenth century.

See A.F. Johnson, *Type Designs* (3rd edn, 1966); Stanley Morison, 'Early humanistic script and the first roman type', *Libr.* (1943), pp. 1-29; and Philip Gaskell, 'A nomenclature for the letterforms of roman type', *Libr.* (1974), pp. 42-51.

See also **Aldus Manutius** (*c.* 1450–1515); **Gothic type**; **Jenson, Nicholas** (*c.* 1420–1480); **Modern face**; **Old face**

Rood, Theodoric (fl. 1478–1486)

Printer. Rood was the first printer in Oxford, but little is known of him, except by bibliographical inferences from the 17 extant books and fragments from his press. His types are of a design associated with Cologne, and it is, therefore, assumed that he was a German. It is not known whether he was invited to Oxford, although as he worked with Thomas Hunt, a University Stationer, and it can be assumed that there was some connection. Certainly, the books which he produced were academic texts and Latin grammars intended to appeal to a scholarly market. His first book was an edition of Rufinus's commentary on the Apostles' Creed (then ascribed to St Jerome), which he dated 'M.cccc.lxviij'; it is agreed that the date is a misprint, but the assumption that the correct date was 1478 has recently been challenged, and it seems that the first Oxford book may have been published in 1479. Rood's enterprise was unsuccessful; Oxford alone could not sustain it, and the market for learned books elsewhere in England was even smaller. His printing house vanished in 1486, and it was to be nearly two centuries before the University finally succeeded in establishing its own learned press.

See Harry Carter, *A History of the Oxford University Press, vol. 1* (1975); and A.C. de la Mare and Lotte Helinga, in *TCBS* (1978), p. 184.

See also **Oxford University Press**

Rotary press

See **Press**

Rotunda

Type design. One of the four basic groups of Gothic type. Rotunda is Italian

Gothic, based in a hand used in the Law School at Bologna University. As the name suggests, the letters are open and well-rounded, although somewhat narrower than in the rather similar Fere-humanistica. The design is first found in Northern Italy in the early 1460s, but in its native land it was soon displaced by Roman. It did, however, become the standard Gothic in Spain and France; in the latter country it was still used for law printing in the middle of the sixteenth century.

See A.F. Johnson, *Type Designs* (3rd edn, 1966).

See also **Fere-humanistica**; **Gothic type**; **Roman**

Roxburghe Club

Bibliophilic society. The Roxburghe Club was founded in 1812 on the initiative of Dibdin, to celebrate the Roxburghe sale which marked the climax of the bibliomania. Dibdin brought together a small group of bibliophiles, most of them aristocratic, and the Club has retained essentially that character ever since. The members prepared publications for presentation to each other, and had them printed to a very high standard. The earliest publications followed the contemporary taste for type facsimiles, but in the 1830s editions of early English texts became the fashion, followed in the 1860s by some of the earliest photographic facsimiles and very fine chromolithographic facsimiles of illuminated manuscripts. In recent years, the publications have taken on a more distinctly scholarly character to the extent that some, despite their cost and rarity, have become standard works.

See Lord Mersey, *The Roxburghe Club: Its history and members* (1926); and Nicholas Barker, *The Publications of the Roxburghe Club 1814–1962* (1964).

See also **Bibliomania**; **Book collecting**; **Chromolithography**; **Dibdin, Thomas Frognall** (1776–1847); **Facsimile**; **Type facsimile**

Royalty

Book trade term. A royalty is a payment to the author of a book, based on a percentage of the retail price of each copy sold. This is usually 10 per cent. Royalties gradually replaced the older practice of payment by half-profits in the late nineteenth century, largely under pressure from the newly-founded Society of Authors, which rightly considered royalties to be a more equitable system.

See James Hepburn, *The Author's Empty Purse* (1968).

See also **Half profits**; **Society of Authors**

Rubrication

The practice of using red ink for the first letter of a word, usually at the beginning of textual sub-division. This was common in medieval liturgical manuscripts, and was imitated by the early printers in editions of such texts. Even in printed books, rubrication was normally done by hand in a space left for the purpose.

See Colin Clair, *A History of European Printing* (1976).

Running title

Printer's term, used also by bibliographers. The running title is the title of the book or chapter printed at the head of each page of the text, as part of the headline. It is sometimes an abbreviated form of the full title. The value of running titles to bibliographers is that they were often kept as standing type as part of a skeleton forme; if individual sorts can be identified, the bibliographer can trace the successive uses of the skeleton, and perhaps the order of the formes to the press. A record of running titles is a normal part of a full bibliographical description.

See Fredson T. Bowers, 'Notes on running-titles as bibliographical evidence', *Libr.* (1938/39), p. 139.

See also **Descriptive bibliography**; **Forme**; **Headline**; **Skeleton forme**; **Sort**; **Standing type**

Rylands, John (1801–1888)

See **John Rylands University Library of Manchester**

Sabin, Joseph (1821–1881)

Bibliographer. Sabin was born in England and learned bookbinding from a bookseller in Oxford. In 1848, he emigrated to the United States and spent the rest of his life there working as a bookbinder, auctioneer and bookseller in New York City and Philadelphia. In the late 1840s he began to compile a list of all books relating to the Americas, and after 1865 devoted himself entirely to this enterprise. A prospectus for his *Dictionary of Books Relating to America* was issued in 1866, followed by the first volume in 1867. By the time of his death, however, Sabin had published only 12 volumes, and the work was eventually completed, under the auspices of the Bibliographical Society of America, only in 1936 (vol. 24). The *Dictionary* (sometimes called from the half-title *Bibliotheca Americana*) is the basic work of American bibliography. There is an *Author/Title Index* by Joseph Edgar Molnar (3 vols, 1974).

There is a notice of Sabin in the *Dictionary of American Biography*, vol. 8 (1935).

See also **Americana**; **Bibliographical Society of America**

Sadleir, Michael (1888–1957)

Bibliophile and bibliographer. The son of Sir Michael Sadler, Vice-Chancellor of Leeds University and subsequently Master of University College, Oxford, Sadleir was educated at Rugby and Oxford, and then went into publishing, the profession in which he spent the rest of his life. He made a name as a minor novelist, and one of his later books, *Fanny by Gaslight* (1940), is a classic of its kind. His great interest was the nineteenth-century novel, of which he assembled a large collection, beginning with Trollope but moving out into fiction of all literary levels. As a bibliographer, his importance is that he was the first person to apply modern bibliographical techniques to nineteenth-century books, and his *Excursions in Victorian Bibliography* (1922) was the first work to come to grips with such specifically nineteenth-century problems as edition bindings and half-titles. Bindings of this period were indeed a special interest; his *Evolution of Publishers' Binding Styles, 1770–1900* (1932) is both the first and the best account of the subject. His greatest work, however, was his *XIX Century Fiction* (2 vols, 1951). It is a descriptive catalogue of his own collection rather than a bibliography, but the collection was so comprehensive that it has become a standard work.

Large parts of Sadleir's collection are, happily, still extant. His Trollopes are at Princeton University, his Gothic romances at the University of Virginia, and his unique collection of three-deckers and yellowbacks at the University of California, Los Angeles.

Graham Pollard's obituary of him in *Libr.* (1958), pp. 129-38 was written from many years of personal knowledge; appended to it is a list of Sadleir's works by Simon Nowell-Smith. See also Roy Stokes, *Michael Sadleir 1888–1957* (1980) which has a biographical preface and extracts from both his fiction and his bibliographical works.

See also **Bibliography**; **Book collecting**; **Edition binding**; **Half-title**; **Three-decker**; **Yellowbacks**

St Dominic's Press

See **Gill, Arthur Eric Rowton** (1882–1940).

Sangorski and Sutcliffe

Bookbinders. The firm flourished in London in the late nineteenth and early twentieth centuries, specialising in highly decorated gilt bindings. They now command little admiration, although in their day they were favoured by many bibliophiles, and are to be seen on many books in most collections formed at that time.

See Howard M. Nixon, *Five Centuries of English Bookbinding* (1978).

Sans serif

Type design. Literally 'without serifs', a precise description of the design. The first sans serifs were cut in the early nineteenth century. The name was, apparently, coined by Figgins in 1832, when he made the first successful sans serif design. In the nineteenth century, sans serifs were normally used for advertising and display, but in 1927 Eric Gill cut a sans serif book type which was used by a number of private and semi-private presses, and even found its way into commercial book printing in the 1930s.

See A.F. Johnson, *Type Designs* (3rd edn, 1966); for the Gill Sans Serif, see Nicolas Barker, *Stanley Morison* (1972).

See also **Figgins, Vincent** (1766–1836); **Gill, Arthur Eric Rowton** (1882–1940); **Serif**

Script type

Type design. As the name suggests, script types are designed to resemble handwriting; consequently, their most characteristic features are that the letterforms are somewhat irregular, and that when printed the letters appear to be linked. All early type designs were based on contemporary styles of handwriting, but the conscious attempt to imitate the appearance of the written page began in the early sixteenth century, usually in books which were intended as writing manuals. Of these designs the most successful was Civilité. All the early script types were based on Gothic hands, or on the Secretary hand derived from it. Latin script types, based on Italian hands, began to be cut only in the seventeeenth century. In the eighteenth century, they became more common, and in England are particularly associated with the name of John Trusler (1735–1820) who, from 1771, used his own design for printing sermons which had the somewhat disreputable purpose of making the printed text look like a manuscript when it was being read from the pulpit. Today, script types are normally used only for such items as business and invitation cards.

See A.F. Johnson, *Type Designs* (3rd edn, 1966); and Stanley Morison, 'On script types', *Fleuron* (1925), p. 1.

See also **Civilité**

Senefelder, Alois (1771–1834)

Inventor of lithography. Born in Prague, the son of an actor, Senefelder wished to follow his father onto the stage; he was, however, frustrated in this by his family who sent him to university to study law. In the event, his father died before Senefelder had completed his studies and he did indeed become an actor. He was unsuccessful, as he was in subsequent attempts to make his name as a playwright. In about 1793, the publication of one of his plays brought him into contact with the printing trade, and he began to try his hand at printing for himself to save money. He tried various relief and intaglio methods on metal plates, but in 1796 he began to experiment with relief etching on stone. He then became aware of similar work by Simon Schmidt in Munich, where he was then living. By 1797 he had advanced to the point of experimenting with planographic printing, and in 1798 finally discovered the basic principles of what he called 'chemical printing'. Within a few years this came to be known as lithography. Senefelder travelled to London to promote his invention, having persuaded the brothers Friedrich, Philip and Johann André to give him financial support. He took out a British patent for lithography in 1801 but made it over to Johann André within a few weeks. The Andrés then helped him to secure patents in Vienna and Bavaria. Like Gutenberg, Senefelder was a poor businessman although the Andrés were kinder than Gutenberg's associates, for he was able to keep some of the income from the Viennese and Bavarian patents. By the time that Senefelder died, still experimenting with improvements to his technique, lithography was in use throughout Western Europe.

See Michael Twyman, *Lithography 1800–1850* (1970); Senefelder's own account of his invention is in his book translated as *A Complete Course of Lithography* (1819).

See also **Ackermann, Rudolph** (1764–1834); **Etching**; **Intaglio**; **Lithography**; **Relief printing**

Serial publication

A work published at regular intervals over a period of time. The most common serial publications are newspapers and magazines, which appear at predetermined intervals and are numbered serially. Another form of serial publication, however, is the part book, also regular and numbered, but of finite length since publication ceases when the work is complete.

See also **Magazines**; **Newspapers**; **Part books**

Serif

Technical term in typography. The serif is the small stroke at the head and foot of the letter, which is normal in almost all roman and italic types. It is a residual survival of the book hands from which the early letterforms were copied. The word itself came into use in about 1800; formerly serifs were known as *headings* and *footings*.

See A.F. Johnson, *Type Designs* (3rd edn, 1966).

See also **Italic**; **Letterform**; **Roman**; **Sans serif**

Setting by formes

See **Casting-off**; **Forme**

Share books

Book trade term. In origin, share books were editions which were jointly financed by two or more booksellers or printers to spread the risks and capital costs of publication. In this sense, there were share books in the early sixteenth century. The term is, however, usually reserved for those books whose copyright was jointly owned by groups of London booksellers in the seventeenth, eighteenth and nineteenth centuries. The practice evolved out of the operation of the congers in the late seventeenth century when joint wholesaling was undertaken. This developed into joint copyright ownership, especially in the very profitable standard works of literature, history and theology which were frequently reprinted. By the 1730s, when the system was fully developed, many hundreds of copies were owned in this way and the shares, some as minute as 1/132, were bought and sold at the jealously defended trade sales. The system survived into the nineteenth century, although it was in decline from the mid-1770s onwards, and had all but vanished by 1900.

See Graham Pollard, 'The English market for printed books', *PH* (1978), p.7.

See also **Conger**; **Copyright**: **Trade sales**

Sheet

Papermakers' term used by bibliographers. The sheet is the complete piece of paper made in the hand papermaking process. This may seem self-evident, but the concept is an important one in bibliography, particularly in the determination of format which is always a statement describing the way in which the sheet has been folded or cut.

The maximum size of the sheet was effectively determined by the largest size of mould that the papermaker could conveniently handle; the very largest (called Super Royal) was about 90 × 60 cm (or, approximately, 36 × 24 inches). Such sheets were, however, uncommon; the usual sheets for book printing were Demy size, typically about 50 × 40cm (= approx 20 × 16in), Crown (about 45 × 35cm = 18 × 14in), Foolscap (about 40 × 35cm = 16 × 14in) and Pot (about 40 × 30cm = 16 × 12in). Within each of these categories the size was somewhat smaller in the sixteenth century, and somewhat larger in the eighteenth century.

See Graham Pollard, 'Notes on the size of the sheet', *Libr.* (1936/37), p. 337; and Philip Gaskell, 'Notes on eighteenth-century British paper', *Libr.* (1957) p. 34.

See also **Format**; **Papermaking**

Siberch, John (1476–1554)

Printer. Siberch, a native of Siegburg in Germany, was educated at Cologne University and went into the book trade. He married (*c.* 1512) the daughter of Gerhard van Amersfoort, a bookseller who had wide-ranging contacts with humanist printers in Cologne and the Low Countries and some commercial dealings with England. By 1514, Siberch was working for the Cologne bookseller, Hans Beck, and came to know Erasmus and other humanists. These humanist connections included a number of scholars at Cambridge, notably Richard Croke who may have been responsible for inviting Siberch to England. In 1520 Siberch arrived in Cambridge where he was the first printer. It is unlikely that either Siberch himself or his Cambridge sponsors saw his press as a commercial venture; it was a scholarly enterprise from which a number of humanist works appeared. It was also a short-lived enterprise; in just over three years at Cambridge Siberch is known to have produced 14 books. In fact, the English market was too small to support a learned press, and the brave effort of the Cambridge humanists was in vain. Siberch returned to Germany and died in his native town.

See Otto Treptow, *John Siberch. Johann Lair von Siegburg*, trans. Trevor Jones, abridged and ed. John Morris and Trevor Jones (CBS, monogr. 6, 1970).

See also **Cambridge University Press**

Side notes

Printer's term. Side notes are notes to a text printed in the inner or outer margin, rather than at the foot of the page. Such notes were common in medieval manuscripts, and were, like other features of such manuscripts, imitated by the early printers. By the late sixteenth century, however, they had been almost entirely displaced by footnotes which presented fewer technical difficulties to the printer.

See Moxon, p. 228, for the technical aspects of side notes.

Siderography

See **Steel engraving**

Signature

Printer's term, used also by bibliographers. The signature, printed in the direction line, is a guide to the binder which enables him to fold, gather and collate the sheets in correct sequence. The normal form of a signature was a letter on the first recto of the gathering, with each succeeding recto having the letter and a number, beginning with 2 on the second leaf. Until the end of the eighteenth century the usual practice was to sign each recto up to and including the first leaf after the centre-fold of the gathering. Although signatures were usually alphabetic, numbers were sometimes used, and, in the fifteenth century, sequences of symbols such as * ,)(, and so on are found. In the latter case, the printer usually added a register as a further guide to the binder. After about 1800, numerical signatures became common, but they gradually died out when the binding processes were mechanised and are rarely seen today.

For the bibliographer, as for the binder, the signatures are an indispensable tool; they help to establish the make-up of the book and the completeness of the copy in hand. A register of signatures or the collation of an ideal copy is an invariable part of a bibliographical description. Signatures can also be used as a system of reference. Such a reference as $A2^v$, meaning the verso of leaf A2, is more practical than relying on the often erratic pagination of early printed books.

See Gaskell, p. 51; and R.A. Sayce, *Compositorial Practices and the Localization of Printed Books 1530–1800* (OBS, occ. pub. 13, 1979).

See also **Bookbinding**; **Collation**; **Descriptive bibliography**; **Direction line**; **Gathering**; **Recto**; **Register**; **Verso**

Simpkin, Marshall

Wholesale booksellers. The firm had its origins in 1814, when W. Simpkin and R. Marshall bought the bookselling business of their employer, Benjamin Crosby. Crosby had followed Lackington's example of buying large stocks from the publishers at low prices, but rather than remaindering them he travelled the country and established himself as a wholesaler to provincial booksellers. Simpkin and Marshall developed this trade, and by the middle of the nineteenth century Simpkin, Marshall and Co (as the firm became in 1838) was the largest wholesale bookseller in the country and virtually the only supplier of most of the provincial trade. Their only serious competitor was W.H. Smith, and for most of the nineteenth century Smiths tended to concentrate on newspapers and magazines while Simpkin, Marshall dealt in books.

Sixteenmo

Simpkin, Marshall became something of a book trade institution, and continued to flourish during the first four decades of the twentieth century. Their offices, warehouses and stock were, however, destroyed in the Blitz in 1941, and despite efforts both within the trade and by a new figure on the scene, Robert Maxwell, the business never recovered. It ended in bankruptcy in 1955.

For an account of Simpkin, Marshall at its height, see Henry Curwen, *A History of Booksellers* (1873); and for its sad demise, see Ian Norrie, *Mumby's Publishing and Bookselling in the Twentieth Century* (1982).

See also **Lackington, James** (1746–1815); **Smith, William Henry** (1792–1865) **and Smith, William Henry** (1825–1891); **Wholesaling**

Sixteenmo

Bibliographical format. A sixteenmo, written 16° and very occasionally called 'sextodecimo', is a sheet printed with 32 pages to fold to 16 leaves. This produces a small, rather squat, page, and a very thick gathering. To overcome the latter problem, 16's were often bound in 8s, i.e. with two gatherings to the sheet. 16° was used from the sixteenth to the eighteenth centuries for books where a small size was an advantage, such as pocket books, almanacs, school books and children's books.

The best imposition diagrams for 16° are those in William Savage, *A Dictionary of the Art of Printing* (1841, repr. 1968).

See also **Format**; **Gathering**; **Imposition**

Skeleton

See **Skeleton Forme**

Skeleton Forme

Printer's term used by bibliographers, sometimes simply as 'skeleton'. When the forme had been printed and was returned to the compositor for distribution, he left the furniture and sometimes the headlines in the chase for re-use in making up the next forme. This was known as the skeleton forme. In theory, only two skeletons were required for a book: one on the press and one being distributed and reimposed. In practice, it was rarely as neat as this, but skeletons were very convenient and their use was widespread. The bibliographer can most easily detect the use of skeletons when some typographical peculiarity enables him to identify individual settings of the running title and thus trace the recurrence of a particular headline through a book.

See Gaskell, p. 109; and Moxon, p. 229.

See also **Chase**; **Compositor**; **Distribution**; **Forme**; **Headline**; **Running title**; **Typesetting**

Slip songs

Bibliographical term. A slip is a long narrow strip of paper consisting of a quarter, or occasionally a fifth, of the sheet. It was most often used for printing a song, usually on a topical theme and with a woodcut at the head. Such slip songs were common in the eighteenth century, especially in the earlier decades when they were a popular medium for Jacobite propaganda.

There is no study of slips as such, but many are listed by D.F. Foxon, *English Verse 1701–1750* (1975), and he discusses them in vol. 2, p. 210.

Sloane, Sir Hans (1660–1753)

Book collector and *de facto* founder of the British Museum. An Irishman educated in England and France, Sloane was a highly successful physician who collected almost everything. He amassed fossils, anatomical specimens and antiquities as well as books and manuscripts. By the time of his death he had about 50,000 books, including some 3500 manuscripts. He kept his collections in his house in Great Russell Street, London, until 1742 when he moved to Chelsea. In his will, Sloane ordered his Trustees to offer everything to the Crown for £20,000, and, after some debate, Parliament voted the money. The same legislation established the British Museum to house and care for the Sloane and other collections which were brought together at Montagu House.

A catalogue of the manuscripts was compiled by Samuel Ayscough and incorporated in his *Catalogue of the Manuscripts Preserved in the British Museum* (1782); this is an unreliable work, but has now, at last, been replaced by a good modern catalogue.

See Edward Miller, *That Noble Cabinet* (1973).

See also **British Museum**

Slug

See **Line casting**

Small Pica

See **Type size**

Smith, William Henry (1792–1865) and Smith, William Henry (1825–1891)

Booksellers and newsagents. The elder Smith was the son of Henry Smith, a London newsagent in a small way of business; Henry, however, died a few months after his son was born, and the business was run by his widow until William Henry was old enough to join her in 1812. He embarked on a programme of expansion which took advantage of the rapid increase in newspaper sales in the 1820s and 1830s under the combined impact of steam printing, reduced prices and greater prosperity. The firm, originally H. and W. Smith, became W.H. Smith in 1828, and W.H. Smith and Son in 1846 when the younger William Henry joined it. Smiths reached its apotheosis in the Victorian age when the firm involved itself with the rapidly expanding railway network. In 1848, they signed a contract with the London and North Western Railway which gave them the exclusive right to sell books and newspapers on LNWR stations; the first stall was opened at Euston in the same year. Similar contracts with other companies followed, and Smiths also began to develop a network of provincial shops and warehouses. In this way they became wholesale newsagents on a national scale, achieving something close to a monopoly of sales of London newspapers in the provinces. Again their railway links proved crucial for they were able to hire special newspaper trains at favourable rates. The firm has gone from strength to strength; it is now a limited company, and it still has a wide network of bookshops throughout the country. In some smaller towns Smiths are the only booksellers.

See Charles Wilson, *First with the News. The History of W.H. Smith 1792–1872* (1985).

See also **Advertisements**; **Newspapers**

Society of Authors

Professional body of authors in the United Kingdom. The Society of Authors was founded in 1884 on the initiative of Walter Besant (1836–1901), a popular novelist and journalist who was subsequently knighted for his services to literature and authors. Besant, like other professional writers, felt the need for a united front against the publishers which could argue the case for the rights of authors. This was and is the primary function of the Society, which is particularly concerned with such matters as royalties, of which it was an early and consistent advocate, copyright and, in recent years, tax liabilities and Public Lending Rights. The Society provides advice, including legal advice, to its members, as well as acting as a pressure group.

Membership is open to all who have published a 'full-length work' in the United Kingdom. The Society's address is 84 Drayton Gardens, London SW10 9SD.

Victor Bonham-Carter, *Authors by Profession* (2 vols, 1978–84) is largely a history of the Society and its activities.

See also **Copyright**; **Royalties**

Sophistication

See **Forgery**

Sort

Printer's term. The word is used by printers to mean an individual letter or character on a piece of type.
    See Moxon, p. 352.

Sothebys

Auction house. Sothebys is certainly the largest, and probably the most famous, auction house in the world. It began as a firm of booksellers and has always been particularly active in the field of books and manuscripts. The founder of the firm was Samuel Baker (1712–1778), a bookseller who held his first auction in 1745 over a decade after he first entered the trade. Auctions were an increasingly popular means of dispersing libraries, and Baker soon established himself as the leading book auctioneer in London; his early sales included the library of Richard Mead. In 1767 he took George Leigh (1742–1816) into the firm which became Baker and Leigh. After Baker's death Leigh continued as both bookseller and auctioneer, although it was auctioneering which now began to dominate his activities. He was joined by Baker's nephew, John Sotheby (1740–1807), whereupon the firm became Leigh and Sotheby. Leigh outlived Sotheby, but was joined by his son, Samuel Sotheby (1771–1842), who was eventually succeeded by his own son, Samuel Leigh Sotheby (1805–1861). By the early nineteenth century the firm was unquestionably at the head of the trade; it benefited immensely from the sales which followed the French Revolution and from the mania for book collecting which swept through the English aristocracy in the late eighteenth and early nineteenth centuries. After the death of S.L. Sotheby, his partner John Wilkinson took over the business and brought in E.G. Hodge as a partner; from 1861 until 1922 the firm was known as Sotheby, Wilkinson and Hodge. It was under that title that it conducted most of the great book sales of the late nineteenth century, including those of Ashburnham and Huth among many others. It was, indeed, at the very heart of the antiquarian book trade in Britain, and was also attracting an increasing number of American customers towards the end of the nineteenth century. By the outbreak of World War I, however, the somewhat loose management style was putting the firm into financial difficulties; and a group of younger partners began a reorganisation which involved both a move to the present premises in New Bond Street and expansion into other fields such as paintings and furniture. In 1922, the firm became Sotheby and Co., and so it has remained.

In recent years, Sothebys has been under some pressure from its competitors, but it has continued to expand, notably by buying auction houses overseas of which the most spectacular was Parke Bernet of New York, the leading book auction house in the United States. The tentacles of Sothebys now extend from Monaco to the Gleneagles Hotel, and books are only one part of a vast international business.

Admidst all the changes and upheavals, one constant in the Sotheby tradition has been the scholarship of its partners and staff. Since the last nineteenth century they have commanded the universal respect of the book world for their vast knowledge of the items which pass through their hands, and Sothebys catalogues are a major source of bibliophilic reference.

Frank Herman, *Sotheby's. Portrait of an auction house* (1980) is full of detail, but it was officially inspired and is perhaps a little bland. Sothebys catalogues, from the beginning of the firm, have been published on microfilm (1973), and are available in many research libraries; as far as possible, the films were made from marked copies, giving prices and buyers' names.

See also **Ashburnham, Bertrand, 4th Earl of Ashburnham** (1797–1878); **Auction sales**; **Bibliomania**; **Book collecting**; **Mead, Richard** (1683–1754)

Spencer, Charles, 3rd Earl of Sunderland (1674–1722)

See **Spencer, George John, 2nd Earl Spencer** (1758–1834)

Spencer, George John, 2nd Earl Spencer (1758–1834)

Book collector. Born into one of the most ancient of English families, and destined to be the ancestor of even more illustrious descendants, Spencer had a brief political career before he retired to his home at Althorp to devote himself to what was already probably the finest private library in Europe. It had been started in the early eighteenth century by his ancestor Charles, 3rd Earl of Sunderland (1674–1722), a contemporary of the Harleys, and in some ways their equal as a bibliophile and collector. Spencer himself added to the library on a huge scale, especially in the fields of incunabula and early English literature. He employed Dibdin to catalogue the library, and it was through Dibdin's *Bibliotheca Spenceriana* (4 vols, 1814–16) and *Aedes Althorpianae* (2 vols, 1821) that the world learned of the treasures of Althorp. Even at the height of the bibliomania it was an outstanding collection, and Spencer himself was, inevitably, a founder member of the Roxburghe Club which his descendants continue to patronise. The great majority of the incunabula, including an incomparable collection of Caxtons, was bought by Mrs Rylands in 1882, and are now in the John Rylands University Library of Manchester where they are among that library's greatest treasures.

There is a life of Spencer in *DNB*, but for the library see Dibdin's catalogues; Seymour de Ricci, *English Collectors of Books and Manuscripts (1530–1930)* (1930); and E. J. O'Dwyer, *Thomas Frognall Dibdin* (1967).

See also **Bibliomania**; **Book collecting**; **Dibdin, Thomas Frognall** (1776–1847); **Incunabula**; **John Rylands University Library of Manchester**; **Harley, Robert, 1st Earl of Oxford** (1661–1724) **and Harley, Edward, 2nd Earl of Oxford** (1689–1741); **Roxburghe Club**

Spine

See **Bookbinding**

St Paul's Churchyard

The area around St Paul's Cathedral in London was the centre of the English book trade from the sixteenth to the eighteenth centuries. When de Worde left Westminster in 1501 he established himself in Fleet Street and was joined there by other printers; some however moved further east and by the early sixteenth century Julian Notary (fl. 1498–1520) and others were established in the precincts of the cathedral. For the next 150 years, the area around St Paul's was full of booksellers' stalls, although printing houses tended to be a little further away. When the Stationers' Company acquired its new Hall in 1554 it was on a site just to the west of St Paul's, and the present Hall, originally built after the Great Fire of London (1666) stands on the same site. It was, however, the Great Fire which marked the beginning of the decline of the area as the centre of the trade. Although the rebuilding of Stationers' Hall ensured that many booksellers did indeed move back to Ludgate Hill, the building of the new cathedral, and the greater control exercised over the use of the Close, gradually forced the trade westwards. This trend was emphasised by the growing fashion to live west of the City, and by the middle of the eighteenth century the booksellers were beginning to regroup on the Strand and in Piccadilly. The great days of St Paul's Churchyard had really ended with the medieval cathedral itself.

See Marjorie Plant, *The English Book Trade* (3rd edn, 1974); and Cyprian Blagden, *The Stationers' Company* (1960).

See also **de Worde, Wynkyn** (*c.* 1455–1534); **Stationers' Company**

Stamp

See **Bookbinding**

Stamp Acts

Legislation for the taxation of paper and certain publications. The record of payment of the excise duty on these and other items was a stamp impressed either on the article itself or on its label; hence it was known as the Stamp Tax, or Stamp Duty. Stamp duties were introduced on many commodities in the late seventeenth century; the first application to vellum and paper was in 1694 when it was imposed on certain classes of legal documents. In 1711, under an Act of 1710, almanacs were taxed and in the following year the duties were extended to newspapers and pamphlets. The newspaper duties proved to be the most enduring of these, and were increased on many occasions in the eighteenth and early nineteenth centuries. Although the Stamp Tax was intended originally as a means of raising revenue, it was subsequently used as a means of restricting the circulation of newspapers by raising the price to a level which few could afford to pay. This was especially true during the French Revolutionary Wars (1793–1815); by 1820 the price of a newspaper had reached 6d or 7d, which was far too high for a working man. The pressure to reduce or repeal the paper and newspaper duties, known to their opponents as the 'taxes on knowledge', began in the 1830s, and bore fruit in 1836 when the duty was reduced to 1d. The newspaper tax was finally abolished in 1854.

For the early history of the taxes, see Edward Hughes, 'The English stamp duties, 1664–1774', *EHR* (1941), p.234; and John Feather, 'The English book trade and the law 1695–1779', *PH* (1982), p.51. For their later history, see Joel H. Wiener, *The War of the Unstamped* (1969).

See also **Almanacs**; **Newspapers**

Standing type

Printer's term, used also by bibliographers. Standing type is type left undistributed after printing has been completed so that it can be reused for a subsequent impression. Usually, it is kept locked in the chase, so that the forme remains intact. Standing type was uncommon until the eighteenth century because printers wanted to economise on the use of type, and it was cheaper to reset for a reprint. By the middle of the nineteenth century, the practice had been largely displaced by stereotyping.

In bibliographical terms, when standing type is re-used the result is an impression of the edition.

See Gaskell, pp.116, 314.

See also **Chase**; **Forme**; **Impression**; **Stereotyping**

Stanhope, Charles, 3rd Earl Stanhope (1753–1816)

See **Stanhope Press**; **Stereotyping**

Stanhope press

Printing press. Charles, 3rd Earl Stanhope (1753–1816), had a turbulent political career in which he embraced a number of radical causes but he was also, throughout his life, a scientist and inventor. He became interested in printing in the 1790s, and made a number of minor improvements to the common press. In 1800–2 he built a cast-iron hand press, the first successful metal press. Although it was essentially an iron version of the common press, it did have one great advantage: because it was possible to cast an iron platen to a larger size than a wooden platen could be planed, printing at one pull became possible for the first time over the whole sheet.

Stanhopes were installed by Oxford University Press in 1805, and thereafter were rapidly adopted by almost all book printers. They themselves were displaced by the Columbians and Albions in the 1830s and 1840s; both of these had more satisfactory mechanisms than the rather complicated pull bar of the Stanhope.

See Horace Hart, *Charles Earl Stanhope and the Oxford University Press* (OHS *Collectanea* 3 (1896), repr. ed. James Mosley (1966)).

See also **Albion press**; **Columbian press**; **Common press**; **Oxford University Press**; **Printing**

State

Bibliographical term. A state, unlike an edition, issue or impression, is a variant which is accidentally rather than intentionally created. The simplest case is when there are press variants resulting from stop press corrections. A forme showing such corrections then exists in an uncorrected and a corrected state, since the variation is a consequence of accidental error in setting the uncorrected state. It is the corrected state which represents the printer's original intention. Normally, formes in corrected and uncorrected states will be bound randomly and hence it is the forme rather than the book which has states. The borderline between state and issue can be somewhat vague; the bibliographer does well to apply common sense to the matter, while generally inclining to describe a variant as a state rather than an issue unless the intention to issue can be clearly shown.

See G. Thomas Tanselle, 'The bibliographical concepts of issue and state', *SB* (1975), p. 17.

See also **Edition**; **Forme**; **Issue**; **Impression**; **Press variants**

Stationer

Book trade term. In origin, a stationer was *stationarius*, a man with a shop or stall in a fixed location, rather than an itinerant tradesman. By the thirteenth century, the word was exclusively used for sellers of manuscripts and writing materials. Gradually, it became a generic word for all those engaged in the book trades, and was used in this sense from the fifteenth to the late seventeenth centuries. After that time, it was displaced a generic term by 'bookseller', and took on its modern meaning of dealer in paper products.

See Graham Pollard, 'The Company of Stationers before 1557', *Libr.* (1937/38), p. 1.

See also **Bookseller**

Stationers' Company

Livery Company of the City of London which was (and to some extent still is) the trade guild of the book trade. All those involved in manuscript production came together in a single guild in 1403, and when de Worde and others began to print in the City it was to this guild that they gravitated. The real power in the guild, however, was held by the wealthy merchants who were importers of paper and, to a much lesser extent, of printed books. It was not until the second half of the sixteenth century that the printers took control. In 1557, the Company received a Royal Charter from Mary I, which was confirmed by Elizabeth I in 1559. This marked the beginning of the Stationers' golden age, for the Charter gave the members of the Company a monopoly of both printing and bookselling except in the universities. In return for these privileges, the Master and Wardens, the elected senior officers of the Company, acted as *de facto* censors, for they were required to satisfy themselves that a book was suitable for publication before allowing it to be entered in the Hall Book, or Stationers' Register. Such entry was compulsory. The powers of the Company were confirmed and strengthened by Star Chamber decrees in 1586 and 1634, but with the abolition of Star Chamber in 1641 and the outbreak of the Civil War in 1642, it became impossible to enforce either the monopoly or the Company's own regulations. Control was reasserted to some extent in the 1650s, but after the Restoration in 1660 the Company lost its crucial power of censorship in the Printing Act 1662. The same Act, however, did restore its other powers, including its monopoly and such associated rights as the limitations on the numbers of apprentices and master printers.

During the period 1557–1640, the Stationers' Company exercised an unbroken and almost unchallenged stranglehold on the English book trade. Executive decrees and its own regulations, the latter enforced by the Court of Assistants elected from among the senior Liverymen of the Company, ensured that the trade was controlled in every respect, both political and commercial. From this tradition of central control of the book trade there emerged the small group of leading members of the trade whose descendants and successors continued to dominate the trade long after the power of the Company itself was broken in 1640. In the 1560s, the printers had used their monopoly of book production facilities to assert their own influence over the Company, but gradually the booksellers came to the fore as the ownership of rights in copies became the dominant fact of economic life in the book trade. By 1620 the booksellers were firmly in control, and in the late seventeenth century it was the booksellers, often using the mechanism of a formal petition from the Company or the Court of Assistants, who took the lead in seeking the Printing Act, in protecting the trade's interests in its provisions and in seeking replacements for it when it lapsed in 1694. It was they also who formed the early congers which led to the development of the share-book system which effectively preserved this oligarchic monopoly of the trade for a century or more after the Stationers' Company itself, from which that oligarchy had originated, had ceased to be of any real importance.

The Company did, however, survive as a trade guild, largely because of its ownership of the English Stock which provided it with a sound financial base, and which encouraged members of the trade to be members of the Company in order to share in the considerable profits which the Stock continued to generate. Most members of the trade went to the trouble and expense of becoming Freemen long after this ceased to be a legal requirement for them. In 1842, the Company's importance was revived by the Copyright Act of that year, under which registration of a book at Stationers' Hall was compulsory if the publisher sought to protect his copyright. This provision was repealed in 1911. In 1933, the Company joined forces with the Newspaper Makers Company, and, as the Worshipful Company of Stationers and Newspaper Makers, it still flourishes in a social and charitable role, although it has little direct corporate influence on the affairs of the trade.

For the history of the Company, see Cyprian Blagden, *The Stationers' Company 1403-1959* (1960); and Philip Unwin, *The Stationers' Company 1918-1977*(1978). The archives of the Company are of central importance to the history of the book trade in England and fortunately, despite the destruction of Stationers' Hall both in the Great Fire and again in the Blitz, they have substantially survived. They are at present (1985) being issued on microfilm, and when complete, there will be a printed guide by Robin Myers, the Company's Archivist. Some documents have already been published. Of these, the most important are the Stationers' Register from 1557 to 1640 (ed. Edward Arber, 5 vols, 1875-94) and from 1641 to 1708 (3 vols, 1913-14); the records of the Court of Assistants from 1576 to 1602 (ed. W.W. Greg and E. Boswell, 1930) and from 1602 to 1640 (ed. William A. Jackson, 1957); and the lists of apprentices bound and freed from 1602 to 1640 (ed. D.F. McKenzie, 1961), from 1641 to 1700 (ed. D.F. McKenzie, OBS, new ser. 17, 1974), and from 1701 to 1800 (ed. D.F. McKenzie, OBS, new ser. 19, 1978).

See also **Censorship**; **Conger**; **Copyright**; **de Worde, Wynkyn** (*c.* 1455-1534); **English Stock**; **Printing Act 1662**; **Share books**; **Stationers' Register**

Stationers' Register

Scholars' name for the register of ownership of copies kept by the Stationers' Company. Its official name was the 'Register of Copies', or later the 'Hall Book'. From 1557, a stationer was required to enter each 'copy' or book which he proposed to print. The purpose was to ensure that he had an official licence which permitted publication, but by the end of the sixteenth century an entry was taken to mean that the person in whose name the entry was made had the sole right to print that particular copy. This is the origin of the concept of copyright. Up the 1640 the Register is remarkably complete, and after the Printing Act 1662 it is reasonably so. When that Act lapsed in 1694 many booksellers continued to enter their copies in the belief that this protected their rights; the Copyright Act 1710 required registration. During the eighteenth century, however, this requirement was increasingly ignored. Under the Copyright Act 1842 the ownership of copyright was made dependent upon entry in the Register, and from that date until 1911, when this provision was repealed, the Register is comprehensive. Since 1911, it has rarely been used.

The Stationers' Register is one of the central documents for the historian of the English book trade, especially for the period before 1640. The Registers for this period were edited, rather idiosyncratically, by Edward Arber (5 vols, 1875-94); this is usually known as 'Arber's *Transcript*'. A much less satisfactory edition of Registers for the period 1641-1708 has been privately published (3 vols, 1913-14). For the period 1557-1640, *STC* provides (as Arber did not) an author index to the Register, since it notes the date of entry against each title whenever this is applicable; William P. Williams, *An Index to the Stationers' Register, 1640-1708* (1980) is an invaluable aid for the later seventeenth century. The significance of the Registers and the forms of entry are discussed by W.W. Greg, *Some Aspects and Problems of London Publishing from 1550 to 1650* (1956).

See also **Copyright**; **Printing Act 1662**; **Stationers' Company**;

STC

Reference book. The acronym invariably used for A.W. Pollard and G.R. Redgrave, *A Short-title Catalogue of Books Printed in England, Scotland, & Ireland and of English Books Printed Abroad 1475-1640* (1926), certainly the best known and arguably the most important of the Bibliographical Society's publications. Each entry consists of the author's name (if known); a short title; the format; a very abbreviated imprint; the date of publication; and the location of up to five copies on both sides of the Atlantic. The record of copies was substantially augmented for the UK by David Ramage (1958), and for the USA by W.W. Bishop (1950). There is an index of printers and booksellers by Paul G. Morrison (1961). *STC* was the inspiration for Wing, the *Eighteenth-Century Short Title Catalogue*, and the *Nineteenth-Century Short Title Catalogue*.

A revision of *STC*, sponsored by the Bibliographical Society, began in 1946 under the editorship of William A. Jackson and F.S. Ferguson; both were dead before the first part (vol. 2, covering letters I-Z) was published in 1976, edited by Katherine F. Pantzer. Vol. 1 was published in 1986 and a third volume of indices will follow. The revised *STC*, increasingly known as *STC-2*, is more elaborate than its predecessor, and contains the fruits of vast collective efforts in bibliographical scholarship, especially for some of the more complicated forms such as newsbooks and almanacs.

See also. **Bibliographical Society**; *Eighteenth-Century Short Title Catalogue*; *Nineteenth-Century Short Title Catalogue*; **Wing**

Steel engraving

An intaglio process of graphic printing. The process was invented by Charles Warren (1762–1823) as a consequence of his interest in developing a secure method of printing banknotes. Previous experimenters had developed a complex process which involved the use of multiple iron plates, called *siderography*, but it was too difficult to be entirely satisfactory. Steel was an attractive material for the purpose because of its inherent hardness, but it was this very hardness which created the problem since it made it impossible to use engravers' tools on its surface. Warren solved the problem by coating the steel with iron filings and then heating it, which had the effect of softening the surface. After engraving, the plate was fired to restore the original hardness. The plate could then be used for up to 200,000 impressions without any deterioration in the quality of reproduction. Warren perfected the process in 1818, and by the mid-1820s it was in widespread use for book illustration; its use declined in the late 1830s, under the double challenge of lithography and wood engraving. Like all other processes it was finally displaced by photomechanical techniques in the late nineteenth century.

See the comprehensive study by Basil Hunnisett, *Steel-engraved Book Illustration in England* (1980).

See also **Intaglio**; **Lithography**; **Photomechanical printing**; **Wood engraving**

Stereotyping

Relief printing technique. Stereotyping is the process of producing an exact copy of typeset matter from which an impression can be taken on the press. A mould is made from the type, in which a plate is then cast. This plate can be printed in exactly the same way as the original type. The economic advantages of stereotyping over resetting or keeping standing type are considerable: type can be distributed and re-used immediately; no typesetting is required for a reprint; the mould can be used to make a second or subsequent plate if necessary; and a plate is easier to handle than a forme. The process was apparently invented in Holland by Johann Müller in the first years of the eighteenth century and was introduced into Britain by William Ged, an Edinburgh printer, in the 1730s. In neither country, however, did it attain any real importance, although Ged did produce a few books, and some of Müller's plates of a Dutch Bible were still in use in the 1790s. The platemaking procedure was, however, forgotten, until it was reinvented by Alexander Tulloch in Glasgow in the 1780s. Stereotyping only achieved any commercial importance when Charles, 3rd Earl Stanhope, employed Andrew Wilson to perfect and use the process from 1802 onwards.

The early moulds were made of Plaster of Paris which was too brittle to be entirely satisfactory; from 1829 onwards, however, plaster moulds were displaced by moulds made of flexible laminated paper, known as *flong*. Throughout the nineteenth and early twentieth centuries stereotyping was used for reprinting and was a major factor in reducing the price of books. After the development of the rotary press it became an even more attractive proposition, since, unlike type, plates could be used on the rotaries. Flongs were also sent from one printer to another, and even from Britain to America for the American reprints of British books.

Bibliographcally, each use of the plates creates an impression of the edition.

The classic description of the process is in L.A. Legros and J.C. Grant, *Typographical Printing-surfaces* (1916). For its early history, see John Carter, 'William Ged and the invention of stereotype', *Libr.* (1960), p.161; and Michael L. Turner, 'Andrew Wilson: Lord Stanhope's stereotype printer', *JPHS* (1975), p.22.

See also **Distribution**; **Forme**; **Impression**; **Relief printing**; **Standing type**; **Typesetting**

Stipple engraving

An intaglio process of graphic printing. Stipple engraving is a combination of engraving and etching. The line and basic tonal lines are etched, before the plate is then worked with a special tool called a 'stipple graver'. This implement has a curved end which produces soft-edged dots on the plate; according to the greater or lesser number of dots the image is darker or lighter. Stipple thus produces an approximation to continuous tone. The process may have been of Italian origin; it was introduced into England in the 1760s by Francesco Bartolozzi (1727–1815) and it became an especially English technique. It was primarily used for portraits and for reproductions of paintings.

See Arthur M. Hind, *A History of Engraving and Etching* (3rd edn, 1923).

See also **Etching**; **Intaglio**

Stitched books

Bookbinding technique. All books are stitched in some way (unless 'perfect' bound), but the term is normally reserved for books which are stitched with a single thread passing through both the sheets and the wrappers or boards, with the holes through the edges rather than the centre-fold. The practice was at its height in the eighteenth century, when many pamphlets were issued stitched in this way, usually in blue paper wrappers.

See David Foxon, 'Stitched books', *BC* (1975), p. 111.

See also **Bookbinding**

Stop-press correction

See **Press variant**

Strahan, William (1715–1785)

Printer and publisher. The son of a Scots lawyer, Strahan was apprenticed to an Edinburgh printer but was in London by 1738, and in 1739 went into partnership with a fellow Scot, Andrew Millar. After Millar's death in 1769 Strahan took Thomas Cadell and as his new partner. Strahan himself was closely associated with the literary circle around Dr Johnson, although two of his most famous publications, Smith's *Wealth of Nations* (2 vols, 1766) and Gibbon's *Decline and Fall of the Roman Empire* (6 vols, 1776–88), were distinctly un-Johnsonian in character. His technical standards were extremely high and he was a major influence in the much needed improvement in the quality of English printing in the second half of the eighteenth century. In 1770, with Charles Eyre, he became King's Printer, although the office seems to have brought him more prestige than profit. Strahan's youngest son, Andrew (1749–1831), succeeded both to the business and to his father's share in the King's Printer's patent.

Strahan's business records are among the few archives surviving from the eighteenth-century British book trade and are of great importance to the historian. They are listed and discussed by Patricia Hernlund, 'William Strahan's ledgers: standard charges for printing, 1738–1785', *SB* (1967), p. 89. Hernlund is working on a complete edition of the ledgers. There is a life of Strahan in *DNB*, and an indifferent biography by J.A. Cochrane, *Dr Johnson's Printer* (1964).

See also **King's (or Queen's) Printer**

Strawberry Hill Press

Private press. The press was established in 1757 by Horace Walpole (1717–1797) whose many interests included literature and architecture. The two came together in his house at Strawberry Hill, Twickenham, near London, which he rebuilt in a style which marks the beginning of the Gothic revival in England. He also assembled there a huge library and other collections, and set up his press. He employed various unsatisfactory printers before, in 1765, he appointed Thomas Kirgate who remained at Strawberry Hill until the Press came to an end with Walpole's death. Strawberry Hill books are well printed, although not particularly outstanding, and there are among them a few titles of great literary importance, most notably *Odes by Mr Gray* (1757), the first Strawberry Hill book.

Walpole's own *Journal of the Printing Office at Strawberry Hill* has been edited by Paget Toynbee (1923); and there is a *Bibliography of the Strawberry Hill Press* by Allen T. Hazen (new edn, 1973).

Studies in Bibliography

Bibliographical annual. *SB* is published by the Bibliographical Society of the University of Virginia, and has been edited from the first volume (1948/49) by Fredson Bowers. It has always reflected the editor's concern with textual and analytical bibliography, while never entirely neglecting other aspects of the subject. It is a remarkable journal, and there is probably not a single volume which does not contain at least one article of outstanding importance.

See also **Analytical bibliography**; **Bowers, Fredson Thayer** (1905-   ); **Textual criticism**

Subscription

Book trade term. In essence, a subscription is a commitment to buy a book or periodical made before publication, usually accompanied by at least a part-payment. The practice originated in England in the early seventeenth century, when John Minsheu was unable to find a publisher for his multi-lingual dictionary, *Glosson Etymologikon*. He sought financial support through a printed prospectus (1610) and subsequently also printed the names of the subscribers. This established the pattern, so that books published by sub-scription can normally be identified from the printed list of subscribers' names which appears in them. The system reached its apogee in the eighteenth century when many literary and historical works were published in this way. It soon became a matter of prestige to be seen to subscribe to an important (or fashionable) book. In the nineteenth century, learned societies took over much of the scholarly publishing which had formerly been the province of subscription publishing, but the practice was revived by the private presses in the 1890s and many still use it.

In modern book trade parlance, subscription has a different meaning: it refers to the bookseller's pre-publication orders from a publisher.

In recent years, printed subscription lists have attracted a good deal of scholarly attention for the insights which they afford into social, literary and political groups. A catalogue of books with such lists was the origin of the Pro-ject for Historical Bio-Bibliography, and was published as F.J.G. Robinson and P.J. Wallis, *Book Subscription Lists. A revised guide* (1975, with 4 supple-ments: 1976, 1977, 1980, 1981). For a general discussion, see P.J. Wallis, 'Book subscription lists', *Libr.* (1974), p. 255.

See also **Private press movement**; **Project for Historical Bio-Bibliography**; **Prospectus**

Super Royal

See **Sheet**

Tauchnitz, Christian Bernhard (1816–1895)

Publisher in Leipzig. Tauchnitz was descended from an old Saxon family which had fallen on hard times, and he was apprenticed to his uncle Karl, a printer in Leipzig who is believed to have introduced stereotyping into Germany. In 1837, he established his own business, and in 1841 issued his first English book, Bulwer-Lytton's *Pelham*. This was the beginning of the *Collection of British* (later *British and American*) *Authors* which made his fame and fortune, and which eventually ran to some 5425 volumes. Tauchnitz editions could not be imported into Britain for domestic copyright reasons, but long before there were any international copyright agreements Tauchnitz paid fees to his foreign authors, many of whom became his friends. Indeed, in some cases they revised their works for him, and the Tauchnitz edition is therefore of textual importance. The Tauchnitz edition was the form in which most Europeans read English literature for nearly a century, and the little buff volumes were equally familiar to British travellers on the Continent. The enterprise continued until 1943, when the firm's offices, stock, plates and records were destroyed in an RAF raid on Leipzig.

Bibliographically, Tauchnitz books present one major problem, apart from the sheer quantity of them. From the beginning, Tauchnitz used stereotype plates, and these plates continued to be used for decades without change. Thus a book originally published in, for example, 1860, would still be dated '1860' in an impression printed in 1910. The true date of the impression can only be determined from copies whose wrappers survive, for the wrappers usually have either a genuine date, or a dated list of recent or forthcoming books.

Simon Nowell-Smith first drew the attention of scholars to the importance of the Tauchnitz edition, and summarised his work in *International Copyright Law and the Publisher in the Reign of Queen Victoria* (1968). More recent work includes William B. Todd, 'Firma Tauchnitz: a further investigation', *PH* (1977), p.7; the same author's 'A new measure of literary excellence: the Tauchnitz international editions 1841–1943', *PBSA* (1984); and Karl H. Pressler, 'The Tauchnitz edition: beginning and end of a famous series', *PH* (1980), p.63.

See also **Copyright**; **Impression**; **Stereotyping**

Term catalogues

Book trade catalogues. The first term catalogue, under the title *Mercurius Librarius,* was issued in 1668 by the London bookseller, John Starkey. It listed all books published in London in the previous legal Term, from which it derives the title given to the series by scholars. The catalogues were then issued at quarterly intervals from 1668 to 1709, with a final issue in Easter Term, 1711. The term catalogues are the first serial bibliography of English books; cumulations were published in 1673, 1675, 1680 and 1696. They are a crucial source of information for the historian of the trade for they often give more details than can be found in the book itself, especially on such matters as price and the publishers and distributors.

The whole series, except for that for Michaelmas Term, 1695, was edited by Edward Arber as *The Term Catalogues, 1668–1709* (3 vols, 1903). The 'missing' issue was unknown to Arber, but copies have now been located, and it is to be published by the Oxford Bibliographical Society. The cumulations were reprinted by D.F. Foxon in *English Bibliographical Sources* (1964–67).

See Graham Pollard, 'Bibliographical aids to research. IV. General lists of books printed in England', *BIHR* (1934–35), p. 164.

See also **Trade bibliography**

Textual bibliography

See **Textual criticism**

Textual criticism

The analysis of the history of the transmission of a text undertaken as a preliminary stage in the editing of the text itself. All texts inevitably suffer from verbal and other corruption during their transmission through the various stages from author to reader, whether in manuscript or in print. The art of textual criticism, which aims to eliminate that corruption, was first evolved by scholars in the library at Alexandria in the first century BC, and applied by them, *inter alia,* to assembling the texts which we now know as the *Iliad* and the *Odyssey.* The art was revived in the fifteenth century and applied in the first instance to editing the Bible and Greek and Latin classics. Although the techniques have been refined, the essential principle has not changed since antiquity: that each 'witness' to a text must be critically examined and analysed to establish its authority relative to that of other witnesses.

The bibliographers of the early twentieth century, especially Greg and Pollard, were greatly concerned with the text of Shakespeare, and applied to printed texts the same rigour which their contemporary (and Pollard's Oxford intimate) A.E. Housman brought to the study of classical texts. Inevitably, they used their bibliographical expertise; indeed both argued that the purpose of bibliography was to clear the ground for the textual critic and the editor by increasing their understanding of the printed texts from which they were working. Their particular achievement was the realisation that once it was possible to isolate what had happened in the printing house, what remained had probably been transmitted from the lost manuscript original. This came to be known as 'textual' or 'critical' bibliography. In fact, the relationship between the two disciplines was not quite as close they imagined, as their friend and colleague R.B. McKerrow pointed out in his *Prolegomena to the Oxford Shakespeare* (1939).

Bowers, in this as in other matters, developed Greg's work, and the classic statement of the theory of textual bibliography is to be found in his *Bibliography and Textual Criticism* (1964).

See also **Analytical bibliography**; **Bibliography**; **Bowers, Fredson Thayer** (1905–   ); **Greg, Sir Walter Wilson** (1875–1959); **Pollard, Alfred William** (1959–1944)

Textura

Type design. One of the four basic groups of Gothic type. Textura was the first and most formal of the Gothics, with a narrow letter and a pointed rather than a rounded appearance. Gutenberg's type was a Textura, and they continued to be used for Bibles and liturgies until the sixteenth century. The use of Textura was not confined to Germany, for it was also used in the Netherlands and England. The black letters of seventeenth- and eighteenth-century England are Texturas.

See A.F. Johnson, *Type Designs* (3rd edn, 1966).

See also **Black letter**; **Gothic type**; **Gutenberg, Johann** (1394/99–1468)

Thomas, Isaiah (1749–1831)

Printer and historian of printing. Thomas came from an old New England family which had fallen on hard times. After a minimal education he was apprenticed in 1756 to Zechariah Fowler, a printer in Boston, Massachusetts. He left Boston in 1765, going to Nova Scotia where he started *The Halifax Gazette*, the first of his anti-British newspapers. He returned to Boston in 1770, and became ever more committed to the cause of American Independence which he advocated in his new newspaper, *The Massachusetts Spy*. In 1771, he fled from Boston to nearby Worcester where he was to spend the rest of his life; after the end of the War of Independence he was increasingly regarded as one of the major figures of the Revolution for his role as a propagandist. He also became a major publisher, especially of school books and dictionaries which were of immense influence during the first decades of the Republic. From 1802 he gradually began to retire from business to devote himself to antiquarian matters. These studies reached their fruition in *The*

Thomason, George

History of Printing in America (2 vols, 1810), the first serious book on the subject and now itself an important primary source for the period of Thomas's active life in the trade. He also founded and endowed the American Antiquarian Society which still flourishes in Worcester and is a major centre of scholarship, not least in book history. The Program in the History of the Book in American Culture, under the directorship of David Hall, is one of the important developments in the field of book history in the United States in recent years. The Program sponsors meetings and assists individual scholars with funding their research. It seems likely to develop as the institutional base for much of the larger-scale work in this field in the USA, as it already is for the North American Imprints Program. AAS publishes a regular newsletter on the book history projects, entitled *The Book*, which contains full details of its activities and other items of interest.

A *Memoir* by his grandson forms the preface to the 1874 edition of Thomas's *History*, and is the best source for his life. See also Clifford K. Shipton, *Isaiah Thomas, Printer, Patriot and Philanthropist 1749–1831* (1949).

See also **North American Imprints Program**

Thomason, George (d. 1666)

Bookseller and book collector. Thomason was apprenticed to the bookseller, Henry Fetherstone in 1617, married his master's niece, and gradually took over the business after 1626. He was greatly involved in the affairs of the trade, not least as leader of a group of apprentices who rebelled against the authority of the Stationers' Company in the 1620s. During the Civil War and interregnum he also became involved in politics. He started as a Presbyterian and was elected to the Common Council of the City of London in 1647. Within a short time, however, his views began to change and in 1651 he was briefly imprisoned for royalism.

Thomason is chiefly remembered for the collection of pamphlets which he assembled in the 1640s, 1650s and 1660s. During that period, he bought a copy of almost every pamphlet and newsbook, as well as more substantial works, with the conscious intention of preserving the huge output of the press during those years of political upheaval. After his death, his friend Thomas Barlow, then Provost of the Queen's College, Oxford, but later Bodley's Librarian and Bishop of Lincoln, and himself a major collector, was responsible for the Thomason pamphlets. They underwent a number of misfortunes before, in 1762, they were presented to the British Museum. Even in the Museum they were badly neglected until they were catalogued by G.K. Fortescue (1908). The Thomason Tracts, as they are usually called, are in fact the major source of printed material for English history in the period 1640–60. They are now in very poor condition and have recently been microfilmed to protect the originals from over-use.

See Lois Spencer, 'The professional and literary connexions of George Thomason', *Libr.* (1958), p.102; and the same author's 'The politics of George Thomason', *Libr.* (1959), p.11.

See also **British Museum**

Thong

See **Bookbinding**

Times, The

See **Walter, John** (1738–1812)

Timperley, Charles (1794–1846?)

Printer and historian of printing. After an apprenticeship in his native Manchester, Timperley spent the whole of his life as a journeyman in Northampton and Warwick. His first book, *Songs of the Press* (1833), was followed by a *Printer's Manual* (1838), but his fame rests on his *Dictionary of Printers and Printing* (1839). This is usually consulted in the edition of 1842, under the title of *Encyclopaedia of Typographical and Literary Anecdote*. Although heavily dependent on Nichols, Timperley did a good deal of research, and the *Encyclopaedia* often supplements the information in the *Literary Anecdotes*, as well as being a great deal easier to use.

What little is known of him is recorded in *DNB*. The *Encyclopaedia* has been reprinted with an introduction by Terry Belanger (2 vols, 1977).

See also **Nichols, John** (1745–1826)

Title page

The first page of a book, or the third if there is a half-title. It normally contains the title, author's name and publisher's imprint. Although there are examples of title pages in medieval manuscripts, it is essentially a product of the age of printing. At an early date, Italian printers developed the habit of leaving the first recto blank as a protective covering for the book before it was bound, and by the 1470s they had begun to print an abbreviated form of the title on this page for ease of identification. By the end of the fifteenth century such pages were normal, and by the mid-sixteenth century title pages were often very elaborate, giving details of the book's contents rather than a simple title. Such title pages were displayed on stalls and in shops as advertisements for the book. From the middle of the eighteenth century onwards title pages generally became less verbose, and by about 1820 the title page had taken on its usual modern form.

See Rudolph Hirsch, *Printing, Selling and Reading 1450–1550* (rev edn, 1974).

See also **Advertisements**; **Half-title**; **Recto**

Tonson, Jacob (1655–1736), Tonson, Jacob (1682–1735) and Tonson, Jacob (1713–1753)

Publishers in London. The first Tonson's father was a shoemaker, but his mother was the daughter of Matthew Walbancke, a well-established London bookseller, and Tonson was duly apprenticed to his grandmother after Walbancke's death. He was freed in 1676, and took over the business. Almost immediately, he began to show an interest in literary publishing; his early books included two plays by Aphra Behn, and, in 1679, Dryden's 'improved' version of Shakespeare's *Troilus and Cressida*. This began a long and fruitful association between the two men, in the course of which Tonson published *Absolom and Achitophel* (1681), *The Medall* (1682), *Miscellany Poems* (1684 and later editions), *Alexander's Feast* (1697) and *Aesop's Fables* (1700) among many others. After the poet's death in 1700, Tonson also published the first collected edition of Dryden's plays (1701). Through Dryden, Tonson met Addison, Steele, and other literary men of the period, with whom he was associated in the Kit-Kat Club. He published both *The Tatler* (1709–11) and *The Spectator* (1711–12), and acquired substantial shares in the copyrights of both Milton and Shakespeare. The second Tonson joined him in the business, but his successor was his grandson, Jacob III. The firm was among the most successful of the early eighteenth century, for thanks to Jacob I's literary taste (or commercial acumen or, most likely, both) they owned shares in nearly all of the most valuable copyrights of the period.

Much has been written about the Tonsons. Perhaps the best books are Kathleen M. Lynch, *Jacob Tonson. Kit-Kat publisher* (1971); and G.F. Papali, *Jacob Tonson, Publisher* (1968). For the Tonson copyrights, see Terry Belanger, 'Tonson, Wellington, and the Shakespeare copyrights', in R.W. Hunt, I.G. Philip and R.J. Roberts (eds), *Studies in the Book Trade* (OBS, new ser. 18, 1975).

See also **Copyright**; **Share books**

Tooling

See **Bookbinding**

Trade, The

The term which the book trade has applied to itself since at least the eighteenth century. The most obvious analogous usage is the phrase 'the licensed trade', a term applied to themselves by the brewers and publicans, with whose products the members of the trade have rarely been unfamiliar.

Trade bibliography

Bibliographers' term. In this sense, the phrase means lists of new books issued by or for the book trade. The Frankfurt Book Fair catalogues are early examples. The first English trade bibliography was Andrew Maunsell's *Catalogue of English Printed Bookes* (1595), but only the first part, of books on divinity, was ever published. The real history of trade bibliography in England begins with William London's *Catalogue of the Most Vendible Books in England* (1658), whose more than 3000 titles represented a substantial proportion of the English books then in print. London's work was probably the inspiration for John Starkey who, in 1668, published the first part of *Mercurius Librarius*, the first of the term catalogues. A number of competitors to the term catalogues appeared in the first decade of the eighteenth century, and various monthly lists were also established. All of these were displaced after 1732 by the admirable lists of new publications in each month's issue of *The Gentleman's Magazine*. Not until the second half of the century did another trade bibliography establish itself. In 1779, William Bent published his *General Catalogue of Books*, the first of a series under various titles (*A Modern Catalogue*; *The London Catalogue*; and others) which Bent published between that date and his death in 1823. He also founded *The Weekly Literary Advertiser* (1802), which is the direct ancestor of *The Bookseller* with which it merged in 1860, and which is still flourishing as the trade's own record of its weekly output.

In 1854, Samson Low began to the publish their annual *Catalogue of Books*, which became *The British Catalogue* in 1853, and *The English Catalogue of Books* in 1860. Under that title it was published annually until after World War II, when it eventually succumbed to competition from the *British National Bibliography*, now the only British trade bibliography other than the lists in *The Bookseller* and their annual cumulation as *British Books in Print.*

See A. Growell and Wilberforce Eames, *Three Centuries of English Book Trade Bibliography* (1903).

See also **Bibliography**; **Frankfurt Fair**; *Gentleman's Magazine, The*; **Term catalogues**

Trade Binding

See **Bookbinding**

Trade sales

Book trade term. Trade sales were auctions open only to invited members of the trade, at which copyrights were bought and sold in the eighteenth and nineteenth centuries. The trade sales were an essential part of the share-book system, for it was by restricting sales of shares to carefully selected booksellers that the controlling oligarchy maintained its power within the trade. The first trade sale of which there is a certain record (in the form of a catalogue) was held on 3 April 1718, but it seems likely that sales took place before that date, perhaps even as early as the late 1690s. The copyright sales were clearly inspired by the similar private sales at which books were sold within the wholesaling congers. Many hundreds of sales were held during the next 150 years, and the essential pattern of an auction by invitation (usually preceded by dinner) never changed.

The catalogues of the trade sales are essential documents for the historian of the trade. The survivors (which are, happily, many) are discussed by Terry Belanger, 'Booksellers' trade sales, 1718–1768', *Libr.* (1975), p. 281, which is an important supplement to Cyprian Blagden's paper of the same name (*Libr.* (1951), p. 243) which pioneered the subject.

See also **Auction sales**; **Conger**; **Copyright**; **Share books**

Transactions of the Cambridge Bibliographical Society

Bibliographical journal. *TCBS* is published annually. The articles are normally of some Cambridge interest, either for the subject-matter or because the books or manuscripts which they discuss are in Cambridge libraries. On the other hand, a wide range of subjects is covered, so that *TCBS* is by no means parochial.

The present editor is D.J. McKitterick.

See also **Cambridge Bibliographical Society**

Trusler, John (1735–1820)

See **Script type**

Tympan

See **Common press**

Type

A metal block on which an image is cast from a matrix to be impressed by a relief printing process. Type was invented by Gutenberg; indeed, it is the very essence of his achievement. Gutenberg's types, like those of all of his successors for 400 years, were cast in a lead-based metal, with one letter or character on each type.

On type in general, see Gaskell, p. 9.

See also **Gutenberg, Johann** (1394/99–1468); **Relief printing**

Type facsimile

Book trade term. A type facsimile is an edition which is an exact reproduction of the edition or manuscript being reprinted or printed. Type facsimiles are normally made for antiquarian or scholarly purposes, although very occasionally the purpose is less reputable. Probably the first type facsimile was the edition of Boccaccio's *Decameron* printed in Florence for the bicentenary of the great Giunta edition of 1527, and there are a few other eighteenth-century examples of type facsimiles of printed books. Early type facsimiles of manuscripts included Farley's edition of *Domesday Book* (1783) and Woide's edition of the Codex Alexandrinus of the New Testament (1786). It was, however, in the nineteenth century that the type facsimile had its hey-day. A combination of bibliophilic interest in 'black letter' books, and a growing interest in historical books and documents for scholarly purposes, resulted in the printing of a substantial number of type facsimiles between 1810 and the end of the century. In the 1820s, the practice was particularly associated with the Roxburghe Club, but some learned societies also used the same technique. The development of cheap and simple methods of photographic reproduction, especially offset lithography, has rendered the type facsimile obsolete.

There is no general history of the type facsimile, although the subject is not without some interest and importance. See Joan M. Friedman, 'Fakes forgeries, facsimiles, and other oddities', in Jean Peters (ed.), *Book Collecting. A modern guide* (1977); and Nicolas Barker, *The Publications of the Roxburghe Club 1814–1962* (1964).

See also **Giunta family**; **Offset lithography**; **Roxburghe Club**

Type height

Technical term in typecasting. Type height is the measurement from the base (or 'foot') for the type, which rests on the bed of the press, to the printing surface (or 'face'). The usual height is 0.918 inches, although Oxford University Press retained its own 'Oxford' (or 'Dutch') height of 0.9395 in.

See Gaskell, p. 284.

See also **Typecasting**

Type size

Type is measured by the height of the body, i.e. the measurement from the top to the bottom of the surface on which the face is cast. Until the eighteenth century, and in some cases much later, these measurements were actually in the form of rather imprecise names, the meaning of which varied between places and times. In descending order of size, the most common names in Britain were: Double Pica, Great Primer, English, Pica, Small Pica, Long Primer, Brevier, Nonpareil and Pearl. The usual book types were English and Pica. The old nomenclature was gradually replaced by the more precise point sizes which are now invariably used.

Because of the difficulties of precision, bibliographers normally express type size in the form of a measurement of 20 lines of the printed page, measured from the top of an ascender to the bottom of a descender, and expressed in millimetres.

See Philip Gaskell, 'Type sizes in the eighteenth century', *SB* (1952/53), p. 147.

Type specimens

Printing trade term. A type specimen consists of an impression of one or more founts of type intended either to attract a printer to buy the type, or to attract the publisher to cause it to be used. The former are normally issued by type-founders, the latter by printers, The earliest extant examples of both genres date from the second half of the seventeenth century.

See James Mosley, *British Type Specimens before 1831: a hand-list* (OBS, occ. pub. 14, 1984).

See also **Fount**

Typecasting

The process of making type. In traditional typecasting (or 'typefounding' as it is often called in England), as it was developed in the fifteenth century, the first stage is the cutting of the *punch*. This is a small metal block, usually of steel, about $1^{1}/_{2}$in long, on one end of which the punchcutter engraves the character in relief. Punchcutting is a highly skilled task which few workmen are able to undertake. The engraved punch is then hammered into a block of copper, called the *matrix*. The matrix is normally about $1 \times {}^{1}/_{2} \times {}^{1}/_{4}$in; the punch is hammered (or 'struck') towards the end of one of the largest faces of the matrix. A large number of matrices can be made from a single punch, and a trade in matrices was established at a very early stage in the history of printing. Punches, on the other hand, were closely guarded by their owners.

The actual casting of the type takes place in a *mould*, a metal box in two parts, into which the matrix is inserted. When the parts are brought together, the character on the matrix is exposed at the bottom of a small gap between the two halves of the mould. Into this, the founder pours molten type metal, an alloy of lead, antimony and tin combined in proportions which allow it to cool quickly without contracting and yet remain reasonably hard. When the molten metal has been poured into the mould, the caster flicks the whole assembly by a sharp movement of the wrist of the hand in which he is holding it, to ensure that the matrix is completely filled. It solidifies at once, and is removed by splitting open the mould. The sort is then trimmed (or 'dressed') to shape and size. It was normal to cast an entire fount at the same time.

In the nineteenth century, various attempts were made to mechanise the typecasting process, and indeed the mechanical 'hot-metal' typesetters all incorporate a typecasting machine. Type is rarely cast now, for when sorts are required (which they rarely are) they are normally produced in the caster of a Monotype machine. Indeed probably only a handful of men in the world, most of them of a considerable age, still have the requisite skills.

The classic description of the process is that by Moxon, *Mechanick Exercises*, pp. 99 (punchcutting), 150 (matrix-making), 168 (typecasting). The description by Gaskell, p. 10, is shorter and perhaps more immediately comprehensible. For the early trade in matrices, see Harry Carter, *A View of Early Typography* (1969).

See also **Fount**; **Monotype**; **Sort**; **Type**; **Typesetting**

Typeface

Generic name for the designs of letterforms used in type. For the Latin alphabet there are basically three designs of typeface: Gothic, roman and italic. All are derived from the late medieval and Renaissance handwriting styles which were imitated by the early type designers. Within each group there are many varieties; the basic roman letterforms, in particular, have been subjected to many strange transformations by designers. There are also, of course, typefaces for other alphabets, such as Cyrillic, Greek and Arabic; these are known somewhat parochically as 'exotics'.

On the whole subject, see A.F. Johnson, *Type Designs* (3rd edn, 1966).

See also **Gothic type**; **Italic**; **Roman**

Typesetting

The process of assembling type for printing by a relief process. It is sometimes called *composition*, and the workman who undertakes the task is invariably called a compositor (or, in printing trade cant, a 'comp').

Until the second half of the nineteenth century, typesetting was an entirely unmechanised process. Various attempts were made to construct a typesetting machine, but none was successful until Ottmar Mergenthaler (1854–1899) produced the first line-casting machine in 1886. In Britain and Europe this was superseded for book work by the Monotype machine which casts sorts rather than lines, and this held sway until relief printing, and hence typesetting, was almost entirely displaced by planographic printing in the second half of the twentieth century.

Moxon p. 191, gives a detailed description of typesetting by hand; for the whole subject, see James Moran, *The Composition of Printed Matter* (1965).

See also **Compositor**; **Line casting**; **Monotype**; **Relief printing**; **Sort**; **Type**

Typographical Association

Principal trade union of the provincial printing industry in the nineteenth and early twentieth centuries. Trade unionism has a long history in printing, developing out of the chapels of the earliest printing houses. In the late eighteenth century, a recognisably modern form of unionism emerged, went underground for as long as unions were illegal, and re-emerged very strongly in the mid-nineteenth century. The compositors, with their highly skilled work, which remained unmechanised until the 1880s, were always able to command a hearing from the master printers, and fully exploited their very strong position. In 1849, a number of regional and craft unions came together to form the Typographical Association a few years after their London brethren had formed the London Society of Compositors (1845). In fact, the TA was a good deal more successful than the London unions, and during the rest of the century there was a proliferation of craft unions within the industry in London. Not until 1955 did all the London unions come together as the London Typographical Society, which, in its turn, merged with the TA in 1964 to form the National Graphical Association, now one of the two principle unions in the industry (the other being SOGAT).

See A.E. Musson, *The Typographical Association* (1954); and John Child, *Industrial Relations in the British Printing Industry* (1967).

See also **Chapel**; **Compositor**

Upper board

See **Bookbinding**

Vale Press

Private press. The Vale Press, founded in 1896 by Charles Ricketts, was unique among the early private presses in not having its own printing facilities. Ricketts and his friend Charles Shannon were involved in the design, illustration and binding of the books, but the actual machining was done by Ballantynes of Edinburgh on a rotary press kept for the purpose. A special type, Vale Type, was cut from designs by Ricketts, and this was used for all the books of the Press. Vale types were also used by the Eragny Press. The two Presses were very close in spirit, both being more influenced by art nouveau than by the Arts and Crafts Movement. Ricketts' intention was to print significant works of literature, and this, to some extent, he achieved. The Press closed in 1903.

A bibliography of the Vale Press, by Ricketts, was published in 1904.

See also **Eragny Press**; **Private press movement**

Variant

See **Press variant**

Vatman

See **Papermaking**

Vellum

Writing material. Vellum is made from animal skin, usually calf, but sometimes goat or lamb. The skin is soaked in lime, scraped clean with a knife and finally smoothed with pumice stone to prepare the writing surface. Even so, there is a considerable difference between the rough outer side (the 'hair' side) and the smoother inner side (the 'skin' side). Vellum is a very durable material, and was used for most large and expensive manuscripts in the Middle Ages and Renaissance. It was also used for *de luxe* issues by some of the early printers, but it is somewhat intractable to handle, and is not really practical for use on a printing press, despite the high quality of the results which can be obtained if great care is taken. By the fifteenth century, paper was cheaper than vellum, and it soon displaced it as the normal book material.

Vellum differs from parchment both in materials and manufacture, and the words should not be used as synonyms, although they are indeed very often difficult to distinguish, especially when badly worn.

See Dard Hunter, *Paper Making* (2nd edn, 1947).

See also **Parchment**; **Paper**

Verso

The left-hand page of an open book; the right-hand page is called the recto.

See also **Page**

Victoria Press

See **Faithfull, Emily** (1835–1895)

Village Press

Private press. The Village Press was founded by Frederic W. Goudy (1865–1947) in Chicago in 1903. Goudy had already made one unsuccessful attempt to establish a press which would reflect his attachment to the ideals which had inspired Morris at Kelmscott. Goudy was a type designer as well as printer, and many of his books were printed in his Village Type, which he produced shortly before the Press opened. The type itself, the design of the books and the choice of texts all reflect the influence of Morris. Goudy was in fact one of the most important of Morris's American disciples, and his influence on American printing was in some ways comparable to Morris's influence in England. The style of the Village Press books themselves was somewhat too esoteric to appeal to a mass public, but he raised an awareness of the principles of good typography, and of the crying need for it, and in that sense helped to improve the rather low standards of American printing at the turn of the twentieth century. Goudy moved to New York in 1906, but the Press never really recovered from a fire in which most of Goudy's possessions were destroyed in 1908. For the rest of his life, Goudy was associated with the Lanston Monotype Corporation, and thereby exercised a crucial influence on the development of modern American typography.

There is a *Bibliography of the Village Press* (1938) by Melbert B. Cary, and a valuable book on Goudy by Bernard Lewis, *Behind the Types: The Life Story of Frederic W. Goudy* (1941). More generally, see Susan O. Thompson, *American Book Design and William Morris* (1977).

See also **Kelmscott Press**; **Private press movement**

Walker, Sir Emery (1851–1933)

Typographer. Walker, a Londoner by birth, was trained as an etcher and process engraver, setting up his own business in 1872. In 1883, he met William Morris, a neighbour in Hammersmith, and they found that they shared an interest in typography. In 1888, the two of them and others formed the Arts and Crafts Society, intended to revive good design, and in the November of that year Walker lectured to the Society on the principles of typography. He took his examples from manuscripts and incunabula in Morris's considerable library, and advocated a return to the typography and design of the fifteenth and early sixteenth centuries. It was after this lecture that Morris decided to found the Kelmscott Press, and so Walker can claim to be the father of the private press movement. After Morris's death, Walker joined Cobden-Sanderson in the Doves Press, and for the rest of his life he was deeply concerned with the improvement of the prevailing standards of book production and design. After World War I he was associated with the Ashendene Press, the last British private press in the Kelmscott tradition. For his work, he was knighted in 1930.

See the anonymous *Sir Emery Walker* (1933); and the life in *DNB 1931–1940* by Sir Sydney Cockerell.

See also **Ashendene Press**; **Doves Press**; **Etching**; **Incunabula**; **Kelmscott Press**; **Private press movement**

Walpole, Horace, 4th Earl of Orford (1717–1797)

See **Strawberry Hill Press**

Walter, John (1738–1812)

Founder of the *The Times*. Walter was the son of a prosperous merchant, and was himself a successful London businessman. He found himself in financial difficulties, however, in the early 1780s because of the heavy losses which he suffered through underwriting insurance at Lloyds during the American War of Independence. He met Henry Johnson, the inventor of logography, in about 1783, and took over from Johnson the exploitation of the invention. He bought the old King's Printing House in Blackfriars, and in 1784 opened The Logographic Press where he subsequently printed some 150 books. On 1 January 1785 he produced the first issue of *The Daily Universal Register* which, on 1 January 1788, he renamed *The Times*. In the following year he opened a bookshop in Piccadilly, but by the end of that year he was in serious trouble. He was successfully prosecuted for a seditious libel on the Prince of Wales, and spent several months in prison. When he was released he was ruined. The Press and the bookshop were abandoned, and Walter's sons took over *The Times*. *The Times*, of course, survived this early crisis in its history, and remained in the hands of the Walter family until the early twentieth century.

See Oliver Woods and James Bishop, *The Story of The Times* (1983); and John Feather, 'John Walter and the Logographic Press', *PH* (1977), p. 92.

See also **Logography**

Warren, Charles (1762–1823)

See **Steel engraving**

Watermarks

Papermaker's term. A watermark is produced by a pattern woven into the chains and wires of the papermaker's mould; like them, it causes the sheet to be slightly thinner, so that the pattern can be seen when the paper is held up to the light. Traditionally the design is an heraldic or symbolic device, perhaps incorporating the name of the manufacturer, or the place or date of manufacture. Watermarks began to be used in the late thirteenth century, and became almost universal in European and American papermaking. From the seventeenth century onwards, *countermarks* also began to appear in addition to watermarks; these normally take the form of the initials or name of the papermaker. In such cases, the watermark is woven into the centre of one half of the mould, and the countermark into the centre of the other half.

Watermarks can provide bibliographical evidence in several ways. At the simplest level, they can be used like the chain lines and the wire lines as an aid in the determination of format. More difficult is the use of watermarks for dating paper, and therefore providing at least a *terminus ante quem* for a book written or printed on that paper. First, the mark itself has to be identified, and since many designs were in common use, it is not always easy, especially with the cheap papers used for ordinary book work, to identify the source of the paper at all. Secondly, watermarks are not unique; moulds are used in pairs, and each of the two is intended to be identical. Thus the watermarks are also in pairs, although in practice because of the comparative flimsiness of the wires from which they are constructed, differences can usually be seen. Despite this, however, it is sometimes possible to identify a stock of paper being used by a printer at a particular time, and from this conclusions can be drawn about printing house procedures and perhaps even the chronological sequence in which undated books were actually printed.

'Watermarks' are sometimes artificially inserted into machine-made paper as an affectation.

For the general history of watermarks, see Dard Hunter, *Paper Making* (2nd edn, 1947). For their use by bibliographers, see two classic articles by Allan Stevenson: 'New uses of watermarks as bibliographical evidence', *SB* (1948/49), p. 149; and 'Watermarks are twins', *SB* (1951/52), p. 57. The largest collection of published watermarks is that by C.-M. Briquet, *Les Filigranes* (2nd edn, 4 vols, 1923), but Briquet's reproductions are based on tracings which are necessarily less accurate than modern beta-radiographs, which are photographs of watermarks taken using a radioactive light source. Other collections, which supplement Briquet for the later period, but which were also compiled before the development of beta-radiography, included W. A. Churchill, *Watermarks in Holland, England, France, etc., in the XVII and XVIII Centuries* (1935); and Edward Heawood, *Watermarks, Mainly of the 17th and 18th Centuries* (1950).

See also **Chain lines**; **Format**; **Papermaking**

Watt, Alexander Pollock (1834–1914)

See **Literary agents**

Watt, Robert (1774–1819)

Bibliographer. The son of a farmer, Watt had a rudimentary education before becoming first a ploughboy and then a carter. Through his own great efforts he was, however, able to matriculate at Glasgow University in 1793, and he graduated MD in 1799. He practised medicine for the rest of his life, and wrote a number of medical works. He became interested in the bibliography of his subject, an interest which developed into an attempt to catalogue and classify a representative selection of European books on all subjects. When he died, ill and perhaps even insane, the work was almost completed, and was published posthumously as *Bibliotheca Britannica: Or a general index to British and foreign literature* (4 vols, 1824).

Bibliotheca Britannica is an astonishing book, and still very useful. Its real value lies in vols 3 and 4, which are a subject index and what would now be called a 'key-word' index to the titles and contents of the books listed by author in vols 1 and 2. There is still no substitute for it as a subject guide to the pre-1800 printed literature of Western Europe.

See G.W. Cole in *PBSA* (1939), p. 1. There is a bibliographical *Account of the Life and Works of Dr Robert Watt* by James Finlayson (1897), which is the source of the entry in *DNB*. *Bibliotheca Britannica* has, unfortunately, never been reprinted, and is now very rare and expensive, although copies are available in most research libraries.

Web

See **Papermaking**

Whatman, James (1702–1759) and Whatman, James (1741–1798)

Papermakers. From an old Kentish family, the elder Whatman married a papermaker's widow in 1740, and took over Turkey Mill near Maidstone, a well-established paper mill. He was very successful in his new business, and by the time of his death Turkey Mill was the most productive in the country. Indeed, Whatman's huge output was a major factor in reducing Britain's former reliance on imports for adequate supplies of paper. Whatman was also a very good papermaker. In particular, he developed the technique of making wove paper, in which the wire lines and the chain lines are eliminated by the substitution of a very fine mesh in the mould. This gives both a stronger and a smoother paper. Baskerville encouraged Whatman in the development of wove paper, and was indeed one of the first customers for it. The younger Whatman took over the business after his father's death, and continued the traditions which he had established. He greatly expanded the enterprise and was able to retire in comfort in 1798.

See Thomas Balston, *James Whatman, Father and Son* (1957).

See also **Baskerville, John** (1706–1775); **Chain lines**; **Papermaking**

Wholesaling

Book trade term. As in other trades, wholesaling in the book trade is the activity of a middleman who buys from producers (printers or, more usually, publishers) and sell to retailers (booksellers). Wholesaling in the trade has a very long history, for the fifteenth century merchants in London imported printed books from the Continent and wholesaled them to retailers through country fairs. The fairs began to be used by the London printers and publishers as the trade established itself in the capital in the sixteenth century. The fairs, however, gradually declined in importance, and in the late seventeenth century the leading booksellers formed congers through which books were wholesaled. By the middle of the eighteenth century, the publisher usually designated a particular bookseller or booksellers for wholesaling and named him or them in the imprint. Through these wholesalers, the retailers could obtain the book at the lowest possible price, and thus maximise their own profits. With the vast increase in book production in the nineteenth century, this system was no longer satisfactory, and specialist wholesale houses emerged; the largest of these was Simpkin, Marshall, although W.H. Smith also operated in this field. Smiths are still involved in the wholesaling of paperbacks, but the wholesaling of hardbacks in Britain came to an effective end with the destruction of Simpkin, Marshall's warehouse in the Blitz (1941).

See Graham Pollard, 'The English market for printed books', *PH* (1978), p. 7; Norma Hodgson and Cyprian Blagden, *The Notebook of Thomas Bennet and Henry Clements* (OBS, new ser. 6, 1943); and John Feather, *The Provincial Book Trade in Eighteenth-century England* (1985).

See also **Conger**; **Paperbacks**; **Simpkin, Marshall**; **Smith, William Henry** (1792–1865) **and Smith, William Henry** (1829–1891)

Wilson, Andrew (fl. 1800–1816)

See **Stereotyping**

Wing

Reference book. Donald G. Wing, *Short-title Catalogue of Books Printed in England, Scotland, Ireland, Wales, and British America and of English Books Printed in Other Countries, 1641–1700* (3 vols, 1945–51) is invariably referred to by its author's surname. It was intended as a successor to *STC*, but, although it is undoubtedly a very creditable performance for one man working alone and often in his spare time, it does not achieve the same high standard. Wing, a librarian at Yale University, rarely travelled and too often relied on outdated secondary sources for his information. As a consequence there are many errors both of commission and omission, which are only partly corrected in the unfortunately named *Gallery of Ghosts* (1967). The first volume of a revised edition by Wing himself (1972) repeated and compounded more errors than it corrected as well as introducing new ones. Wing's death in 1973 led to the project being taken over officially by the Modern Language Association, and being given a formal institutional base at Yale; since that time the revised vols 2 and 3 have been published, and are a great improvement. For all its faults, Wing is a standard and indispensable work.

See also **STC**

Wire lines

See **Chain lines**

Wise, Thomas James (1859–1937)

Bibliographer, book collector and criminal. From a humble background and with little education, Wise became a successful and wealthy businessman, while actually devoting increasing amounts of time to his real interests: literature, bibliography, forgery and theft. In particular, Wise was a lover of the Romantic and Victorian poets, and at an early age began to assemble what was to become a very remarkable collection of first and early editions of their works. He was very active in bibliophilic and bibliographical circles, and was instrumental in forming both the Browning Society and the Shelley Society to encourage the study of those poets. He was indeed largely responsible for establishing his favourites as literary classics worthy of collecting and study just like the writers of earlier periods. His pioneering bibliographies, which included the Brontës (1917), Byron (1932), Tennyson (1908) and Browning (1897) among many others, although marred by inaccuracies, set new standards of bibliographical description, as did his catalogue of his own collection, *The Ashley Library* (11 vols, 1922–36). The collection itself is now in the British Library.

Had he stopped there, Wise would be remembered as a flawed but influential bibliographer and a pioneering bibliophile. Unfortunately he did not stop there. As the leading light of the Shelley Society, he had been responsible for the production of type facsimiles of early editions of that poet's works, and using the same printers (Clays, at Bungay in Suffolk, who were entirely innocent of what they were doing) he began, in about 1880, to forge whole editions, usually of single poems or short prose works by the authors on whom he was an acknowledged expert. These were duly supported by entries in his bibliographies, copies were presented to the British Museum to establish their existence and other copies were then fed onto the market, at great profit to Wise, as 'rarities'. Wise never openly dealt in books himself. In the early years of the twentieth century, his principal channel into the trade was the bookseller, Herbert Gorfin (who was probably not innocent), a former clerk in Wise's company whom Wise established in business for the purpose. For many years, Wise was entirely successful, and became one of the grand old men of the bibliographical world; some of his productions, notably Elizabeth Barrett Browning's *Sonnets from the Portuguese* ('Reading, 1847', but actually printed by Clay for Wise after 1880) were among the most desirable rarities for collectors of what were then modern first editions. There is no doubt that Wise made a great deal of money by his gradual release of copies onto the unsuspecting market. The whole enterprise was exposed in 1934 by John Carter and Graham Pollard in their *Enquiry into the Nature of Certain Nineteenth-century Pamphlets* which, in addition to its startling revelations, was also a pioneering work in its use of scientific techniques in the study of paper which actually clinched the case about the true date of the forgeries. Wise never acknowledged what he had done, but was a broken man when he died three years later.

Some 20 years after his death, it emerged that Wise was a thief as well as a forger. David Foxon, then an Assistant Keeper at the British Museum, discovered that a number of leaves in copies of early seventeenth-century plays in the Ashley Library had actually been removed from copies which were already in the Museum during Wise's lifetime; there can be no doubt that Wise himself was responsible for this. Again the motive was financial: in addition to his own copies, Wise also made up copies to sell to John H. Wrenn, a Texas collector, whose books are now in the Harry Ransom Center at the University of Texas at Austin. Foxon published his findings as *Thomas J. Wise and the pre- Restoration Drama* (1959), a pamphlet which hammered the final nail into the coffin of Wise's reputation.

The books by Carter and Pollard and by Foxon are the principal sources for the study of Wise's iniquities. A revised edition of the former completed from Carter and Pollard's own work by Nicholas Barker and John Morris (2 vols, 1982) has further strengthened the case against Wise and greatly expanded the list of suspect books. Wise has been the subject of a number of books, of which the most useful are W.G. Partington, *Thomas J. Wise in the Original Cloth* (1947) and William B. Todd (ed.), *Thomas J. Wise: Centenary studies* (1959). Arundell Esdaile's life of Wise in *DNB 1931–1940* is fair but frank. The interest in Wise will no doubt continue, although there are still many in the book world who share Sir Frank Francis's view, expressed in his preface to Foxon's book, that the whole subject is 'distasteful'.

See also **Book collecting**; **Forgery**; **Type facsimile**

Wood engraving

A relief process of graphic printing. Wood engraving differs from woodcut in that the block is cut on the end-grain of the wood (usually box wood). This permits a finer line which can be more freely drawn, and also allows the engraver to cut away the parts of the block which he does not want to print, producing what is known as 'white-line' engraving. The result is far more subtle than can be achieved with the 'black-line' engraving of woodcut.

The technique was first used in the late eighteenth century and it was perfected by Bewick, the first and greatest master of the art. It continued to be used throughout the nineteenth century, although as a commercial process it declined rapidly after the introduction of photomechanical techniques in the 1880s It was, however, rescued by a number of artists and illustrators, and wood engraving is often found in modern private press books.

See Douglas Percy Bliss, *A History of Wood-engraving* (1928); and A. Garrett, *A History of British Wood Engraving* (1978). For the later history of the art, see Eric de Mare, *The Victorian Woodblock Illustrators* (1981).

See also **Bewick, Thomas** (1753–1828); **Illustrated books**; **Photomechanical printing**; **Private press movement**; **Relief printing**; **Woodcut**

Woodcut

A relief process of graphic printing. A woodcut is cut on the side-grain of box wood, by carving away the non-printing areas, leaving raised lines which are then inked. It is consequently known as 'black-line' engraving. Although the results can be good in very skilled hands, woodcut generally produces a very crude illustration since the lines have to be cut very thick to prevent the tearing of wood fibres along the grain during engraving.

Printing from wooden blocks almost certainly antedates typographical printing, and until the middle of the sixteenth century, when it was gradually displaced by various intaglio processes, it was the normal form of illustration even in the typographic book. Woodcuts continued to be used, although by the end of the seventeenth century they are rarely found in anything more elevated than a chapbook.

See Douglas Percy Bliss, *A History of Wood-engraving* (1928); and, for early examples, Edward Hodnett, *English Woodcuts 1480–1535* (2nd edn, 1973).

See also **Block books**; **Chapbooks**; **Intaglio**; **Relief printing**

Work and turn

See **Half sheet**

Wove paper

See **Papermaking**

Wrangham, Francis (1769–1842)

Book collector and author. The son of a Yorkshire farmer, Wrangham was educated at Cambridge and after some problems in obtaining preferment became Vicar of Hunmanby, Yorkshire, in 1828. From his Cambridge days he was an avid book collector, and he assembled a huge library in Hunmanby vicarage. Although the collection was not specifically bibliophilic, Wrangham did share the taste of many of his contemporaries to a large extent. He also, however, had an interest in fine printing; he bought type facsimiles, and products of the presses of both Brydges and Johnes, as well as publishing his own poems. The latter were issued in small editions often with several variant issues in different wrappers. After his death his library was sold in a sale of nearly 6000 lots (Sotheby, 1843).

See Michael Sadleir, *Archdeacon Francis Wrangham 1769–1842* (1937).

See also **Book collecting**; **Brydges**, **Sir Samuel Egerton** (1762–1837); **Hafod Press**; **Type facsimile**

Xylographica

See **Block books**

Yellowbacks

Editions of fiction published in the nineteenth century with highly-coloured covers. Yellowbacks are so-called from the yellow paper used for their wrappers which were printed with woodcut illustrations in blue, black and red or black, green and red. This design, like the cover of the modern paperback of which the yellowback is a precursor, was intended to catch the customer's eye, especially on the railway station bookstalls for which the yellowbacks were intended. Millions were printed in the period from the 1840s to the end of the century, although few have survived and they are now very rare.

Michael Sadleir formed a superb collection of yellowbacks, which are catalogued in his *XIX Century Fiction* (2 vols, 1952). See also his essay in John Carter (ed.), *New Paths in Book Collecting* (1934).

See also **Paperbacks**; **Sadleir, Michael** (1888–1957)